Revelatory Events

Revelatory Events

Three Case Studies of the Emergence of New Spiritual Paths

ANN TAVES

PRINCETON UNIVERSITY PRESS
Princeton & Oxford

Published by Princeton University Press, 41 William Street, Princeton,
New Jersey 08540

In the United Kingdom: Princeton University Press, 6 Oxford Street,
Woodstock, Oxfordshire OX20 1TR

press.princeton.edu

Cover art courtesy of Shutterstock; cover design by Jen Betit

Library of Congress Cataloging-in-Publication Data

Names: Taves, Ann, 1952–author.

Title: Revelatory events : three case studies of the emergence of new spiritual paths
/ Ann Taves.

Description: first [edition]. | Princeton, NJ : Princeton University Press, 2017. |
Includes bibliographical references and index.

Identifiers: LCCN 2016008010 | ISBN 9780691131016 (hardcover : alk. paper) |
ISBN 9780691152899 (pbk. : alk. paper)

Subjects: LCSH: Experience (Religion)—Case studies. | Revelation—Case studies.
| Spiritual life—Case studies. | Spirituality—Case studies. | Mormon Church. |
Alcoholics Anonymous. | Course in Miracles.

Classification: LCC BL53 .T385 2017 | DDC 204/.2—dc23 LC record available
at https://lccn.loc.gov/2016008010

British Library Cataloging-in-Publication Data is available

This book has been composed in Adobe Garamond Pro

Printed on acid-free paper. ∞

Printed in the United States of America

10 9 8 7 6 5 4 3 2 1

The excerpts from *Twelve Steps and Twelve Traditions*, *Alcoholics Anonymous* (*AA*), and
AA Archival Data are reprinted with permission of Alcoholics Anonymous World
Services, Inc. (AAWS). Permission to reprint these excerpts does not mean that
AAWS has reviewed or approved the contents of this publication, or that AAWS
necessarily agrees with the views expressed herein. AA is a program of recovery from
alcoholism *only*—use of these excerpts in connection with programs and activities
that are patterned after AA but that address other problems, or in any other non-AA
context, does not imply otherwise.

Documents and images that are the property of the Stepping Stones Foundation
Archives, Stepping Stones, the historic home of Bill and Lois Wilson, Katonah, New
York, www.steppingstones.org, are reproduced with permission of the Foundation.
No permission is granted whatsoever for any use, distribution (online or otherwise),
or reproduction.

Portions of chapter 2 were previously published in *Numen* 61/2–3 (2014), 182–207,
and chart 3 and portions of chapter 3 in *Mormon Studies Review* 3 (2016), 53–83.
Permission to reprint is gratefully acknowledged.

CONTENTS

Appendix Charts

Experiences in which people sense unseen presences, see apparitions, hear voices, or feel themselves and the world suddenly transformed, are more common than we suppose. Some people dismiss them. Some find them distressing, sometimes to the point of seeking clinical help. Still others find inspiration in them. In some cases, such experiences lead to personal transformations and occasionally to the emergence of new spiritual paths and religious movements. If we assume that such experiences are neither inherently pathological nor religious and therefore subject to a range of interpretations, then new questions emerge. If we assume that the meaning of such experiences is subject to interpretation and, thus, a matter of discernment, we can ask how people decide what has occurred and why, in some cases, groups form around their claims. This book examines three cases—Mormonism, Alcoholics Anonymous, and *A Course in Miracles* (ACIM)—in which insiders claimed that a seeming "presence" guided the emergence of a new spiritual path—a restored church, a spiritual fellowship, and a network of students. The book reconstructs the historical process whereby small groups coalesced around the sense of a guiding presence and accounts for this process in naturalistic rather than supernatural terms.

I have a long-standing interest in the competing ways that people explain unusual experiences. In my first book on the subject, *Fits, Trances, and Visions* (1999), I traced some of those debates about unusual experiences over time, but for the most part I refrained from trying to explain them. In *Religious Experience Reconsidered* (2009), I took on the challenge of explaining unusual experiences in naturalistic terms. That book's approach to explanation, which focused on the layers of mental processing that interact to form our experience at a given point in time, was largely synchronic. In the present book, I have sought to integrate the explanatory concerns of *Religious Experience Reconsidered* with the historical perspective of *Fits, Trances, and Visions* by focusing on unusual experiences in the context of small group interactions as these interactions unfold over time. The focus here is thus largely diachronic.

My goal in writing this book is twofold. First, I want to demonstrate how we can study a central religious claim—the claim that suprahuman entities guide the formation of new spiritual paths through a revelatory process—

historically.[1] To do this, I reconstruct how people's sense of being guided emerged, what it was like, and how they negotiated discrepancies and contradictions. In developing these reconstructions, I treat the experiences on which these claims were based with the utmost seriousness, while recognizing that their claims were and are contested. Second, I want to explain the emergence of a collective sense of being guided in naturalistic terms drawn from the cognitive social sciences. My goal in doing so is not to debunk or explain away the groups' claims but to learn about the interactive process, the mental mechanisms underlying the unusual experiences, and the interplay between individual differences and group processes.

Although I think—and will argue—that the sense of a guiding presence emerges through a complex interaction between individuals with unusual mental abilities and an initial set of collaborators, an explanation of this sort says little about the content of what is revealed or the value of the spiritual path that emerges. If—as I believe—presences that articulate and guide a group toward collective goals can be understood as creative products of human social interactions rather than actual suprahuman agents, this does not undercut the human need to work out answers to the larger questions these paths seek to address. It just requires us to generate other methods for evaluating the value of the goals and the merits of the paths as means of obtaining them. Nor does a naturalistic understanding rule out the possibility of experiencing ideas or ethical demands that seem to come from beyond ourselves as a sense of inspiration or calling. It does require us, however, to develop means of testing their value and merit.

My overall interest in both reconstructing and explaining the role of presences in group formation required the careful selection of cases in which people claimed to interact with suprahuman presences and left records that enable us to reconstruct the process of emergence as it unfolded. Each of the three case studies presented here had founding figures who interacted with presences they felt were other than themselves; each produced a scripture-like text that has now been translated into multiple languages; and each now

---

[1] In what follows, I refer to "presences," "entities," and "selves" when referring in general to that which guides the groups. Although "guiding presences" is perhaps the most accurate way to refer to what the three groups have in common, sentences such as this require modifiers to convey the nonordinary quality that people are attaching to the presence, entity, or self. After considering a number of options, such as "otherworldly," "discarnate," "superhuman," "transcendent," and "extraordinary," I have settled on "suprahuman" as the most workable in relation to these case studies. Wiktionary defines "suprahuman" as "having much greater powers that are above and beyond that of a normal human" (en.wiktionary.org/wiki/suprahuman). This works if we interpret it as referring to powers that people perceive as above and beyond that of a normal human. Interpreted in this way, suprahuman is a vague term, specified in particular instances by emic views of "normal" and "above and beyond." As such, it accommodates a range of emic views of the relationship between the human and suprahuman from the unusual or exceptional, but still human, to the explicitly supernatural.

attracts a worldwide following. At the same time, each path characterizes itself very differently—Mormonism as a restored church, Alcoholics Anonymous as a fellowship, and ACIM as a spiritual thought system—and each tells a very different story of how they came to be what they are: a religion, a way of life, and a network of students. Most crucially, they each institutionalized the continuing role of the "guiding presence" in different ways— Mormonism subordinated individual guidance to the leadership of the church, Alcoholics Anonymous subordinated individual guidance to the conscience of the local group, and ACIM, insofar as it has institutionalized the guiding presence at all, seems to be doing so via the governing board of the Foundation for Inner Peace, which is responsible for publishing the Course.

The book can be read in several different ways: as an account of the role that guiding presences played in the emergence and formation of the three social groups, as an explanation of the emergence of paths whose origins are attributed to suprahuman sources, and as an illustration of methods that can be used to reconstruct and explain the role of experiences in the emergence of new social formations. Read in the first way, it is intended as a contribution to the study of the new social movements; in the second, as a contribution to creativity studies; and in the third, as a demonstration of how historians can make use of the cognitive social sciences to explain historical phenomena.

ACKNOWLEDGMENTS

Like many who work with living traditions, I shared my case study chapters with knowledgeable insiders and solicited their feedback. In the Mormon case, I consulted with LDS historians who could alert me to sources I had not considered and who commented on my interpretations. I am grateful to Richard Bushman, Terryl Givens, Kathleen Flake, and Steven Craig Harper for feedback on all or parts of chapters 1–3 and to the LDS scholars who attended a workshop on Joseph Smith's translations for feedback on the first portion of chapter 11. In relation to Alcoholics Anonymous, I am grateful to Matt Dingle for feedback on chapter 6 and an extended discussion of his father-in-law, Thomas Powers Sr. I am grateful to Judith Skutch Whitson, the sole surviving member of the group involved with producing *A Course in Miracles*, and Robert Rosenthal and Gloria Wapnick, who were closely connected to those involved in producing the Course, for providing extensive comments on multiple versions of chapters 7–9. Tamara Morgan, Rosemarie LoSasso, and Beverly Hutchinson McNeff also provided helpful information. Above all, I want to thank Judith Skutch Whitson for her enthusiastic assistance with the project; she not only supplied numerous photographs and documents but, most crucially, provided feedback on the emergence of the Course that helped me to realize how central the sense of being guided by a presence was for all three of the groups discussed in this book.

In almost every case, the insiders understood that I was trying to reconstruct what it was like for the initial collaborators (and their critics) as their respective paths emerged. Their feedback not only helped to ensure that I played fair with the sources but in some cases led to important refinements of my argument. At the same time, our viewpoints differ, and the reconstructions, however faithful to the sources, do involve interpretations with which they would not necessarily agree. In the end, I am responsible for the reconstructions in chapters 1–9.

I also have a number of more conventional debts. I am very grateful to Sally Corbett, the executive director of the Stepping Stones Foundation Archives (the historic home of Lois and Bill Wilson), for a marathon session searching for early sources with much good conversation along the way, as well as for her extensive help with illustrations. Michelle Mizra and her colleagues in the Archives Department at the General Service Office of Alcoholics Anonymous were also very generous with their time, providing prompt and helpful responses to all my queries regarding sources and illustrations. Michael MacKay provided generous assistance in acquiring many of the Mormon illustrations. I also benefited from feedback on talks related to the book, particularly on the materialization of the golden plates, given at many colleges and universities in the United States and Europe. Jan Shipps, after reading portions of chapters 1–3 in early drafts, generously arranged for me to present the material on the golden plates at the Mormon History Association, where Laurie Mafly-Kipp and Steve Harper responded.

At UC Santa Barbara, my students in a course on new religious movements gave helpful feedback on the three cases, and the members of the Religion, Experience, and Mind Lab Group offered a much-appreciated context for discussing the ideas and refining the methods. I am particularly grateful to Shelby King, a UCSB graduate student, for her assistance in preparing the manuscript for publication, and to Egil Asprem, a UCSB postdoctoral scholar, for two years of collaboration on the building-block approach, many discussions of the book, and multiple readings of the appendix. Thomas Tweed, Catherine L. Albanese, and two anonymous reviewers read the manuscript as a whole and offered much excellent feedback, both substantive and editorial. Thanks also to Mark Paloutzian for preparing the index, to the production team for their careful attention to copyediting and design, and to Fred Appel for his continuing editorial guidance.

Finally, I am grateful to my department chairs, the UCSB administration, the Center for Advanced Study in the Behavioral Sciences at Stanford University, and the John Simon Guggenheim Foundation for supporting sabbaticals in 2008–9 and 2014. And, last but not least, I thank my husband, Ray Paloutzian, for his continuing and always generous companionship, support, and feedback, both personal and intellectual.

ABBREVIATIONS

MORMONISM

D1   *Documents, Volume 1: July 1828–June 1831.* Ed. Michael Hubbard McKay, Gerrit J. Dirkmaat, Grant Underwood, Robert J. Woodford, and William G. Hartley. Vol. 1 of the Documents series of *The Joseph Smith Papers*, ed. Dean C. Jessee, Ronald K. Esplin, and Richard Lyman Bushman. Salt Lake City: Church Historian's Press, 2013.

D&C   Doctrine and Covenants of the Church of Jesus Christ of Latter-day Saints. Salt Lake City: Church of Jesus Christ of Latter-day Saints, 1981.

EMD   *Early Mormon Documents.* Ed. Dan Vogel. 5 vols. Salt Lake City: Signature Books, 1996–2003.

H1   *Histories, Volume 1: Joseph Smith Histories, 1832–1844.* Ed. Karen Lynn Davidson, David J. Whittaker, Richard L. Jensen, and Mark Ashurst-McGee. Vol. 1 of the Histories series of *The Joseph Smith Papers*, ed. Dean C. Jessee, Ronald K. Esplin, and Richard Lyman Bushman. Salt Lake City: Church Historian's Press, 2012.

JSP   *The Joseph Smith Papers.* Ed. Dean C. Jessee, Ronald K. Esplin, and Richard Lyman Bushman. 14 vols. (to date). Salt Lake City: Church Historian's Press, 2008–16.

MRB   Manuscript Revelation Books. Facsimile ed. Ed. Robin Scott Jensen, Robert J. Woodford, and Steven C. Harper. Vol. 1 of the Revelations and Translations series of *The Joseph Smith Papers*, ed. Jessee, Esplin, and Bushman. Salt Lake City: Church Historian's Press, 2009.

ALCOHOLICS ANONYMOUS

AACOA   *Alcoholics Anonymous Comes of Age: A Brief History of A.A.* By Anonymous. New York: AA World Services, 1957.

BB:1939   The Big Book. *Alcoholics Anonymous.* By Anonymous. 1st ed. New York: AA World Services, 1939.

BB:1955   The Big Book. *Alcoholics Anonymous.* By Anonymous. 2nd ed. New York: AA World Services, 1955.

BB:1976   The Big Book. *Alcoholics Anonymous.* By Anonymous. 3rd ed. New York: AA World Services, 1976.

Dr. Bob   *Dr. Bob and the Good Oldtimers: A Biography, with Recollections of Early A.A. in the Midwest.* By Anonymous. New York: AA World Services, 1980.

GSOA   AA General Service Office Archives, New York.

LOH   *The Language of the Heart: Bill W.'s Grapevine Writings.* By Bill W. AA Grapevine Digital Archives, 1988.

LR   *Lois Remembers: Memoirs of the Co-Founder of Al-Anon and Wife of the Co-Founder of Alcoholics Anonymous.* By Lois W. New York: Al-Anon, 1979.

OWM   *The Book that Started It All; The Original Working Manuscript of Alcoholics Anonymous.* By Anonymous. Center City, MN: Hazelden, 2010.

PIO   *"Pass It On": The Story of Bill Wilson and How the A.A. Message Reached the World.* By Anonymous. New York: AA World Services, 1984.

SSFA   Stepping Stones Foundation Archives, Katonah, New York.

12&12.   *Twelve Steps and Twelve Traditions.* By Anonymous. New York: AA World Services, 1953.

A Course in Miracles

ACIM   A Course in Miracles (refers to both the published book [*A Course in Miracles*] and the thought system that derived from it; also referred to in shortened form as "the Course")

AFF   *Absence from Felicity: The Story of Helen Schucman and Her Scribing "A Course in Miracles."* By Kenneth Wapnick. Temecula, CA: Foundation for *A Course in Miracles*, (1991) 1999.

FACIM   Foundation for *A Course in Miracles*. Temecula, CA.

FIP   Foundation for Inner Peace. Tiberon, CA.

FIP 3rd   *A Course in Miracles.* 3rd ed. Tiberon, CA: Foundation for Inner Peace, 2007.

HS   Helen Schucman. *Autobiography.* Mill Valley, CA: Foundation for Inner Peace, [1975] 2009.

JWD   *Journey Without Distance: The Story Behind "A Course in Miracles."* By Robert Skutch. Berkeley, CA: Celestial Arts, 1984.

Notes   Unpublished Writings of Helen Schucman. Vols. 1–22. Compiled by Kenneth Wapnick Temecula, CA: FACIM, 1990.

Ur   *A Course in Miracles Urtext Manuscripts.* Complete seven-volume combined edition. Ed. Doug Thompson. Jaffrey, NH: Miracles in Action Press, LLC, 2008.

WT   William Thetford. *Life Story.* Mill Valley, CA: Foundation for Inner Peace, (1983) 2009.

Revelatory Events

Introduction

In *Religious Experience Reconsidered*, I argued that we should not focus on "religious experience" as if it were comprised of a fixed and stable set of experiences but on how people decide on the meaning and significance of their experiences. This book tests the method outlined in that book on a particular type of experience that has played a central role in the formation of many spiritual paths—experiences of presence that some consider "revelatory." In using the word "revelatory," I am deliberately adopting a term loaded with theological meaning and recasting it in a way that I believe will allow us to investigate processes that inform many spiritual paths as they emerge, whether they are explicitly viewed as "revealed religions" or not. I refer to such experiences as "events," that is, as "happenings," because "events" provide a promising link between the psychological, which focuses on "event cognition," and the sociocultural, which focuses on narratives of events. Experiences are events—meaningful wholes—that we pick out from the stream of experience. My focus here, as a historian with interests in cognitive science, is on events that people experienced firsthand and the processes whereby they came to believe that something had been revealed by or via a suprahuman source.

REVELATION AS EVENT

In referring to revelatory events, I am focusing on one of the three different ways the concept of revelation is used in the modern context. In addition to particular *events* or *occurrences* (whether mythic or historical) that some construe (explicitly or implicitly) as revelatory, the term is also used to refer to the specific *content* that people claim has been conveyed through a revelatory event or to a general *type of knowledge*. Within a religious tradition based on a revelatory event, people may refer to the content of what was revealed simply as "revelation." Thus, when people refer to God's revelation to Moses on Sinai, they may be referring to the content—the oral and written Torah—rather than to the event in which Moses went up the mountain and spoke with God. When people refer to Christian revelation, they may be referring to the (content) claim that Christ is the incarnate Word (logos) of God rather than to the event of Jesus's birth in Bethlehem. Similarly, when Muslims refer to revelation, they may be referring to the content of the Qur'an rather than to the event in which the angel Gabriel appeared to Muhammad and commanded him to speak. Although the content of revelation differs from one revealed religion to another, these traditions all presuppose that revelation is a valid source of knowledge. Whether this is in fact true has been debated since the Enlightenment and has thus given rise to treatises defending the very possibility of revelation as a legitimate type of knowledge and way of knowing. Although theologians and philosophers of religion continue to devote attention to revelation in the second and third sense, this book looks at revelation in the first sense, that is, as an event or occurrence that some claim is revelatory.

To aid us in thinking about revelation as an event, we can begin with *The Oxford English Dictionary* definition of revelation as "the disclosure or communication of knowledge to man by a divine or supernatural agency." Reframed in the active voice as "knowledge that an individual or group *claims* was disclosed or communicated to them by a divine or supernatural agency," it captures the range of contested phenomena that interest me and the sort of phenomena that will be considered in this book. This definition, which goes back to the fourteenth century, has four distinct components: (1) an act of disclosure or communication that presumably involves some sort of means through which this communication takes place; (2) the knowledge that is disclosed, which presumably involves some sort of content, however enigmatic or mysterious; (3) the human or humans to whom this knowledge is disclosed; and (4) the divine, supernatural, or suprahuman agency that discloses or communicates the knowledge. Revelatory events thus involve two knowledge claims. The first is the commonplace and empirically verifiable claim that knowledge has been communicated or disclosed. The second is the controversial claim that the knowledge came from a divine, supernatural, or suprahuman source.

It is the second claim that makes the knowledge non-ordinary and sets it apart from other kinds of knowledge. The attribution of the communication to a suprahuman source constitutes the knowledge as revelation and the event as a whole as revelatory. Such claims are generally based on the interpretation of unusual or ambiguous events. Those who make such claims are typically aware of a range of alternatives and seek to rule out competing claims. Thus, for example, claims having to do with divine or supernatural agency may be in competition with alternatives that postulate a human source for the knowledge, whether conscious or unconscious, normal or pathological, or an alternative divine or supernatural agent. Both claimants and their critics typically rely on various sociocultural resources to defend their claims, including the arts of persuasion; the systems of diagnosis and discernment advanced by different cultures, traditions, or disciplines; and/ or institutionalized structures of power and authority. As historians, we can compare and contrast the resources at hand and analyze the way that people mobilize them—and to what effect—in particular situations. Points of uncertainty and contestation, and the various resources that are mobilized in response to them, allow us to see both the interpretive options and the social possibilities available in any given context.

Many scholars of religion have been content to analyze the events people consider revelatory without attempting to explain them. Indeed, purely as historians, we have little basis on which to do so. If historians or other scholars want to go beyond analyzing the revelatory process and account for the source of the revelation in question, we enter into the explanatory fray, along with claimants and critics. In the first part of the book, I write as a historian; in the second part, I enter into the fray, drawing on methods and findings from the natural and social sciences to explain the emergence of these new spiritual paths in naturalistic terms.[1]

Although some critics and scholars offer naturalistic explanations in order to debunk revelatory claims, oftentimes characterizing claimants as deluded or out of touch with reality, that is not my goal. Instead, I will be approaching new revelations as new insights that seem to come from beyond the individual or the group and analyzing them in light of recent research on creativity. Doing so allows us to move beyond the polarized perspectives of believers and critics; challenges us to acknowledge presuppositions about reality embedded in our understanding of delusion, self-deception, and psychopathology; and raises theoretical questions regarding the emergence and assessment of novelty that haven't been fully addressed.

CASE STUDIES AND SOURCES

This book analyzes the role of revelatory claims in three groups that emerged in the United States in the nineteenth and twentieth centuries: Mormonism, Alcoholics Anonymous (AA), and the network of students associated with *A Course in Miracles* (ACIM). These three case studies are not only richly documented but also present intriguing comparative possibilities. Each had a key figure whose unusual experiences and/or abilities led to the emergence

---

[1] Philosophers defend a range of versions of naturalism. In its weakest form, naturalism simply rejects supernatural claims. In its strongest form, naturalism assumes that all explanations can ultimately be cast in terms of physics (Papineau 2015; Baker 2013). Here I am assuming a relatively weak version, informed by the "new mechanism" in the philosophy of science (Craver and Tabery 2016), that presupposes: (1) that subjective experience is an emergent property of underlying brain mechanisms that evolved over the course of evolutionary history; (2) that the behavior of biological systems can be explained in terms of mechanisms, layered in part-whole relations, that span multiple levels of organization; and (3) that properties that emerge (organizationally) at higher levels may have causal effects on lower levels.

of a new spiritual path and to the production of scripture-like texts that were not attributed directly to them. Joseph Smith (1805–44), a farmer and treasure seeker in Upstate New York, had a vision in 1823 in which a personage told him of ancient golden plates buried in a hillside, which Mormons claim he recovered, translated, and published as the Book of Mormon (1830) and which led to the founding of a restored church (1830). Bill Wilson (1895–1971), a (failed) stockbroker, had an ecstatic experience of a blinding white light while hospitalized for alcoholism in 1934, which he associated with the feeling of a "presence" and which gave rise to a vision of a "chain reaction of alcoholics, one carrying this message and these principles to the next." The vision, once he rightly understood it, led to the anonymously authored "Big Book" (*Alcoholics Anonymous*, 1st ed., 1939) and the *Twelve Steps and Twelve Traditions* (1953; hereafter *12&12*) of Alcoholics Anonymous. Psychologist Helen Schucman (1909–81) "scribed" the words of an inner voice, which she and her collaborators attributed to Jesus, to produce the best-selling self-study course *A Course in Miracles* (1976).

Each of the founders was embedded in an intense primary group that collaborated on the production of the books on which the spiritual paths were based. Smith's immediate family and a few key supporters were involved in the discovery, recovery, and translation of the golden plates. Wilson, with the support of his wife, his doctor, and a small group of alcoholics, refereed a collaborative process that produced the Big Book. Schucman, with the help and encouragement of her colleague and fellow psychologist, William Thetford, scribed *A Course in Miracles*, the "Workbook for Students," and the "Manual for Teachers." Kenneth Wapnick and Judith Skutch, who joined with Schucman and Thetford after the Course was scribed, worked with them to make it public.

Despite these intriguing similarities, the three groups do not make the same claims for their scripture-like texts, and their respective collaborations generated very different social formations. Mormons explicitly describe the Book of Mormon as new revelation, the Big Book of Alcoholics Anonymous does not mention revelation, and ACIM teaches a new understanding of revelation. Joseph Smith's new revelation led to the founding of a new church, which some now characterize as a world religion; Bill Wilson's sudden experience, which he told critics was simply a conversion experience and not a new revelation, led to the emergence of a worldwide fellowship, which is usually characterized as therapeutic; and *A Course in Miracles*, which characterizes itself as "but one version of a universal curriculum," resulted in a network of foundations, workshops, and study groups.

There is extensive primary documentation that can be used to reconstruct the process through which both the scripture-like texts and the groups themselves emerged. Virtually all the documents related to early Mormonism are available either through the *Early Mormon Documents* (Vogel 1996–

2003; hereafter *EMD*) or the *Joseph Smith Papers* (ed. Jessee, Esplin, and Bushman, 2008–12; hereafter *JSP*). In addition to published materials, such as the original working manuscript of AA's Big Book (Anonymous 2010), Bill Wilson's correspondence and other unpublished materials are available at the Stepping Stones Foundation Archives (SSFA) in Katonah, New York, and the AA General Service Office Archives (GSOA) in New York City. Much of the available material related to Helen Schucman and ACIM has been published or is available on the Internet; unpublished materials are available at the Foundation for Inner Peace (FIP; Tiburon, California) and Foundation for *A Course in Miracles* (FACIM; Temecula, California). There is also an extensive secondary literature surrounding the emergence of all three movements. Even when written by outsiders, however, the secondary literature generally reflects the groups' own sense of their beginnings, viewed retrospectively *in light of what emerged* rather than from the point of view of participants *as the group was emerging*.

METHODS

Methodologically, this project is built on a stipulated analogy that generates a series of comparisons. In Part 1, the point of analogy is more narrowly focused on the three groups, each of which had a founding figure who had unusual experiences of a presence that they felt was other than themselves. In Part 2, the point of analogy expands to include comparisons with others who had experiences in which *it seemed like* they were not the agent or author of their experience, even if they knew that they actually were.

Part 1 reconstructs the interactive process through which a small group of collaborators found meaning in their experiences. It draws on process-tracing methods used in microhistory, historical anthropology (Handelman 2005), microsociology (Collins 2004), and case study research in the social sciences (George and Bennett 2005) to work backward from official accounts of origins to reconstruct the process of emergence using the full range of available primary sources. Within a general process-tracing framework, I analyze narratives of key experiences (aka events or situations), distinguishing between the experiencer's perceptions (what happened) and appraisals (their implicit or explicit explanations of why it happened). Depending on the nature of the sources, I compare multiple accounts of a single event to see how a subject reinterpreted it over time and multiple versions of a more comprehensive narrative (an event series) to analyze the way the narrator positions a particular event within a larger narrative framework. As one reconstruction is added to the next, we can begin to see similarities and differences in how the small groups formed, the way key figures' unusual experiences were understood, the way the scripture-like texts were produced, and the way authority was structured within each of the groups.

The discussion of each group opens with a consideration of how the story of the path's emergence is usually told by followers of the path, briefly introduces the key collaborators, and then indicates, based on the available sources, how we can reconstruct the process *as it unfolded* from the point of view of the interacting subjects. It's important to recognize that while the reconstructed process will break with the more or less "official" story of the path's emergence, it still tells the story from the point of view of the interacting subjects. The difference lies in the timing and the vantage point of the telling. Insiders tell the "official" stories in light of what emerged. Their retrospective accounts make the outcome look much more inevitable than it did as the process was unfolding. Part 1 thus remains faithful to the point(s) of view of those involved in the process of emergence, but does so recognizing that (1) they did not know what was emerging, (2) developments took place amid uncertainty and at times disagreement, and (3) dissenters and skeptics were part of the process. Although my aim is to reconstruct the process from the point of view of the interacting subjects, I occasionally insert comments in my own voice when I think that doing so will make my argument clearer.

In Part 2, I break with the point of view of the three groups to offer a naturalistic explanation of the emergence of these new spiritual paths. The explanation is based on two methodological steps. The first step is a deepened comparison of the process whereby the path emerged in each of the three groups in order to specify the features that need to be explained more precisely. The second step expands the range of comparisons related to the specific features to be explained. This expanded range of comparisons will include experiences in which people felt *as if* they were not the agent or author of their experience and will rely in part on scientific research on hypnosis, delusion, and unconscious motivation. Although critics have often alluded to these lines of research to debunk revelatory claims, I hope to demonstrate how we can make judicious, critically informed use of scientific resources to offer naturalistic explanations of such experiences without being dismissive of them (for a more in-depth discussion of methods, see the appendix).

Main Points

Building on Rodney Stark's (1999) insight that small, intimate, face-to-face groups play a crucial role in the interpretation and elaboration of unusual experiences, I argue that both the interactions of the group and the outcomes of their interaction depend to a significant extent on the form, the content, and the elaboration of the unusual experience—that is, *on what interacting subjects viewed as emerging and how they decided to act on it*. Although the content, significance, and interpretation of the unusual experiences differed and led to the emergence of very different social formations (a restored church, an anonymous fellowship, and an educational network), the meaning-making process in each case allowed multiple factors to coalesce to create self-reinforcing concepts and practices—circular logics—that simultaneously constituted and validated (and thus "bootstrapped") something new into existence. In each case, the group developed procedures that gave voice to the alleged suprahuman source of the emergent path and allowed it to guide the process as it unfolded. This guidance ultimately provided and legitimated the narrative thread that constituted the "official" accounts of the groups' emergence. While there is no one path or product, the emergence of the new paths in each case involved the collective reconfiguration of the self-understanding of the key figure as the conduit of a suprahuman presence. This reconfiguration enabled the emerging group to view this presence as the source of the key text, as guiding the emergence of the group, and calling each of them to reorient their lives in a profound and compelling way.

Stated most concisely, I make two arguments. Part 1: These three spiritual innovations were produced by small groups that believed they were guided by suprahuman presences and were able to generalize their experience so as to attract and incorporate others. Part 2: We can generate a naturalistic explanation of the emergence and role of these suprahuman presences by expanding a social identity approach to the creative process in light of research on nonconscious mental processes grounded in evolutionary and cognitive social psychology.

Theoretical and Methodological Contributions

As indicated in the preface, this project is intended as a theoretical contribution to interdisciplinary research on the emergence of new social formations and on the creative process. At the same time, it illustrates a method that historians and ethnographers can use to set up comparisons between cases in order to analyze and explain similarities and differences in the way the processes unfold.

Theoretically, this project builds on earlier research (Taves 1999, 2009) in which I argue that we will learn more about how people interpret their experiences and those of others if we do not focus on "religious experience" per se but on the uncertainties and disputes surrounding particular kinds of experiences or events, for example, those involving a seeming "presence." Thus, while James Lewis (2003) made a forceful case for studying the role of religious experience in the context of new religious movements, this study offers a broad theoretical framework for analyzing the role of "presences" in the emergence of new social formations. It places the process whereby people determine how such experiences should be interpreted or categorized at the center and thus situates the project in an interdisciplinary space that does not presuppose how the experiences, or the formations that result from them, will be categorized. This broader, more generic terminology allows us to apply the methods used here to new social formations regardless of how they characterize themselves.

The project also reflects the "material turn," widespread in the humanities and the social sciences (Houtman and Meyer 2012), in which scholars have sought to undercut the presumed oppositions between spiritual/material and belief/practice, moving beyond studying beliefs about non-ordinary powers, entities, and worlds to examine the processes—cognitive, experiential, and interactive—whereby people materialize what they view as non-ordinary in the ordinary world. In focusing on revelatory *events*, I am focusing on events in which people claim to perceive non-ordinary presences in the ordinary world. The situations in which this occurs are varied but include interactive visual appearances to an individual or several people, internal textual dictation, the collective conscience of small groups, and revealing and transporting material objects. Claims regarding presence may thus arise in response to various kinds of stimuli: internal thoughts and sensations that subjects claim to experience as not their own, sensations that they claim arise externally but are not reflected in the external environment in an ordinary way, and the objects that people claim such presences have produced or transformed.

Although Max Weber ([1956] 1978), Anthony Wallace ([1956] 2003), and Rodney Stark (1999) all contributed to our understanding of these processes, none devotes sufficient attention to the process of interpretation and decision making as it unfolds from the point of view of the people associated with the emergent group, whether as supporters or critics. To better understand this multilevel process, this study integrates research on appraisal processes drawn from cognitive psychology, attribution theory in social psychology, and framing processes in sociology in order to tease apart subjects' perceptions of what happened and why it happened as they frame and reframe key events over time.[2] This more integrated approach, which is described in detail in the discussion of methods in the appendix, allows us to ground social movement theory in cognitive and social psychological processes.

When this more integrated approach to appraisal processes is combined with research on the abilities of highly hypnotizable individuals, delusions, and unconscious motivation, we can better understand the interplay of variables that lead some people who have unusual experiences (i.e., score high

[2] On event cognition, see Radvansky and Zacks (2014), as discussed in Taves and Asprem (2016); on attribution theory in social psychology, see Malle (2004), as discussed in Taves (2009), 88–119; on framing processes in sociology, see Goffman (1974); Snow et al. (1986, 464); Snow (2007); Johnson and Noakes (2005, 3).

on measures of "benign schizotypy") to seek clinical treatment, while others join new religious or spiritual movements and still others create new ones.[3] Among these variables, appraisal processes within small groups, whether conceptualized as "reality monitoring" or "spiritual discernment," clearly play a crucial role, leading not only to the materialization of spiritual entities, texts, and objects but to the emergence of widely accepted spiritual paths.

I interpret this process of materialization as a creative act, while recognizing that the insiders view themselves not as creators but as followers of suprahuman entities that they allow to act through them. To account for their experience, I draw on a social identity approach to creativity, which explores the way that shifts in self-identity and self-categorization affect the creative process when it takes place in and for groups (Haslam et al. 2013; Postmes 2010). This line of research links psychological and social processes and thus provides the basis for an explanation that is both cognitive and social scientific (Thagard 2012, 35–41; 2014). To explain the emergence of suprahuman entities, however, I had to expand shifts in self-identity to include postulated suprahuman "selves." In doing so, I realized—much to my surprise—how this line of research could lead to a rereading of Durkheim's understanding of the "totem" and, by extension, its role in the emergence of groups (small societies) within the context of complex, large-scale societies.

Methodologically, many still assume that we must choose between engaging in deep, descriptive analysis or explaining phenomena in terms alien to those we are studying. I hope that this book models a way of playing fair with people's deeply held beliefs, whether religious or not, without having to bracket one's own. Certain presuppositions and values inform this effort:

1. *Humanistic Presuppositions*: It's important to take account of how things feel to people on the inside (subjectively). People can undergo radical life transformations and shifts in worldview. We need to recognize novelty as such and seek to understand its emergence.
2. *Scientific Presuppositions*: Scientific explanations presuppose a naturalistic point of view and adopt the most economical explanations. How things feel on the inside (subjectively) isn't necessarily the best way to explain them scientifically. We will understand ourselves better if we can achieve greater consilience between the humanities and the sciences.

---

[3] On the role of appraisal processes in "the path to psychosis," see Peters et al. (1999); Brett et al. (2007); Brett et al. (2009); Heriot-Maitland, Knight, and Peters (2012); Ward et al. (2014). On the incidence of "benign schizotypy" among those drawn to new religious movements, see Day and Peters (1999); Farias, Claridge, and Lalljee (2005); Smith, Riley, and Peters (2009); Farias, Underwood, and Claridge (2013).

Explaining things scientifically neither explains them away nor destroys their value.

3. *Methodological Transparency*: When analyzing the beliefs and practices of others, it's important to be open and clear about the methods and presuppositions we are bringing to our analysis, so that those we are studying can see where they agree or disagree with us.

4. *Methodological Fairness*: Research becomes polemical when we apply methods and theories to others that we are unwilling to apply to our own beliefs and practices. It is good to test our methods and theories on ourselves to see what it is like to be studied in this way.

5. *Methodological Agility*: It is possible (and helpful) to shift back and forth between humanistic and scientific presuppositions, so that we can (a) explore what experiences, beliefs, and practices are like for those who hold them; (b) compare their experiences with those of others, including ourselves; and (c) offer explanations that make sense to us that may differ from those we are studying.

CHAPTER OUTLINE

The book is divided into two unequal parts, each with its own brief introduction. Part 1—"Making Meaning"—reconstructs the emergence of each of the three groups. Each reconstruction is presented in a set of three chapters accompanied by an introduction. The introduction indicates how the story of the group's emergence is usually told and the sources available for reconstructing the process as it unfolded. The chapters are then organized based on the availability of real-time sources rather than chronologically.

Because the Book of Mormon and the revelations that Joseph Smith received in the context of translating it provide the earliest real-time sources, the reconstruction of early Mormonism begins in chapter 1 ("Translation") in the midst of the "translation" of the golden plates. Chapter 2 ("Materialization") moves back in time through a reading of extant retrospective (post hoc) sources to reconstruct how Smith and his family might have materialized ancient golden plates if we presuppose that (a) there were no actual ancient golden plates and (b) the ancient plates were real for Smith in some nondelusional sense. Chapter 3 ("Beginnings") turns to a close reading and comparison of the origin narratives that Smith and others recounted in the 1830s in the wake of the publication of the Book of Mormon and the founding of the new church.

Again, due to the nature of the evidence, the chapters devoted to Alcoholics Anonymous begin not with the meeting between Bill Wilson and Dr. Bob Smith in 1935 that marks AA's official beginning, but with the real-time sources that survive from the drafting of AA's Big Book in 1938. Chapter 4 ("Stories") traces the emergence of a gap between Wilson's personal version of his story and his public account of AA's beginnings. Chapter 5 ("Fellow-ship") analyzes the development of AA's spiritual path (the Twelve Steps) in the late thirties and its social organization (the Twelve Traditions) in the forties, focusing on the role of experience in the former and anonymity in the latter to account for the gap that emerged between the public "Mr. AA" and the private Bill Wilson. Chapter 6 ("Seeking") highlights spiritual inter-ests and abilities that Wilson shared with Joseph Smith and Helen Schuc-man but that he suppressed for the sake of the movement.

Correspondence between Helen Schucman and William Thetford during the summer that the Voice emerged allows us to begin the first of the three chapters on ACIM, where ACIM begins its own story—with Schucman and Thetford's decision to try to find a way to overcome their interpersonal dif-ficulties. Chapter 7 ("Emergence") uses these sources to analyze the emer-gence of the Voice. Chapter 8 ("Teaching[s]") draws on unpublished ver-sions of the Course to analyze the interactions between Schucman, Thetford, and the Voice in the early stages of scribing it. Chapter 9 ("Roles") analyzes how roles shifted, as first Kenneth Wapnick and then Judith Skutch were integrated into the Course's inner circle.

Part 2 is comprised of three chapters that compare and explain the pro-cess whereby the three paths emerged. Chapter 10 ("Groups") compares the process of group formation and the emergence of suprahuman entities and guidance processes, and extends the social identity approach to creativity to encompass suprahuman entities. Chapter 11 ("Selves") compares Smith as translator of the golden plates with Schucman as scribe of the Course and, through a series of additional comparisons, attempts to account for the pro-duction of complex texts that followers believe neither Smith nor Schucman could have produced on their own. Chapter 12 ("Motives") uses research on motivation—the factors that activate, direct, and sustain goal-directed be-havior—to consider why some and not others were motivated to participate in the process of group formation and how competing motives directed to-ward different goals were given voice as alternate "selves." The conclusion highlights the distinctive feature of the three cases—their claim that a supra-human presence was involved in the emergence process—and discusses its implications for understanding emergent groups, the creative process, and key aspects of Emile Durkheim's *Elementary Forms of the Religious Life*.

PART I

Making Meaning

Although an individual who had unusual experiences played a central role in launching each of the spiritual paths, they and their collaborators interpreted their experiences in very different ways and conceived of their paths in very different terms. The Church of Jesus Christ of Latter-day Saints (LDS Church) understands itself as a religion founded by a prophet who received revelation and translated new scriptures, while AA and ACIM emphatically declare that they are not religions and that their founders were not saints or prophets or gurus. Yet both AA and ACIM are avowedly "spiritual" movements. AA conceives itself as a "way of life" and a fellowship comprised of small groups that center on the Twelve Steps and Twelve Traditions. According to Step Twelve, the steps culminate in a "spiritual awakening" and, according to Tradition Twelve, "anonymity is the spiritual foundation of all our traditions, ever reminding us to place principles before personalities." ACIM is "a complete self-study spiritual thought system that teaches that the way to universal love and peace—or remembering God—is by undoing guilt through forgiving others, healing our relationships and making them holy" (http://www.acim.org/AboutACIM/).

Organizationally, they are also quite different—Mormonism is a church structured by means of doctrine and covenants, AA is a democratic fellowship of small groups centered on the Twelve Steps and structured organizationally by the Twelve Traditions and Twelve Concepts, and ACIM is a networked movement of students that is resourced by several foundations and makes use of study groups, conferences, workshops, and websites, but has no formal organization apart from the two foundations tasked with publishing, distributing, and teaching the Course. Mormonism, which claims to be the true path to a religious goal, does not allow dual membership in another religion. AA, which claims to be—and has been widely recognized as—a spiritual path that is compatible with any religious goal or none at all, encourages dual memberships. Students of the Course differ regarding the extent to which the Course can be combined with other systems of thought, but given its lack of organization, they have no way to adjudicate the issue officially.

The development of each type of path presented distinctive challenges. For Mormonism, the challenge was to convince others that the golden plates were real and that Smith was the seer, revelator, and prophet of the restored church. With AA, the challenge was to convince alcoholics that it offered a transformative path and religious groups that the new path was not a (heretical) competitor. With ACIM, the challenge was to convey the radical nature of its vision and, in light of that, to clarify its relation to other paths. Despite these distinctive challenges, each group developed a guidance procedure that they believed gave a suprahuman source input into the process, through ongoing revelation to Smith (and subsequent prophets) in Mormonism, a Higher Power operating through the conscience of the group in the case of AA, and inner guidance from the Holy Spirit in the case of ACIM. This guidance procedure, once in place, provided a means of overcoming these challenges and ensuring that the emergent process stayed on its "prescribed" course.

Toward the end of the emergence process, each group coalesced around an overall understanding of what had happened, which they captured in more or less official narratives of their group's emergence. These quasi-official origin accounts not only defined what it meant to be a member of the group, but also *constituted the group as a social formation*. In the Mormon case, Joseph Smith's 1839 history was canonized as scripture along with the Book of Mormon, the Doctrine and Covenants (D&C), and a few other inspired writings. AA's official understanding of its history is represented in brief in the prefaces to the Big Book and more expansively in the histories published by AA World Services (*Alcoholics Anonymous Comes of Age* [*AACOA*; 1957], *Dr. Bob and the Good Oldtimers* [*Dr. Bob*; 1980], and *Pass It On* [*PIO*; 1984]). Helen Schucman's preface to *A Course in Miracles* (Schucman [1977] and Schucman [1992]) provides a brief history of how it came to be; it was supplemented in the late seventies and early eighties by interviews from the collaborators that expanded on the preface. Robert Skutch's *Journey Without Distance* (*JWD* [1984a]) provides the earliest attempt at a comprehensive insider account, and Kenneth Wapnick's *Absence from Felicity* (*AFF* [1991]) provides a history of Schucman and the Course from the point of view of a close collaborator.

Because each group framed these events and appropriated their framed version to constitute themselves as a formation—a church, a fellowship, or a spiritual thought system—the challenge in Part 1 is to reconstruct the process as it unfolded, beginning with the sources that are as close to real time as possible. The nature of the sources is discussed in detail in the introduction to each of the case studies. Because the nature of the sources differs in each case, the chapters devoted to each case study unfold in different ways.

In Part 1, I often break with historical convention and refer to individuals by their first rather than their last names. I do so in the chapters on AA in order to comply with the requirements of the Stepping Stones Foundation Archives (SSFA) and General Service Office Archives (GSOA), which ask historians to maintain the anonymity of AA members by identifying them by their first name and last initial only. I often refer to individuals by their first names in the chapters on Mormonism and ACIM in part to keep naming conventions more uniform in Part 1, but also because it reflects the more intimate nature of microhistory, where first names are routinely used in the primary sources and are necessary at times in order to distinguish family members. In the introduction and in Part 2, in which I express my own views and focus on the main characters in the case studies, I generally refer to them by their last names.

A Restored Church

When Mormons today tell the story of their church's origins, they usually begin where Joseph Smith began in his 1839 version of his history, which is excerpted and canonized in Mormon scripture, that is, with an account of what Mormons now refer to as his "first vision" (*JSP*, H1:204–46; *EMD* 1:59–72). The 1839 account situates his first vision in 1820 in Manchester Township in Upstate New York, near the village of Palmyra, in the context of revivals of religion. Once convicted of their sins by revival preachers, converts were expected to select and join one of the many Protestant denominations. In the story, the young Joseph Smith, at about the age of fifteen, sought forgiveness for his sins but was confused by the multitude of denominations and retired to the woods to ask God which one he should join. In response, according to this account, the Heavenly Father and his Son, Jesus, appeared in a pillar of light and, standing above him in the air, told him that he should join none of the churches, because they were all wrong. He recounted that when he told a Methodist preacher about his vision, the preacher dismissed it with great contempt and that others persecuted him because he claimed to have seen this vision.

The next major event occurred in September 1823 at his home in Manchester, when, while calling upon God, a light lit up his room and a glorious personage dressed in white appeared at his bedside. The personage said he was a messenger sent by God to tell him of a book "written upon gold plates, giving an account of the former inhabitants of this continent and . . . [containing] the fullness of the everlasting Gospel . . . as delivered by the Saviour to the ancient inhabitants." The plates were buried along with two stones of the sort used by seers in former times, referred to in the 1839 account as Urim and Thummim, which would enable him to translate the book. The personage instructed him to recover the plates, allowing him to see where they were buried so clearly that he recognized the place when he visited it the next day. Although he was able to find and see the plates, he was forbidden by the messenger to remove them and was told to return every year until the time came to retrieve them.

In September 1827, four years after the discovery of the golden plates and almost exactly nine months after his marriage to Emma Hale, he was finally able to recover them. Others were so eager to take them from him that Joseph and Emma took the plates to Harmony, Pennsylvania, where her family lived, to begin the work of translating them. Martin Harris, a relatively well-to-do farmer who lived near Palmyra, soon joined them to help with the translation. In mid-June 1828, two months into the translation process, Harris asked Smith to ask the Lord for permission to take the writings home to show them to his wife, Lucy. While he was in Palmyra, the initial 116 pages disappeared and were never recovered. Smith completed the translation with the help of Oliver Cowdery, who arrived in Harmony in April 1829, and the three of them moved to Fayette, New York, in June 1829, to the home of David Whitmer, where they completed the translation later that month. Also in June 1829, Smith received a revelation indicating that three witnesses would be allowed to see the plates directly—Oliver Cowdery, David Whitmer, and Martin Harris. Their testimony, along with the testimony of eight additional witnesses, was included in the Book of Mormon when it was published in March 1830, and was followed by the founding of the restored Church of Christ a month later.

Key Collaborators

The Smith family, comprised of Joseph Smith Jr. (1805–44), his parents, Joseph Smith Sr. (1771–1840) and Lucy Mack Smith (1775–1856), and his siblings—particularly Alvin (1798–1823), Hyrum (1800–1844), Samuel (1808–44), Sophronia (1803–76), William (1811–93), Katherine (1813–1900), and Don Carlos (1816–41)—collaborated in bringing forth the Book of Mormon and establishing the church. Joseph Smith Sr. married Lucy Mack in Tunbridge, Vermont, in 1796, where he was a member of the Universalist Society. They and their children moved from Vermont to Palmyra, New York, in 1816, living there and in neighboring Manchester Township until 1831. Lucy Mack Smith, along with Hyrum, Samuel, and Sophronia, joined the Presbyterian Church of Palmyra in the mid-1820s.

Emma Hale Smith (1804–79), the daughter of Isaac Hale and Elizabeth Lewis, was born in Harmony, Pennsylvania, where she and her family belonged to the Methodist Church. She married Joseph Smith Jr. in January 1827. Emma and Joseph Smith Jr. initially settled in Manchester near his parents. With Emma's help, Joseph recovered the golden plates in September 1827. In December 1827, they moved to her parents' farm in Harmony, Pennsylvania, where Emma assisted in the translation of the plates.

FIGURE 1.1. Lucy Mack Smith (*left*), Joseph Smith (*center*), Emma Hale Smith (*right*). LMS image © Intellectual Reserve, Inc.

Martin Harris (1783–1875) moved with his parents to Palmyra, New York, in 1793. He married his first cousin, Lucy Harris, in 1808, and together they farmed some 320 acres in Palmyra. He was religiously unsettled—reportedly investigating many denominations—before deciding to assist Smith with "the Lord's work" in December 1827. In February 1828, he shared copies of the Book of Mormon characters with experts and assisted Smith with the translation from mid-April to mid-June 1828 in Harmony, Pennsylvania. In June 1828, he took the first 116 pages to Palmyra to show his wife, at which point the pages disappeared. In the wake of the loss, Harris remained in Palmyra and translation was discontinued. Harris visited Harmony again in March 1829, was one of the three witnesses to the gold plates in June 1829, and helped pay for the printing of the Book of Mormon. He and his wife were separated in June 1830.

Oliver Cowdery (1806–50) was born in Vermont and raised as a Congregationalist. He moved to western New York in the mid-1820s. He taught school in Manchester, New York, in 1828–29, at which time he heard about the golden plates from Lucy and Joseph Smith Sr. He traveled to Harmony, Pennsylvania, in April 1829 and served as principal scribe for most of the Book of Mormon.

Joseph Smith Jr. and Oliver Cowdery baptized each other in May 1829, and baptized Hyrum and Samuel Smith in June 1829. They baptized Joseph Smith Sr., Lucy Mack Smith, and Martin Harris in April 1830 and Emma Hale Smith, William Smith, Katherine Smith, Don Carlos Smith, and probably Sophronia Smith in June 1830. The six original members of the church (founded in April 1830) were all drawn from this group, as were two of the three witnesses to the golden plates (Oliver Cowdery and Martin Harris) and three of the eight witnesses (Joseph Sr., Hyrum, and Samuel) in June 1829. They all moved to Kirtland, Ohio, in 1831.[1]

SOURCES AND BEGINNINGS

Although the LDS Church follows this 1839 account and begins its history with Smith's first vision, believers in the early 1830s began the story not with the first vision but with the discovery of the golden plates in 1823.[2] This starting point is assumed in the accounts of Smith's close associate, Oliver Cowdery, and the church's first historian, John Whitmer (*JSP*, H1:6) and, in the words of LDS historians, records predating 1832 "only hint at JS's earliest manifestation" (*JSP*, H1:6). That the starting point shifted over time should not be surprising. By all accounts, Smith claimed access to continuing revelation, and on this basis, he and others edited and revised both their histories of the church and the revelations allegedly vouchsafed to Smith. This process of revising in light of new revelation means that, although early Mormonism is richly documented, most of the accounts of unusual experiences are embedded in layers of interpretation. To reconstruct the process through which this new church emerged, we need to peel back layers of later interpretation to reconstruct how those involved in the process viewed events and understood their experiences as they unfolded.

The Joseph Smith Papers Project, which is publishing critical editions of texts related to Joseph Smith, is providing scholars with access to the earliest known versions of texts, along with subsequent emendations and revisions. This massive undertaking makes it possible for historically minded scholars to approach the emergence of the movement in a new way. Rather than attempting another chronological narrative premised on reconstructing a plausible beginning, we can start with the earliest period for which we have real-time sources and work our way forward and back in time, focusing on questions of interest, in this case, the role of unusual experiences in the emergence of the movement.

If we take the earliest sources as our starting point, they focus our attention on the late 1820s, that is, on the period during which the plates were being translated (Calendar of Documents, in *JSP*, D1:391–428). These include:

- 1825, 1 November, Agreement of Josiah Stowell and Others (including Joseph Smith), Harmony Township, Susquehanna Co., PA (authenticity not confirmed; *JSP*, D1:345–52; see also *EMD* 4:407–13).

---

[1] For brief biographies, see http://josephsmithpapers.org/reference/people#a.
[2] For firsthand accounts of the first vision, see http://josephsmithpapers.org/site/accounts-of-the-first-vision.

- 1826, a court record that predates the recovery of the plates (not extant; for a discussion of later versions, see *EMD* 4:239–56).
- 1827, copies of Book of Mormon characters, Harmony Township, PA (not extant; for a discussion of later versions, see *JSP*, D1:353–67).
- 1828, reference to a (now missing) letter written by Joseph Smith Jr. to Asahel Smith (see *EMD* 1:553); Revelation, July 1828 (*JSP*, D1:6–9 [D&C 3]).
- 1829, a letter from Jesse Smith to Hyrum Smith (*EMD* 1:551–54); numerous revelations, February–Summer (*JSP*, D1:Parts 1–2 [D&C 5–10, 11–16, 17–18, 19]); the manuscript of the Book of Mormon, the Book of Mormon copyright, title page, and preface (*JSP*, D1:58–65, 76–81, 92–93); and the testimony of the three and eight witnesses (*JSP*, D1:378–87).
- 1830, the published Book of Mormon; another court record (original not extant, reprinted in the *New England Christian Herald*, 7 November 1832 [facsimile ed., Signature Books]); the Articles and Covenants (April, *JSP*, D1:116–25); numerous revelations, April–December (*JSP*, D1:Parts 3–4 [D&C 21–37]); and the vision of Moses (June, *JSP*, D1:150–55).

The most extensive documentation of this early period is provided by the revelations received during the process of translation (1828–29), which were transcribed in two manuscript revelation books between 1830–31 and published in the Book of Commandments (1833) and the Doctrine and Covenants (D&C; 1845), and by the text of the Book of Mormon itself, read in the order in which it was most likely dictated.[3] Apart from the 1825 agreement with Josiah Stowell and the 1826 court record, both of which are preserved in later versions, we have no real-time access to events until July 1828, when D&C 3—the first real-time recorded revelation—opens a window in the wake of the loss of the first 116 pages of the manuscript. Chapter 1 thus opens with an in-depth analysis of D&C 3, read as a window on that moment rather than as it was interpreted and reinterpreted in later accounts.

In reconstructing these events, we do not have to limit ourselves to the perspectives of insiders. Although insiders generated most of the early real-time documentation, we have a few early sources that offer a more skeptical perspective: Jesse Smith's 1829 letter to Joseph's brother Hyrum and the transcripts of the 1826 and 1830 court cases that involved Smith. We also have numerous later accounts from both believers and skeptics who were present or heard about the events as they unfolded. Thus, in addition to the later accounts by Joseph Smith, his immediate family, and others who partici-

---

[3] LDS scholars generally agree on the order, which is clearly laid out in Grant Hardy's reader's edition of the Book of Mormon (2003). For discussion, see Welch (2005, 115–16n111).

pated in the translation of the plates, we have accounts that reflect the perspectives of Smith's skeptical in-laws (the Hales and Lewises) in Harmony, Martin Harris's wife Lucy, various neighbors in Manchester, and insiders who later dissented, such as Oliver Cowdery, David Whitmer, and David's brother John. LDS scholars have provided careful reconstructions that interweave the real-time sources for this period with later insider and outsider accounts of the process.[4] In what follows, I rely on these chronologies, starting with the sources that are as close to real-time documentation as we can get, while using later accounts of both insiders and outsiders gingerly, looking for points where later sources agree with each other or with the best real-time sources.

[4] See "Chronology, 1827–1831," in *JSP*, D1:443–48; "Chronology of the Translation" (Hardy 2003, 643–49); and "The Miraculous Translation" (Welch 2005, 76–117).

CHAPTER I

Translation

The revelation to Joseph Smith that Mormons now refer to as "D&C 3," that is, the third revelation in the current edition of the LDS Church's canonized Doctrine and Covenants, provides our first direct window into the emergence of early Mormonism. Although there is evidence to suggest that Joseph Smith received what he and others viewed as revelations prior to this one, this is the first revelation that was written down at about the time it was received (*JSP*, D1:6). This and subsequent revelations were recorded on loose pages, which John Whitmer began transcribing into a manuscript book titled the "Book of Commandments and Revelations" in 1831. In the absence of the originals, which weren't kept, we don't know exactly when or how the earliest revelations were recorded, but John Whitmer supplied headings that indicated, in most cases, when, where, why, and to whom the revelation was given. From Whitmer's heading, we learn that Smith received the first recorded revelation in July 1828 in Harmony, Pennsylvania, "after he had lost certain writings which he had Translated by the gift & Power of God" (Revelation, July 1828, *JSP*, D1:6–8 [D&C 3]). This chapter centers on that revelation, using it to reconstruct, as carefully as we can, not only the event itself but the events that led up to and followed from it, as they likely appeared to those who were involved at the time.

THE CONTEXT

Based on the real-time sources already cited and an array of later sources from those directly involved in the events, including Joseph's mother Lucy Smith, Emma's father Isaac Hale, and Martin and Lucy Harris, we can confirm and flesh out many of the basic historical facts that Smith recounted in his 1839 history related to the first real-time revelation, bracketing or noting interpretations that were contested. Geographically, it is important to note that the revelation was given to Smith in Harmony, Pennsylvania, where he and his wife Emma were living near her extended family, and not at the Smith family farm in Manchester Township in Upstate New York, although events unfolded between these two locations. As Smith indicated in his 1839

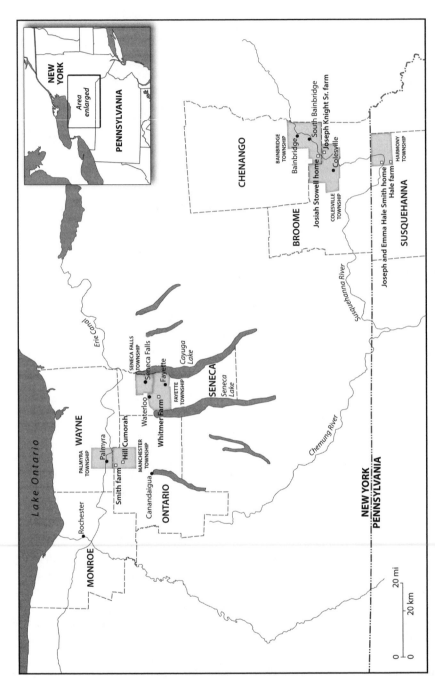

FIGURE 1.2. The Finger Lakes Region of New York and Upper Susquehanna Valley in Pennsylvania, 1828–31. © Intellectual Reserve, Inc.

history, he boarded with the Hales in Harmony when he, in company with Josiah Stowell, his father, and a number of others, were searching for a mine they believed had been opened and abandoned by Spaniards in the late eighteenth century (*EMD* 4:407–13). According to the 1826 trial transcript in which Stowell's nephew brought charges against Smith for "imposture," Smith testified that, while living at Josiah Stowell's for five months, he had spent some time "employed in looking for mines," but most of the time, he said, he had worked on Stowell's farm and attended school (*EMD* 4:249). He acknowledged that "he had a certain stone, which he had occasionally looked at to determine where hidden treasures in the bowels of the earth were, that he professed to tell in this manner where gold mines were a distance underground, and had looked for Mr. Stowel [*sic*] several times." Stowell corroborated Smith's testimony, indicating that "he positively knew that the Prisoner [Smith] . . . possessed the art of seeing those valuable treasures through the medium of said stone" (*EMD* 4:251). In a statement given in 1834, Isaac Hale confirmed that he met Smith in 1825, when he was "in the employ of a set of men who were called 'money-diggers'; and his occupation was that of seeing, or pretending to see [minerals and hidden treasure] by means of a stone placed in his hat, and his hat closed over his face" (*EMD* 4:284). While Isaac Hale confirmed that he refused to consent to Joseph and Emma's marriage, he did so, he said, because he disapproved of Smith's money-digging (*EMD* 4:285), not because Smith claimed to have seen a vision in 1820 or 1823, as Smith implied in his 1839 history.

After they were married in January 1827, Joseph and Emma Smith moved to Manchester to live with Joseph's parents, and, in September 1827, they ostensibly recovered ancient golden plates from a hillside near the Smith family farm. The alleged recovery of the plates did arouse considerable interest, especially in treasure-seeking circles, and others did attempt to gain access to the plates (*EMD* 4:15–16). Joseph and Emma moved to Harmony in December 1827, where Emma's father had offered to help them get established in farming if Joseph would give up "money-digging" (*EMD* 4:285). Martin Harris, a substantial, well-respected farmer from Palmyra, New York, contacted the Smith family in October 1827 after hearing about the recovered plates and gave Joseph and Emma fifty dollars in November to help with their move to Harmony (*EMD* 2:307–10). In Harmony, sometime between December 1827 and February 1828, Joseph Smith produced one or more documents containing "characters" that he said he copied from the plates, perhaps with the help of Emma and Emma's brother Reuben (MacKay 2013; *JSP*, D1:354–55). Harris visited Harmony in February 1828 and, with Smith's permission, took a "characters" document to show several scholars, among them the linguist Charles Anthon at Columbia University (*EMD* 2:253–54). Harris's wife Lucy apparently wanted to accompany him but did not (*EMD* 1:351).

Sometime in this period, Joseph, Emma, and perhaps also Reuben Hale began translating the plates. Martin and Lucy Harris visited Harmony together, most likely in late February or early March, and, in early April 1828, Martin returned to help full-time with the translation (*EMD* 1:353). As Smith recounts in his 1839 history, he and Harris worked for about two months, with Smith dictating and Harris transcribing. In mid-June, Harris took the first 116 manuscript pages home to Palmyra to show them to Lucy and others, leaving Harmony just before Emma delivered the Smith's first child, who died the same day, on 15 June 1828. Joseph stayed with his wife for about two weeks before leaving for Manchester to see why Harris had not yet returned. Over breakfast at the Smith family home, he learned from Harris that the manuscript was lost (see *JSP*, D1:443, *EMD* 1:363–64, and sources cited in *EMD* 4:275–76). Smith received the first recorded revelation after he returned to Harmony in the wake of learning of this loss.

A TURNING POINT

If we now turn to the content of the revelation itself, we find real-time evidence that the loss of the manuscript precipitated a crisis. The key portion of the text reads as follows:

> behold thou art Joseph & thou wast chosen to do the work of the Lord but because of transgression thou mayest fall but remember God is merciful therefore repent of that which thou hast done & he will only cause thee to be afflicted for a season & thou art still chosen & will & will again be called to the work & except [p. 1] Thou do this thou shalt be delivered up & become as other men & have no more gift & when thou deliveredst up that Which that which God had given thee right to Translate thou deliveredest up that which was Sacred into the hands of a wicked man who has Set at naught the Councils of God & hath broken the most Sacred promises which was made before God & hath depended upon his own Judgement & boasted in his own ~~arm~~ wisdom & this is the reason that thou hast lost thy Privileges for a Season for thou hast suffered that the council of thy directors to be trampeled upon from the begining for as the knowledge of a Saveiour hath come to the world so shall the knowledge of my People the Nephities [*sic*] & the Jacobites & the Josephites & the Lamanites come to the ~~Lamanites~~ . . . for this very Purpose are these Plates prepared which contain these Records that the Promises of the Lord might be fulfilled which he made to his People & that the Lamanites might come to the knowledge of their Fathers . . . Received in Harmony Susquehannah Penn. (*JSP*, D1:8–9)

The revelation presupposed the discovery and recovery of buried plates that were inscribed in an ancient language and could be translated by means of a gift that had been granted to Smith, who had been chosen for this work. The loss of the manuscript led Smith to fear that he was no longer chosen and thus threatened to derail the whole translation project. The crisis was resolved through the intervention of an otherworldly personage, who revealed to Smith that he was "still chosen" and would "again be called to the work." It was this intervention that was recorded and later transcribed as the first entry in the manuscript "Book of Commandments and Revelations."

Historians have rightly viewed this crisis as a major turning point. But what kind of turning point? Jan Shipps describes it as the point at which "Joseph Smith don[ned] the prophet's mantle" (1974, 17); Richard Bushman as the point at which Smith "cast aside" the magic of treasure seeking and "found his prophetic voice" (2005, 69); Dan Vogel as the point at which "Smith was transformed from a translator of God's words to ancient prophets into a prophet himself" (2004, 129). From a process perspective, however, describing him as a prophet in 1828 is premature. The headnote for the first revelation in the manuscript revelation book refers to him simply as "Joseph the Seer," as do many of the other revelation headnotes in the manuscript book (MRB, 9; see also 27, 35, 41). The manuscript book itself was titled "A Book of Commandments and Revelations of the Lord Given to Joseph the Seer and Others by the Inspiration of God and Gift and Power of the Holy Ghost" (ibid., 3). John Whitmer, who likely supplied the headings, as he transcribed the revelations into the manuscript book, regularly referred to Joseph as "the Seer" in his history (*EMD* 5:233–38), despite the fact that the revelation of 6 April 1830 (*JSP*, D1:129 [D&C 21]), which legally constituted the church, instructed believers to view him as "a seer & Translater & Prop[h]et," as well as "Apostle" and "Elder." Subsequent early revelations characterized Smith as the church's president, as "a Seer a revelator a translator & a prophet" (11 November 1831-B, *JSP*, D2:135 [D&C 107]), and as a "Seer, Revelator and Prophet" (5–6 December 1834, *JSP*, H1:32). Given that John and David Whitmer ultimately dissented from the LDS Church and the absence of such terms in the revelations apart from the headnotes, it seems prudent not to read back any labels for Smith into these early sources.

This is not to deny that the loss of the manuscript precipitated a crisis or that the recording of the revelation marked a turning point, but it allows us to specify the shifts in both process and content with more precision. Although we don't know for sure when or how the earliest revelations were recorded, the fact that they were recorded reflected an acknowledgment on the part of those who transcribed and preserved them, not only that it was possible to communicate with suprahuman entities in the present but that their communications needed to be recorded. The act of transcription recorded and, at the same time, formalized these communications as "revelations" (Shipps 1974, 18). In terms of content, the communication testified to Smith's gift and his continued calling as a translator. This suggests that the revelation was not simply a communication but an intervention into the process. The text simultaneously recorded the intervention of a suprahuman entity in the process of translation (to testify to Smith's gift and his continued calling) and formalized the intervention as a "revelation."

KEY TERMS AS BUILDING BLOCKS

Three key terms are at work in this first recorded revelation—revelation, gifts, and translation—each of which served as a fundamental "building block" in the process of generating the manuscript of the Book of Mormon. Although this point may seem obvious, I want to stress that all three were *complex cultural concepts, simultaneously internal to the process and constitutive of it.* They came together in the context of the first real-time recorded revelation in a new way, simultaneously establishing real-time revelation as a formal recorded practice and reaffirming Smith's gifts as a translator. Each has a history of use before and after this event, which allows us to situate them in a *developmental trajectory.*

The idea of explicit "revelations," which this first recorded revelation instantiated, was preceded by communications from suprahuman entities, often in response to inquiries made in prayer. The revelation itself refers to these past communications as "revelations," when the speaker notes that "a man"—presumably alluding to Smith—"may have many Revelations . . . yet . . . incur the vengeance of a Just God" if he transgresses. Moreover, the recording of this revelation did not necessarily presuppose belief in continuing revelation as the church later came to understand it. The early revelations, written on individual sheets of paper, were not transcribed into a manuscript book until 1831 and were not published until 1833, at which point they were understood within a framework of "continuing revelation" to the church. During the translation process, those involved may have simply viewed them in practical terms, as divine interventions needed to keep the process on track. They might have believed that the revelations were given to individuals, as David and John Whitmer later concluded, "for their individual instruction" during the translation process and not, as the church later claimed, to the church through its president (as seer and prophet) as continuing revelation (*EMD* 5:207). We can distinguish, as the Whitmers did in retrospect, between new revelation that functioned to facilitate the translation process and the institutionalization of an open-ended process of continuing revelation (via the presidency) as a distinctive mark of the restored church. While the progression from recording, to transcribing in a manuscript book, to publication and canonization as revelations of the church may seem inevitable in retrospect, they were steps in a developmental process that could have occurred otherwise, as the dissenters came to acknowledge (introduction in *JSP*, MRB, xxv–xxviii).

The idea of "gifts" also has a developmental history. The revelation itself was centrally concerned with the gift of translation, which the earliest version of the text characterized as the "right to Translate," but which Sidney Rigdon later amended to read the "sight and power to Translate" (*JSP*, MRB,11). The speaker said that he had lost these "Priveleges" due to his transgressions, but that, if he repented, he would "again be called to the work" and the translation process, which depended on this gift, would go forward.

Although his initial gift was simply that of "translator," the idea of gifts was significantly enlarged over the coming months to include the gift of "revelation" (Revelation, April 1829-B, *JSP*, D1:45 [D&C 8]) and the gift of "seership" (Mosiah 8:11–13). In Mosiah 8:11–13, a portion of the Book of Mormon dictated in early April 1829, a seer was explicitly characterized as one to whom God had given the "gift" of interpreting "the language or the engravings" recorded on ancient plates by means of "interpreters." This characterization specified the role of the seer beyond that of ordinary local seers, who were generally viewed simply as people who could see what others could not by means of special tools or techniques. It also dramatically elevated the seer's status, such that the seer was not only "greater than a prophet" but "a revelator and a prophet also."

Smith had previously demonstrated gifts as a local "seer" engaged in treasure seeking or "money-digging" to the satisfaction of some of his contemporaries, including Josiah Stowell. Others, however, were skeptical, including Stowell's nephew, who brought charges against him in 1826. Sometime after his trial, Smith and others began to view his gift of seeing in the more exalted terms expressed in Mosiah 8 (Bushman 2005, 69). With the founding of the church in 1830, Smith's gifts as seer, translator, revelator, and prophet were all explicitly recognized. In the wake of the translation and publication of the Book of Mormon, others would claim that they too had gifts of seership and prophecy, and these claims were adjudicated through new real-time revelations to Smith, thus confirming his status as the primary and authoritative "prophet, seer, and revelator" (see Revelation, September 1830-B [D&C 28], *JSP*, D1:183–86).

The concept of "translation" presupposed that Smith had recovered ancient records inscribed on metal plates that required translation and that the "right to Translate," as a gift and a privilege given by God, could also be taken away. In this case, the speaker indicated that Smith had lost his "Privileges for a Season," not only because he delivered the manuscript to Harris, but also because he "suffered that the council of thy directors [interpreters] to be trampeled [*sic*] upon" (*JSP*, D1:8–9).[1] This was likely a reference to the objects that he (and, as it turned out, Book of Mormon "seers") used to translate. In the revelation itself, we thus see indications that the translation did not involve the usual process of translating words from one language to another but involved special objects that were known by various names. The title page of the Book of Mormon acknowledged the unusual nature of the process as well, indicating that the translation or "interpretation" of the records "[came] forth by the gift and power of God" (*JSP*, D1:65).

If we view the concepts of revelation, gifts, and translation as building blocks with developmental histories that come together in a new way in the context of the first recorded revelation, we can use the revelation, along with later documents, to reconstruct both the crisis and the alleged supernatural response. In doing so, we need to recognize that later accounts provide considerably more detailed descriptions, including descriptions of how Smith initiated the revelation, who spoke, and what was lost and recovered. Although the text of the revelation suggests that he lost his "gift" or ability to translate, later accounts describe the coming and going of material objects. In his 1832 history, Smith indicated that the Lord chastened him for his repeated inquiries on Harris's behalf and as a result "the Plates was taken from me by the power of God" (*JSP*, H1:16). In Lucy Smith's manuscript history, she indicated that Joseph had to "give back the plates" for a time, but in the 1853 version, she amended the text to indicate that objects used to translate, which she referred to as the Urim and Thummim, were taken and returned, not the plates (*EMD* 1:370). In his 1839 history (*JSP*, H1:246), Smith wove all these details together, indicating that the "heavenly messenger" took the Urim and Thummim away because Smith "wearied the Lord" with his repeated inquiries as to whether Harris could take the manuscript but returned them to him after he returned to Harmony. The return of the Urim and Thummim allowed him to inquire of the Lord and obtain the revelation. After receiving the revelation, both the plates and the Urim and Thummim were taken from him and then returned after a few days (*JSP*, H1:246, 252). Lucy's account indicates that whatever was lost was returned on 22 September 1828, that is, after a few months.

---

[1] There are references to two different kinds of "directors" in the Book of Mormon: a compass-like device (see Mosiah 1:16, D&C 17) and the "stone," which the Lord said he would prepare for his "servant Gazelem, a stone which shall shine forth in darkness unto light, that I may discover unto my people which serve me . . . yea, their secret works, their works of darkness, and their wickedness and abominations" (Alma 37:23–24). The reference to the stone as "these directors" (v. 24) is amended to read "interpreters" in post-1920 LDS versions of the Book of Mormon (Skousen 2009, 769), thus linking the stone/directors with the interpreters that seers use to translate plates in the Book of Mormon (Mosiah 8:13) and the interpreters that Smith ostensibly recovered with the golden plates. If Smith believed that the stone allowed him to see secret works of darkness, including perhaps "wicked" intentions, chastisement for not heeding the "counsels of the directors" would make considerable sense. On the confusing terminology surrounding objects, see Welch (2005, 107–8n40).

LDS scholars have struggled to reconcile the early and late accounts. According to Hardy (2003, 644–45), the angel Moroni took the plates and interpreters in July (D&C 3), extended forgiveness in the summer with D&C 10, and returned the plates and interpreters on 22 September 1828. According to Welch, "portions of [D&C 10] may have been received . . . [during July 1828], although it took its final form [in] . . . May 15–May 25, 1829" (2005, 88).[2] Welch indicates that "[i]t was promised that Moroni would return the plates to Joseph on this familiar date [22 September 1828]," but notes that, according to David Whitmer, "the plates . . . were not returned, but instead Smith was given by the angel a Urim and Thummim of another pattern" and that, according to William McLellin, who collected testimony from those closer to the events, "The Plates and gift of translation was restored to him, but not the Interpreters. He translated the entire book of Mormon by the use of a little stone he had in his possession before he obtained the plates" (Welch 2005, 88, 107n40).

Rather than attempting to reconcile these discrepancies, I think it makes more sense to try to reconstruct the process of emergence using D&C 3 as a baseline. Based on D&C 3, I think we can assume that Smith had experiences prior to July 1828 that he may have interpreted as revelations, that he had (or claimed to have) abilities that he interpreted as gifts, and that there were at least two kinds of objects present prior to Harris's departure— "plates" believed to contain "records" of ancient peoples and "directors" upon whose "council" he had "trampled." To sketch developments relative to this baseline, I will focus on three developmental trajectories: shifts in how Smith's gifts were conceived and enacted in the context of revelatory events, shifts in how believers viewed the material objects associated with the translation process, and shifts in the translation process as a result of Smith's efforts to enlist a "first follower" from outside the family.

The First Revelation as Event

D&C 3 offers us content, but tells us little about the event itself, that is, where it took place, who was present, and how the revelation was received. From the scribal heading (1831), we learn only that it was given to Smith in July 1828 in Harmony; from Smith's histories (1832, 1839) and his mother Lucy's history (1844–45), we learn that he was alone when he received it. We

[2] For a discussion of the difficulties involved in dating D&C 10, see *JSP*, D1:38–39. Although the editors consider the possibility that it was a composite revelation, a portion of which might have been received in the summer of 1828, they conclude that it was not written down until April or May 1829 and that as a whole it more closely resembles other revelations from that period. Evidence for the later dating includes the fact that it was "written in the first-person voice of Jesus Christ, [which] more closely resembles JS's April 1829 texts . . . than it does the July 1828 revelation, which speaks of God in the second person," a point that will be taken up below.

do not know when or how it was transcribed (*JSP*, D:6–7), but, according to Lucy Smith, Joseph told her about the revelation when she and his father visited him in Harmony in September 1828, two months after he received it (*EMD* 1:369–70). Historians typically reconstruct the event based on Smith's 1839 history, indicating, as he does there, that he obtained it by "enquiring of the Lord through [the Urim and Thummim]" (*JSP*, H1:246; *JSP*, D1:6), that is, in a manner consistent with most of his subsequent recorded revelations. Evidence internal to the revelation and Lucy Smith's account of what Joseph told her two months afterward suggest that the speaker may not have been the Lord and that the speaker's words may not have been mediated by an object.

In discussing the revelation so far, I have referred to the speaker simply as "the speaker," since it does not disclose its identity. It addresses Joseph Smith directly and refers to God and the Lord in the third person, self-identifying indirectly in referring to "my People the Nephities [*sic*] & the Jacobites & the Josephites & the Lamanites" (*JSP*, D1:9). In subsequent revelations to Smith in March and April 1829, the speaker self-identifies as the Lord, God, or Jesus Christ (*JSP*, D1:39), leading some to assume that Smith thought the Lord was speaking in the first revelation as well. According to Lucy Smith's account, however, Joseph told her that while he was "humbling [him]self in mighty prayer before the Lord," asking to be forgiven for all that "[he] had done which was contrary to his will[,] . . . *an Angel stood before me and answered me* saying that I had sinned in that [I] had delivered the manuscript into the hands of a wicked man" (*EMD* 1:369–70; emphasis added). After recounting this appearance of the angel, Lucy said Joseph received the following "revelation from the Lord," whereupon she inserted the text of the 1844 version of D&C 3. In his 1839 history, Smith indicated that, while he was out walking, "*the former heavenly messenger appeared* and handed to me the Urim and Thummin [*sic*] . . . and I enquired of the Lord through them" (*JSP*, H1:246; emphasis added).

Rather than viewing the appearance and the revelation as two separate events, I think it is more likely that the text of the July 1828 revelation was obtained through a prayer-induced visionary experience of "a heavenly messenger." Such an interpretation is congruent with the third-person references to "God" and "the Lord" in the recorded revelation, with Lucy Smith's account of an angelic appearance, and Joseph Smith's account of the appearance of "the former heavenly messenger," that is, the ancient Nephite who appeared in his 1823 vision. Most crucially, a visionary appearance would not have required the use of a mediating object and thus is a more plausible response to a situation in which it seemed that his powers had failed him, that is, one in which it appeared to him and/or others that he was no longer "chosen," that he had "no more gift," and that his "privileges" had been withdrawn. I am suggesting, in other words, that the crisis had little to do with the alleged comings and goings of the plates or other objects and everything to do with Smith's confidence in his gifts and/or the credibility of his claims in the eyes of others. The loss of his gifts implies that the objects used to translate were not working and as a result the translation could not proceed. There is no need to add the loss of the objects or the plates to the loss of his gifts; that loss in itself was sufficient to bring the process to halt.[3]

If this reconstruction is accurate, there is a marked difference between the first recorded revelation and those Smith received in March and April 1829 when the derailed translation process was back on track. In these subsequent revelations, the speaker self-identifies as the Lord, God, or Jesus Christ (Revelation, March 1829, *JSP*, D1:13–19 [D&C 5]; Revelation, Spring 1829, *JSP*, D1:37–44 [D&C 10]), thus amplifying the source of the revelation and in turn elevating Smith's status. By the spring, he is no longer receiving revelations *from* an ancient Nephite but is now receiving revelations *like* an ancient Nephite. This suggests that Smith's role as seer was clarified and defined at about the time he was dictating the book of Mosiah with its elevated definition of the Nephite seer as greater than a prophet or revelator.

In terms of content, comparison of the first with subsequent early revelations highlights two important shifts: (1) a shift from prayer-induced visionary appearances of spiritual messengers to object-mediated inquiries of the Lord and (2) a shift from a seer who used special objects to seek buried treasure to the more elevated understanding of a seer as a receiver of revelation who—like the Nephite seers—relied upon special objects to interpret ancient records. In terms of process, the recording of revelations formalized the expectation that an otherworldly voice could and would intervene in the translation process. The shift from appearances to object-mediated inquires marked the emergence of formal procedures for enlisting the Lord's guidance in the translation process. Taken together these shifts resulted in an elevated understanding of Smith and the task that he and his collaborators had undertaken, and created guidance procedures for keeping the translation process on track.

STONES AS NON-ORDINARY OBJECTS

Apart from references to the gift or privilege of translation and the cryptic reference to the "counsel of [his] directors," the early revelations say little

---

[3] Although we only have evidence of what Smith claimed he saw in these objects, I am working with the assumption in chapters 1–3 and chapter 11 that Smith may well have "seen things" in his seer stone while treasure seeking and while translating. We know that some people are much better visualizers than others and, I think, given his visionary experiences and his reputation as a local seer, that Smith probably had such abilities. This doesn't mean that what he visualized was real. As I discuss in chapter 11, I think that he most likely had the ability, which has been demonstrated in so-called highly hypnotizable individuals (HHs), to visualize things that aren't actually there *as if they were*, that is, in a way that goes beyond simply imagining them (Heap, Brown, and Oakley 2004). As with the abilities of HHs, I am assuming that contextual factors could have affected Smith's ability to draw upon his "gifts" and thus given him the impression that they were "withdrawn."

about how the translating was done. In the preface to the first edition of the Book of Mormon, Smith simply said that he "translated by the gift and power of God." Other early sources, however, mention objects. Jesse Smith's letter to his nephew Hyrum on 17 June 1829 refers to "your Brother's [that is, Joseph's] spectacles," which he used to "decypher hieroglyphics" (*EMD* 1:553). In an interview with Peter Bauder in October 1830, Joseph Smith reportedly told the newspaper editor, "he was enabled to translate the characters on the plate into English . . . only by the aid of a glass which he also obtained with the plate" (*EMD* 1:17). In his 1832 history, Smith indicates, "the Lord had prepared spectacles for to read the Book" (*EMD* 1:30). Lucy Smith claims to have seen and handled the spectacles "with no covering but a silk handkerchief" the day after her son allegedly recovered the plates (*EMD* 1:328–29). In an 1838 diary entry (*EMD* 1:52), Smith indicates that he told the Mormon elders that he obtained "the Urim and Thummim with them [the plates]; by the means of which, I translated the plates."

The Book of Mormon also discusses objects used to translate, referring to them as "interpreters" in Mosiah 8:13, 28:13–14 and "directors" in Alma 37:21, 23–25. Mosiah's interpreters were comprised of "two stones which was fastened into the two rims of a bow" and handed down with the plates "for the purpose of interpreting languages" (Mosiah 28:13–14). The "directors [*sic*]" in Alma 37 was "a stone" that would "shine forth in darkness" that "Gazelem" would use to "bring forth . . . all their [the Jaredites'] secret works and their abominations," the record of which had been preserved on "twenty four plates."

We can get a clearer sense of the role of objects in the process of translation if we step back and focus not on what they were called but on the later eyewitness accounts of what Smith was actually doing when he translated. Based on a careful analysis of the later sources, LDS scholars Richard Van Wagoner and Steve Walker (1982) concluded, and scholars now generally agree (Anderson 1984; Quinn 1998; Ashurst-McGee 2000; MacKay and Dirkmaat 2015), that Smith dictated most of the early revelations and most, if not all, of the Book of Mormon text to a scribe while looking at a stone placed in a hat to block out the light.[4] There is also general agreement that the stone or stones he used to translate and receive revelations were the same as those he used to find lost objects and search for buried treasure. Scholars also agree that he gave up regular use of a seer stone sometime in early 1830 and thereafter received revelations and made translations (e.g., of the Bible)

---

[4] There are two widely held LDS theories of method: the stone in the hat method, which reflects the testimonies of the direct witnesses, and the Truman Coe finger on the text method, which more likely reflects stories from the Kirtland era (see Gardner 2011, 7–8, 115). Although LDS scholars generally agree that the former is more historically accurate, the LDS Church's public representations reflected the latter method until quite recently (MacKay and Dirkmaat 2015; Turley, Jensen, and Ashurst-McGee 2015).

FIGURE I.3. Joseph Smith translating with Martin Harris as scribe. The plates are elsewhere. (Artist's depiction, based on historical sources. © Anthony Sweat.)

for the most part without a mediating object (*JSP*, D1:xxxiii). According to David Whitmer, Smith gave the stone he used to translate to Oliver Cowdery. It was eventually acquired by Brigham Young and has been preserved since that time by the LDS First Presidency (Van Wagoner and Walker 1982, 58–59; MacKay and Dirkmaat 2015, 136–37n26). Apart from the printer's copy of the manuscript of the Book of Mormon and portions of the original, it is the only material artifact remaining from the translation process.[5]

This bare-bones account tells us very little about how believers and critics viewed the use of a stone in the process. In considering their views, we can start with discovery of the surviving stone. Willard Chase, a neighbor of the Smiths, reported that he discovered the stone in 1822 while he was digging a well with the help of Joseph and his brother Alvin. According to Chase, after digging down about twenty feet, "we discovered a singularly appearing stone, which excited my curiosity." He brought it to the top of the well and, while they were examining it, "Joseph put it into his hat, and then his face

---

[5] With the inclusion of photographs of the brown seer stone in the *JSP*'s *Revelations and Translations, Volume 3: Printer's Manuscript of the Book of Mormon*, which appeared in August 2015, the LDS Church brought Smith's use of a seer stone to the attention of a general LDS audience. Although many have assumed that documents containing characters that Smith copied from the plates have also survived from this period, scholars have concluded that this is unlikely (see *JSP*, D1:Appendix 2, 353–67; MacKay, Dirkmaat, and Jensen 2013).

into the top of the hat." The next day Smith came back and asked Chase if he could have the stone, "alleging that he could see in it" (*EMD* 2:65–66). With Smith's discovery that "he could see in it," the stone went from being a singular stone (a non-ordinary object) to an object with non-ordinary powers. Whether in claiming to "see in it," Smith attributed special powers to the stone, viewed it as awakening real or pretend powers in himself, or some combination thereof, is not clear. Contemporaries interpreted his claim that "he could see in it" in light of all these possibilities.

When Smith was brought to court in 1826 by Josiah Stowell's nephew, the witnesses focused on his abilities, or lack thereof. Many of the witnesses testified to his "pretended . . . skill of telling where hidden treasures . . . were by means of looking through a certain stone." Others, however, including Stowell, testified to their faith in Smith's skill, specifically his ability to "divine things by means of said Stone and Hat" (*EMD* 4:248–56). In an 1870 interview (*EMD* 2:321), Martin Harris recounted a story in which he set out to prove to skeptics that the stone itself had special properties that enabled Smith to translate. The story was set in the period in which he and Smith were translating the first 116 pages of the manuscript, during which time, Harris said, they sometimes grew tired of translating and "exercise[d] by throwing stones out on the river." On one such occasion, "Martin found a stone very much resembling the one used for translating, and on resuming their labor of translation, Martin put in place the stone that he had found." Martin reported that on starting to translate, "Joseph exclaimed, 'Martin! What is the matter? All is as dark as Egypt.'" When Joseph asked why he had replaced his stone, Martin said, "to stop the mouths of fools, who had told him that the Prophet had learned those sentences and was merely repeating them." To counter critics who apparently claimed that the "translation" was a product of Smith's mind, Harris set out to prove that the translation was dependent on Smith's special stone.

Joseph and Heil Lewis, cousins of Joseph's wife Emma, attributed non-ordinary power of a negative sort to the stone and to Smith, characterizing him as "a practicing necromancer." Emma's cousins, who were slightly younger than Joseph, lived near her parents in Harmony when Joseph and other treasure seekers boarded at the Hales' in 1825 and when Joseph and Emma returned to live there from December 1827 until June 1829. In highly critical statements given later in life, they described Smith's role in the treasure seeking. "All that Smith did was to peep with stone and hat, and give directions where and how to dig, and when and where the enchantment removed the treasure [when it could not be recovered]" (*EMD* 4:312). When Smith attended a Methodist class meeting held in their home in June 1828, "[they] thought it was a disgrace to the church to have a practicing necromancer, a dealer in enchantments and bleeding ghosts, in it" and told him that they would initiate an investigation of his conduct if he didn't withdraw his name from the Methodist class book (*EMD* 4:311). In his 1835 history, Oliver Cowdery discussed Smith's treasure-seeking days, saying he would have left the topic "unnoticed," if Smith had "not been accused of digging down all, or nearly so, the mountains of Susquehannah, or causing others to do it by some art of nicromancy [*sic*]" (*EMD* 2:464).

Emma Smith's cousins, like others close to the translation process, believed that treasure seeking and translation were conducted with the same stone and hat. Smith's father-in-law, Isaac Hale, later indicated that "the manner in which he pretended to read and interpret [the golden plates] was the same as when he looked for the money-diggers, with a stone in his hat, and his hat over his face, while the Book of Plates were at the same time hid in the woods" (Van Wagoner and Walker 1982, 52). Those who believed that local seers, such as Smith, had the ability to "divine things" by means of the stone and the hat, those who believed he was practicing dark "arts of necromancy," and those who felt he was mounting an elaborate deception, all held beliefs about the kinds of powers that could plausibly be attributed to people, objects, and suprahuman beings. While Joseph and Hiel Lewis attributed "the same unreasoning and blind credulity" to both the treasure seekers and those who believed that Smith "by inspiration found and translated his golden bible" (*EMD* 4:313), those who believed that Smith had recovered ancient records reinterpreted the stones in light of newly recounted narratives (Gardner 2011, 127–29).

Instead of viewing spectacles, directors, interpreters, and Urim and Thummim as designating *different* objects, we can view them as progressively elaborated interpretations of the stone(s) that Smith used in the translation process.[6] Each of the terms contextualized the stone(s) in progressively larger narratives that simultaneously undercut competing treasure-seeking narratives and gave the stone(s) new meaning and significance within a developing Mormon narrative. We can place these terms and their associated stories in a plausible developmental sequence. The first story was most likely Joseph's story of recovering something he could use to translate the plates, whether "spectacles" or "a glass he obtained with the plates." The story of an object recovered along with or after the plates was most likely followed by the Book of Mormon stories; first the stories in Mosiah about the "interpreters"—"two stones which was fastened into the two rims of a bow" that could be used to translate ancient records, and then the stories in Alma about the "directors"—"a stone" that "Gazelem" would use to bring forth the content of the Jaredites' twenty-four plates. In 1833 W. W. Phelps connected the objects described in the Book of Mormon with the biblical "Urim and Thummim" (e.g., 1 Sam. 14:41–42). Smith subsequently em-

---

[6] I am not ruling out the possibility that there were actual "spectacles," but according to LDS historians MacKay and Dirkmaat (2015, 62), the lenses of the spectacles *were* seer stones.

braced this idea in his canonized history, as did the later tradition, such that "Urim and Thummim" were adopted as generic terms designating objects that were used to discern the mind or will of the deity (Van Wagoner and Walker, 49–50, 53). Later revelations further integrated these stories by interpreting Gazelem as a reference to Joseph Smith (D&C 78:9; 82:11; 104:26, 43–46) and elaborating on the cosmic significance of the Urim and Thummim (D&C 130).

If we return to what was lost and recovered in conjunction with the disappearance of the manuscript, the confusion seems more understandable. These are all retrospective reconstructions by believers who were (and are) seeking to relate the objects in Smith's narrative of the recovery of the golden plates, in the Book of Mormon, and in the Bible with the physical object—a stone in a hat—that was used to receive the early revelations and translate the Book of Mormon. Assuming that Smith translated at least some of the lost pages with his seer stone, as Martin Harris and others indicate, and that he had used his stone in the past to locate things, I find it significant that he wasn't able to use his stone to locate the lost manuscript (Vogel 2005, 127). This inability is congruent with the idea that (1) he had lost his gift and (2) that he had somehow "trampled on the council of his directors." It is more evidence to suggest that Smith lost and recovered his ability to see things in his stone, without losing possession of the stone, and that the appearance and disappearance of other allegedly material objects, such as the spectacles and the golden plates, must be accounted for in other terms.

THE PLATES AS NON-ORDINARY OBJECT

Although LDS historians, such as Bushman (2004, 269) and Givens (2002, 12) have stressed the evidence for the materiality of the plates and, to a lesser extent, the spectacles, they tend to downplay the evidence that insiders did not view them as material in the ordinary sense of the term. In saying this I do not mean to deny the presence of an ordinary material object, but to argue that there were, in effect, two types of objects: ordinary material objects and believed-in objects. The ordinary material objects included something made out of metal that had "leaves" that could be felt through a cloth and a box containing an object of significant weight. The ancient golden plates were a believed-in object that could be transported by angels, viewed from a distance via seer stones, and seen directly only with the eyes of faith. Believers—not surprisingly—conflated these two types of objects in response to Joseph Smith's claim that the Lord had commanded them not to look at the ancient plates directly.

We can begin with the evidence for an ordinary material object, which is of three sorts: first, accounts of feeling and "hefting" the plates while covered with a cloth or contained in a box; second, the accounts of the three and eight witnesses, who claim to have seen the plates directly; and third, relatively detailed visual descriptions that characterize the plates in terms of their size and appearance and have been used to create models of them.

Although Joseph, his parents, and others, such as David Whitmer, provide detailed descriptions that have been used by believers to create models of the plates (see *EMD* 1:171, 221, 462, 5:38), most of the sources agree that no one was allowed to look at the plates directly from the time they were recovered in September 1827 until they were shown to the witnesses in late June 1829, after which time they were no longer available. Most of the evidence offered by Smith's immediate family and those directly involved in the translation process is of something material, which, though obscured by a cloth or kept hidden in a box, nonetheless could be felt and "hefted." Joseph's younger siblings, William (*EMD* 1:479, 497, 505, 508, 511) and Catherine (*EMD* 1:521, 524), both recount that they had hoped to see the plates when Joseph brought them home, but that when he said they were not allowed to look at them directly, they obeyed. Joseph's wife Emma provided a more detailed account that ran along similar lines (*EMD* 1:539–40). Martin Harris, who helped with the translation, reported that "[t]hese plates were usually kept in a cherry box made for that purpose, in the possession of Joseph and myself. The plates were kept from the sight of the world, and no one, save Oliver Cowdrey [*sic*], myself, Joseph Smith, jr., and David Whitmer [i.e., Smith and the three witnesses], ever saw them" (*EMD* 2:306). The signed testimony of the three and the eight witnesses provides relatively little physical detail. The three—Cowdery, Whitmer, and Harris—simply testified "we beheld & saw the plates & the engravings thereon" (*EMD* 5:347), while the eight testified that the plates, which "we did handle with our hands & we also saw the engravings thereon," had "the appearance of gold" (*EMD* 3:471).

The more detailed descriptions of the plates seem not to reflect what people saw firsthand, but the way Joseph described the plates to them. Joseph Knight, who was staying with the Smiths the night Smith ostensibly recovered the plates, recounted that Smith described the plates to him the next morning, indicating "the Length and width and thickness of the plates[,] and[,] said he[,] they appear to be Gold." But, according to Knight—and Smith's mother Lucy agrees on this point—Knight did not see the recovered plates, which were still not present in the house but presumably hidden for safekeeping (*EMD* 4:15). The later descriptions offered by Joseph (1:171), his parents (*EMD* 1:221, 462, 456), and others (*EMD* 5:38) are similar to the one that Smith offered to Joseph Knight and suggest that the models of the plates are based not on what they actually saw, but on how Smith described the plates to them.

If we look beyond this inner circle of believers, all of whom testified to the materiality of the plates, opinion as to their existence was sharply divided. There were many, mostly associates or former associates of Smith's in the local treasure-seeking network, who clearly believed the plates existed, viewed them as gold treasure rather than a gold bible, and went to great lengths to get them away from Smith, but without success. Then there were those who viewed Smith as a charlatan and a deceiver who fabricated plates in order to promote his revelatory claims, including Martin Harris's wife Lucy (*EMD* 1:353–55, 382–86), Emma Smith's family (*EMD* 4:284–88), and neighbors such as the Ingersolls (*EMD* 1:385–86, 2:39–45).

What I find most striking, though, is that discussions of the materiality of the plates, whether by insiders or outsiders to the tradition, downplay the non-ordinary properties that believers (and treasure seekers) associated with the material objects. Thus, if we examine key events in the material history of the plates, we find that their material presence remained under the control of supernatural entities that had the power to manifest or withdraw them as they saw fit. "The Testimony of the Three Witnesses" published with the Book of Mormon provides the most obvious example. Smith did not simply show the plates to the three witnesses; instead, they testified that they were shown the plates "by the power of God & not of man," and specifically, that "an angel of God came down from Heaven & he brought & laid before our eyes that we beheld & saw the plates & the engravings thereon" (*EMD* 5:347). In contrast, the published "Testimony of the Eight Witnesses" indicates that Joseph Smith Jr. showed them the plates, not an angel.[7] Nonetheless, according to his mother, Lucy, Joseph didn't bring the plates to the grove so that the eight could handle them. Rather, she indicates, the eight "repaired to a little grove where it was customary for the family to offer up their secret prayers[,] as Joseph had been instructed that the plates would be carried there by one of the ancient Nephites." Moreover, she adds, "[a]fter the witnesses returned to the house the Angel again made his appearance to Joseph and received the plates from his hands" (*EMD* 1:395–96).

Lucy Smith recounts other occasions in which an angel transported the plates from one place to another. Prior to traveling from Pennsylvania back to New York, the Lord told Joseph to leave the plates in Pennsylvania and "he would receive the plates from the hand of an angel" after he arrived at the Whitmers' house in New York (*EMD* 1:391). Both Joseph's history (*EMD*

[7] While there is general agreement that the three witnesses saw the plates in a vision, skeptics and believers tend to disagree with respect to the testimony of the eight, with believers arguing that the eight saw and handled the plates directly (Givens 2002, 39–40; Anderson 2005) and skeptics arguing that they did not (Vogel 2002, Palmer 2002, Vogel 2012). Although Anderson (21–22) quotes Lucy Smith's account, both he and his interlocutors focus on what the witnesses saw in the grove without commenting on how Lucy Smith indicates the plates got there. Thanks to Mark Ashurst-McGee for bringing this discussion to my attention.

1:73) and Lucy's manuscript history (*EMD* 1:370–71) indicate that an angel took the plates back after Martin Harris reported that the first part of the manuscript had disappeared. When the plates were hidden, Joseph monitored them from a distance using his "interpreters." Thus, according to his mother, "Joseph kept the urim and thumim constantly about his person as he could by this means ascertain at any moment [if] the plates were in danger" (*EMD* 1:333–34, 338). The treasure seekers used the same method to try to find the plates. According to Lucy, the "mob" enlisted Sally Chase, another local seer of some repute, to use her "green glass" to find "the exact place where Joe Smith kept his gold bible hid" (*EMD* 1:342–43).

In short, insider accounts depict the plates as a material object that angels, "ancient Nephites," and, in particular, the angel Moroni, who was himself "an ancient Nephite," could display, deliver, and take away as appropriate. Even though the inner circle that saw and touched the plates generally acknowledged that they had either seen the plates "in vision" or obscured by a covering, believers and nonbelievers found the "magical realism" of the plates hard to grasp.[8] In 1837–38 a number of well-placed believers left the church when Martin Harris testified, according to Warren Parish, that "he never saw the plates . . . except in vision, and . . . that any man who says he has seen them in any other way is a liar, Joseph [Smith] not excepted" (*EMD* 2:289) and, according to Stephen Burnett, that neither the three nor the eight witnesses had seen "the plates with his natural eyes only in vision or imagination" (*EMD* 2:291). Although Harris's testimony apparently caused considerable consternation, Parrish noted that it was supported by the revelation Smith received in June 1829, preserved in the canonized Doctrine and Covenants (D&C 17:5), which indicated that the three witnesses would see the plates, "as my servant Joseph Smith, Jun., has seen them; *for it is by my* [God's] *power that he has seen them*, and it is because he had faith" (*EMD* 2:289n2; emphasis added).[9] In other words, God, or Smith in revelatory

---

[8] The term "magical realism" refers to "narrative fiction that includes magical happenings in a realist matter-of-fact narrative," such that the supernatural is presented as an ordinary, everyday occurrence (Bowers 2004, 4).

[9] It is not clear what was so disturbing about Harris's testimony, partly because we don't know exactly what Harris said (for text and commentary, see *EMD* 2:288–93). Although he may have said that the testimony of the eight was false, he most likely said, under some duress, that the eight—like the three—saw the plates "in vision," which then, as now, is not how believers typically interpret the witness of the eight. Whether he said "Joseph Smith not excepted" isn't clear either, as it appears in Parrish's but not Burnett's account. There is no indication that Harris considered his testimony as a repudiation of the Book of Mormon; indeed, Burnett reports him as saying "he knew it was true." Most likely, then, Harris simply reiterated his long-standing testimony to have seen the plates "with the eye of faith [although covered with a cloth] . . . just as distinctly as I see any thing around me" (*EMD* 2:292n11) and, when pressed on the matter in the heat of an emotional meeting, claimed that the same was true for the eight as well. Since he allegedly said that "he should have let it pass as it was . . . if it had not been picked out of him" (*EMD* 2:292), I suspect that Harris typically left people to believe what they wished about the testimony of the eight, because he knew some people had dif-

FIGURE 1.4. Joseph Smith translating with Emma Smith as scribe. The plates are present but hidden under a cloth. (Artist's depiction, based on historical sources. © Anthony Sweat.)

mode, depending on how you look at it, conceded that Smith himself only saw the plates through the power of God in faith.

The ancient golden plates, like Smith's seer stones, were believed-in objects, that is, material objects to which insiders attributed non-ordinary properties. The objects, though, were of different sorts. Smith kept his seer stones in open view and they have survived down to the present day. Following the command of the Lord relayed to them by Smith, he and his collaborators kept the plates concealed. Because family members and others who participated in the translation process believed in the reality of the ancient golden plates, they did not challenge Joseph's statement that God had commanded them not to look at them directly. Outsiders found this puzzling. When Joseph's brother William told an interviewer that, while disappointed that they could not view the plates directly, the family had obeyed, the interviewer was surprised. "[M]ost people," the interviewer told the elderly William, "would ha[v]e examined them any way." At that, the interviewer said, "the old man suddenly straiphtened [straightened] up

---

ficulty with the idea that all the witnesses had seen through the eyes of faith. Given the evidence already presented, that people, including Smith, either saw ancient plates directly in vision or through the eyes of faith when covered or in a box, I take the consternation surrounding Harris's testimony as evidence of believers' difficulty grasping the "magical realism" of the plates.

and looked intently at him and said[, ']The Lord knew he could trust Joseph[,] and as for the rest of the family[,] we had no desire to transgress the commandment of the Lord but on the other hand was exceeding anxious to do al[l] we were commanded to do[']" (*EMD* 1:508). Joseph's wife Emma made much the same point, though less emphatically, saying, "I did not attempt to handle the plates nor, uncover them to look at them. I was satisfied that it was the work of God, and therefore did not feel it to be necessary to do so" (*EMD* 1:540).

Joseph's directive, understood by insiders as a divine injunction, functioned to set the plates apart in a Durkheimian sense. Although Joseph could supply the directive, others had to observe it in order for it to have any effect and, insofar as they did, they participated in the materialization of ancient golden plates. They did so by fusing an ordinary material object that could be viewed and "hefted" and a non-ordinary believed-in object that could be seen only through the eyes of faith. In cognitive science terms, believers linked their believed-in representation of the ancient golden plates with an ordinary, albeit concealed, material object, while skeptics did not. Belief in the existence of ancient golden plates and special objects that gave Smith the power to translate them distinguished insiders from outsiders and thus played a crucial role in constituting the emergent group as a group.

First Follower and First Critic

While it seems as if Smith's immediate family members rapidly overcame their disappointment at not being able to view the plates directly, Martin and Lucy Harris offer a more complicated window on the process of believing or not believing. Apart from Martin Harris and Joseph Knight Sr., who was present at the Smith's home the morning Joseph claimed to have recovered the plates, the story of the golden plates up through the arrival of Oliver Cowdery is a family story. The copyright for Lucy Smith's history—"The History of Lucy Smith . . . containing an account of the many persecutions, trials and afflictions *which I and my family have endured* in bringing forth the Book of Mormon and establishing the church"—emphatically depicts it as such (Easton-Flake and Cope 2014; emphasis added). But the movement wouldn't have grown if Smith hadn't been able to attract followers from outside his family. Although Joseph Knight was allied with the family, he did not participate in or help support the translation and publication of the Book of Mormon, as Harris did. If we look beyond Joseph and Emma's immediate and extended families, Martin Harris emerges as the movement's crucial "first follower" and Lucy Harris as, in many ways, its "first critic."

If we think about what it means to join an emergent group, it seems safe to say that anyone who does so must weigh the strength of their current ties with the prospects afforded by the new group. Scholars have long observed that religious "seekers," that is, those with relatively weaker ties to extant groups and those who are prone to unusual experiences, are more likely to join a new group. Family members typically differ from outsiders in that they have a preexisting relationship with the person who is making new revelatory claims. Still, they have to decide how to respond to the new revelatory claims, and the nature of their preexisting relationships colors the way they respond. The most crucial factor in this regard is trust. Joseph's immediate family was divided religiously and infused with a seeker spirit, but if they had not trusted Joseph, they most likely would not have believed him when he said the Lord had commanded them not to look at the plates. This trust extended, albeit more gradually, to Joseph's father's family, all of whom, apart from his Calvinist uncle, Jesse, joined the new church. Emma's family—Joseph's in-laws—were not only committed Methodists but had known Joseph in his treasure-seeking days; they did not trust him, opposed Joseph and Emma's marriage, and did not join the new church. Martin and Lucy Harris, by way of contrast, had a much more limited relationship with Smith and had to decide whether or not he could be trusted. Martin decided he could be trusted, Lucy decided he could not, but it took both of them a while to arrive at their opposing views.

As already noted, we have later accounts of the events leading up to D&C 3 from many of the key participants, but much of the evidence is inconsistent. It is not clear, for example, when Martin Harris learned of the plates. Both Lucy Harris and Lucy Smith indicate that Martin knew of the plates before they were recovered (*EMD* 2:35, *EMD* 1:330), but Martin said he didn't hear the news "about Joseph Smith, jr., having a golden bible" until a few weeks afterward (*EMD* 2:307–8). Both Lucy Smith and Martin Harris agree, however, that there was considerable back-and-forth between the Smiths and Harrises in the weeks immediately following the alleged recovery of the plates in which Martin, who was aware of Smith's reputation as a "money-digger," sought to investigate the truth of Smith's claims (*EMD* 1:344, 2:308). It is also clear that the Harrises had financial resources and the Smiths did not (*EMD* 2:34) and, thus, that the back-and-forth between the Smiths and Harrises in October and November 1827 concerned money and the nature of the plates.

We know little about Lucy Harris's religious views, but Martin is consistently described as unsettled yet opinionated (Walker 1986; Taylor 1999). Rev. John A. Clark, an Episcopal priest from Palmyra who interviewed Harris in 1827 and 1828, provides an apt summary: "in his religious views, he seemed to be floating upon the sea of uncertainty. He had evidently quite an extensive knowledge of the Scriptures, and possessed a manifest disputatious turn of mind. As I subsequently learned, Mr. Harris had always been a firm believer in dreams, and visions, and supernatural appearances, such as apparitions and ghosts, and therefore was a fit subject for such men as Smith and his colleagues to operate upon" (*EMD* 2:262). There is also evidence to suggest that both Martin and Lucy Harris were emotionally volatile. Lucy Harris described her husband as "quick in his temper and in his mad-fits frequently abuses all who may dare to oppose him in his wishes" (*EMD* 2:34). Lucy Smith described Lucy Harris as "habitually of a very jealous temperament and being hard of hearing she was always suspicious of some secret . . . designedly kept from her" (*EMD* 1:344).

Evidence from both Lucy Smith and Martin Harris indicates that trust, finances, and personality were all at play in the exchanges between the Smiths and Harrises just prior to the Smiths' move to Harmony. Initially, it appears, *both* Harrises were willing to help fund the translation and printing of the plates, if they were of God. According to Lucy Smith, both Lucy Harris and her sister offered the Smiths money to support the project when Lucy Smith visited the Harrises at Joseph's request. Lucy Harris apparently returned the visit before Martin did, at which point she said "that she would see the Gold plates if he really had any and she was resolved to help him in publishing them." According to Lucy Smith, Joseph told Lucy Harris "he was not permitted to exhibit [the plates]" and that he "always prefer[red] dealing with men rather than their wives," which "highly displeased Mrs Harris" (*EMD* 1:346–47).

Moreover, while his wife was initially supportive, Martin depicted himself as highly uncertain. Martin clearly knew of Smith's money-digging activities; if Joseph did tell him about the plates a year or two before he recovered them, as his mother indicates, he may have characterized them as gold plates, that is, as gold treasure, and Martin may have thought of them as such rather than as a gold bible (Walker 1986, 38). According to Martin (*EMD* 2:309), when he and Joseph did meet, Joseph told him that the angel had instructed him to "quit the company of the money-diggers" and "look in the spectacles" to see "the man that would assist him." The man, of course, turned out to be Martin Harris. Harris, clearly uncertain as to whether he could trust Smith, responded: "if it is the devil's work I will have nothing to do with it; but if it is the Lord's, you can have all the money necessary to bring it before the world." Although Joseph claimed he was following the directives of an angelic messenger, Martin parried with scripture—"cursed is every one that putteth his trust in man"—and told Joseph he must not blame him for "not taking [his] word." Still, Martin said, if the Lord would show him directly "that it is his work," he would give Joseph all the money he wanted (*EMD* 2:309). That night, Martin prayed about the matter and God showed him that it was his work "by the still small voice spoken in the soul" (*EMD* 2:310). Shortly thereafter, when Martin ran into Joseph in a "public house" in Palmyra, he offered Smith fifty dollars to pay off his debts and move to Harmony "to do the Lord[']s work" and Smith did not refuse (*EMD* 1:348–49).

Offering Smith the fifty dollars was just the first step, however. Although Smith's 1839 history makes it sound as if it was his idea to copy the characters from the plates after he arrived in Harmony, Lucy Smith's history indicates that Joseph and Martin had agreed on this before Joseph and Emma left (*EMD* 1:350). Moreover, Smith's 1832 history indicates that, due to Martin's righteousness in giving Smith the money, the Lord appeared to Harris in a vision, which prompted him to travel to Harmony to tell Joseph that "the Lord had shown him that he must go to new York City with some of the c[h]aracters so we [Joseph and Martin] proceeded to coppy [*sic*] some of them" (*EMD* 1:30). Smith's earliest account, in other words, suggests that copying the characters off the plates and taking them to New York *was Harris's idea* (*EMD* 1:30). If this was the case, and I see no particular reason to doubt Smith's earliest recollection, it would suggest that this was a further step in Martin Harris's efforts to test the reality of Smith's claims. According to Lucy Smith, Lucy Harris wanted to accompany Martin to New York, but he didn't think that was a good idea, so he left suddenly, leaving it to Lucy Smith to break the news to his wife that he had gone. So again, Lucy Harris wanted to be involved and was rebuffed (*EMD* 1:350–51).

Smith's 1839 history also differs from earlier accounts of Harris's visit with Professor Charles Anthon in New York City. The 1839 account indicates that Harris brought a sample of characters and a partial translation, which Anthon initially said was correct. Smith's 1832 history, Rev. Clark's report of his 1828 interview with Harris, and Anthon's 1834 testimony all indicate that Harris only brought characters and that Anthon could not read them (*EMD* 1:30, 2:267, 4:380). Clark, who indicated that Harris visited him in order to tell him of Smith's discovery of the plates and show him a transcription of the characters, said that his and Anthon's *inability* to read the characters convinced Harris that Smith's account could be relied on. After visiting Anthon, Clark reported, "Martin had now become a perfect believer. . . . The very fact that Smith was an obscure and illiterate man, showed that he must be acting under divine impulses" (*EMD* 2:267). Clark said his own "ignorance of the characters in which this pretended ancient record was written, was to Martin Harris new proof that Smith's whole account of the divine revelation made to him was entirely to be relied on" (*EMD* 2:266). The proof of this was biblical, but drew not on Isaiah's prophesy, as Smith later did, but rather from a passage in Corinthians: "God had chosen the foolish things of the world to confound the wise" (1 Cor. 1:27; *EMD* 2:267).[10]

MacKay and Dirkmaat (2015, 65–71) speculate that initially Smith did not realize that he had been given the spectacles in order to translate the

[10] According to MacKay, none of the extant "characters documents" were composed by Smith, and they do not match the document described by Anthon; they are at best copies of one or more of these early documents (see MacKay 2013; *JSP*, D1:353–67).

plates and that it was not until Harris returned to tell him that the "learned" could not translate the characters that he began translating with the spectacles. If they are right, it highlights the interactive nature of the process and the role that Harris's need to test Smith's claims played in it. As a fellow visionary, Harris, like Smith, called on the Lord for guidance: first, to determine whether the plates were actually God's work and, second, to find out how he should proceed (*EMD* 2:310). He apparently told Smith that "the Lord had shown him that he must go to [N]ew York City with some of the c[h]aracters" (*EMD* 1:30), not the other way around. Finally, although it is not clear who came up with the idea that the experts' inability to recognize the characters demonstrated that God had chosen Smith to "confound the wise," the back-and-forth between Smith and Harris reveals the informal, improvisational nature of the guidance process in the months leading up to the loss of the manuscript.

As Smith drew Harris more deeply into the translation project, they both resisted Lucy Harris's desire to be involved, leaving her so angry and suspicious that she refused to share a bedroom with her husband after he returned from New York (*EMD* 1:353). When Martin Harris decided to move to Harmony to help Smith with the translation full-time, his wife wanted to go with him. He agreed she could come for a week or two, but then was to return home. According to Lucy Smith, Lucy Harris spent the entire time in Harmony searching for the plates and doing all she could to "injure Joseph in the estimation of his neighbors" (*EMD* 1:353–55). It was in this context of growing estrangement between the Harrises that Martin asked if he could take the manuscript home to show his family what he had been doing, hoping, in the words of Lucy Smith, that it would "have a salutary effect upon his wife[']s feelings" (*EMD* 1:357).

Whatever happened to the 116 manuscript pages—and the matter was hotly disputed—the fact of their disappearance brought Martin Harris's participation to a halt, thus derailing the translation process. Little progress was made until Oliver Cowdery arrived in Harmony to assist Smith full-time in April 1829. In March 1829, Martin Harris visited the Smiths in Harmony, during which time he expressed his desire for "[a] witness that . . . Joseph hath got the things [the plates] which he hath testified that he hath got" (Revelation, March 1829, *JSP*, D1:16 [D&C 5]). Isaac Hale may have been referring to this revelation when he reported seeing Smith and Harris comparing pieces of paper on which they had written "my servant seeketh a greater witness, but no greater witness can be given him." These words, they told Hale, were those of Jesus Christ (*EMD* 4:287). D&C 5 indeed said that Martin Harris could not see the plates at that time, but indicated that the Lord would in due time allow "three of [his] Servants [the as yet unspecified witnesses] . . . [to] view these things as they are" (*JSP*, D1:16–17).

The initial impetus for Harris's visit to Harmony is not clear, however. The *JSP* editors suggest, following Martin Harris's 1870 testimony (see *EMD* 2:332), that Martin went to Harmony *because* his wife had threatened him with a lawsuit (*JSP*, D1:14–16). According to Lucy Smith (*EMD* 1:382), who was not predisposed to take Lucy Harris's side, Martin himself may have started things off by announcing that he wanted to visit Joseph in the wake of Samuel Smith's return from a visit. Since, as far as we know, this would have been his first visit since the loss of the manuscript, Lucy Harris may well have gotten angry, fearing that a visit would draw her husband back into the gold plates business. When Lucy Harris learned "of his intention [to visit Harmony]," Lucy Smith said, it "fixed in her mind a determination to prevent him from going also to bring Joseph into a difficulty that would be the Means of hindering him perhaps entirely" (*EMD* 1:382). To that end, Lucy Smith said, she "flew through the neighborhood like a dark spirit from house to house . . . for miles" looking for evidence "to prove that Joseph had not the record which he pretended to have[,] that he pretended to be in possession of certain Gold plate[s] for the express purpose of obtaining money from those who might be so credulous as to believe him" (*EMD* 1:382–83). Knowing that his wife was planning to bring a lawsuit would have motivated Martin to gather countervailing evidence (hence his request to see the plates) on a visit that was initially just motivated by a desire to see how things were going.

In the trial, which took place in Lyons, New York, three neighbors testified against Smith, along with Lucy Harris; the judge, however, dismissed the case in response to Martin Harris's positive testimony (*EMD* 1:387). The opposing arguments are illuminating. The critical witnesses swore, based on what Smith had allegedly told them, that the box that allegedly contained the ancient gold plates in fact did not, and that, therefore, Smith was clearly trying to deceive people—most notably Martin Harris—in order to get their money. When Harris was called to the stand, he stressed that he had given Smith fifty dollars of his own free will to do "the work of the Lord," but had never been pressed for more. He did not claim to have seen the plates "which he [Smith] professes to have," but witnessed to his belief in their truth and salvific power (*EMD* 1:385–86). Martin Harris was baptized into the new church on 6 April 1830. He and Lucy separated a month later.

Lucy and Martin Harris may well have had marital difficulties that predated Smith's claims to have recovered ancient golden plates, but Smith's claims clearly exacerbated tensions to the point that Martin became physically abusive toward his wife (*EMD* 2:35). Their way of handling their differences aside, their growing estrangement is highly revealing. Most crucially, the series of events from the alleged recovery of the plates through D&C 3—Joseph's production of the characters document(s), Martin's visit to the linguistic experts, Lucy's search for the plates, and Martin's need to show Lucy the manuscript—can all be read in light of Smith's desire to enlist a first follower and Martin and Lucy Harris's need to test Smith's claim to have recovered ancient golden plates before investing time and money in the translation project. Although Smith clearly wanted a male first follower with financial resources, the battle lines of future arguments for and against Smith's claims emerged in the unfolding of the events leading up to the first recorded revelation. The critics—represented by Lucy Harris—maintained that there were no ancient golden plates, that there was something else in the box or under the cloth, and that therefore Smith was clearly perpetrating a hoax, presumably a money-making hoax. I will take up this inference in chapter 2. The followers—represented by Martin Harris—believed in the reality of the ancient plates based on their own faith-confirming experiences (the Lord's still, small voice in Martin's case) and their belief that God gave gifts "to the foolish to confound the wise" (in this case Smith's ability to translate characters that experts did not recognize). Smith's alleged ignorance and his inability to dictate a complex narrative were thus key elements of the believers' case for the supernatural origins of the Book of Mormon from the outset. I will return to this issue when I compare the translation of the Book of Mormon and the scribing of *A Course in Miracles* in chapter 11.

Finally, if we compare Martin Harris as Smith's "first follower" and Oliver Cowdery as his "second follower," we find similarities and significant differences. Both were religious seekers with an openness to finding ultimate meaning in dreams and visions. Both were drawn to Smith by the stories they heard circulating about the golden plates; both checked them out reasonably carefully; both were ultimately convinced by what they viewed as evidence of Smith's special abilities and their own sense of divine guidance. Objectively speaking, however, Cowdery came relatively unencumbered. He was not married and he wasn't particularly wealthy; his involvement didn't put an established partnership at risk. Still, issues came up. Cowdery's issues had less to do with the reality of the ancient plates than with authority: Cowdery wanted to know if he, too, could translate the plates (D&C 8) and if he, too, could receive revelations (D&C 28). These issues were all resolved by asking the Lord, who responded with real-time recorded revelations that kept the translation and then the church-building process on track. The retrospective accounts offered by Joseph Smith, Lucy Smith, and Isaac Hale all suggest that Joseph and Emma Smith and Martin Harris were seeking guidance prior to the loss of the manuscript, but it wasn't recorded and preserved. Doing so further externalized the guidance process, locating it primarily in Smith's hands and giving it an authority that stabilized the relationship between Smith and Cowdery, if not indefinitely, at least until the early thirties.

CHAPTER 2

Materialization

When Jan Shipps challenged scholars to address "the charlatan-true prophet dichotomy that has plagued Mormon history from the beginning" (1974, 14), relatively little scholarly research had been published on early Mormonism. Since that time much has changed. Numerous biographies of Joseph Smith have been written, primary sources are readily available, scholarship has flourished, and there is much upon which historians—Mormon and non-Mormon—can agree. Seer stones, money-digging, magic, and anti-Mormon polemic have all been integrated into the scholarly narrative of early Mormonism. But the puzzle has not been solved; it has simply become more narrowly focused on a question Shipps deliberately decided to bracket: the existence of the golden plates.

According to Richard Bushman, the Mormon claim that there were actual ancient golden plates created a divide between insiders and outsiders, including LDS and non-LDS historians, and led insiders and outsiders to divergent characterizations of Joseph Smith. Non-Mormons, assuming there were no plates, presumed there was something "fishy" going on, as Bushman (2004, 269) puts it, and this then colored their entire assessment of Smith. Explanations of the gold plates down to the present tend to presuppose an either/or choice: ancient golden plates either existed or they did not. If they existed, then Smith was who he claimed to be. If they did not and Smith knew it, then he must have consciously deceived his followers in order to convince them that they existed. Alternatively, if Smith believed there were plates when in fact there were not, then he was deluded.

In keeping with these either/or choices, nonbelieving contemporaries of the Smiths and nonbelieving historians in the present typically explain Smith's claims regarding the plates in terms of deception, fantasy, or a prank that got out of hand. Within two years of the alleged removal of the plates from the hill in 1827, the Smiths' neighbor, Peter Ingersoll, claimed that the box that supposedly contained the plates really contained only sand (*EMD* 2:44–45). In his notes on Ingersoll's statement, Dan Vogel speculates that Ingersoll was the first of the three unnamed witnesses at the trial (*EMD* 2:44n14). Historian Fawn Brodie, relying on this source, suggested that "[p]erhaps in the beginning Joseph never intended his stories of the golden plates to be taken so seriously, but once the masquerade had begun, there was no point at which he could call a halt. Since his own family believed him, . . . why should not the world?" (1995, 41). Historian Dan Vogel views the materiality of the plates as "the most compelling evidence" for "conscious misdirection" on Smith's part (2004, xi). Speculating that Smith most likely made the plates himself out of tin, Vogel characterizes the recovery of the plates as a mix of deception and fantasy, the sort of "pious fraud" that he associates with shamans and magicians (ibid., xi–xx, 44–45, 98–99).[1]

Although I think there is too much conflicting evidence to come to a firm conclusion about what Smith really believed about the plates, I think we can expand the range of possibilities beyond the either/or choices that scholars have typically advanced. In making this case, I want to stress that the evidence is all late, that my proposal is conjectural, and that, as a mediating position, readers can easily tilt it in more or less skeptical directions. In light of the intense polarization of views, my aim is to highlight modes of religious thinking, some of which are reflected in the Book of Mormon, which Smith might have embraced and which, if he did, would expand our options for thinking about his motives. To get at this, I will assume for the sake of argument that there were no plates, or at least no ancient golden plates, and at the same time take seriously believers' claim that Smith was not a fraud. If we start with those premises, then we have to explain how the plates might have become *real* for Smith as well as his followers. The challenge, however, is not just to explain how they might have become real for Smith, but how they might have become real for him *in some non-delusory sense*. This shift in premises forces us to consider a greater range of explanatory possibilities and has the potential to expand our understanding of the way new spiritual paths emerge.

To open up some new options, we can turn to a letter written by Jesse Smith, Joseph's staunchly Calvinist uncle, to Joseph's older brother Hyrum in June 1829, in response to letters that Joseph and his father had written to Jesse and other members of their extended family living in St. Lawrence County, New York, after the loss of the initial pages of the translation in 1828 (*EMD* 1:552; for context, see *EMD* 1:567). In a scathing attack, Jesse Smith denounced "the whole pretended discovery" and compared Joseph to the Israelites in the desert bowing down before the golden calf. Joseph, Jesse wrote, was like a "man [who] . . . makes his own gods, [then] falls down and worships before it, and says this is my god which brought me out of the land of Vermont." In Joseph's case, though, it was not a golden calf but a "gold

---

[1] Characterizing shamans as "pious frauds" begs the question, as the literature on shamans and shamanic practices is at least as complicated and contentious as the literature on Joseph Smith (for an overview, see Znamenski 2004).

book discovered by the necromancy of infidelity, & dug from the mines of atheism." His Calvinist sensibilities outraged, Jesse summarized the letter he had received from Joseph a year earlier, complaining, "he writes that the angel of the Lord has revealed to him the hidden treasures of wisdom & knowledge, even divine revelation, which has lain in the bowels of the earth for thousands of years [and] is at last made known to him." To this very early account of the new revelation, Jesse then adds: "he says he has eyes to see things that are not, and then has the audacity to say they are."

This is an extraordinarily rich passage that opens up two lines of inquiry: first, the allusion to the golden calf, idolatry, and Joseph Smith as the "maker of his own gods" and, second, Jesse Smith's astute, albeit somewhat puzzling, observation that his nephew had "eyes to see things that are not, and then [had] the audacity to say they are." The first opens up issues related to ma- terialization, specifically, the complex relationships between materiality and sacrality, on the one hand, and between human creativity and divine mani- festation, on the other. The second takes us into the problems surrounding perception. What exactly does it mean to say someone has eyes to see things that are not? I will take up the problem of materialization in this chapter and turn to matters of perception in chapter 11.

THE SOURCES

Given the absence of real-time sources for either the discovery or recovery of the plates, what basis do we have for reconstructing these events? Dan Vogel is definitely right to note that the surviving descriptions of the discovery and recovery of the plates are all rather late and differ on important points. His concerns regarding the historicity of Smith's accounts of his visions are valid, and his decision to treat the accounts as "evolving stories he told about them rather than as actual events" (2004, 44) is understandable and consistent with the way that many historically minded New Testament scholars treat gospel narratives. Instead of treating the surviving accounts simply as stories without any basis in history, however, we can compare the accounts, focus- ing on what happened and what people did, that is, on the sequence of events that they depict, rather than the way the narrator interpreted the events. Regularities with respect to what happened in accounts that disagree in their interpretation or appraisal of what happened allow us to reconstruct what may have occurred in a basic behavioral sense, as well as the very dif- ferent ways that people understood what occurred.

Approached in this way, we find considerable agreement in the early, generally quite brief accounts of the discovery of the plates that circulated after the plates were recovered but before the Book of Mormon was pub- lished in 1830. All agree that a noncorporeal being, whether described as an angel, a personage, or a spirit, appeared to Joseph Jr. in a vision in 1823 and told him about "plates of gold" or "treasure" buried nearby that he must recover. Although the accounts of finding the plates were similar to the accounts circulating about Smith's treasure-seeking activities, in the accounts of the plates, the golden object was *also* a "book" or "a record" or "account of the ancient inhabitants," which the "angel" or "spirit" is depicted as having preserved so that it could be given to a special individual at a later time.

In the earliest such description, which Jesse Smith quoted from a (now lost) letter to the extended family in fall 1828, Joseph wrote that "the angel of the lord has revealed to him the hidden treasures of wisdom & knowledge, even divine revelation, which has lain in the bowels of the earth for thousands of years [and] is at last made known to him." This passage echoes the statement Joseph Smith made in court in March 1826, about a year and a half earlier, when charged with "pretending . . . to discover . . . lost goods." As noted previously, Smith acknowledged, "he had a certain stone, which he had occasionally looked at to determine where hidden treasures in the bowels of the earth were; that he professed to tell in this manner where gold mines were a distance under ground." In both accounts he referred to "hidden treasures" made of gold buried in "the bowels of the earth," but with this difference: in the former case, an angel revealed the hidden treasures that contained divine revelation of "wisdom & knowledge," whereas in the latter, Smith was hired by Stowell to search for buried wealth, "on account," as his mother put it, "of [Stowell] having heard that he [Joseph] possessed certain keys, by which he could discern things invisible to the natural eye." Witnesses at the trial, like his extended family a few years later, disagreed sharply over whether Smith could actually see things that others could not. Members of Stowell's family, who thought he was being conned by Smith, testified that they had investigated Smith's abilities to "discern objects at a distance" by means of a stone and "came away disgusted, finding the deception so palpable." Stowell, however, testified to his "faith in [the] Prisoner[']s skill," as did another treasure seeker confident in Smith's abilities to "divine things by means of said Stone and Hat" (*EMD* 4:249, 253, 255).

In June 1829, a few months after Jesse wrote his letter to Hyrum, Joseph Smith recorded the copyright for the Book of Mormon. The copyright provided a capsule description of the new revelation, describing it as "an account written by the hand of Mormon [an ancient American prophet and seer] upon plates . . . sealed up by the hand of [Mormon's son] Moroni & hid up unto the Lord, to come forth in due time by the way of the Gentile [Joseph Smith], the interpretation thereof by the gift of God." The account preserved by Mormon was in turn "an abridgment of the record of the people of Nephi; and also of the Lamanites, . . . written by way of commandment; and also by the spirit of prophesy & revelation" (*JSP*, D1:80). The copyright encapsulates what Susan Staker has described as the central narrative thread that runs through the Book of Mormon, that is, an account of seers who are also revelators and prophets and who handed down records from one generation to the next in order to ensure that through them "shall all things be revealed—or rather shall secret things be made manifest—and hidden things shall come to light . . . which otherwise could not be known" (Mosiah 8:17, Staker 2002). While much elaborated, we are still talking about plates hidden in the earth and seers to whom secret things are made manifest.

Following the publication of the Book of Mormon, Smith went into more detail in public about how he discovered and recovered the plates. In an interview with Peter Bauder in October 1830, Smith reportedly told the newspaper editor the following:

> [A]n angel told him he must go to a certain place in the town of Manchester, Ontario County, where was a secret treasure concealed, which he must reveal to the human family. He went, and after the third or fourth time, which was repeated once a year, he obtained a parcel of plate resembling gold, on which were engraved what he did not understand, only by the aid of a glass which he also obtained with the plate, by which means he was enabled to translate the characters on the plate into English. He says he was not allowed to let the plate be seen only by a few individuals named by the angel, and after he had a part translated . . . the angel took them and carried them to parts unknown to him. (*EMD* 1:17)

Although some scholars have made much of the fact that Joseph Smith Jr. refers to an angel or to seers and prophets in the accounts just quoted, while other early accounts allegedly circulated by his father, Joseph Smith Sr., refer to a "spirit" (*EMD* 2:245), I find these accounts surprisingly consistent. Indeed, according to Willard Chase, Joseph's father explained that the spirit was "the spirit of the prophet who wrote this book, and who was sent to Joseph Smith, to make known these things to him" (*EMD* 2:67). Taken together, they suggest that by the time the plates were recovered in 1827, the Smiths, father and son, both attributed the discovery of the plates to a vision in which a long-deceased prophet, however characterized, told Joseph Smith Jr. of their existence and how to recover them. That people struggled to characterize a long-deceased prophet, who had returned to deliver something as a "spirit" or an "angel" or even a "ghost," seems perfectly plausible and in keeping with the insider narrative, if read in light of the various ways early nineteenth-century Americans might have characterized a long-deceased person who presented him- or herself to the living. Joseph's wife's cousins, Joseph and Hiel Lewis, may have precipitated the polarized readings with their claim that, in Smith's narrative as recounted to them, "there was not one word about 'visions of God,' or of angels, or heavenly revelations. All his information was by that dream, and that bleeding ghost. The heavenly visions and messages of angels, etc., contained in Mormon books, [they claimed] were after-thoughts revised to order" (*EMD* 4:305).

Joseph Smith Jr., and other family members who were present at the time the discovery allegedly took place, provided more elaborate accounts of the discovery of the plates beginning in the 1830s. Of the seven such accounts, three are from Joseph Smith, dated 1832, 1835, and 1839; two are from his mother, dated 1841 and 1853; and two from his youngest brother, William, dated 1845 and 1883. Willard Chase, a hostile witness, also provided a detailed account in 1833. Whereas the accounts offered by Joseph Jr., Lucy, and William provide much more detail regarding the vision(s) themselves and events leading up to the discovery, Chase's account elaborates on the discovery and recovery of the plates. Although there is, as already noted, considerable variation in the specific content of these accounts, there is significant overlap in their description of the basic events, which we can divide into three episodes: the vision(s), the discovery, and the recovery.

Dream-Vision(s)

We get details on the visions and other events leading up to the discovery of the plates in the accounts provided by Joseph Jr. in 1832 (*EMD* 1:28–30), 1835 (*EMD* 1:44), and 1839 (*EMD* 1:66); his mother, Lucy, in 1845 and 1853 (*EMD* 1:90–95); and his brother, William, in 1841 (*EMD* 1:478–79) and 1883 (*EMD* 1:496) (for detailed comparisons, see the appendix, chart 1). Their accounts agree that an angel (or messenger or personage) appeared to Joseph Jr. either once or three times during the night in the midst of the harvest season in 1823 to tell him where to find engraved plates of gold that had been deposited in the vicinity by the ancient inhabitants of the continent. All but one of the accounts indicates that the messenger appeared again the following day. The six that elaborate on this indicate that when he arose in the morning, Smith did not go to look for the plates but rather went to work in the fields to help his father (and brother[s]) with harvesting. Appearing sick, he was sent home by his father or brother. On the way home, his strength failed him, he fell to the ground, the messenger reappeared, repeated the message from the night before, and told him to tell (or in his mother's account reminded him to tell) his father about the vision or, in William's account, to tell the whole family. In each case, the telling is well received. In Smith's 1835 account, his father "wept and told [him] that it was a vision from God to attend to it," whereupon he did. Similarly, in the 1839 version, his father replied "that it was of God, and [told him] to go and do as commanded by the messenger." In William's earlier version, the family was "astounded, but not altogether incredulous" and in his later one, "the whole family were melted to tears, and believed all he said . . . and anxiously awaited the result of his visit to the hill Cumorah, in search of the plates." Lucy Smith's 1845 account doesn't indicate how her husband responded, but her later version indicates that "his father charged him not to fail in attending strictly to the instruction which he had received from this heavenly messenger."

In sum, the family's accounts agree that Smith didn't immediately seek out the plates upon waking. Instead, he went to work in the fields as usual, was sent home by his father because he seemed ill, collapsed on the way home, was visited again by the angel who told him to tell (or reminded him to tell) his father (or his family) what he had seen, and, upon doing so, was told by his father that what he had seen was "a vision from God" (1835) or simply "of God" (1839) and that he needed to "attend to it" (1835) or "do as commanded" (1839). Smith's father's account of events, as recounted by Willard Chase, though from a more hostile source, is not inconsistent with this analysis. In Chase's account, the "spirit" says nothing about telling his father or any family member and instead provides detailed instructions regarding what Smith was to wear, the sort of horse he should ride, and the way he should interact with the spirit before and after retrieving the plates. The account indicates, however, that Joseph's father helped him with the preparations: "they [Joseph and his father] accordingly fitted out Joseph with a suit of black clothes and borrowed a black horse" (*EMD* 2:66–67). Despite the differences in content, in this version too, Joseph must have told his father about the vision, which his father clearly took seriously or he would not have helped his son to meet the spirit's demands.

I infer from this (1) that Smith did not feel an immediate need to act on the night's events or at least that other duties (harvesting) seemed more important and (2) that the angel's reappearance and instruction (or reminder) to tell his father (or family) and his father's statement that the events constituted "a vision from God" or were "of God" and/or his family's belief prompted him to act (to "attend to it" and "do as commanded"). The intervention of Smith's father (or family) at this point was thus crucial. The sequence of events suggests some hesitation on Joseph's part—if not outright uncertainty—as to how the events of the previous night should be appraised. His father's conviction that it was "of God" in Joseph and Lucy Smith's accounts, his family's astonished belief in William's account, and his father's assistance in Chase's account confirmed that the vision was authentic and there were plates to be found.

DISCOVERY

For the next portion of the narrative, in which Smith went to the hill and discovered the plates, he was the only witness. In all three of his accounts, he went to look for the plates after the angel appeared the next day and, in his second and third accounts, after his father told him that the visions were "from God." In all three accounts, he found the place where the plates were buried without difficulty. In all three accounts, he then attempted to remove the plates, but was unable to do so, after which the angel reappeared to explain why. The accounts differ in various particulars. In the third, we get an elaborate description of the plates, the "interpreters," the breastplate, and the stone box that contained them, none of which appears in the two earlier accounts. The more interesting differences, however, lie in the sequence of events surrounding the finding of the plates, his attempts to remove them, and the reappearance of the angel. Moreover, if we focus on the events as they unfold, we find interesting parallels between Joseph Smith's first two accounts and his father's account as reported by Willard Chase.

If we compare these four accounts (see appendix, chart 2), we find not only that Smith's third account provides much more detail about the objects he discovered, but that the matter-of-fact tone in which he reports his failure to remove the plates is belied by the three earlier accounts. In them, his failure to recover the plates arouses strong emotion. In a dreamlike sequence in the Chase account, which is at best thirdhand, Smith is kept from the plates by a toad that morphs into a man who strikes him and morphs into a spirit who strikes him again. He is frightened, but what frightens him is not clear—the toad-man-spirit, being struck, or his inability to recover the plates. In Smith's 1835 account, he does not mention his feelings explicitly, stating only that "the powers of darkness strove hard against me." In his 1832 account, however, he is more specific, indicating that his three failed attempts to get the plates left him "excedingly [sic] frightened" and led him to suppose that the appearances of the heavenly personage were in fact only "a dream of Vision." It is this thought, we may suppose, that he presumably attributed to "the powers of darkness" in the second account and that, upon consideration, he "knew" was not true.

Smith's first and second accounts, in other words, insert a realistic doubt about the reality of the vision—perhaps it was only a dream—perhaps it was not a "vision of God" as his father had suggested, perhaps what he was experiencing on the hill was only a waking dream, and the plates were not real after all. This, I think, is the thought that he "knew" was not true, in light of his father's conviction about "what was the case." Upon appealing to the Lord/God (in the first two accounts), the angel/spirit reappeared and offered an explanation that in its basic structure (i.e., failure is due to transgression) paralleled the explanations Smith routinely offered for why buried treasure got away. In the first account, however, he explained the transgression in a way that is elaborated more fully in later accounts, to wit, that he had "saught [sic] the Plates to obtain riches and kept not the commandment that I should have an eye single to the glory of God" (EMD 1:30).

Thus, I am hypothesizing that Smith's inability to recover the plates led to feelings of fear, which he explicitly acknowledged in his 1832 account and personified as combat with powers of darkness in his later accounts, fueled by fear that what he took to be real (at his father's suggestion) was in fact imaginary. Challenged by his inability to retrieve the plates, he struggled with doubts about their reality but then reaffirmed his father's suggestion in the face of his doubts, explained the absence of the plates as a disappearance, and their disappearance as the result of his transgressions. In short, without his father's firm belief that the appearances of the "personage" were real, that the knowledge being conveyed was authentic, and that its instructions were to be obeyed, the evidence suggests that Joseph might not have acted on it on his own.

RECOVERY

Smith's accounts give us very little information as to how he finally recovered the plates. In his 1832 account, he simply says that "on the 22d day of Sept[ember] of this same year [1827] I obtained the plates" (*EMD* 1:30). In the 1835 account, the angel told him to come again "in one year from that time." "I did so," he continued, "but did not obtain them also the third and the fourth year, at which time I obtained them, and translated them into the english [*sic*] language, by the gift and power of God" (*EMD* 1:45). Smith's 1839 history also indicates that he was instructed to return annually "untill the time should come for obtaining the plates." On each of these occasions, Smith says, "I found the same messenger there and received instruction and intelligence from him at each of our interviews respecting what the Lord was going to do, and how and in what manner his kingdom was to be conducted in the last days" (*EMD* 1:67). When the time finally arrived "for obtaining the plates," he went as usual "to the place where they were deposited, [and] the same heavenly messenger delivered them" over to him (*EMD* 1:68).

When he saw but was unable to remove the plates, Smith's account of his failure, as recounted to his family, paralleled the stories he and others told of buried treasure spirited away by mysterious treasure guardians (Vogel 2004, 47–50; Ashurst-McGee 2006). Historians typically interpret the four years as a period of transition in Smith's own self-understanding from village seer to prophet, whether conceived as a natural progression or as a more abrupt break with the past (see Shipps 1974, Taylor 1999, Ashurst-McGee 2000, Gardner 2011, 99). There is evidence to suggest that some early Mormons integrated Smith's treasure-seeking past into their understanding of the church. Thus, shortly after leaving the church in 1831, Ezra Booth wrote that "it passe[d] for a current fact in the Mormon church, that there are immense treasures in the earth, especially in those places in the state of New-York from whence many of the Mormons emigrated last spring: and when they become sufficiently purified, these treasures are to be poured into the lap of their church" (Howe [1834] 2015, 270). For our purposes, it is crucial simply to note that however the treasure was reframed, the reframing took place in conversation with the divine messenger. Although he would not succeed in recovering the plates for another four years, he visited the hill annually as instructed by the messenger. During these visits, Smith indicated (*EMD* 1:67), he "received instruction and intelligence" from the messenger of the Lord and, according to his mother, he in turn recounted what he learned about the ancient inhabitants of the continent to his enthralled family "as though," his mother recalled, "he had spent his life with them" (*EMD* 1:295–96).

Insider explanations of the four-year delay—then and now—have focused on two conditions that Smith ostensibly had to meet in order to recover the plates: he had to develop the right attitude (the object was a gold bible not a gold treasure) and solicit the assistance of the right companion (ultimately, his wife, Emma). Here I want to suggest another possible reason for the delay, premised on my working assumption that there were no actual ancient golden plates. Recovery of the plates may have depended on Joseph realizing that he had to actively materialize the plates "in faith," rather than passively waiting for them to be "given" to him ready-made, as it were.

The historical evidence for this is speculative and derives primarily from Lucy Smith's description of the way Joseph told his family that the time had come to recover the plates (*EMD* 1:325). Arriving home one evening shortly before his last visit to the hill, Joseph reported to his anxious parents that he had just received "the severest chastisement that [he] had ever had in his life . . . [from] the angel of the Lord." The angel told him that he had been "negligent [and] that the time ha[d] now come when the record should be brought forth." But, he added confidently, "Father give yourself no uneasiness as to this reprimand [for] I know what course I am to pursue an[d] all will be well." I am hypothesizing that until this point, insofar as Smith was thinking about recovering the plates, he knew that someone else had to be involved, but still did not know how he was actually going to recover them. If, as I am assuming, he did in fact materialize the plates, the "chastisement from the angel" evidently convinced him that he needed to take a more active course.[2]

This more active course, I am hypothesizing, involved creating what was in effect a representation of the plates, perhaps using sand and later tin or lead, as detractors claimed, in the knowledge that they would become the sacred reality the Smith family believed them to be only insofar as the angel made them so.[3] As such his representation of the plates, placed under the

---

[2] I am assuming that "chastisement from an angel" could be construed in naturalistic terms as a mental dialogue between two inner voices, one of which Smith attributed to an angel.

[3] Disparate descriptions make it difficult to be more specific about how they might have been made. Martin Harris estimated that "the box . . . weighed forty or fifty pounds" (*EMD* 2:306). In contrast to Harris, who hefted but did not claim to touch the object, Emma Smith (*EMD* 1:539) re-

cloth or in the box, can be understood as representing or even cocreating the plates along a continuum of possibilities, ranging from the way a crucifix represents the crucifixion, an Eastern Orthodox icon points to the reality it depicts, the way Eucharistic wafers are thought to be transformed into the literal body of Christ, or the way that Mary "created" Jesus in her womb. We can, in other words, situate what I am construing as Smith's actions in creating plates in relation to this range of possibilities within the Christian tradition more broadly.

I am not arguing that Smith necessarily thought about what he was doing in light of these options. The logic of the insider stories nonetheless points in the direction of a theologically informed process of co-creation, and a similar logic is evident in key chapters in the Book of Mormon, which suggests that such a process would have been in keeping with the new revelation.[4] Thus, in Ether 4, Moroni (the ancient Nephite who appeared to Joseph Smith as an "angel") describes how the plates came to be in the first place. According to Moroni, the Lord instructed him to write on "these plates the very things which the brother of Jared saw" and to "seal up the interpretation thereof" along with "the interpreters," hiding them in the earth until the day "that they shall exercise faith in me [the Lord] . . . even as the brother of Jared did," at which time, the Lord said, "will I manifest unto them the things which the brother of Jared saw, even to the unfolding unto them all my revelations" (Ether 4:3–7).[5]

What Jared's brother saw, due to his "exceeding faith," was the bodily form of the Lord Jesus Christ, initially just the Lord's finger and then the whole "body of [his] spirit" (Ether 3:6–9, 15–16). Jared's brother demonstrated his exceeding faith—and this is the key point—by preparing sixteen small stones, carrying them to "the top of the mount," and imploring the

---

counted feeling the pages/leaves under a cloth. In recently discovered minutes of a court case where Smith was tried for breaching the peace on 30 June 1830, Josiah Stowell said that he had seen "a corner of it [the golden bible]; it resembled a stone of a greenish caste [*sic*]; should judge it to have been about one foot square and six inches thick; he [Smith] would not let it be seen by any one; the Lord had commanded him not; it was unknown to Smith, that witness saw a corner of the Bible, so called by Smith; [Smith] told the witness the leaves were of gold, there were written characters on the leaves" (*New England Christian Herald*, 7 November 1832 [facsimile ed., Signature Books]). A greenish cast would suggest copper rather than lead or gold, and pages could be made out of copper more easily than lead. An 1835 article adds: "The probability is that Smith, who had been a book-pedlar, and was frequently about printing establishments, had procured some old copper plates for engravings, which he showed for his golden plates" (*Christian Journal*, Exeter, NH, 1835, in Welch 2005, 185). Although believers tend to conflate the various descriptions, I think it is more likely that Joseph saw the plates in a vision, described what he saw to those close to him, and then made one or more objects to represent what he saw: initially, perhaps, a box containing something heavy and then later an object with leaves.

[4] Thanks to Loyd Ericson at Kofford Books for bringing the brother of Jared to my attention.

[5] The Book of Ether claims to be Moroni's abridgment of the twenty-four gold plates that recorded the history of the Jaredites, one of several ancient peoples who, according to the Book of Mormon, came to the Americas from the ancient Near East (see Bushman 1984, 118; Hardy 2010, 227–47).

FIGURE 2.1. A Book of Mormon illustration depicting the Lord touching the stones hewn by the brother of Jared and causing them to shine in the dark (Ether 3:1–6, 6:1–3). © Intellectual Reserve, Inc.

Lord, who "hast all power," to make them shine (Ether 3:1–4). In response to his plea, "the Lord stretched forth his hand and touched the stones [that Jared's brother had made] one by one with his finger" (Ether 3:6) and "caused [them] to shine in darkness" (Ether 6:1–3). Jared's brother "molten[ed]" the sixteen small, clear white stones from a rock,[6] because the Lord had commanded him to do something (construct waterproof vessels to save his people from impending floods), but had not provided all that was needed to complete the task (a means of getting light into the sealed vessels). Smith, too, believed he had been commanded to do something (bring forth the golden plates from the hill), but after numerous attempts had been unable

[6] As Brooke (1994, 159–60) indicates, the verb "molten" appears in other contexts (1 Nephi 17:9, 16) where it suggests metalworking. The smelting of transparent stones from a rock suggests something more complex than ordinary metalworking, perhaps even some kind of transmutation of an esoteric variety in keeping with Brooke's general reading of early Mormonism. In any case, this passage is redolent with symbolism that is elaborated later. Thus, D&C 130 explicitly links the white stone to the cosmic Urim and Thummim, the new name bestowed on each person who enters the celestial kingdom, and the white stone in Revelation 2:17. But as Brooke (258–59) points out, the Masonic tradition associates the white stone of Revelation 2:17 with the alchemical philosopher's stone and the alchemical work of transmutation, which suggests esoteric possibilities that Smith might have had in mind if, as I am suggesting, he made plates and asked the angel to transform them. Thanks to Sally Gordon for urging me to consider possible esoteric interpretations.

to complete the task. In the same way that the Book of Mormon depicts Jared's brother's solution to the lighting problem as a demonstration of his faith, so too Smith may have understood himself as demonstrating his faith by figuring out how to recover the ancient plates, that is, by taking home-made plates to "the top of the mount" (the Hill Cumorah) and imploring the Lord to transform them into the ancient golden plates he saw in his 1823 dream-vision.

Although we can only speculate on the course Smith pursued to recover the plates, there is a final parallel worth noting between Smith and the brother of Jared, this one explicit: both stories begin with severe chastisement and end in revelation. It turns out that after a period of four years, the Lord came to the brother of Jared and for three hours "chastened him because he remembered not to call upon the name of the Lord" (Ether 2:14). Jared's brother repented; the Lord forgave him and instructed him to build the vessels, which then led to the events just described. In 1827, four years after the angel's first visit, Smith received "the severest chastisement that [he] had ever had [in] his life . . . [from] the angel of the Lord" for his negligence in recovering the plates.[7] Regardless of how we conceive the relationship between Smith and the text, "active materialization" does seem to be compatible with the Jaredite tradition.[8]

Jared's brother notwithstanding, it is the idea of "active materialization" that gives rise to charges of fraud and deception and, if not fraud and deception, then idolatry and delusion. As already noted, Vogel considers the materiality of the plates "the most compelling evidence" that Smith consciously misdirected his followers, and compares the making of the plates with the practices of adepts who commingle trickery and sincere belief. Smith's logic, however, may have been less like an adept deceiving his subjects and more like a Catholic priest making Christ present in the Eucharistic wafer.[9] In the

[7] According to Terryl Givens (2002, 220), the story of Jared's brother opens in Ether 2:14 with "what must surely be the longest dressing-down in sacred history" and ends with "the most spectacular epiphany recorded in the Book of Mormon." In using this story to illustrate the Book of Mormon's dialogic understanding of revelation, Givens notes that "the brother of Jared asks the Lord to touch and illuminate 16 molten stones," but he does not reflect on the fact that Jared's brother crafted the stones or on the parallels between Smith and Jared's brother.

[8] The plausibility of this reading is strengthened by the explicit reference to the brother of Jared in the June 1829 revelation (D&C 17) given through Joseph Smith to Cowdery, Whitmer, and Harris, who had just learned from the "translating" of Ether 5:2–4 that "three [who had assisted in bringing forth the work] shall be shewn [the plates] by the power of God." The revelation indicates that Cowdery, Whitmer, and Harris will not only see the plates through the power of God and their faith, just as Smith had seen them, but also "the brestplate, the sword of Laban, the Urim and Thumin [sic] [which were] given to the brother of Jared upon the mount, when he talked to the Lord face to face" (Revelation, June 1929-E, *JSP*, D1:84 [D&C 17]).

[9] Others connect the interweaving of the spiritual and material with a magical worldview (see Quinn 1998; Taylor 1999, 149). Fleming (2014) connects it with theurgy rooted historically in Christian Platonism. Calvinists, of course, historically viewed the Catholic understanding of transubstantiation as magical.

first case, the adept knowingly misleads his viewers, albeit for their own good. In the second, a priest calls upon the Holy Spirit to transform the bread and wine into the body and blood of Christ.

In comparing the gold plates and the Eucharistic wafer, I am not making an argument for the reality of ancient plates (or the real presence of Christ) but raising the possibility that when materializing the plates, Smith might have been thinking more like a good Catholic than a good Calvinist. The comparison, in other words, allows us to consider the possibility that Smith viewed something that he had made (metal plates) as a vehicle through which something sacred—the ancient golden plates—could be made (really) present. In both the Catholic and Mormon case, the sacred character is visible only to those who believe. In both, the materialization unfolds in accord with a story. In the case of the Eucharist, the story of the Last Supper; in the case of the Mormon prophet, the story of the angel and the buried plates. Moreover, in both cases, believers claim that this is not just an enactment. The priest doesn't just pretend that the wafer is the body of Christ. Standing in for Christ, he says, referring to the wafer, "this is my body." Nor did Smith claim that the plates were a representation of ancient gold plates; he claimed that they really were. In much the way that Jesus is said to have held up human-made bread and said to his disciples "this is my body," Joseph Smith may have made plates, placed them in a box, and said to his family: "These are the golden plates." While some in each tradition may view these statements as figurative, others—orthodox Catholics and orthodox Latter-day Saints—might view them as literally true in light of their belief in the power of divinity to manifest itself in material bodies and objects. In cognitive science terms, we are considering the extent to which Smith—as well as his followers—came to identify a human-made object with a mental representation of ancient golden plates in faith.

If we consider the divine prohibition against viewing the plates as relayed by Smith, the obedient response of insiders, and their willingness to protect the plates from skeptical outsiders, we can envision an alternative way to view the materialization of the plates that involved neither recovery and translation in any usual sense nor necessarily deception or fraud, but rather a process through which a small group who believed in the power of revelatory dream-visions, in ancient inhabitants of the Americas, and in golden records buried in a hillside came to believe that a material object covered by a cloth or hidden in a box were the ancient plates revealed to Joseph Smith by the ancient Nephite, Moroni. Highlighting the crucial role played by his family, who shared Smith's belief in ancient Nephites, the angel Moroni, and ancient buried plates long before Smith claimed to recover them, suggests a broader view that embeds the recovery of the plates in a process of materialization that stretched (at least) from Smith's dream-vision in 1823 to the publication of the Book of Mormon in 1830. Within this framework, I

FIGURE 2.2. Portraits of the Three Witnesses of the Book of Mormon with the Hill Cumorah (*below*), an angel (*above left*), and an angel showing the plates to the witnesses (*upper right*). (Engraving by HB Hall & Sons, 1883.)

hypothesize Smith arrived at an understanding of the relationship between materiality and sacrality, reflected in the Book of Mormon, that allowed him to materialize believed-in plates. In contrast to the either/or positions commonly embraced by many scholars, I see evidence in the insider accounts and the Book of Mormon to suggest a shared insider understanding of the relationship between human creativity and divine manifestation that was more in keeping with the "both/and" views of the Catholic tradition than the "either/or" views of Calvinists.

The Materialization Process

In keeping with this view, we can view the materialization of the plates as a process that unfolded over a period of years beginning with the dream-visions of September 1823 and culminating in the publication of the Book of Mormon. Within that time span, believers claim that the plates were materially present for approximately two years. In that two-year window, I am proposing that believers materialized the plates in three steps. The *first step* involved the creation of one (or more) representation(s) of the plates that could be hefted in a box and touched through a cloth, but not viewed directly. The *second step* involved the creation of the first characters document, which Harris took to Anthon. Anthon's inability to translate the characters was interpreted first in light of 1 Corinthians 1:27 and later Isaiah 29:11–12 as justification for Smith's "translation" by means of the "interpreters." The *third step* involved the direct seeing of the plates in a vision by those already deeply invested in the translation process and strongly disposed to believe. While many Mormons take the witness of the three and the eight as testimony to the materiality of the plates, according to the Lord (D&C 17:5), the witnesses saw as Joseph Smith saw, that is, through the power of God in faith. Thus, their testimony should not be taken as testimony to the materiality of *ancient* golden plates but rather as testimony to the witnesses' ability to see reality in the way Joseph Smith did, that is, as a supernaturally charged reality in which angels produced, transported, and ultimately withdrew a believed-in simulation. In naturalistic terms the witnesses testified to the powers of the human mind not only to see things others could not see but to the power of human minds to see things together in faith.

CHAPTER 3

Beginnings

Chapter 2 concluded by stressing that the testimony of the witnesses tells us more about their ability to see reality the way that Joseph Smith did— through the eyes of faith—than about the materiality of the ancient golden plates. When Martin Harris asked if he could see the plates when he visited Harmony in March 1829, the Lord made a similar point in a revelation (D&C 5), reminding Harris that believing his words was more important than seeing the plates. Although the Lord indicated that he would allow three of his "Servants" to see the plates, he stressed that without belief in his (the Lord's) words, people would not be convinced by any amount of seeing. Indeed, he said, "woe shall come unto the Inhabitents of the Earth *if they will not hearken unto my words*[,] for Behold if they will not believe my words they would not believe my servants if it were possible he could show them all things" (Revelation, March 1829, *JSP*, D1:16–17 [D&C 5]; emphasis added). As this revelation makes clear, the central act of faith lay in believing that the Lord was speaking through Smith and that it was the Lord—and not Smith—who was guiding the process.

THE NEW REVELATION

In returning to the question of how and why Mormons arrived at the official story of their origins as depicted in Smith's 1839 history, we need to start therefore with the words of the Lord, recognizing that in the eyes of Smith and his followers, the Lord was guiding the process through the revelation of the Book of Mormon and the real-time revelations that accompanied it. We need to consider not only *what* the Lord was revealing, but what the Lord had conveyed to them about *why* he was revealing it. What, in other words, was the point of the new revelation? If we read through key early revelations—D&C 3 (July 1828), D&C 5 (March 1829), the title page of the Book of Mormon (June 1829), and the Articles and Covenants of the Church of Christ (1830)—in light of the contents of the Book of Mormon, we can get a pretty clear idea of what the Lord was revealing to his followers and why he was doing so.

We learn from the July 1828 revelation (D&C 3) that the "Purpose" for which "these Plates . . . which contain these Records [were prepared was so] that the Promises of the Lord might be fulfilled which he made to his People [the Nephities & the Jacobites & the Josephites & the Lamanites] & [so] that the Lamanites might come to the knowledge of their Fathers & that they [the Lamanites] may know the Promises of the Lord that they may believe the Gospel & rely upon the merits of Jesus Christ & that they might be glorified through faith in his name & that they might repent & be Saved" (Revelation, July 1828, in *JSP*, D1:9 [D&C 3]). The Lord had made promises to his people here in the New World, but knowledge of those promises had been lost. The Lamanites and the Ishmaelites, the only ancient peoples who had survived down to the (then) present, had lost the knowledge of the promises the Lord made to his people; they had "dwindled in unbelief because of the iniquities of their Fathers" who fought and destroyed the other ancient peoples "because of their iniquities & Abominations." The records on the plates were given so that the Lamanites could regain this knowledge, repent, and be saved.

The March 1829 revelation (D&C 5) focused not on "my People," that is, the ancient inhabitants and their descendants, but on "the People of this generation" more generally. With respect to them, the Lord indicated (*JSP*, D1:17 [D&C 5]) that he was prepared to "work a reformation among them," putting down "all lyings and deceivings" and establishing his church among them as "taught by [his] Disciples," if they believed in his word. If, however, they "harden[ed] their hearts," refusing to believe in his word, then the "Sword of Justice" would fall upon them and they would be delivered up to Satan.

The copyright and the title page for the Book of Mormon linked these two purposes, explaining that it was "*written to the Lamanites, which are a remnant of the House of Israel; and also to Jew and Gentile*" (emphasis added). It also explained how it had been preserved (it was "written and sealed and hid up unto the Lord that they [the records] might not be destroyed"), how it had been recovered ("by the way of Gentile [i.e., Joseph Smith]"), and how Smith interpreted the plates ("by the gift of God"). It then summarized the twofold reason *why* the records had been preserved: first, so that "the remnant[s] of the House of Israel" might know the "great things the Lord hath done for their fathers; and that they may know . . . they are not cast off forever," and, second, to convince "the Jew and Gentile that Jesus is the Christ, the eternal God, manifesting himself unto all nations" (*JSP*, D1:65). For those familiar with the contents of the new book, this was an apt summary, though it most likely left outsiders wondering who exactly the Lamanites were and why the Gentiles still needed to learn that Jesus is the Christ.

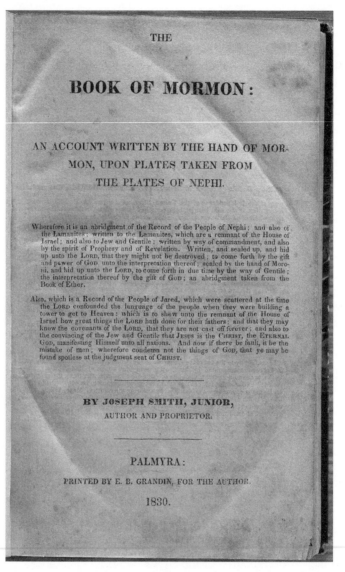

THE

BOOK OF MORMON:

AN ACCOUNT WRITTEN BY THE HAND OF MOR-
MON, UPON PLATES TAKEN FROM
THE PLATES OF NEPHI.

Wherefore it is an abridgment of the Record of the People of Nephi; and also of the Lamanites; written to the Lamanites, which are a remnant of the House of Israel; and also to Jew and Gentile; written by way of commandment, and also by the spirit of Prophesy and of Revelation. Written, and sealed up, and hid up unto the LORD, that they might not be destroyed; to come forth by the gift and power of GOD unto the interpretation thereof; sealed by the hand of Moroni, and hid up unto the LORD, to come forth in due time by the way of Gentile; the interpretation thereof by the gift of GOD; an abridgment taken from the Book of Ether.

Also, which is a Record of the People of Jared, which were scattered at the time the LORD confounded the language of the people when they were building a tower to get to Heaven: which is to shew unto the remnant of the House of Israel how great things the LORD hath done for their fathers; and that they may know the covenants of the LORD, that they are not cast off forever; and also to the convincing of the Jew and Gentile that JESUS is the CHRIST, the ETERNAL GOD, manifesting Himself unto all nations. And now if there be fault, it be the mistake of men; wherefore condemn not the things of GOD, that ye may be found spotless at the judgment seat of CHRIST.

BY JOSEPH SMITH, JUNIOR,

AUTHOR AND PROPRIETOR.

PALMYRA:

PRINTED BY E. B. GRANDIN, FOR THE AUTHOR.

1830.

FIGURE 3.1. The title page of the original 1830 edition of the Book of Mormon.

The Articles and Covenants, adopted by the newly founded Church of Christ in April 1830, were more forthcoming. In addition to the first brief history of the church, we learn that the "book [not only] contains a record of a fallen people [but] . . . also the fullness of the gospel of Jesus Christ to the Gentiles and also to the Jews." In addition to providing "the fullness of the gospel," it proved to Gentiles and Jews "that God doth inspire men and call them to his holy work in these last days." In other words, the book made a case for continuing revelation; it established that there was more to the gospel than people knew and that God was calling people to some kind of task ("his holy work") in the short time remaining ("these last days"). Finally, we learn that people's salvation depended on how they received the book, whether in "faith and righteousness" or "in unbelief to their own condemnation" (Articles and Covenants, ca. April 1830, in *JSP*, D1:121 [D&C 20]). While outsiders learned that there was more and that their salvation depended on it, they were not told *why* they needed more.

With the publication of the Book of Mormon (March 1830) and the founding of the Church of Christ (6 April 1830), Smith and his followers had reached a turning point. A first set of tasks had been accomplished and new ones now surfaced. Up until this point, insiders had been able to follow the unfolding of the process from the inside. As participants in the process, they were privy to revelations as they were received and to the Book of Mormon narrative as it was dictated and transcribed. Now, with the book published and the church founded, followers were "called to a holy work in these last days," which was, in effect, to convince others—the Lamanites (Native Americans) and the Gentiles (ordinary Christians)—of what they had come to believe.

Initially, it was not clear to outsiders whether the new revelation supplemented or completely superseded the Christianity they knew. Shortly after the founding of the church, a group of Baptists indicated that they believed in the Book of Mormon and wished to join the church without being rebaptized (*JSP*, D1:137n140). When Smith inquired of the Lord on this point (Revelation, 16 April 1830, *JSP*, D1:137–38 [D&C 22]), the Lord indicated that all the "old covenants" had been replaced by "a new and everlasting covenant" and that believers could not enter by means of "dead works, *for it is because of your dead works* that I have caused this last covenant and this church to be built up unto me" (emphasis added). As critics were quick to point out, this was not a small matter. The claim that all the old covenants—not just with the Jews but also with other Christians—had been replaced by a new covenant effectively negated the claims and baptismal practices of all other Christians. As the *Painesville (OH) Telegraph* pointed out, the Mormon missionaries were claiming, "the ordinances of the gospel [had] not been regularly administered since the days of the Apostles" (16 November 1830, *JSP*, D1:138n146).

The idea that the old covenant had been broken and a new covenant revealed was at the heart of the earliest understanding of the new church. In the preface to the "Book of Commandments and Revelations," which Smith received as a revelation in November 1831, these themes were repeated. According to the Lord, those who did not believe would be cut off "for they have strayed from mine ordinances & have broken mine everlasting Covenant." The Lord explained, he had spoken to Smith "from heaven . . . [so] that mine everlasting Covenant might be established" and gave his "Servant Joseph [the] power to translate . . . the book of Mormon . . . to lay the foundation of this Church . . . the only true & living Church upon the face of the whole Earth" (Revelation, 1 November 1831-B, *JSP*, D1:103–5 [D&C 1]).

From a letter written by Lucy Mack Smith to her brother, Solomon Mack, and her sister, Lydia Mack Bill, in January 1831, out of concern for "the welfare of [their] souls," we can learn how someone deeply involved in the new church presented its claims and the evidence offered to support them. The main points are familiar: God was soon to "make his appearance on the earth . . . to take vengance [*sic*] on the wicked & they that know not God." God was again attempting "to recover his people the House of Israel" and had "commenced this work" by sending "forth a revelation in these last days" that contained "the fullness of the Gospel to the Gentiles." Following this overview, she recapped the highlights of the Book of Mormon and then briefly described how the new revelation came forth, rehearsing Moroni's burial of the plates and their recovery by her son Joseph, who, "after repenting of his sins and humbling himself before God[,] was visited by an holy Angel."

In recounting what her siblings would learn from reading the Book of Mormon, Lucy Smith explained why a new revelation, a new covenant, and a new church were needed:

> [B]y [reading] this our eyes are opened that we can see the situation in which the world now stands that the eyes of the whole world are blinded, that the churches have all become corrupted, yea every church upon the face of the earth; that the Gospel of Christ is nowhere preached. [T]his is the situation which the world is now in, and you can judge for yourselves if we did not need something more than the wisdom of man for to show us the right way. God seeing our situation had compassion upon us and has sent us this revelation that the stumbling block might be removed, that whosoever would might enter. He now established his church upon the earth as it was in the days of the Apostles. He has now made a new and everlasting covenant and all that will hear his voice and enter he says they shall be gathered together into a land of promise. (Lucy Mack Smith to Solomon Mack Jr., 6 January 1831, *EMD* 1:216)

Their Bible, Lucy thus explained, was insufficient because the churches were all corrupted and the Gospel of Christ was nowhere preached. They needed a new revelation both to open their eyes to the true situation—that the churches were all corrupted—and to "show [them] the right way" to a church restored "as it was in the days of the Apostles." Believers in the new revelation could not enter the new church by means of the "dead works" of corrupt churches, but only through rebaptism into the true church founded on "a new and everlasting covenant."

Lucy Smith's letter spelled out the work that the Lord's followers were called to do in the last days: they were to get the message to the Lamanites that they were not "cast off forever" and also to the Jews and Gentiles, alerting them to the new revelation, the restoration of the church, the impending judgment, and "the gathering of the house of Israel" that was to take place at a still undisclosed location in these "last days" (introduction, *JSP*, D1:xxxiii–xxxv). Her letter also pointed to two frequently voiced objections: "we have Bible enough and want no more" (*EMD* 1:215) and "many think hard [of us] when we tell them that the churches have all become corrupted" (*EMD* 1:216).

These were likely the two main objections of those who rejected the new revelation. Those who belonged to churches may have thought some or even many of the other churches were wrong, but undoubtedly would have been hard-pressed to agree that *theirs* was wrong. Those who would have agreed with the Mormons that all the churches were wrong—known as "restorationists"—typically turned to the Bible, not to new revelation, to restore Christianity to its "primitive" simplicity (Hughes 1996). Whether they belonged to a church they thought was right or to the restorationist movement, most Christians assumed that the "full Gospel" was present in the New Testament and that nothing could or should be added to it.

In her letter, Lucy Smith made very limited use of the Bible to support her claim that new revelation was needed. She pointed to the absence of miraculous "signs" in the present, like those depicted in the early church in the book of Acts, as evidence that the churches were not teaching "the true doctrine of Christ," and she referred to the writings of Isaiah to support her claim that God wanted to gather his people (*EMD* 1:216–17). Most of the support for her claim that new revelation was needed came from the Book of Mormon itself. It was there that her siblings would learn that "many plain and most precious things" had been removed from the Bible by the "abominable church," leaving the Gentiles in a "state of awful wickedness" (1 Nephi 13:28–32); that the situation in the world was one in which "the churches . . . [all] contend one with another" (2 Nephi 28:3–4); that the Lord would "raise up [a seer] out of the fruit of [the biblical Joseph's] loins" to bring forth his word and overcome "the confounding of false doctrines and . . . contentions, and establish peace" (2 Nephi 3:11–12); and that, if they did not repent, they would "bring down the fulness of the wrath of God upon [themselves] as the inhabitants of the land have hitherto done" (Ether 2:9, 11). Moreover, without the Book of Mormon, they would not know who the ancient inhabitants of the land were and what they had done to bring down the fullness of God's wrath.

Much of the evidence for her claims, in other words, was self-authenticating. This evidence would have made sense to insiders, but for most outsiders, a self-authenticating revelation was not enough. For those who thought the Bible they already had was sufficient, the fact that the new revelation said—based on its own authority—that they were wrong most likely seemed circular. The case for new revelation and a new church would be much more compelling if the problem—the corruption of all the churches—could be derived from a source outside the new revelation itself. In the early thirties, many converts were drawn to the new church by reports of signs and wonders, much like those they had read about in the early church in the book of Acts (Staker 2009, 71–91). Over the course of the thirties, however, Mormons increasingly turned to the histories of the emergence of their church. Over time, these histories more deeply embedded the history of the church in a narrative of prophetic authority going back to Moses.

Histories

If we return now to our central question—how and why Mormons got to the official story of their origins as expressed in Smith's 1839 history, we can situate the question in relation to two fundamental transitions: (1) from producing new scripture to evangelizing based on it and (2) from revelation-guided production of a sacred history that began in biblical times (the Book of Mormon) to human narration of the story of how and why the Lord was intervening in the nineteenth century to provide continuing access to revelation (church history). Insiders, guided by real-time revelations, dictated and transcribed the Book of Mormon, absorbing the narrative as it unfolded. Evangelizing required insiders to formulate the message for outsiders, who had not heard the story, in a way they could understand. But without knowing the sacred history as related in the Book of Mormon, as those involved in the translation process did, the public summaries, such as the book's title page, were cryptic and hard to grasp. Moreover, as Lucy Smith pointed out, many outsiders reacted negatively to what they did grasp—that their church, along with all the others, was corrupted and that their Bible was not enough to restore it to its proper apostolic form.

In the wake of these transitions, insiders had to figure out how to convey the new revelation as effectively as possible to outsiders. Revelation-based guidance did not end, but it was an insider activity; only those who believed that the Lord was guiding his newly restored church—that is, church members—were open to guidance through revelations to Joseph Smith. The new revelation—the sacred history recounted in the Book of Mormon—took place in the distant past, although, like the Bible, it made allusions to the present. Histories of the new church quickly emerged as a separate, human-authored genre that attempted to explain to insiders, outsiders, and future generations how and why the Lord had intervened as he had in the nineteenth century (cf. *JSP*, H1).[1] They began not in the far distant past but in the nineteenth century, and not only provided a description of how events had unfolded but also a rationale and justification for what had emerged. Church histories thus offered reasons for insiders and outsiders to accept the new book as revelation, the new church as authentically restored, and Smith's role and function as seer, prophet, and revelator. Histories functioned as a bridge between insiders and outsiders, simultaneously explaining and legitimizing the message and structure of the restored church for a mixed audience of insiders and potential converts. Rehearsing the narrative solidified insiders' identity as insiders and, when accepted by outsiders, offered a means of incorporating them into the church.

If we consider references to events leading up to the founding of the church as protochurch histories, the focal event in the earliest accounts was the appearance of the angel Moroni to Smith in 1823 to announce the presence of new revelation preserved on golden plates. This is how Joseph Smith recounted the story in his letter to his father's family in 1828; how Lucy Mack Smith recounted it in her letter to her siblings, Solomon and Lydia, in 1831; and, generally, how it was understood in the early 1830s (*JSP*, H1:6). The brief history of the church that appeared in the Articles and Covenants (ca. April 1830 [D&C 20]) offered a bit more of a preamble, telling us that, after Smith ("the first elder" of the church) "had received remission of his sins, he was entangled again in the vanities of the world, but after truly repenting, God visited him by an holy angel . . . by the means of which was before prepared that he should translate a book" (*JSP*, D1:121). This is the first hint of a story that begins prior to Moroni's appearance in 1823, but it is not clear why the story should begin with the "remission of his sins" or how this helps us to understand the import of either the new scripture or the new church.

If the story initially began with the discovery and recovery of the ancient golden plates, why does the story get a new beginning—Smith's first vision—starting in the thirties? I think Smith started telling the story of this earlier experience in the context of proselytizing, because it helped him to explain to ever wider audiences how he and his followers knew that all the extant churches were wrong and why the Bible that their listeners already had was not enough to get things right. In other words, the need to explain "the reason why he [Smith] preached the doctrin[e] he did" (*EMD* 1:36)—to quote an early convert—led Smith to reflect on when he had first realized

---

[1] For a complete listing of histories written by Joseph Smith or others empowered by him in the thirties and forties, as well as Lucy Mack Smith's history, see the Histories section of *The Joseph Smith Papers* online at http://josephsmithpapers.org/the-papers#/H2L.

that all the churches were wrong. In his histories, Smith said he struggled with the question of which church was correct in the context of revivals of religion as a young teenager. I see no reason to doubt that he did. Not only is there evidence to corroborate the presence of revival activity nearby during his early adolescence (Harper 2012, 74–80; Fluhman 2012, 18–19), but his description in his later account (*EMD* 1:58–59) of the way the Methodists, Baptists, and Presbyterians worked together to promote "this extraordinary scene of religious feeling in order to have everybody converted," but then lost their "seemingly good feelings" as "the Converts began to file off some to one party and some to another" rings true. I am suggesting, though, that the memory of his earlier struggles with this question came to the fore in the context of explaining why a new revelation was needed, that is, at the point when he needed to provide external (as opposed to internal Book of Mormon) evidence for the problem that the new revelation and the restored church were intended to solve.

The First Vision

If we compare the earliest accounts of Smith's first vision, which he recounted in 1832, 1835, and 1838, we find that Joseph and Lucy Mack Smith agreed on the problem for which the new book and new church were the solution—the corruption of all the churches—but how they learned that this was the case shifted from the Book of Mormon itself (in Lucy Smith's 1831 letter) to early nineteenth-century revivals of religion, that is, to the context in which Smith received his "first vision," as Mormons came to call it. This is not to argue that Smith made up his first vision experience. That's possible, but I think it is more likely that he recalled the personally significant "remission of sin" experience that he alluded to in the 1830 Articles and Covenants, realized that it was the context in which he had initially concluded that all the churches were wrong, and therefore started recounting the experience not only as personally significant but also as the context in which he became aware of the problem addressed by the new revelation and restored church. As such, it was a logical place to begin "a history" of his life and "an account of the rise of the church of Christ" rooted in the nineteenth century rather than ancient America, which is what he set out to do in 1832. This is also how he told the story when he recounted it in public in the early thirties. Thus, as Curtis's account of Smith's visit to Michigan in 1834 attests, he explained to his listeners that the reason he preached the doctrine he did was not because the angel Moroni appeared to him in 1823, but because, in the context of "a revival of some of the sec[t]s," he had become anxious as to which was correct and went to "enquire of the lord [*sic*] himself," as to which was right. After some struggle, Curtis recounted, Smith said "the Lord manifested to him that the different sects were [w]rong also that the Lord had a great work for him to do" (*EMD* 1:36).

If we compare Smith's three accounts from 1832 (*EMD* 1:26–31), 1835 (*EMD* 1:43–44), and 1839 (*EMD* 1:59–62), along with reports from those who heard him speak (Andrus in 1833 and Curtis in 1834), we can identify a consistent set of features that may represent the way he would have recounted the event about the time it occurred and some significant differences that he elaborated in response to events of the thirties (see appendix, chart 3).[2] The consistent features include:

1. He felt mentally distressed in the context of "contentions and divisions" (1832) among the different religious groups.
2. He "cried unto the Lord" (1832), "called upon the Lord" (1835), and "offer[ed] up the desires of [his] heart to God" (1838–39).
3. "A pillar of light came down from above" (1832), "a pillar of fire appeared above my head [and] . . . rested down up[on] me" (1835), "a pillar [of] light . . . descended . . . upon me" (1838–39).
4. He saw one (1832) or two (1835, 1838–39) personages and they spoke to him.
5. When he recounted his experience, no one believed him (1832, 1838–39).

These common features, which may indicate how he initially understood the event, suggest that key features of an initial recounting may have been mental distress in the context of sectarian differences, an appeal to the Lord, a vision of a pillar of light, the appearance of one or more personages who delivered a message, and subsequent disbelief on the part of others.

There are, however, a number of significant differences with respect to how he knew all the churches were wrong, who he encountered, what they said, and how others responded. I will describe the differences and then offer my interpretation (for an alternative interpretation, see Harper 2012 and Harper's interpretation in Taves and Harper 2016).[3]

How He Knows All the Churches Are Wrong: In the 1832 account, he indicated that he "had become convicted of [his] sins" in the context of the

---

[2] This chart was expanded in light of Steven C. Harper's research to include the accounts of those who heard Smith preach.

[3] Taves and Harper (2016) is the published version of a formal dialogue about the first vision accounts that LDS Church historian Steven C. Harper and I presented at the 2014 meeting of the American Academy of Religion. To refine our views and identify more clearly where we agreed and disagreed, I suggested that we enter into a dialogue based on the chart that I had developed for this chapter (see appendix, chart 3).

contentions between the denominations and, as a result, began searching the scriptures only to discover, *based on his own reading of scripture*, "that they [the different Christian sects] had apostatized from the true and live-ing [*sic*] faith and there was no society or denomination that built upon the Gospel of Jesus Christ as recorded in the new testament." In Smith's later versions and in the Curtis account, he does not search the scriptures to learn that there is no "denomination that built on the Gospel," but rather scriptures come to mind (Matt. 7:7 and James 1:5 in 1835 and James 1:5 in Curtis 1838–39) that instruct him to bring his concern to the Lord. In the 1838–39 account, the James 1:5 passages came to mind dramatically "with power" and "great force," in contrast to the 1835 or Curtis account where one or two passages dawned on him more gradually. The differences between the later versions and the Curtis account, all of which involve asking the Lord, are not as important as the difference between the early method of "searching the scriptures" and the "ask and you will be told" method of the later accounts. The difference is not a mere nuance, because *he took out the part about searching the scriptures* and *replaced it* with the "ask and you will be told" method. He didn't combine the two methods as some readers have assumed.

Interpretation: I think that he may have concluded that all the churches were wrong in his early teens based on his own interpretation of scripture. A revival context in which his sense of his own sinfulness was awakened and he was expected to seek forgiveness within one of the extant "sects" provides a plausible context for such searching. But it was undoubtedly also suggested by the fact that others in his family held similar views. In light of his conclusion, he appealed directly to the Lord for forgiveness and had a sense that the Lord appeared to him and forgave him. Like Bushman (2005, 35–41) and Vogel (2004, xv), I think he recalled this experience of forgiveness in 1832.[4] I think that he started using the "ask and you will be told" method of praying in the late twenties, most likely when he began initiating revelations by "inquiring of the Lord."

The distinction between the two methods is important, since most Protestant Christians, believing that revelation had ended and that the "canon" of scripture had been "closed," read scripture intensively as their primary source of religious knowledge. In his 1839 account, Smith criticized the ex-

---

[4] According to Bushman, "He [Smith] initially thought, I believe, of the First Vision as a personal experience. It was his encounter with God that would reassure him of the favor of Heavenly Father. And only later did he come to see it as his call as a Prophet. The call of a prophet is a form of religious experience in Moses and Isaiah and all sorts of prophets. And gradually Joseph saw that this was the founding moment of his life as the restorer of the Gospel. But it took time for it to emerge in its full significance." Samuel Alonzo Dodge, interview with Richard L. Bushman, 2009, transcript in possession of Steven C. Harper (quote used here courtesy of Steven C. Harper).

egetical method as unreliable, stating explicitly: "the teachers of religion . . . understood . . . scripture so differently as [to] destroy all confidence in settling the question by an appeal to the Bible." Bickering over the meaning of scripture, in other words, was another sign that all the churches were wrong and, more crucially, external evidence of the need for new revelation. If differences could not be settled through an appeal to the Bible, then something more was evidently needed. By shifting methods, he allowed the Lord to answer directly.

The 1832 account thus provided external (non–Book of Mormon) evidence that all the churches were wrong based on Smith's exegesis of scripture. This point potentially spoke to those who "think hard [of us] when we tell them that the churches have all become corrupted," as Lucy Smith put it (*EMD* 1:216), by claiming that the corruption of the churches could be demonstrated on the basis of scriptures they already believed in. But it didn't explain why the Bible wasn't enough. The 1839 version offered a more comprehensive external explanation of how Smith knew all the churches were wrong (direct revelation from the Lord) based on the scriptural injunction to "ask and you will be told" and also explained why the Bible was not enough to solve the problem (because the teachers of religion couldn't agree on how to interpret it, which was in turn another sign of the contention that needed to be overcome).

Who He Encounters: This too varies among the accounts. "The Lord" appeared in the 1832 and the Curtis account, an angel in the Andrus account, a personage and many angels in 1835, and two personages in 1839. Although Mormon readers, beginning in the 1880s, highlighted the significance of the two personages who appear in the canonized 1839 account in light of later theological concerns (Allen 1992, 46–50), the appearance of a negative encounter in the later accounts is a more noteworthy change in the context of the thirties. Thus, in the 1832 account, Smith simply "crie[s] unto the Lord for mercy" and the pillar of fire appears. In Smith's later versions and in the Curtis account, Smith describes an intervening "struggle" (Curtis), an inability to pray and a "noise" (1835), and being "seized upon by some power" that felt dark and destructive (1838–39) prior to the pillar of light appearing. There are interesting parallels between the struggles depicted in Smith's 1835 and 1839 accounts of his first vision and Smith's vision of Moses's initial encounter with God, which he received in June 1830. In that encounter, Moses was tempted by Satan, "began to fear exceedingly," and called upon God, who then spoke with him again (*JSP*, D1:152–55).

Interpretation: This suggests to me, as it does to Bushman (see note above), that Smith was starting to think more about how prophets were called and that his memories of his "forgiveness experience" gradually came to sound more like Moses's, that is, more like a prophetic call than an evangelical conversion experience. I think that this integration took place over the course of the thirties, such that his vision of Moses's calling—his prophetic template as it were—only gradually reshaped his memories of his own experience. Although I am suggesting that the inclusion of the struggle with "dark powers" theme in his first vision accounts made the accounts more congruent with his prophetic template, I think he knew this feeling from his 1823 efforts to recover the plates from the hill in the wake of his Moroni vision. All of Smith's accounts of that experience, which, as discussed in chapter 2, were included in the 1832, 1835, and 1839 histories, contained this element of struggle, but the meaning of the struggle was progressively elaborated over time from a struggle with doubt (1832) to a struggle with Satan (1839) and incorporated, I am suggesting, into his memory of his first vision as well.

What the Personage(s) Said: In Smith's 1832 version, a personage told him his sins were forgiven and then proclaimed that the world "lieth in sin" and that his "anger is kindling against the inhabitants of the earth," but he didn't tell him that all the churches were wrong (*EMD* 1:28). In the observer's accounts and Smith's 1838–39 account, the divine personages do. In the 1839 history, the Lord then justified his statement "that all their Creeds were an abomination in his sight [and] that those professors [of religion] were all corrupt" with quotes from Isaiah 29:13 and 2 Timothy 3:5.

Interpretation: There are two key changes in what the personage(s) said. First, there is a shift in what happened. In the 1832 and 1835 accounts, his sins were forgiven. In the other accounts, he was told that all the churches were wrong and that he was called to do something. This is a crucial shift from an account of forgiveness to a prophetic call account that parallels Moses's prophetic calling as revealed in Smith's vision of Moses. Second, as time goes on, the personages quote more scripture, mostly from the biblical prophets. There are no references to scripture in the 1832 history in the context of the first vision or the Moroni visitation. The one reference—to Isaiah 29—appears in relation to the visit to Charles Anthon. In the 1835 account, the angel cites Malachi 4 in defense of the Mormon claim that the end is near. In the 1839 history, the claim that the churches are corrupt is backed by quotes from Isaiah and 2 Timothy. In the 1839 version of Moroni's visit, the ancient Nephite provided Smith with extensive support from the biblical prophets. After he told Smith where he had deposited the plates, "he commenced quoting the prophecies of the old testament," beginning with Malachi. After an extended discussion of Malachi, Moroni turned to the eleventh chapter of Isaiah and the second chapter of Joel (*EMD* 1:64–65).

Much as Jesus in Luke 24:17 "interpreted to them [two of his grieving disciples on the road to Emmaus] the things concerning himself [in all the scriptures] . . . beginning with Moses and all the prophets," so too in the 1839 history, the Lord and his messenger, Moroni, interpreted the new revelation in light of Smith's vision of Moses and the writings of the later prophets. [In rereading the new revelation in light of already believed-in scripture, the 1839 history authorized the new revelation by means of the old, thus grounding its claims in a widely acknowledged external source of authority.] Mormons no longer had to rely as heavily on people reading the Book of Mormon as a self-authorizing revelatory text or on signs and wonders, but could show outsiders how their claims were anticipated and prefigured in already believed-in scripture. In the words that appear in the mouths of supernatural figures, we can see how Smith and his followers were—over time—rereading received scripture in light of their new revelation and were increasingly able to defend their new revelation in light of that rereading.

How Others Respond: In 1832, Smith said he "could find none that would believe the hevnly vision" (*EMD* 1:28). In 1839, a minister told him "it was all of the Devil, that there was no such thing as visions or revelations in these days, that all such things had ceased with the apostles and that there never would be any more of them" (*EMD* 1:61–62). Moreover, in the 1839 account, his story excited "great persecution" and "all [the sects] united to persecute me." He says he was "hated and persecuted for saying that [he] had seen a vision" (*EMD* 1:62).

Interpretation: In our discussion of these issues, Steven Harper stressed the importance of Smith's emotional "diatribe" against the evangelical clergy (Taves and Harper 2016, 70–71). While I agree that the passage is important, I don't think Smith was responding to a lifetime of persecution, as Harper contends, but to the evangelical clergy's increasingly vehement rejection of his claims *in the thirties*, which is when they become widely known. When we compare the versions, we see a heightening of the persecution theme. In the 1832 version, Smith simply said "that none would believe the heavenly vision." I doubt anyone had difficulty with the idea that the Lord forgave him in a vision. What they didn't believe, as Lucy Smith's letter, written just a year earlier, documents, was his claim that all the churches were wrong. As Lucy indicated, "many think hard [of us] when we tell them that." Moreover, in the 1839 version, the clergy were not persecuting him simply because he claimed that he had had a vision, as Smith makes it seem when he compares his experience with that of the apostle Paul (*EMD* 1:42). The minister in question said, "there was no such thing as visions *or revelations* in these days, that all such things had ceased with the apostles" (emphasis added). The insertion of "or revelations" here strikes me as highly significant. It seems to speak directly to the post–Book of Mormon claim to have produced new revelation. This is totally anachronistic in relation to 1820 but highly plausible post-1830.

AUTHORITY

Switching to the "ask and you will be told" method in later versions shifted the authority for his claim that all the denominations were wrong from his exegesis (which would make him just another fallible "teacher of religion") to the Lord's revelation. This shift, in turn, set up his prophetic calling, displacing other options, for example, as a teacher of religion or a seer, neither of which he wanted to stress in 1838–39. The insertion of the "dark powers" theme suggested parallels with his vision of Moses's call and the parallels between his experience and that of the prophets. The insertion of more and more biblical citations, primarily from the writings of the prophets (Malachi, Isaiah, and Joel) into the speeches of the Lord in the first vision and Moroni in the 1823 vision, not only provided external authority for Book of Mormon claims, it aligned the revelations through Smith with earlier revelations through the prophets. Finally, the heightening of the persecution theme between the 1832 and the 1839 versions firmly grounds the histories in the 1830s when Mormon claims regarding new revelation and a restored church led to increasing conflict and, indeed, persecution. We can see in these shifts the emergence of an origin narrative that justified the new revelation and the restored church, not in terms of the internal Book of Mormon narrative upon which it was built but in terms of the lived experience of early nineteenth-century Protestants, who believed in the Bible yet found themselves caught in the midst of religious rivalries and competing interpretations of scripture.

The 1839 history not only gave Mormons a way to explain their origins to others, it also helped them to better understand who Joseph Smith was. In the eyes of many who knew him in Manchester and Palmyra in the twenties, he was a "money-digger," a "treasure seeker," and a local "seer." In Book of Mormon terms, he was a seer, prophet, and revelator, and, as the Book of Mormon made clear, a seer was greater than a prophet. Although the earliest Mormon documents routinely refer to "Joseph the seer," this title was gradually downplayed with the founding of the restored church. With the institution of the first "ordinance" (baptism) in 1829 and the organization of the church in April 1830, new forms of authority were introduced, including the roles of elders, priests, teachers, and deacons (*JSP*, D1:xxxvi–xxxix, 123–24). With the founding of the church, Smith's authority as an apostle and elder came to the fore. In April 1830, Smith was "ordained an apostle of Jesus Christ, an elder of the church" (*JSP*, D1:120). The revelation of 6 April 1830 referred to him as "a seer & Translator & Prop[h]et an Apostle of Jesus Christ an Elder of the Church" (*JSP*, D1:129).

In Smith's 1832 history, the explicit emphasis is on his priestly and apostolic authority. When he outlined the topics he would cover in his "account of the rise of the church of Christ," he listed four things: his reception of "testamony from on high" (the first vision), "the ministering of Angels" (the Moroni visitation), "the reception of the holy Priesthood," and "a confirmation and reception of the high Priesthood after the holy order of the son of the living God [and] . . . the Kees of the Kingdom of God confered upon him" (*JSP*, H1:10). Here the explicit emphasis is not on Smith as seer, prophet, translator, or revelator but on priesthood authority and the keys of the kingdom (apostolic authority). This emphasis was in keeping with revelations on priesthood authority (*JSP*, D2:289 [D&C 84] and *JSP*, D2:334, 346 [D&C 88]), which are dated immediately after this.

Because Smith had many titles, it is easy to conflate them as if they were all equally important at any given point in time. The historical evidence suggests that this was not the case. Instead, the evidence suggests that different titles were emphasized depending on the context and the kind of authority that he was claiming. In the late twenties, in the context of dictating the Book of Mormon, the emphasis was on "Joseph the seer," with the understanding that seers were greater than prophets because they had the ability to translate ancient records with special objects. With the founding and organization of the church in 1830, Smith and his followers started to downplay seer authority in favor of his priesthood and apostolic authority, which aligned with churchly ordinances and offices, and thus his authority within the church. Internally, this emphasis never disappeared, but it was complemented with a growing emphasis on Smith as prophet rather than seer, which emerged during the thirties as he and his followers built a case for the primacy of prophetic authority by integrating the Book of Mormon, as new revelation, into a long history of revelation to Moses and the prophets. Even though the Lord instructed Cowdery to ordain Smith as "seer & Translater & Prop[h]et" (Revelation, 6 April 1830, *JSP*, D1:129 [D&C 21]), it was probably no accident that, when recalling the event later, both Cowdery and David Whitmer transposed the order, referring to his ordination as "Prophet[,] Seer and Revelator" (*JSP*, D1:113n5).

An Anonymous Fellowship

Alcoholics Anonymous (AA) dates its beginning as a fellowship to 10 June 1935, the day cofounder Dr. Bob Smith took his last drink. This anniversary was marked at AA International Conventions beginning with the Twentieth Anniversary International Convention in St. Louis in 1955 and every five years thereafter. In conjunction with its twentieth anniversary, Bill Wilson prepared and AA published the second edition of *Alcoholics Anonymous* (the Big Book; hereafter cited as BB:1955), and, with the assistance of others, Bill Wilson researched and wrote AA's first history, *Alcoholics Anonymous Comes of Age* (Anonymous 1957; hereafter cited as *AACOA*). As part of his efforts to preserve the history of AA, he interviewed "old-timers" in the Midwest and, for the first time, dictated his autobiography. In the forward to the second edition of the Big Book (BB:1955), he summarized the basic story of AA's first twenty years.

> The spark that was to flare into the first A.A. group was struck at Akron, Ohio, in June 1935, during a talk between a New York stockbroker and an Akron physician. Six months earlier, the broker had been relieved of his drink obsession by a sudden spiritual experience, following a meeting with an alcoholic friend [Ebby T.] who had been in contact with the Oxford Groups of that day. He had also been greatly helped by the late Dr. William D. Silkworth, a New York specialist in alcoholism . . . Though he could not accept all the tenets of the Oxford Groups, he was convinced of the need for moral inventory, confession of personality defects, restitution to those harmed, helpfulness to others, and the necessity of belief in and dependence upon God. Prior to his journey to Akron, the broker had worked hard with many alcoholics on the theory that only an alcoholic could help an alcoholic, but he had succeeded only in keeping sober himself. The broker had gone to Akron on a business venture which had collapsed, leaving him greatly in fear that he might start drinking again. He suddenly realized that in order to save himself he must carry his message to another alcoholic. That alcoholic turned out to be the Akron physi-

FIGURE 4.1. AA's Twentieth Anniversary Convention at Kiel Auditorium in St. Louis, Missouri, 1955.

cian. . . . He sobered, never to drink again up to the moment of his death in 1950. This seemed to prove that one alcoholic could affect another as no nonalcoholic could. . . . Hence the two men set to work almost frantically upon alcoholics . . . Their very first case, a desperate one, recovered immediately and became A.A. number three. . . . When the broker returned to New York in the fall of 1935, the first A.A. group had actually been formed, though no one realized it at the time . . . A second small group had promptly taken shape at New York [followed in 1937 by a third in Cleveland]. . . . This determination [to place their message and unique experience before the world] bore fruit in the spring of 1939 by the publication of this volume.

The standard narrative placed the meeting of Bill Wilson and Dr. Bob Smith at the center. Although Wilson's sudden spiritual experience relieved him of "his drink obsession," he had no success in his work with other alcoholics until he went to Akron, where "he suddenly realized that in order *to save himself* he must carry his message to another alcoholic" (BB:1955, xv–xxi). In this account, there is something in the nature of Wilson's and Smith's connection that set a "chain reaction" in motion and established AA as a movement with Bill W. and Dr. Bob as its cofounders. When Bill's wife, Lois Burnham Smith, looked back in 1949 (Lois W. 1949), however, she said "it was hard to say just when Alcoholics Anonymous began." She said it could have been when Ebby T. came to see her husband at their home in Brooklyn or the moment of his sudden experience at Towns Hospital shortly thereafter, but for her, she said, "it was the day I first saw the released expression on my husband's face [when she arrived at Towns shortly after his sudden experience]."

KEY COLLABORATORS[1]

William Griffin Wilson (1895–1971) grew up in East Dorset, Vermont, the eldest of two siblings. His parents divorced when he was ten; his father left for Alaska, his mother moved to Boston to study osteopathic medicine, and he and his sister, Dorothy, moved in with their prosperous maternal grandparents. He attended Norwich University, a military college in Vermont, and met Lois Burnham, whose family summered in nearby Manchester, Vermont, while he was a student. He left college before completing his degree to serve in World War I, marrying Lois just before he was shipped overseas. He struggled to find a job upon his return, eventually becoming involved with stocks and investments. His drinking, which began in the military, was immediately excessive, and, in the wake of the stock market crash, went out of control. He was admitted four times to Towns Hospital—a well-known treatment facility for alcoholics—in 1933 and 1934. In November 1934, Ebby T., a childhood friend and adult drinking buddy, told Wilson he had "gotten religion" and quit drinking with the help of the Oxford Group, which precipitated Wilson's own turn to religion and his December 1934 admission to Towns Hospital, where he had a "sudden experience," after which he remained sober. After his discharge, Wilson attended Oxford Group meetings, invited alcoholics into their Brooklyn home, and visited patients at Towns. In May 1935, eager to rebuild his financial situation, he went to Akron, Ohio, to take part in a proxy fight. Alone at the Mayflower Hotel, he was tempted to drink, but instead made a legendary call to a minister, which led to Henrietta Seuberling, Dr. Robert Smith, and the official June 1935 founding of AA. The Wilsons continued to struggle financially. In 1939, they were forced to give up the Burnham family home, moving to the

---

[1] The Stepping Stones Foundation Archives and General Service Office Archives require historians to maintain the anonymity of AA members by identifying them by their first name and last initial. In practice, it is not clear to what extent this requirements holds after an individual dies. Some would argue that if an individual so indicates while living, their full names can be used after their death without breaching the tradition of anonymity. With respect to the Wilsons and Smiths, I have relied on the precedent established in *Pass It On: The Story of Bill Wilson*, published by AA World Services in 1984. With the exception of Thomas Powers Sr., whose son-in-law indicated Powers granted permission for his last name to be used posthumously, the anonymity of all other known AA members is protected.

AA clubhouse in Manhattan in 1940, and to their permanent home, Stepping Stones, in Bedford Hills, New York, in 1941 (*PIO*; Kurtz 1991).

Lois Burnham Wilson (1891–1988) was the eldest of six children born to churchgoing Swedenborgian parents in Brooklyn Heights, New York, where her father practiced medicine. She attended the Friends School and Packer Collegiate Institute in New York and spent summers in Manchester, Vermont. Bill and Lois met at nearby Emerald Lake, where both their families spent time. They were married in the Swedenborgian Church in New York in 1918, just before Bill's regiment left for Europe. Along with Wilson's physician, Dr. William Silkworth, she vouched for the authenticity of his sudden experience at Towns Hospital, participated with him in Oxford Group meetings, and welcomed recovering alcoholics into their home. Beginning in the forties, she toured the country with Bill, giving talks to family members about AA as a way of life and, in 1951, she and neighbor Anne B. organized the many local AA Family Groups into Al-Anon. She published her autobiography, *Lois Remembers*, in 1979. The Wilsons' home in Bedford Hills was designated a National Historic Landmark in October 2012 and the Stepping Stones Foundation Archives houses their personal papers (*LR*; Borchert 2005).

Dr. Robert Holbrook Smith (1879–1950) grew up in a devout, churchgoing Congregationalist family in St. Johnsbury, Vermont, the only child of a prominent judge and civic leader. Forced to attend church several times a week, he rejected formal religion at an early age. He graduated from Dartmouth College in 1902, received his medical degree from Rush Medical School in Chicago in 1910, and married Anne Ripley in 1915. After a two-year internship at the City Hospital in Akron, Ohio, he opened a private practice in Akron, where he lived the rest of his life. Smith's drinking became an issue in medical school and increased during the twenties and thirties, affecting both his family and his medical practice. At the suggestion of his wife, they began attending Oxford Group meetings in 1933. The meetings, which would eventually provide the spiritual format for AA, awakened Smith's interest in spirituality but did little for his drinking problem. In June 1935, Bob and Anne Smith met Bill Wilson at the home of Henrietta Seuberling, the Oxford Group member who Wilson had called during his crisis at the Mayflower Hotel. Smith remained sober from shortly after their meeting until his death in 1950. "Dr. Bob," as he is known in AA, was at the center of AA's growth in the Midwest and the official "cofounder" of AA (*Dr. Bob*).

Anne Ripley Smith (1881–1949) grew up in Oak Park, Illinois, and met Bob Smith while she was a student at Wellesley College. Upon her graduation, she taught school in Oak Park until she and Bob were married. In addition to the support she provided her husband and the many alcoholics who gathered in their home, she played an important behind-the-scenes role in the development of AA spirituality during the thirties and in laying the groundwork for Al-Anon and AA Family Groups in the forties (*Dr. Bob*; Dick B. 1998; *LR*).

SOURCES AND BEGINNINGS

In contrast to early Mormonism, where Joseph Smith and his followers elaborated on Smith's unusual experiences to produce new scriptures and a new church, Bill Wilson and his collaborators downplayed his unusual experiences, insisting that they were not revelation, he was not a saint or prophet, and AA was not a new religious movement. Nor, they claimed, was their response to alcoholism a purely psychological matter. They characterized themselves as a fellowship and their program as a spiritual way of life, which they maintained—and others came to agree—was compatible with various forms of "organized religion" or no religion at all.

To understand how and why these differences emerged, we need to analyze the role that Wilson's sudden experience played in the emergence of the movement initially, and as Wilson and others interpreted and reinterpreted it over time. The fact that both Smith and Wilson were not only gifted storytellers but had a sense of being guided by forces beyond themselves makes doing so more complicated. Both Smith and Wilson had a tendency to see things in past events that others—especially empirically minded historians—have had difficulty detecting. In the case of early Mormonism, we examined how Smith interpreted and reinterpreted his visions, his revelations, and scripture in light of later continuing revelation. In a similar fashion, AA historians indicate that Wilson often recounted stories to make a point rather than to relate events as they actually happened. He was, they say, "never likely to pass up the opportunity to deliver a parable where he thought it could do some good, never afraid to use himself as a negative example (something he would not do to anyone else) when he thought he could make a point or highlight a principle, and never reluctant to stretch a fact for the sake of emphasis" (*PIO*, 237–38).

Like early Mormonism, where the sources for Smith's first visions were all retrospective, the sources for Wilson's sudden experience at Towns Hospital in December 1934 are retrospective as well. Although the first account appears in the 1938 draft of "Bill's Story" that he prepared for inclusion in *Alcoholics Anonymous* (BB:1939), letters and other sources dating from shortly after his sudden experience allude to it. The key sources for "Bill's Story" are as follows:

- 1933–39: Anne Smith's handwritten sixty-four-page spiritual journal, which she kept while attending Oxford Group meetings in the thirties (portions are excerpted in Dick B. 1998).
- 1934–35: Letters from Bill Wilson to his brother-in-law, Leonard Strong, dated December 1934, written (apparently) after Ebby T. visited and before he entered Towns Hospital for the last time; a letter dated early 1935 from Bill to Roger, an alcoholic he had met at one of his previous stays at Towns; letters to his mother in March 1935; and Lois's draft of her "sharing" at an Oxford Group meeting, which an archivist dated as occurring in 1935.
- 1938 [?]: Bill's "Original Story," a thirty-six-page single-spaced account preserved at the Stepping Stones Foundation Archives (SSFA) (WGW Collection 103: Writings, Box 31, Folder 3) that opens with his parents' decision to separate when he was about ten and ends abruptly in the midst of a very long discussion of what he had learned from Ebby T. without ever mentioning his sudden experience at Towns Hospital. The archival folder dates it as 1939, but there is no internal evidence for this, and it seems highly unlikely when compared with the version of "Bill's Story" that Bill sent to Dr. Bob in spring 1838.
- 1938: "Bill's Story" ([GSOA] 1938 draft), which Bill sent to Dr. Bob in spring 1938. This is most likely a much-edited version of the "Original Story" in the Stepping Stones Foundation Archives. Like the later lithograph, manuscript, and published versions, the 1938 draft runs from his visit to Winchester Cathedral in England at the end of World War I through his Towns Hospital experience to the emergence of the fellowship.
- 1938: Two prepublication versions of the Big Book: the lithograph version, which was circulated to clergy, physicians, and others for comment prior to publication, and the manuscript version, which was edited for publication in response to the feedback on the lithograph version. The former is held by the AA Archives; the latter has been published (Anonymous 2010, cited as *OWM* in the main text). In both, "Bill's Story" has already assumed its published form, apart from one significant insertion in *OWM*.
- 1939: "Bill's Story" as published in the Big Book and left unchanged in further editions.
- 1940: Letters from Bill Wilson to Dr. Bob Smith.
- 1941: "Bill's Story" as told to Jack Alexander for the *Saturday Evening Post*.
- 1944: "Bill's Story" as told at the Yale Summer School of Alcohol Studies, founded in 1943 by E. M. Jellinek, the head of Yale Universi-

ty's Center for Alcohol Studies, the first interdisciplinary research center devoted to alcohol-related problems and treatment (see "The History of the Center of Alcohol Studies" at http://alcoholstudies. rutgers.edu/history).

- 1950–60s: Numerous versions of "Bill's Story" as told to AAs (members of Alcoholics Anonymous) and references to his sudden experience in letters to AAs.
- 1954—Bill Wilson's dictated autobiography, published as *Bill W.: My First 40 Years* (Hazelden, 2000).

Since most of these accounts of "Bill's Story" were embedded in the telling of AA's story, and thus intentionally recounted to further the process of emergence, they allow us to track the role of Wilson's sudden experience in the emergence of AA, just as we tracked the role of Smith's visions in the emergence of Mormonism, and they will give us a good sense of the organizational needs—the principles—that Wilson sought to illustrate in interweaving his story with that of AA. Some versions were recounted for other less public reasons. Thus, the allusions to his experience in his 1935 letters, the 1938 draft of his story, his personal correspondence with alcoholics in the fifties and sixties, and his dictated—but unpublished—autobiography provide a sense of what his sudden experience meant to him personally.

The reconstruction of the emergence process that follows is divided into three chapters—"Stories" (chapter 4), "Fellowship" (chapter 5), and "Seeking" (chapter 6)—designed to highlight and explain the divergence between Wilson's public and personal accounts. Chapter 4 analyzes how Wilson told and retold his story publicly in the context of AA in the thirties, forties, and fifties. Chapter 5 traces the growing distinction between Wilson's personal spirituality and the generic spirituality of AA through a focus on the emergence of the Twelve Steps, which AA viewed as leading to a "spiritual awakening," and the Twelve Traditions, which, with anonymity as its "spiritual foundation," formed the basis for AA's distinctive social organization. Chapter 6 allows us to see the personal views that Bill downplayed for the sake of AA more clearly. Personally, Wilson did not view his sudden experience as the great event that transformed his life simply because it released him from his alcoholic cravings (the AA perspective), but also as an opening to another reality that convinced him of certain spiritual facts and initiated a lifelong process of psychospiritual investigation that included spiritualism, parapsychology, Catholicism, mysticism, and LSD. Whereas AA embodied a tacit perennialism in its structure and organization that could be overridden by various theological perspectives, Bill Wilson was an explicit perennialist with Catholic proclivities who viewed his own unusual experiences—spiritualist, mystical, and drug-induced—as different ways of entering into the unseen Reality.

CHAPTER 4

Stories

In light of AA's many possible beginnings, how did the fellowship arrive at the official account of its 1935 origins in the meeting of Bill W. and Dr. Bob, which it routinely marks in its anniversary celebrations? If we turn to the first edition of *Alcoholics Anonymous* (BB:1939), we find key elements of the later version of AA's beginnings, including the idea of a message passed from one alcoholic to another and specific lines of transmission, but it is clear that the story has not yet fully emerged. In the foreword to the first edition, which states that the purpose of the book is "to show alcoholics precisely how we have recovered," the idea of a fellowship of alcoholics that transmits the message of recovery from one to the next is implicit (BB:1939, xxxi). In recounting his story, Bill said that the idea that he could pass on to other "hopeless alcoholics . . . what had been so freely given to [him]" came to him immediately after his sudden experience at Towns Hospital in 1934. "Perhaps [he wrote] I could help some of them. They in turn might work with others" (BB:1939, 14). This thought galvanized Bill and Lois in the wake of his release from Towns. They both threw themselves into helping other alcoholics and "a fellowship [grew] up among us" (BB:1939, 15; Hartigan 2001, 67–69). Chapter 7 ("Working With Others") reinforces this theme, opening with the statement that "practical experience shows that nothing will so much insure immunity from drinking as intensive work with other alcoholics" (BB:1939, 101), and in each of the personal narratives, the narrator recounts how another alcoholic passed the message on to him or her.

If we look at the arrangement of the first edition, we can also discern the specific line of transmission that structures the later narrative of AA's beginnings. "Bill's Story" has pride of place as chapter 1 and Dr. Bob's ("The Doctor's Nightmare") launches the collection of "Personal Stories." Bill and Bob's meeting and their subsequent recruitment of Bill D. (referred to as AA No. 3 in the second edition) are recounted in chapter 11 (BB:1939, 165–79). But these links are not explicit. Bill and Bob are not characterized as co-founders, their names are not mentioned in chapter 11, and Bill D.'s story, which follows Dr. Bob's in the second edition, is not included in the first. Based on the first edition, we could just as well imagine a line of transmission from Ebby T., whose intervention forms the centerpiece of "Bill's Story" (BB:1939, 18–24), to Bill, and from Bill to Bob, and then to two early East Coast "converts"—Hank P., whose story follows Dr. Bob's in the first edition, and Fitz, whose story is fifth.

All of which is to say that in 1938–39, a link had been forged between Bill and Bob, but the meaning of the link had not been fully elaborated. At that point there were neither official "cofounders" nor an official founding moment. The idea of a fellowship that passed the message of recovery from one alcoholic to the next was in place, and the means of transmitting the message was laid out in the chapter on working with others, but a perceived line of transmission had not yet been clearly established. Moreover, aspects of the story that would seem crucial later were missing from the first edition. There is no indication of the order in which people gained sobriety and no indication of Bill's failure to restore anyone to sobriety before he met Dr. Bob and thus, of course, no explanation of why this might have been the case.

Two years later the basic outlines of the story were in place. In a feature story published in the *Saturday Evening Post*, Jack Alexander (1941) offered an account of AA, including its beginnings, based on an investigation of the emerging movement, that Bill helped him to set up. Bill indicated that they pulled out all the stops, "[taking] him in tow for nearly a whole month. . . . We gave him our records, opened the books, introduced him to nonalcoholic Trustees, fixed up interviews with A.A.'s of every description, and finally showed him the A.A. sights from New York and Philadelphia all the way to Chicago, via Akron and Cleveland" (*AACOA*, 35). Although he was initially very skeptical, Alexander was slowly convinced that he was witnessing something significant. In recounting his change in attitude (Alexander 1945), he said he was particularly impressed by the newspapermen at the meetings in Chicago, because he and they spoke the same language, but he said "the real clincher . . . came in St. Louis" where he had grown up. There, he said, "I met a number of my own friends who were A.A.s, and the last remnants of skepticism vanished. Once rollicking rumpots, they were now sober. It didn't seem possible, but there it was."

For our purposes, what's interesting is that the transparency paid off in a story that reflected their own view of themselves at the time. Referring to Bill pseudonymously as "Griffith" and Bob as "Armstrong," Alexander (1941) recounted a version of AA beginnings within two years of the publication of the first edition of the Big Book (BB:1939) that was congruent with how AA would come to write its own history. Not only does the movement now have a name, but it "owes its existence to the collaboration of a New York stockbroker and an Akron physician." We hear nothing about Bill's old drinking buddy, Ebby T., who "got religion" under the influence of the Oxford Group, visited the Wilson home, and testified to his newfound sobriety just prior to Bill's final stay at Towns Hospital, only that "five months before coming to Akron, he [Griffith] had gone on the water wagon through the ministration of the Oxford Group in New York." We do learn, however, that after he went on "the water wagon," he "work[ed] on other alcoholics." Doing so "stave[d] off his own craving[, but] . . . *he effected no recoveries . . . Dr. Armstrong became Griffith's first real disciple*" (emphasis added). A line of transmission is now explicitly traced from the Oxford Group to Bill to Bob and two others in Akron before Bill returned to New York. Both men, with the support of their wives, opened their homes to alcoholics; both couples were living on borrowed money. But "by the spring of 1939, the Armstrongs and the Griffiths had between them cozened about one hundred alcoholics into sobriety." Soon the movement spread. "Twenty pilgrims from Cleveland caught the idea in Akron and returned home to start a group of their own. From Cleveland, by various means, the movement has spread to Chicago, Detroit, St. Louis, Los Angeles, Indianapolis, Atlanta, San Francisco, Evansville, and other cities. . . . Fewer than half of the A.A. members has ever seen Griffith or Dr. Armstrong."

The two years between the publication of the Big Book and the *Saturday Evening Post* article were difficult ones and did much to shape the way the chain of transmission was depicted. As Alexander indicated, both Bill and Bob were in severe financial trouble. Bill and Lois were forced to give up their home in Brooklyn in April 1939, just as the Big Book was published. Taken in by sympathetic AAs for some months, they settled in tiny rooms in the newly purchased AA clubhouse in New York in February 1940, where they lived until they finally moved to their permanent home in Bedford Hills in April 1941. Bob and Anne almost lost their home as well. Through these difficult times, they remained sober, as did Bill D., but Ebby and Hank P. both started drinking again (Hartigan 2001, 129–32; Thomsen 1999, 225–28, 236–37, 267–68).[1]

[1] Ebby, Bill, and Lois all recognized that AA might have recognized Ebby as its founder. Ebby apparently felt "he never got the recognition that he should" and "felt he was more the founder of what was to become AA than anyone else" (Mel B. 1998, 77, 80–82). Bill (W. 1954) acknowledged that Bill D. was "'A.A. No. 3,' [after Bill and Bob, only because] . . . my first friend, Ebby, was to fall by the 'wayside.'" Although Bill felt an enormous debt to Ebby and looked out for him in various ways until he died, Ebby drifted in and out of their lives and—as Lois indicated (*LR*, 118–19)—was not deeply involved in launching AA. The situation with Hank P. was more complex. Hank was Bill's first "convert" after he returned from Akron and his closest collaborator on a day-to-day basis. During this early period, the AA "office" where Bill, Hank, and Ruth Hock worked on the Big Book was Honor Dealers (Hank's oil franchise), Works Publishing (which published the Big Book), and the Alcoholic Foundation (*PIO*, 190–93). Over time, the working relationship between the three of them disintegrated. According to Hartigan (2001, 129–32), Hank was in charge of Works Publishing's finances but couldn't provide an accounting of them, most likely due to the blurring of lines between personal, dealership, and AA expenses. Other lines were blurred as well. Hank, whose wife was filing for divorce, was having an affair with Ruth Hock, whom he wanted to marry. He also wanted to keep the AA office in New Jersey. Bill wanted to move the office to its own location in New York, and Ruth didn't want to marry Hank. It was in this context that Hank resumed drinking and turned against Bill, blaming him for the financial mismanagement and his loss of Ruth.

Not only did Dr. Bob and Bill D. stay sober, while Ebby and Hank P. did not, but AA grew much more rapidly in Akron and Cleveland than it did in New York. These developments led Bill to conclude that the AA story should downplay his role and play up the movement's growth in Akron and Cleveland. When a journalist tried to place him and his sudden experience at the center of the narrative, he objected. In a letter to Dr. Bob, dated 16 January 1940, he gave his reasons. "In the first place," he wrote, "I did not think there was enough emphasis on the western situation and far too much upon the part I had played personally. Moreover, the idea that the whole scheme was a sudden conception or revelation coming to me was inaccurate" (Fitzpatrick 2012, 153). The center of the movement was not New York, Bill was not the founder, and the idea did not come to him as "a sudden conception or revelation." By the time Jack Alexander was researching AA, Bill went to great lengths to make sure he recognized both Dr. Bob and the rapid growth of AA in Ohio and the Midwest. Moreover, instead of highlighting Ebby's intervention and his own sudden spiritual experience, Bill stressed that his efforts to reach other alcoholics had effected no recoveries prior to Dr. Bob. In Alexander's piece, we don't learn how Bill explained this failure. The reason for his failure, which he linked directly to his initial interpretation of his sudden experience, became a major talking point in his story as he told it in the forties.

"Bill's Story" in the Forties

During the forties, according to AA historians, "Bill . . . developed a format for his talks that he usually pretty much stuck to, whether he was speaking to A.A. groups or to non-A.A.'s. He would go right back to the very beginning and tell the now-familiar 'bedtime story'—his own drinking, his 'hot flash,' his recovery, and how A.A. was born and grew" (*PIO*, 347–48). His June 1944 talk at the Yale Summer School of Alcohol Studies provides an early example (Bill W. 1945). It opened with his hospitalizations at Towns and ran through the "first four years" of AA, that is, from his meeting with Dr. Bob through the publication of the Big Book. The initial portion, which included Lois's conversation with Dr. William Silkworth, a lengthy description of Ebby's interventions, and a brief description of his sudden experience, follows his account in the Big Book closely. In the next three paragraphs, however, he reflected on his sudden experience in relation to the events that followed it, including his efforts to reach alcoholics in New York before he went to Akron, the shift in his motivation when he reached out to Dr. Bob, and what he and Bob learned about the source of their recovery in their early efforts to help others to recover. These additional reflections framed his sudden experience at Towns Hospital in a new way within the AA story (see appendix, chart 4).

Speaking to the Yale audience, Bill said that in the immediate aftermath of his experience, he thought his "sudden illumination" was "the end . . . of all my troubles" (Bill W. 1945). At the time, he said, he thought his experience gave him a "Divine Appointment" and that "God had selected [him], by this sudden flash of Presence, to dry up all the drunks in the world." He felt "inspired" and thought he "knew just how to do it." "I really thought," he continued, "I had been endowed with the power to go out and produce a 'hot flash' just like mine in every drunk." After trying "like thunder" for six months, however, he said, no one had "dried up" and his failure led him to start questioning his methods. The doubts that emerged in New York deepened when he got to Akron, where he was tempted to drink after his negotiations fell through, and he began to question whether his "spiritual experience . . . was . . . real" (ibid.).

In his 1944 version, his failure to convert anyone in New York led him to question his message. Then in Akron, his desire to drink led him to question the meaning of his sudden experience. In this moment of doubt, he realized that although his efforts to convert other alcoholics had done nothing for them, they had kept him sober. His 1944 version underscored this insight: "notice," he said, "how my motivation was shifting all this time. No longer was I preaching from any moral hilltop or from the vantage point of a wonderful spiritual experience. No, this time I was looking for another alcoholic, because I felt that I needed him twice as much as he needed me." It's at this point—and with that new insight—that, according to his 1944 account, he reached out to Dr. Bob. The story of AA's beginning now pivots not simply on the meeting of Bill and Bob, but on the *way* they connect through mutual need. Mutual need forged the first link in the chain and created the "founding moment."

The 1944 account contains three newly articulated themes that Wilson returned to repeatedly in the years to come: his initial "prideful" feeling that he was special and had a "divine appointment to fix all the drunks in the world," an explanation of his failure to convert any drunks before he met Dr. Bob, and his successful connection to Dr. Bob in the wake of his realization that he needed other alcoholics as much as they needed him.

Divine Appointment: In his talks and his correspondence, Bill repeatedly returned to his "prideful" notion that his sudden experience was a sign that God had singled him out. He wrote to a Catholic (Clem L.) on 8 April 1948 (GSOA), saying, "my first spiritual experience brought with it a conviction of divine appointment to fix all the drunks in the world. At the time I took that to be the Word of God. But I now regard such thoughts as conceited in the extreme." In fact, he said, now that "so many good people, especially Catholics, are pointing me out as something special, I confess an increasing aversion to the idea. I think I know myself too well. I am not deserving of such an outstanding distinction. After all, who is to say *who* is divinely appointed?"

When Bill circulated the manuscript of *AACOA* for feedback prior to publication, Fr. John Ford, a Jesuit on the faculty of Weston College, raised some pointed concerns about the expanded account of his sudden experience. Worried that Bill might be making claims regarding "divine intervention" that would set him in opposition to Catholic teaching, Ford asked him to explain his understanding of the experience he had in Towns Hospital. In a letter to Ford on 14 May 1957 (GSOA), Bill wrote that he considered it "a conversion experience" in light of the fruits it produced, but, he added, "I no longer distinguish my own conversion experience from the basic one I see running all throughout A.A." He conceded that his experience had been "a little out of the ordinary . . . [in] its extreme suddenness, brilliance, assurance, and, ever after, the continuous feeling of what I consider to be the presence of God," but, he said, other AAs have had "experiences [that] seem to have been even more sweeping and convincing." In response to Ford's concern that he might be comparing himself to St. Paul, he reassured him that he had "long since laid aside any pretension to having received a miraculous and calculated intervention of God in the sense that St. Paul receive[d] his." He did so, not because he necessarily rejected the idea of a special intervention, but because he felt "it would be utterly presumptuous" for him to judge and because doing so risked "unloos[ing] [his] pride *once more*" (emphasis added).

Explaining Failure: Bill linked his false sense of "divine appointment" with his failure to sober up any alcoholics prior to meeting Dr. Bob. He vacillated, however, on the reason for his failure, sometimes attributing it to his attitude (his "pride" or "conceit") and sometimes to his expectation that "every drunk should have his hot flash" (John J. 1945). On other occasions, such as his twentieth anniversary celebration in 1954, Bill chalked up his failure to "preaching . . . teaching . . . [and] playing 'The Messiah'" (Fitzpatrick 2012, 54; also 122–23). In many of these accounts, Bill credited Dr. Silkworth with setting him straight. "Just before leaving for Akron," he said, "Dr. Silkworth [gave] me a great piece of advice. . . . 'Look, Bill,' he . . . said, 'you're having nothing but failure because you are preaching at these alcoholics. You are talking to them about the Oxford Group precepts . . . Then you top it off by harping on this mysterious spiritual experience of yours. No wonder they point their finger to their heads [implying that he's crazy] and go out and get drunk" (*AACOA*, 67–68).

Insight in Akron: In his 1939 account there is no indication that he failed to sober up anyone before he met Bob in Akron. In recounting his story to

Alexander in 1941, he made it clear that working with other alcoholics helped keep him sober, even if they didn't sober up themselves, but this recognition wasn't linked to the events in Akron. In the 1944 account, the positive effect of his attempts to help others dawned *on him* when his own alcoholic cravings threatened to get the best of him in Akron. "Then," he said, "it burst upon me, what I need is another alcoholic . . . You see, up to this time I'd been lecturing, I'd been preaching, I'd been teaching. Now I began to think: 'For my salvation, I need another alcoholic to work on' " (Bill W. 1945). This realization marked the high point of the revised account.

In the new account, the center shifted from Ebby's visit to Bill and Bill's sudden experience of release to Bill's insight in the Mayflower Hotel, where he was staying in Akron, and his subsequent connection with Bob. Bill's failure to save any alcoholics before he met Bob provides the transition from the Ebby-Bill meeting to the Bill-Bob meeting. The Ebby-Bill meeting, capped by Bill's sudden experience, failed to bear fruit, at least initially, because Bill misinterpreted his "mission" in the wake of his "hot flash." His failures in New York and the intervention of Dr. Silkworth culminated in the insight that "burst upon" him in Akron. This insight led to a "fruitful" connection between Bill and Bob, which resulted, after few adjustments, in the recovery of others. Bill's insight in the Mayflower Hotel is now the centerpiece of the story: links are forged in the chain from one alcoholic to another on the basis of their identification as alcoholics. That sense of identification, of mutuality, provides the foundation that allows the alcoholic to embrace a new approach. Simply "preaching" or "teaching" a new approach is doomed to failure. In these accounts of AA's beginnings, Bill's sudden experience, or at least the message he drew from that experience, far from launching AA, threatened to derail it altogether. If Dr. Silkworth hadn't pulled him aside before he left for Akron, he said, "A.A. might never have been born" (*AACOA*, 67).

Reconstructing Wilson's Experience in the Thirties

So how closely do these later stories correspond with the way Bill understood his encounter with Ebby at the time, and the way he recounted his sudden experience to Dr. Silkworth and his wife Lois in the hospital? Or, more broadly, with the way he recounted these experiences prior to his trip to Akron, that is, between December 1934 and May 1935? The real-time evidence from this period includes a letter from Bill to his brother-in-law, Leonard Strong, dated December 1934, written after Ebby visited and before he entered Towns for the last time; a letter in early 1935 from Bill to Roger, an alcoholic he had met at one of his previous stays at Towns; letters to his mother in March 1935; and Lois's draft of what she shared at an Oxford

Group meeting (most likely) in 1935. From these sources, it is clear that Bill had "gotten religion" and was spending time at Towns Hospital working with other alcoholics in early 1935.

These sources do not describe when and how he "got religion" in any detail. In his letter to his brother-in-law, describing his visit to the Calvary Church mission after Ebby's visit, most likely written before he entered Towns for the last time, he told Leonard, who had financed his previous visit to Towns, that he had realized that his pride—his "absolute refusal under any and all circumstances to eat humble pie" and admit that he could not "take care of everything"—was at the root of his drinking. He told Leonard that the "upshot of it [Ebby's visit] was I got right down on my knees with a lot of other bums, went to the heart of it and admitted I was wrong—Maybe Leonard that's what religion is. Anyhow that's what I have" (WGW to Strong [December 1934], WGW Collection 102: General Correspondence 1934–35, Box 27, Folder 16 [SSFA]). After he got out of Towns, he wrote to his friend, Roger, whom he'd met during a previous stay, telling him about Ebby's transformation and adding:

> The upshot of it all was, that to my amazement, I got religion too, and am spending some time at Towns working on some of the hopeless cases. Of course there has not been time to demonstrate much of anything but the Doctor is perfectly willing to admit that this Oxford crowd has a lot on the ball. That I am riding on the Holy Roller Coaster may seem incredible to you. (WGW to Roger, n.d. [early 1935], WGW Collection 102: General Correspondence 1934–35, Box 27, Folder 17 [SSFA])

His self-deprecating reference to the "Holy Roller Coaster" is reminiscent of his later references to his "hot flash," but we get little indication of what exactly happened. In her letter to Bill on 24 March 1935, his mother said that the things he wrote "seem like the miracles of old" and added that "[his] enthusiasm must be contagious among the patients," but again we get no details (WGW Collection 102.3: Family Correspondence 1934–36, Box 25, Folder 6 [SSFA]).

The most solid real-time evidence that he actually had a sudden experience at Towns comes from Lois's typed draft of the "testimony" or "sharing" she planned to give at an Oxford Group meeting sometime in 1935. She describes having done everything she possibly could to reform Bill, short of "handing the problem over to God."

> And then all of a sudden without my having a thing to do with it[,] Bill was well ["cured" is crossed out]. I was not even instrumental in getting Bill in touch with the Oxford Group. An old friend who was

also an alcoholic got us both to go to Oxford group meetings. From the moment that I saw him I knew that Bill was definitely "cured." I was very grateful to the Group with one half of me & furiously jealous of them with the other. (Oxford Group Sharing 1935, LBW Collection 203: Writings, Box 35, Folder 8 [SSFA])

This line—"From the moment I saw him I knew that Bill was definitely 'cured' "—is echoed in Lois's later accounts of seeing Bill's face when she arrived at Towns Hospital shortly after his "sudden experience." It was, as she later said, the moment in which she felt AA began (Lois W. 1949; *PIO*, 124).[2]

We can deepen our reconstruction through an analysis of various versions of Bill's story, which he drafted for inclusion in the Big Book in the late thirties. Comparison of the early versions, along with his many later recountings for AA audiences and his initially unpublished autobiography (1954), reveal important differences in the way he recounted his story initially and for publication and in how he recounted his sudden experience at Towns over time. Stable features in the accounts suggest elements that may have been integral to his experience with Ebby and at Towns.

A comparison of his early unpublished accounts (SSFA, GSOA, and *OWM*) with his published story (1939) and his unpublished autobiography (1954) indicates that an earlier experience of "presence" at Winchester Cathedral in 1918, which Bill largely excised from his published account, played a major—albeit unstable—role in his framing of his story (see appendix, chart 5). A comparison of his 1938 (GSOA) account of his cathedral experience, which he initially associated with Ebby's visit, with his accounts of his sudden experience at Towns (1939–66) indicates that he gradually reinterpreted his Towns experience in light of his presence experience at the cathedral (see appendix, chart 6). Finally, a comparison of his earliest account of Ebby's visit (SSFA) with all the accounts of his experience at Towns suggests that the feeling of a clean wind blowing on a mountaintop may have been integral to both his experience with Ebby and his experience at Towns, although attached to different sensations—"a great surge of joy" in the first instance and an intense burst of "electricity" or "light" in the second (see appendix, chart 7).

Each of these findings has important implications. The image of the wind on the mountaintop points to an underlying mechanism that may have enabled Bill to stop drinking, which will be discussed in chapter 12; his gradual reinterpretation of his Towns experience in light of his cathedral experience reflects the deepening of his understanding of the process of

---

[2] Wilson said he received the "so-called belladonna treatment" when he first visited Towns (BB:1939, 7). Since belladonna is a hallucinogen, there has been some discussion of whether the drug caused his experience (see, e.g., Raphael 2000, 87–88). Chesnut (n.d.) argues that while he may have been given a small dose during his December stay, it was no longer the standard treatment.

spiritual transformation over time, which will be taken up in chapter 6; and the downplaying of the presence theme in Bill's published story highlights the emerging gap between Bill's personal understanding of what occurred and the needs of his listeners, a central focus of this chapter and the next.

Winchester Cathedral: Bill's "Original Story" (SSFA), a thirty-six-page single-spaced account preserved in the archives at the Stepping Stones Foundation, provides the longest account of his visit to the cathedral in Winchester, England, in 1918. The account appears well into his narrative (page nine), which opens with his parents' decision to separate when he was about ten and ends abruptly in the midst of a very long discussion of what he learned from Ebby without ever mentioning his sudden experience at Towns Hospital. This version appears to be an unfinished, unedited first draft, in which themes that would later become whole chapters in the Big Book ("There is a Solution," "How it Works," and "We Agnostics") came spilling out as he recalled Ebby's visit.

The cathedral experience appears in a slightly edited version at the beginning of the draft version of "Bill's Story" (1938 GSOA draft) preserved in the AA Archives in New York. This version, which Bill sent to Dr. Bob in spring 1938, along with a draft of chapter 2 ("There is a Solution") and a rough outline for the envisioned book, is likely a much-edited version of his "Original Story" in the Stepping Stones Foundation Archives. Like the later lithograph, manuscript, and published versions, the 1938 GSOA draft runs from his visit to the cathedral through his Towns experience to the emergence of the fellowship. The later (lithograph, manuscript, and published) versions, however, drastically abridge the Winchester Cathedral story, transforming it from an experience of "an all enveloping, comforting, powerful presence" inside the cathedral, followed by reflection on an inscription on a tombstone in the cathedral cemetery, to one in which he merely reflects on the tombstone.

Despite this and other significant variations among the early accounts, Bill consistently placed his recollection of his cathedral experience at the point in his story when he was convinced that Ebby had been transformed by a power greater than himself. In his "Original Story," which breaks off before his final visit to Towns Hospital, Bill recalls the cathedral experience at the point when he realized he could not deny that Ebby had been utterly transformed.[3] Thus, he wrote:

> [H]ere I was sitting opposite a man who talked about a personal God who told me how he had found Him, who described to me how I might do the same thing and who convinced me utterly that some-

---

[3] The last name of the Hampshire Grenadier on the tombstone at Winchester Cathedral was an alternate spelling of Ebby T.'s last name, which most likely heightened the associations (*PIO*, 60).

thing had come into his life which had accomplished a miracle. The man [Ebby] was transformed; there was no denying he had been re-born. He was radiant of something which soothed my troubled spirit as tho the fresh clean wind of a mountain top blowing thru and thru me—I saw and felt and in a great surge of joy I realized that the great presence which had made itself felt to me that war time day in Win-chester Cathedral had again returned.

Similarly, in the 1938 draft in the GSOA and in *The Book that Started It All: The Original Working Manuscript of Alcoholics Anonymous* (*OWM*) versions, he said that "the real significance of my Cathedral experience burst upon me" when he realized that Ebby's life was "on a different footing" (*OWM*, 38).

Towns Hospital: The most striking feature of the "Original Story" for read-ers familiar with Bill's later accounts of his experience at Towns Hospital is undoubtedly that the image of "the fresh clean wind of a mountain top blowing thru and thru me" is here associated with Ebby. In his "Original Story" he used the image of "the fresh clean wind of a mountain top" to describe the way Ebby's face "soothed [his] troubled spirit," a feeling that was followed by "a great surge of joy" and the realization that "the great presence . . . had again returned." The image of wind on a mountaintop is also a stable feature of Bill's accounts of his sudden experience at Towns Hospital. If we compare his published account with his later versions (see appendix, chart 7), we find that it is comprised of three subevents, two of which appear in all the accounts: (1) an intense burst of "electricity" or "light"—later interpreted as "ecstasy" (or lifting up), which merges into (2) a feeling of being lifted up as though on a mountaintop with a great wind blowing, and (3) a subevent that varies in terms of content and position. Bill's use of the mountaintop image for these two ostensibly different expe-riences suggests (a) that he experienced surges of intense feeling both while talking to Ebby and at Towns and (b) that this image carried particular significance for him. Although the imagery used to characterize his Towns experience shifts, the more stable elements suggest an underlying physiolog-ical experience of the intense light and a feeling of being lifted up, which he characterized with the mountaintop image, as he did the surge of joy he experienced with Ebby.

Bill's reference to his *realization* that "the great presence had returned" suggests real-time reflection on his part. I suspect that his association of the wind on the mountaintop with his feeling of calm and surge of joy in the Ebby experience, and with the feeling of being lifted up at Towns, came to him, not as real-time reflection but as an image that helped him to express his experience in words. This image, I am hypothesizing, may have just come to him, seemingly spontaneously as part of the experience itself and not while reflecting on it. If this is the case, we can ask, why this image? Bill's autobiography opens with a memory that may help us to understand its power and significance. This memory, which he claims was his earliest, was of Mount Aeolus. As he recounts:

> I was born in the Green Mountains of Vermont, alongside of a tower-ing peak called Mount Aeolus. I was raised in the parsonage there, although my parents were not in the business of being clergy. One of my earliest recollections is looking out of the window from my crib just as the sunset developed over the great mountain and becoming very conscious of it for the first time. It is an impression which never left me. Somehow, today when I go there, there is no spot quite like this— . . . that spot whose ancestry and whose native ruggedness en-dowed me, I fancy, with both strength and weakness.

Three of Bill's biographers link Mount Aeolus to a story about Bill's grand-father Wilson that is remarkably similar to Ebby's and Bill's experiences. According to Francis Hartigan, Bill's grandfather had a serious drinking problem that he was unable to control. "[I]n a desperate state one Sunday morning, he climbed to the top of Mount Aeolus. There, after beseeching God to help him, he saw a blinding light and felt the wind of the Spirit." In the wake of the experience, he "stormed into the church . . . relate[d] his experience to the shocked congregation . . . [and] never drank again" (Har-tigan 2001, 10–11; Lattin 2012, 16–17; Cheever 2004, 17). Although none of his biographers give a source for the story, Hartigan may have heard it from Lois Wilson. In his autobiography, Bill simply said, "My grandfather Wilson was a very serious case of alcoholism, and it no doubt hastened his death, although some years prior to this he had, to everyone's great surprise, hit the sawdust trail, to speak figuratively, at a revival meeting in the Congrega-tional Church and was never known to drink afterward" (Bill W. 2000, 6). If Hartigan provides an accurate account of a story that Bill heard as a child, it may have provided a preconscious interpretation that surfaced and shaped Bill's emotional response when he realized that Ebby had been transformed and that came to mind when he narrated his sudden experience to Lois and Dr. Silkworth. We will return to this potential link between Bill and his grandfather through Ebby when discussing mechanisms of transformation in chapter 12.

Although two of the subevents—the experience of light and the wind on the mountaintop—remain consistent through all his accounts, there are sig-nificant shifts in Bill's framing of his Towns experience and the third subev-ent in his accounts of the forties and fifties that bring it more into line with his Winchester Cathedral experience (see appendix, chart 6). Thus, when he recounted his Towns experience in 1944, he eliminated the didactic introduction, reframing it along the lines of his cathedral experience, such that he cried out to God in desperation and the experience came "suddenly" out of "darkness" in both. In the fifties accounts, we find that the third subevent also takes on features of his cathedral experience. In these later accounts, Bill reported feeling "surrounded by a Presence" (1951, 1954a,b) and interpreted his experience using phrases—"the God of the preachers" and "the great reality"—that first appear in his cathedral account. In his autobiography, however, he not only included the original experience of presence at the cathedral, he also recalled earlier experiences with Lois on the cliffs at Newport, Rhode Island, before he sailed and aboard the *Lancashire* en route to England, that seemed to prefigure the cathedral experience. In contrast to his Big Book version, however, he gave no indication of recalling the cathedral experience while talking to Ebby; instead, he claimed that all these presence experiences (on the cliffs, aboard the *Lancashire*, and at the cathedral) flashed through his mind just prior to his sudden experience in Towns Hospital.

Presence: The evidence that Bill only belatedly associated his experience at the cathedral with his experience at Towns does not undercut the importance of the presence theme in the initial framing of his story. Indeed, this theme runs as a thread through the 1938 draft version in the GSOA. In that version, he first glimpsed the presence ("the great reality") at the cathedral, the memory of the experience returned to him as he recalled rejecting religion as a child, and the meaning of the cathedral experience "burst upon" him when he recognized that Ebby had been transformed by a power beyond himself. Thus, the 1938 draft tells the story of a *recurrent presence*, fleetingly glimpsed at the outset, recalled in the midst of Ebby's intervention, but only tacitly realized in a more enduring way as a result of Bill's full surrender, just prior to his sudden experience.

The lithograph, manuscript, and published versions disrupt this narrative and fundamentally reshape the point of his story. In these versions, Bill deleted the experience of a presence at the cathedral and focused instead on the tombstone in the churchyard, which offered an "ominous warning" that failed to halt his descent into alcoholism (BB:1939, 10). Moreover, in the published version, the connection between Ebby's transformation and Bill's experience at the cathedral is broken with the last-minute insertion of Ebby's "novel idea" that Bill choose his own conception of God (*OWM*, 24–25, 37, 195). With these changes, the story becomes one of descent into alcoholism, Ebby's intervention, and Bill's release as a result of his full surrender.

In both the "recurring presence" and the "descent" versions, Ebby's intervention played a crucial role, but the nature of his role differed. In the earliest versions, Ebby's intervention allowed Bill to recover his previous, fleeting sense of divine presence. In the published version, Ebby's intervention (apparently) led to Bill's first experience of God's presence, and the references to Winchester Cathedral no longer make much sense. It is not clear why an "ominous warning" marked a transition from his childhood memories of rejecting religion to a statement that he had always believed in a power greater than himself or why he would characterize "the real significance" of his experience at the cathedral as one in which "for a brief moment, [he] had needed and wanted God" (BB:1939, 22).[4]

Although the framing of his experience at Towns in light of his cathedral experience most likely came later, he may have made a general connection between his previous feelings of presence and the Oxford Group understanding of God's presence at the time. The best evidence for this comes from Lois, who indicates that Bill immediately joined an Oxford Group "team" in the wake of his discharge from Towns Hospital. The teams were small groups of six to twelve people who sat quietly "listening for the guidance of God for each one" (*LR* 1987, 93–94). As Lois indicates, he soon rejected his team's collective sense of guidance in favor of his own, which suggests that he had a sense of a presence guiding him at that point. During the three months he spent with Anne and Bob Smith in Akron during the summer of 1935, Bill joined the Smiths in their morning "quiet time" (Dick B. 1998), which was also devoted to feeling God's presence and finding guidance for the day ahead (Chesnut 2006, 60–79). When Bill sent the draft of his story to Bob in 1938, he closed his letter with a reference to guidance, saying that rather than trying to "be too literary," it would "be much better [for story writers] to be guided" (Fitzpatrick 2012, 141). Another letter, a year later, suggests that it was this feeling of "Presence" that they were hoping to convey to other alcoholics. Thus, discussing their feelings of discouragement when alcoholics slipped, Bill added: "After all we cannot do much ourselves for other people except to present them with an opportunity; the opportunity to feel the Presence and know the power and love of the Father of Lights" (20 September 1939, in Fitzpatrick 2012, 144).

Bill's autobiography, which remained unpublished for almost three decades after he died, reinstated the earliest—recurring presence—version of his narrative. In his taped autobiography, he described two additional "spiritual experiences"—on the cliffs at Newport overlooking the sea with Lois and aboard the British ship *Lancashire*—that preceded his experience at Winchester Cathedral (Bill W. 2000, 45, 47–48). The significance of the original Winchester Cathedral experience for Bill personally is underscored by the fact that he returned to the cathedral in 1950, at which time, he said,

[4] Bill may have realized that his editing had destroyed the narrative logic of his references to Winchester Cathedral. His proposed revisions for the second edition of the Big Book, which AAs did not allow him to make out of a desire to keep the original unchanged, indicate that he was prepared to edit out all the references to Winchester Cathedral, which would have made his story more internally consistent and eliminated all traces of the "recurrent presence."

FIGURE 4.2. Bill Wilson at Winchester Cathedral, June 21, 1950, by Lois Wilson. Lois wrote in their scrapbook from their European tour: "It was thrilling to go to Winchester where Bill had been so moved in 1918. The interior of this cathedral is the most impressive that we have visited. We also saw the gravestone of the Hampshire Grenadier that had amused Bill 32 years ago. The cycle was completed." Courtesy of the Stepping Stones Foundation Archives.

his original "spiritual experience repeated itself." On both occasions, he said, he experienced "a tremendous sense of presence," even though, when he first visited England, he said he had no defined belief and "was not a conscious believer in God" (Bill W. 2000, 49–50).

PEDAGOGY

If the recurrent presence theme represented his best and most meaningful memory of how things unfolded, as his elaboration on it in his autobiography suggests, why did he downplay it in the Big Book (BB:1939 and subsequent editions) and later in *Alcoholics Anonymous Comes of Age* (1957)? In both cases, I think that the reason was pedagogical. The earliest versions and the autobiography were personal versions of his story—the way he personally remembered his spiritual life unfolding—but not the version that he thought alcoholics would find most helpful. The downplaying of the presence theme in Bill's published story highlights the emerging gap between Bill's personal understanding of what occurred and the needs of his listeners.

Although Bill made mutuality and the need to identify with other alcoholics the explicit point of his 1944 version of his story, the stories in the Big Book were also revised with this idea in mind. In the letter he sent to Dr. Bob, along with his 1938 draft, Bill reflected on how the stories, which he envisioned as the natural "heart of the book," should be written to have the greatest effect.

> Probably emphasis should be placed on those qualities and actions which caused them to come into collision with their fellows and those things which lay beneath the tendency to excessive drinking; the queer state of mind and emotion preceding the first drink. The first medical attention required. The various institutions visited; these ought to be brought in. There ought to be a description of the man's feelings as he met our crowd, his first sense of God being with him, his feeling of hopelessness and now his sense of victory, his application of principles to his everyday life, including domestic business, and relations with other alcoholics; the release he gets from working with others, the victories God has given him, the problems which still face him and his progress with them; these are other possible points. (quoted in Fitzpatrick 2012, 140–41)

These guidelines suggest an early version of the three-part pattern of the typical AA story: what we used to be like, what happened, and what we are like now. Although his aim was to have members write their own stories, many needed help and virtually all were edited to convey the message as effectively as possible. Bill's editing of his own story brought it into line with the pattern that he recommended in his letter to Dr. Bob.

Although their stories were edited in order to effectively convey their message of hope and recovery, how best to depict the role of religious experience in the process was a subject of much debate. In his penciled notes for the marketing prospectus for the Big Book, written in 1938, Hank P. indicated that "religious experience [is] . . . one of the most talked of things among us." What exactly he meant by this is unclear, however, as he immediately added: "We are actually *irreligious*—but we are trying to be helpful—we have learned to be quiet—to be more truthful—to be more honest—to try to be more unselfish—to make other fellow's troubles—our troubles—and by following four steps [the Oxford Group's Four Absolutes] we, most of us, have a *religious experience*" (Hank P., "Observations," AA 501 [SSFA]; emphasis added).

This tension between being "irreligious" and having a "religious experience" came to a head in the heated disagreements over the God-language in the initial draft of the Twelve Steps. These disagreements resulted in a compromise in which "God" was replaced with "a Power greater than ourselves" in Step Two, "God" with "God as we understand Him" in Step Three, and "on our knees" was removed from Step Seven (*OWM*). Looking back on these debates in June 1954, Bill claimed that these modifications were "none of [his] doing. I was on the pious side then, you see, still suffering from this big hot flash of mine. The idea of 'God as you understand him' came out of that perfectly ferocious argument and we put that in" (Texas State Convention, transcript, GSOA). The downplaying of his recurrent experience of presence and last-minute insertion of the passage in which Ebby suggested that he "choose [his] own conception of God" (BB:1976, 12) suggests Bill's recognition of the need to tone down his personal experience, however meaningful it might have been to him.

Within a few years of its publication, it became clear that these revisions hadn't been extensive enough. As Ruth Hock wrote to Dr. Bob in February 1941 (quoted in Kurtz 1991, 99), "many" got the idea from the first edition "that in order to recover, or stay sober at all, it [was] necessary to have a sudden illuminating spiritual experience.'" The problem was serious enough that they revised Step Twelve in the second printing of the first edition of the Big Book (see BB:1939, 59, 222), changing the wording from "Having had a spiritual experience as a result of these steps" to "Having had a spiritual awakening." They also added a new appendix titled "Spiritual Experience," which explained that "our first printing gave many readers the impression that these personality changes, or religious experiences, must be in the nature of sudden and spectacular upheavals. Happily for everyone, this conclusion is erroneous. In the first few chapters [i.e., in "Bill's Story"] a number of sudden revolutionary changes were described. Though it was not our intention to create such an impression many alcoholics have nevertheless concluded that in order to recover they must acquire an immediate and overwhelming 'God-consciousness' followed at once by a vast change in feeling and outlook."

The tone of Bill's 1940s version of AA's beginnings was designed to further counter the impression that an "immediate and overwhelming" experience was needed for recovery. He did so, as AA historians indicated he often did, by attributing this mistaken view to himself, not to his listeners and, at the same time, exaggerating, even caricaturing, his experience in order to make his point more vivid. His sarcastic references to his experience at Towns

Hospital as a "sudden illumination," a "sudden flash of Presence," and a "hot flash," as well as to his benighted sense of "Divine Appointment" and his efforts to convince others by "preaching," recast his own experience in negative terms in order to undercut members' tendencies to take his experience as normative. He adopted a similar strategy when he highlighted the "mistakes" that he and Bob allegedly made when they initially reached out to other alcoholics in Akron. It is hard not to read Bill's story of how his and Bob's efforts were slowed by their tendency to preach as commentary on the 1941 revision of Step Twelve. Once they realized that AA was not based on "a set of fixed ideas [read: Oxford Group principles] but [was] a growing thing, growing out of experience," their results improved. The source of their recovery was "a spiritual awakening growing out of painful adversity" and not, we are led to infer, a sudden "spiritual experience."

In recounting how he had misinterpreted his sudden experience, Bill highlighted and exaggerated his failings in order to create a bond of mutuality between himself and his listeners. In doing so, he was following the AA story format: sharing the mistakes he had made in the past (the descent), what he had learned (the turning point), and what he was doing now (recovery). Bill recast his story and exaggerated some of his mistakes, not to make a historical point about the past but in order to create a bond with his listeners and, thus, to effectively convey the message he felt was needed in the present. In telling his story this way, he was "walking his talk." He was not "preaching" to his audiences, as he said he did in his early days; he was sharing his failures with them, as he had with Dr. Bob, creating a bond of mutuality and identification, before recounting what he had learned from his "mistakes." He did this in his correspondence with AAs as well. When Ernesto B. described his own sudden experience in a letter to Bill on 13 November 1964 (GSOA), Bill adopted the "we language" of the Big Book, identifying with Ernesto as a fellow "sudden experiencer" who—like Bill—was eager to bring the message of recovery to others. "So," Bill wrote, "when we carry the message, we just have to remember that we should try to present it in such a way that the newcomer can make a beginning. There is no point in scaring him off unnecessarily."

AUDIENCES

Bill didn't try to obscure the changes in his story. Speaking to an audience at LeMoyne College in 1954, he tried out a new, longer version of his story that he was preparing for the Twentieth Anniversary Convention and for inclusion in *Alcoholics Anonymous Comes of Age*. After offering a more detailed account of his sudden experience, he paused to note: "[Back in 1934] I began telling all the alcoholics about this strange experience of mine which I have just related to you. *Then*, it was a rather perilous thing to do. . . . Now since AA works, I can get away with it!" (GSOA). A decade later, he indicated to Ernesto B. (13 November 1964) that "in more recent years I have no hesitancy about telling large audiences about my own spiritual experience. But I always make haste to say that it is no different than that received by every other good A.A.—excepting that it was very sudden and most convincing. This is a good stance to take, I think" (GSOA). Writing to Bill B. on 17 May 1965, Bill again noted the difference between the accounts of his sudden experience that were published in 1939 and 1957. "Something," he wrote, "is said in the Big Book about the nature of my experience. But at that time, one had to go slow in a textbook. Later on, in the book, 'A.A. Comes of Age,' I think I enlarged upon it somewhat more."

As AAs became more confident that the spiritual awakening generated by the Twelve Steps could take many different forms, the risk that they would view Bill's sudden experience as the sole route to recovery decreased. Starting in the fifties, Bill was able to recount his experience in more detail, while always taking pains to stress that his experience was "no different" from that of any other AA. Nonetheless, the fact that he recorded, but did not publish, his autobiography suggests his complicated awareness of the competing demands of recovery and history. In light of AA's "studied policy of playing the founding of this movement down," he did not publish his autobiography but dictated it to provide Ed Bierstadt, who was helping with the research for AA's first history (*AACOA*), "a sort of backbone from which to branch out." In so doing, however, he did have future biographers in mind and intended "the early part of this narrative . . . to set the record somewhere near straight" (Bill W. 2000, 2).

Bill's constant awareness of the needs of the movement meant that, although he could provide what he viewed as a more complete, historically accurate version of his story, there were aspects of his life, including his infidelities and the unconventional aspects of his spiritual quest, that we now know he did not share widely and that did not become a part of AA history. Bill probably would have been more forthcoming about these aspects of his life had he not felt constrained by his concern for the movement. He anticipated that historians would eventually surface these aspects of his life but felt that holding back would allow AAs to realize that AA existed independent of his personal views and failings. Telling his story with the needs of his audiences in mind thus created a gap between the stories he told publicly and the story he told for the historical record in his autobiography and in his early unpublished accounts.

In teasing apart the different versions of Bill's story and locating them in relation to their audiences, we can see the gap emerging. The evidence that he downplayed the theme of a recurrent presence in favor of a story of

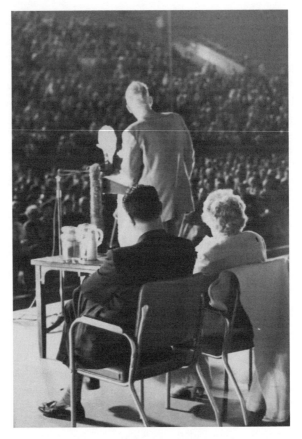

FIGURE 4.3. Bill W. speaking on Friday night of AA's Twentieth Anniversary Convention, Lois Wilson seated onstage (*right*), July 1960, Long Beach, California. Courtesy of the Stepping Stones Foundation Archives.

descent-and-recovery provides real-time evidence that Bill self-consciously revised the Big Book version of his story to meet the needs of other alcoholics. In the wake of publication, he realized that he had to counteract Big Book readers' tendency to assume that a sudden spiritual experience was necessary. He did this in his 1940s accounts of AA's beginnings by vividly contrasting his initial efforts to sober up alcoholics by "preaching" about his "hot flash" with his later recognition that he needed other alcoholics to stay sober as much as they needed him. By downplaying his experiences of presence, he tacitly created and underscored a distinction between the nonspecific spiritual awakening associated with the Twelve Steps and the particularities of his own spiritual experience. Over the next two decades, as Bill articulated and implemented AA's distinctive and perhaps unprecedented organizational structure, the split between Bill Wilson and "Mr. AA" grew more pronounced. In chapter 5, I will consider the role of anonymity ("Mr. Anonymous") in the development and positioning of AA as a "way of life" rather than a new religious movement, before returning to a consideration of Bill Wilson's personal spiritual journey in chapter 6.

Fellowship

If we want to understand how Bill Wilson's sudden experience led to the emergence of AA as a spiritually grounded "way of life" rather than "the Wilson Movement" with Bill Wilson as its leader (*LR*, 114), we need to look more closely at the process that generated the fellowship's distinctive form of organization. At the Twentieth Anniversary Convention in 1955, Wilson gave three talks on the "three legacies" of AA—Recovery, Unity, and Service—symbolized by AA's triangle in a circle logo. Recovery of the individual alcoholic was grounded in the Twelve Steps, which were finalized with a revision of Step Twelve in the second printing of the first edition of the Big Book in 1941; Unity of the fellowship in the Twelve Traditions, which were developed during the forties and formally adopted at AA's First International Convention in 1950; and Service to the fellowship, in the Twelve Concepts for World Service, developed in the fifties and formally adopted in 1962 (*AACOA*, 49–222). Although the Twelve Concepts give symmetry to the triangle, AA's novelty as a social formation lies in the distinctive balance between the needs of the individual in the Twelve Steps and the needs of the group in the Twelve Traditions. Indeed, the degree of independence that AA granted to the individual in relation to the group was so great that outsiders wondered how the fellowship could possibly hold together, much less expand at a prodigious rate. Looking at the process through which this "new form of human society" emerged from the inside, Bill chalked it up to two factors: the tyranny of alcohol and the guidance of a Power greater than themselves (Bill W. 1946; *LOH*, 32–36).

The role that alcoholic desperation played in the process was quite obvious. Reflecting in 1946 on the third of "Twelve Suggested Points for AA Tradition" that he had recently published in the *AA Grapevine*, Bill commented that "Tradition [Three] carries the principle of independence for the individual to such an apparently fantastic length that, so long as there is the slightest interest in sobriety, the most unmoral, the most antisocial, the most critical alcoholic may gather about him a few kindred spirits and announce to us that a new Alcoholics Anonymous group has been formed. Anti-God, anti-medicine, anti-our recovery program, even anti-each other—these rampant individuals are still an AA group if *they think so!*" (*LOH*, 33; emphasis in the original). Asked why a society embracing such a generous view of membership didn't fall apart, Wilson pointed to the role of alcohol. "While it is perfectly true that no AA group can possibly coerce an alcoholic to contribute money, to conform to the Twelve Steps . . . or to the Twelve Points of AA Tradition, each AA member is, nevertheless, most powerfully compelled, in the long run, to do those very things." Alcohol lurks as a "cunning, ruthless" tyrant, whose "weapons are misery, insanity, and death" (*LOH*, 34).

Although desperate self-interest drove many alcoholics to AA, participation in AA often initiated a process of transformation, which he characterized as a "cycle [that] is ever the same."

> First, we turn to AA because we may die if we don't. Next, we depend upon its fellowship and philosophy to stop our drinking. Then, for a time, we tend once more to depend upon ourselves, seeking happiness through power and acclaim. Finally, some incident, perhaps a sharp reverse, opens our eyes still wider. Then, as we learn our new lesson and *really accept its teaching*, we enter a new level of better feeling and doing. Life takes on a finer meaning. We glimpse realities new to us; we apprehend the kind of love which assures us that it is more blessed to give than to receive. These are some of the reasons why we think that Alcoholics Anonymous may be a new form of society. (*LOH*, 36; emphasis in original)

The deeper acceptance of AA's teaching involved recognizing that, in Wilson's words, "Someone much greater than I [was] at work! Someone who sought to transform me; who would, if I permitted, sweep away my less worthy desires and replace them with truer aspirations," in which, if he were "humble enough, [he might] find peace" (*LOH*, 35). The transformative process led, in the words of Step Twelve, to "a spiritual awakening" and the recognition that "each of us may implicitly trust in him who is our loving guide from within—and from above" (*LOH*, 36).

Bill and other old-timers viewed AA's distinctive social organization as emerging in the same way, that is, through a process of trial and error driven by a desperate need for recovery and guided, as they believed, by a Power greater than themselves. In time, he placed the principle of anonymity—understood in terms of the spiritual virtues of humility and self-sacrifice—at the core of this transformative process and at the foundation of AA as a society. Just as a "spiritual awakening" was the result of practicing the Twelve Steps, so anonymity was understood as the "spiritual foundation" of the

Twelve Traditions and, according to Tradition Twelve, ever reminded AAs "to place principles before personalities." Reflecting back on AA's history in his last public talk on 10 October 1970, he said, "the 'Concept of Anonymity' . . . was [the blessing] most responsible for our growth as a fellowship and most vital to our continuity." Knowing that AA "must and will continue to change with the passing years," he stressed, "the principle of anonymity must remain our primary and enduring safeguard. As long as we accept our sobriety in our traditional spirit of anonymity we will continue to receive God's Grace." Today this parting advice from Bill is posted, along with a final message from Dr. Bob, on the wall at the entrance to AA's General Service Office in New York City.

As a spiritual path, AA centers on the Twelve Steps as worked in the context of groups that maintain their unity through their embrace of the Twelve Traditions. Taken together the Twelve Steps and Twelve Traditions simultaneously position AA as a fellowship that is compatible—but not aligned—with either "organized religion" or "organized medicine" and grounds the recovery of the individual and the unity of the organization in the spiritual principle of anonymity. We can see how the process unfolded by taking a closer look at the hammering out of the Twelve Steps in conjunction with producing the Big Book and the development of the Twelve Traditions in the forties in response to the rapid growth of the fellowship.

THE TWELVE STEPS

Although Bill provided the first detailed account of the process of producing the Big Book at the AA Texas State Convention in June 1954 as he was preparing to write *Alcoholics Anonymous Comes of Age*, his later descriptions fit well with the real-time evidence. The basic steps in the process, as outlined in *AACOA*, were as follows. Bill dictated rough drafts of the first ten or eleven chapters to Ruth Hock. Each chapter draft was read to the New York group at its weekly meeting and sent to Dr. Bob for checking and criticism in Akron. Bill indicated that the chapters "got a real mauling" from the New York group, but were warmly received in Akron. In response to feedback, Bill "redictated them and Ruth retyped them over and over."[1]

The fifth chapter, titled "How It Works," presented particular challenges. In the four years since Ebby's visit to Bill, they had "gradually evolved what we called 'the word-of-mouth program.' Most of the basic ideas had come from the Oxford Groups, William James, and Dr. Silkworth." The program, at that point, boiled down to six steps. Although derived in large part from the Oxford Groups, Bill noted that "several of [their] . . . ideas and attitudes

---

[1] *AACOA*, 159; further citations to this source are cited by page number directly in the text in this section.

had been definitely rejected, including any which could involve us in theological controversy" (160). Bill divided the six steps into twelve (161). The resulting steps were then discussed in Akron and New York. The debate, as indicated in chapter 4, was particularly intense over the religious issues. Bill described three viewpoints. The conservatives thought that "the book ought to be Christian in the doctrinal sense of the word and that it should say so." The liberals "had no objection to the use of the word 'God' throughout the book, but . . . were dead set against any other theological proposition . . . Spirituality, yes. But religion, no—*positively* no" (162). The atheists and agnostics, who made up the "radical left wing," wanted to delete the word "God" from the book entirely. They wanted "a *psychological* book which would lure the alcoholic in. Once in, the prospect could take God or leave Him alone as he wished" (163; emphasis in original).

At the same time, they were working on the story section. In Akron, Dr. Bob and James S., a former newspaperman, gathered the stories. "In most cases Jim interviewed the prospects and wrote their stories for them. Dr. Bob wrote his own." There was no one comparable to James in New York, so the New Yorkers wrote their own stories and Bill and Henry (Hank P.) edited their "amateur attempts" over their protests (164). As they were completing the manuscript, Fitz (a conservative), Henry (a radical), Ruth, and Bill returned to the Twelve Steps and hashed out a compromise. "In Step Two we decided to describe God as a 'Power greater than ourselves.' In Steps Three and Eleven we inserted the words 'God *as we understood Him.*' From Step Seven we deleted the expression 'on our knees.' And, as a lead-in sentence to all the steps we wrote these words: 'Here are the steps we took which are suggested as a Program of Recovery.' A.A.'s Twelve Steps were to be *suggestions* only" (167; emphasis in original).

When the manuscript was complete in late January 1939, they decided to "try the book out on [their] own membership and on every kind and class of person that has anything to do with drunks." They were especially concerned that it might "offend our friends of religion" (165). The overall reaction, Bill said, was wonderful, but many suggestions were offered, two of which, he said, were crucial. The first, from a New Jersey psychiatrist, "was to remove all forms of coercion, to put our fellowship on a 'we ought' basis instead of a 'you must' basis." They recognized the importance of this and made this shift throughout the text. Worried about how the Catholic Church would react to the book, they sent the manuscript to the Catholic Committee on Publications, via Morgan R., a very recently sober Catholic—and the only Catholic in the New York group. The committee responded very positively, offering only a few suggestions for improving the section on meditation and prayer (167–69).

While the four hundred mimeographed prepublication copies were circulating, a final controversy erupted over the title of the book and, by extension, the movement. Bill indicated that, "[t]hough [he] had labeled the mimeographed issue 'Alcoholics Anonymous,' this title was still unacceptable to a great many people." Various titles for the book had been debated in New York and Akron while the book was in preparation. The two top contenders were *Alcoholics Anonymous*, which was favored by the New Yorkers, and *The Way Out*, which was favored by the Akronites. The impasse was broken by a check of the Library of Congress records, which revealed that there were already twelve books titled *The Way Out* and none titled *Alcoholics Anonymous*. The more revealing aspect of this controversy comes, however, from Bill's admission that, while he initially favored *Alcoholics Anonymous*, he "began to have certain doubts and temptations . . . as the book-naming discussion went on." If it was titled "The Way Out," he realized, "I could add my signature, 'By Bill W.'! After all why shouldn't an author sign his book? I began to forget that this was everybody's book and that I had been mostly the umpire of the discussions that had created it. In one dark moment I even considered calling the book 'The B. W. Movement.' I whispered these ideas to a few friends and promptly got slapped down. Then I saw the temptation for what it was, a shameless piece of egotism" (165–66).

Although we have no detailed real-time evidence as to how the initial stages of the process unfolded, there is little doubt about its collaborative nature. There is debate over whether Bill drafted all eleven of the initial chapters, with some claiming that Hank P. drafted chapter 10, "To Employers," but all agree that the chapter drafts were discussed in both Akron and New York, that there were disagreements over the way it should be positioned and titled, and that the final draft was circulated widely prior to publication for comment. The marked-up version of the final draft documents the shift in voice from "you must" to "we ought" and the many small changes made throughout the manuscript to effect this shift. It also indicates that two of the changes in the Twelve Steps—the addition of "as we understand Him" to Step Eleven and the deletion of "on our knees" from Step Seven—were made in the final stage of the editing process rather than before. Finally, we have no independent evidence of Bill's doubts and temptations regarding the title of the book until 1946, when he recounts this story in more detail in a letter to a minister in Georgia in the context of concerns over "anonymity breaking." Each of these aspects of the process—its collaborative character, the shift in voice, and Bill's second thoughts about the book title—played a critical role in the formation of the movement. The first two will be considered in relation to the Twelve Steps and the last deferred to the discussion of anonymity breaking and the Twelve Traditions.

A Collaborative Process: At some point Fr. Edward Dowling, the Jesuit priest who became Wilson's confidant and spiritual director during the forties and fifties, said that the genius of AA was not what they put into the

Twelve Steps but what they took out of them. I think this is right. The col-laborative process, through which first the "word-of-mouth program" and then the Big Book emerged, stripped the program of most of its distinctively Christian features and positioned it as spiritual rather than religious (Fuller 2001, 112–15). A word search confirms that the text contains relatively few references to "religion" (7) and "religious" (18).[2] When they do appear, they refer to religion in the abstract, the "world's religions," religious organiza-tions (e.g., bodies, denominations, societies, and affiliations) and religious attitudes, whether positive or negative. There are many references to "God" (64), "spiritual" (60), "Power" (16), "way of life" (10), and "spirituality" (2), which are virtually all positive. The Big Book recognizes that the reader may be resistant to such language, so stresses that "When, therefore, we speak . . . of God, we mean your conception of God. This applies, too, to other spiri-tual expressions which you find in this book. Do not let any prejudice you may have against spiritual terms deter you from honestly asking yourself what they mean to you" (BB:1976, 47). The terms are interconnected, and although God is the most commonly used term, "Power" and "spiritual" are the governing concepts. Thus, in speaking to an agnostic or atheist, the book instructs the AA member to "make it emphatic that he does not have to agree with your conception of God. He can choose any conception he likes, provided it makes sense to him. The main thing is that he be willing to believe in a Power greater than himself and that he live by spiritual prin-ciples" (ibid., 93).

The pruning process began as the "nameless drunks" distanced them-selves from the Oxford Group and continued during the preparation of the Big Book. Of the three New York factions that hammered out the position-ing of the text, the liberals, who were comfortable with God-language and spiritual terms, but not "religion," occupied the middle ground. They wanted a text that, in their words, did not "try to dogmatically pour people into moulds" (OWM, 13, 190). In airing their differences and reaching com-promises, the three factions together hammered out a path that they hoped would be accessible, not only to liberals but also to agnostics, atheists, and those with more conventional religious views. By characterizing God generi-cally as "a Power greater than ourselves," encouraging alcoholics to define their own "God," and redefining the result of the process as a "spiritual awakening" rather than a "religious experience," they made the steps generic and flexible enough that all three factions could get on board. They charac-terized the result as a "spiritual way of life" or just "a way of life" and the program itself as a "simple kit of spiritual tools." The resulting steps were thus neither religious nor secular, but staked out a middle ground they

[2] Word counts were taken from the searchable version of *Alcoholics Anonymous*, 4th ed., at http://anonpress.org/bb/.

viewed as spiritual. In drafting and redrafting the chapters, Bill said he went "pretty much down the middle, writing in spiritual rather than religious or entirely psychological terms" (*AACOA*, 17).

The middle ground not only positioned their program in relation to individual alcoholics, but also positioned AA, as a nascent society, in relation to other social formations. In drafting the book, they were acutely aware that there were others invested in the problem of alcoholism whom they did not want to offend, especially physicians and clergy. In explicitly differentiating themselves from "organized religion" and "organized medicine," they hoped to gain the support of both. Early AAs were particularly eager to gain the approval of the Catholic Church, which, as the largest denomination in the United States, held sway over a vast pool of potential members. Although Dr. Bob was affiliated with a Catholic hospital as of 1934 and began treating alcoholics there covertly in 1939 with the help of Sister Ignatia, there were few Catholics involved in the nascent movement when the Big Book was written. Wilson later indicated that the "main reason" they "omit[ted] any material that would identify us with the Oxford Group" was to avoid "possible trouble with the Catholic Church" (quoted in Kurtz 1991, 52). In reaching out to various religious and medical leaders for feedback, they sought to ensure that AA's approach was compatible with theirs and that individual AA members could combine AA spirituality with any "organized religion" or medical treatment.

In positioning itself in this way, AA aligned itself with an array of "nonsectarian" movements that had emerged in the latter part of the nineteenth century, including spiritualism, New Thought, Theosophy, and many of the fraternal orders, such as the Masons. These movements historically coexisted alongside and interpenetrated rather than competed with "official" religious organizations. They constituted an organizational "third way" that with some exceptions did not adopt a formal "church" structure, did not view themselves as "organized religions," and for the most part were not viewed that way by others. Characterizing themselves variously as nonsectarian, spiritual, metaphysical, or occult, they—like Alcoholics Anonymous—viewed themselves neither as "[organized] religions" (the first way) nor completely nonreligious (the second way) (Taves and Kinsella 2013, 87).

While attitudes toward organized religion varied among these groups and among the individuals within them, the third-way organizations typically embraced a theology that was either universalistic and/or esoteric rather than exclusivist. In contrast to many organized religions that claimed to present an exclusive or at least privileged route to a religious goal, these third-way organizations claimed to identify that which was common to all religions. Although the alleged common core, which they often claimed to have accessed through experiential and/or esoteric means, differed from group to group, these third-way groups shared the belief that there *was* a common core. They expressed this belief by describing themselves as "nonsectarian" in the nineteenth century and as "spiritual" in the twentieth century, opening their membership to all who were open to the common core as they understood it, and viewing membership in their group as compatible with membership in organized religions (Taves and Kinsella 2013, 87).

AA adopted this approach without overtly aligning itself with these earlier movements or making any explicit claims about a common core. They simply sought to make the core of their program—the Twelve Steps—acceptable to as many constituencies as possible through a continual process of testing their approach with alcoholics and interested professionals. In doing so, however, the Steps still made a basic spiritual claim and isolated a tacit, pragmatically defined "common core," to wit, that willpower was not enough to overcome the problem of alcohol addiction and that the solution lay in (1) turning their will and their lives over to a "Power greater than themselves" (or "God as they understand Him"); (2) discerning, confessing, and making amends for the effects of their previous failures; and (3) seeking through prayer and meditation to maintain conscious contact with this Power and align their will and life with it.

The Voice of the Text: The shift in the voice of the Big Book from a didactic second-person ("you must") to the first-person plural ("we alcoholics") of the current text not only aligned the voice of the text with the collaborative process that produced it but also with the spirituality that informed it. In discussing the final revisions of the Big Book, AA historians have recognized the practical importance of the shift, but they haven't reflected on what the shift did, perhaps because from an AA perspective, its import is so obvious. Although all versions of the foreword opened with "We, of Alcoholics Anonymous, are more than one hundred men and women who have recovered from a seemingly hopeless state of mind and body," the mimeographed version switched to the third person in the second sentence, stating that the main purpose of the book was "to show alcoholics how they can recover" and then adopted the second person throughout the rest of the book. In the final version, the purpose of the book was "to show how *we* have recovered," thus setting the voice of the Big Book in the first-person plural (*OWM*, 192). In the original version of the text, the use of you-language made a direct connection between the author and the reader but did so didactically—telling readers what they ought to do—while revealing little about the speaker. In shifting to first-person plural, the voice of the text revealed itself—we did this, we learned that, our experience was. This shift was congruent with the shift from "preaching" to "mutuality," which Bill stressed in the later versions of his story, and with the emerging AA message.

The "we" that speaks—a group of one hundred men and women—was large enough that the "we" in question could not be individually named as they might have been in an ordinary multiauthored work. In the emergence of a collective voice, we can see the emergence of an author who speaks in the voice of the whole. The "we" that speaks also prefigured the group's explicit commitment to anonymity as the spiritual foundation of the traditions and the spiritual significance of placing principles before personalities. The voice of the text thus highlighted the claim that the text reflected the principles of the fellowship and not the personal views of individual human authors.

Finally, it does not require a leap of the imagination to go from an author who speaks *as* the voice of the whole to an Author who speaks *through* the whole. Many AAs view the authorship of the Big Book in both these ways. The changes promoted and reinforced "a long-held belief by many in the simultaneous presence of inspiration from a 'Power greater than ourselves' and the loving hand of careful human editing" (*OWM*, 191). Ascribing authorship to the anonymous "we" allowed AAs to ascribe the changes to a Power that worked through the editing process. In doing so, they tacitly prefigured Tradition Two, which grounds ultimate authority in "a loving God as He may express Himself in our group conscience."

THE TWELVE TRADITIONS

The Twelve Traditions institutionalized the tacit, pragmatically defined core of the program, stabilizing and perpetuating it by means of a novel organizational structure rather than by means of explicit universalist theological claims, which exclusivist traditions would have rejected. Although Bill drafted the long and short versions of the Twelve Traditions, he did so in conversation with the fellowship as a whole over the course of the forties. In the wake of the publication of the *Saturday Evening Post* article in 1941, the movement expanded rapidly and the Central Office was flooded with letters requesting clarifications on procedures and help in adjudicating disagreements. The traditions, some of them already recognized and in practice, were formally articulated and refined through the back-and-forth between the Central Office and the groups. Bill published the long version of the Twelve Traditions in the *Grapevine*, the new AA newsletter, in 1946, and after much promotion and discussion, the short version of the Twelve Traditions was formally adopted at the AA Convention in 1950 (*PIO*, 305–6; Kurtz 1991, 112–16).

With the exception of Tradition Six, the first nine traditions structure the relationship between individuals and the group and thus provide AA's internal structure as a voluntary organization. Tradition One places the "common welfare" of the group above that of the individual. As AA commentary explains, AA explicitly rejected a top-down hierarchical structure governed by a central authority as a means of maintaining the unity of the group, instead locating authority in "a loving God as He may express Himself in our group conscience," that is, in the "conscience" of the local AA group (Tradition Two). Group membership was open to all who wanted "to stop drinking" (Tradition Three), regardless of "race, creed, politics, and language" (*12&12*, 141). Traditions Four, Five, and Seven defined the local groups as autonomous "except in matters affecting other groups or A.A. as a whole" (Four), as self-supporting (Seven), and specified that their primary purpose was "to carry [the] message to the alcoholic who still suffers" (Five). Tradition Eight maintained AA as a voluntary organization, while allowing "service centers" to employ "special workers." Tradition Nine proclaimed that "A.A., as such, ought never be organized; but we may create service boards or committees directly responsible to those they serve." The commentary on Tradition Nine declares AA an exception to the general rule that "power to direct or govern is the essence of organization everywhere" (*12&12*, 172–73), arguing that those elected to serve at the local, intergroup, or worldwide level were caretakers and expediters who could at most make suggestions. While AA's claim that it is "a society without organization" (*12&12*, 175) seems unwarranted, characterizing itself as such distinguished it from both organized religion and organized medicine.

It was, however, the last three traditions, along with Tradition Six, that did the actual work of positioning AA in relation to other social formations. Tradition Six specified that AA groups could never lend the AA name to any outside enterprise and Tradition Ten declared that AA would take no position "on outside issues." Tradition Eleven embraced "personal anonymity at the public level [as] the cornerstone of our public relations policy" and instructed AA members to "maintain personal anonymity at the level of press, radio, and films." Tradition Eleven was not simply about public relations, however; it was also "a constant . . . reminder that personal ambition has no place in A.A.," hence, a matter of spiritual practice. Tradition Twelve brought this point home, stating, "Anonymity is the spiritual foundation of all our traditions, ever reminding us to place principles before personalities."

Although with the publication of the Big Book, the "nameless drunks" officially adopted Alcoholics Anonymous as the name for their fellowship, the concept of anonymity only gradually acquired spiritual connotations. At first, AAs thought of anonymity primarily in terms of protecting members and their families from the stigma attached to alcoholism (*12&12*, 184). As word of AA spread in the early forties and members sought to share their recovery with others, AAs started to reflect on how anonymous they should be (*12&12*, 185). Reflection on what this meant in practice led, over the course of the forties, to the deeper, more spiritual understanding of the concept of anonymity expressed in Tradition Twelve.

ANONYMITY

Explicit reflection on the meaning of anonymity was triggered by Marty M.'s public disclosure of her association with AA in her lectures on behalf of the National Committee for Education on Alcoholism (NCEA) in the mid-forties.[3] At that time, according to Bill, most AAs "believe[d] in anonymity," but AAs were unsure when anonymity was called for and under what conditions it could or should be broken. In a January 1946 *Grapevine* article, Bill laid out suggested guidelines that allowed a great deal of flexibility for individuals and groups as long as they weren't publicly identifying themselves with the movement at the level of press, radio, or any other medium of "public circulation." It was in those contexts, he indicated, that AAs should "with very rare exceptions" maintain their anonymity. "If for some extraordinary reason, for the good of AA as a whole, a member thinks it desirable to completely drop his anonymity, he should only do so after consulting the older members of his local group. If he is to make a nationwide public appearance as an AA the matter ought to be referred to our Central Office" (*LOH*, 15–16).

It was this question of exceptions for the good of AA as a whole that came to a head in relation to Marty M.'s lectures for the NCEA. Marty, in-line with Bill's initial suggestions, had discussed whether she should publicly reveal her connection to AA with Bill, who initially agreed that it was a good idea. Bill and Bob, without identifying their connection to AA, also allowed their names to be included as members of the advisory board on NCEA's letterhead. Not too long after Marty M. began giving lectures across the country in late 1944, the issue exploded (Kurtz 1991, 118–19). In a letter dated 22 November 1946, Bill acknowledged the scope of the problem. "[T]here is a pile of discussion going on in the groups about her and the relation of Yale to the Alcoholics Anonymous movement. Some of this talk is very badly motivated and unfair, but there is a powerful undercurrent of feeling now running all over the country which inquires whether Marty, in breaking her anonymity, has not laid A.A. wide open to a precedent by which any number of other people can do likewise for far less worthy causes" (WGW to Abbo T., GSOA; Brown and Brown 2001, 179–83).

Marty M.'s "anonymity breaking," as it came to be called, precipitated explicit discussion of whether there could be *any* exceptions at this level. As of June 1946, Bill still thought that "in a few rare cases," such as Marty M.'s, it could be justified (WGW to Sam D., 22 June 1946, GSOA). By Novem-

---

[3] *PIO* (307) dates Bill's reflections on anonymity to Rollie H.'s anonymity break in 1940, but I found no real-time discussion of Rollie's break in the archives' files on anonymity. Bill's *Grapevine* articles and his correspondence on anonymity all date from 1946, the year that the Marty M. situation exploded. Kurtz (1991, 85–87) indicates that initial reactions to the Rollie H. publicity were much more positive.

FIGURE 5.1. AA members maintaining their anonymity in the press, *(Dayton, OH) Journal Herald*, 17 May 1942. © *Dayton (OH) Daily News.*

ber, he was having second thoughts and, in a *Grapevine* article in March 1947, he said it was a mistake (*LOH*, 45; WGW to Abbo T., 22 November 1946, GSOA). Although the long version of Tradition Eleven published in April 1946 simply called for "modesty and anonymity" in "our relations with the outside world" (*LOH*, 23), the discussion of the final version in the *Grapevine* in October 1948 emphatically stated that "no member ought to describe himself in full view of the general public as an AA, even for the most worthy purpose" (*LOH*, 92; *12&12*, 180).

Starting in 1946, a significant portion of the correspondence from the Central Office was devoted to discouraging anonymity breaking at the level of press, radio, and other public media (*AACOA*, 209). Notices were sent to newspapers and magazines explaining AA's concerns. The Central Office sent letters to individuals who broke anonymity, describing past experiences that had led most AAs to agree that any short-term benefits were outweighed by the long-term consequences. These efforts rapidly reduced the number of anonymity breakers from more than three hundred in the midforties to a dozen in 1950 and three in 1954 (WGW to George H., 30 October 1950; WGW to Marge N., 9 September 1954, GSOA).

Not surprisingly, Bill developed a series of talking points on the issue of anonymity breaking in which he shared his experiences. In public he often used the story of Rollie H., a national league baseball player and known alcoholic who generated enormous publicity in 1940 when he attributed his comeback to AA (Kurtz 1991, 85–87). The nationwide newspaper coverage drew in many new members and, Bill said, "gave me ideas. Soon I was on the road, happily handing out personal interviews and pictures. To my delight, I found I could hit the front pages, just as he could. . . . For two or three years I guess I was A.A.'s number one anonymity breaker." Noting that there is no evidence to suggest that Bill actually hit the road or the front pages in the immediate aftermath of the Rollie H. episode, AA historians used this claim to illustrate Bill's tendency to use his own experience—real or exaggerated—to establish a bond of mutuality with his audience (*PIO*, 237–38). It also highlights the way he reinterpreted behaviors that might have seemed acceptable at the time in light of later experience.

This brings us back to Bill's story of the temptations he faced in the context of naming the Big Book, a story that he rarely recounted in public, but that he did recount in some detail to Rev. Sam D., a Protestant minister, in June 1946, at the height of the uproar over Marty M.'s anonymity breaking. Rev. D., who was lecturing widely, didn't understand why it would be considered a violation of policy if "the speaker permits the use of his name only for the purpose of promoting AA principles" (Sam D. to Margaret R. Burger, 15 June 1946, GSOA). In his reply on 22 June 1946 (GSOA), Bill characterized the naming of the Big Book as "the most far reaching" decision he had ever made and cast it, in retrospect anyway, in terms of anonymity breaking.

Just as you are now searching your soul about anonymity in public, so did I have to go through that very process in 1939, the year our book Alcoholics Anonymous went to print. I was then called upon to make a decision, perhaps the most far reaching one I have ever taken. Had it not been for the wise council of my friends in A.A. I must humbly confess that I probably would have abandoned my anonymity before the general public. Two courses were then open to me. Because two titles to the book had been proposed and both were equally popular. Here they were:

1. THE WAY OUT By Wm. G. Wilson

2. ALCOHOLICS ANONYMOUS

I don't mind saying, Sam, that the first one looked mighty attractive to me. To justify myself I used to say "Well Bill, you have sure learned enough humility by now. So the mere signing of this book will never go to your head. The leaders of every other movement are publicized. All movements have to be personalized. They have to have personal symbols to lend them power and character. So why shouldn't I sign this book? A good title too—'The Way Out'! I almost succumbed to these rationalization[s,] but my friends tipped the scale the other way. They said to me, 'What if you get drunk—take a good look at Dick P[.]—and Bill, what kind of an example do you think you would sell-ing to the rest of us egocentrics? Even if *you* could stand a lot of news-paper publicity, *we couldn't*. Lots of us would get drunk and let our movement down. And anyhow, isn't the American public pretty well fed up on personal ballyhoo, however good[?]" Well, Sam, my friends wouldn't let me do it, and how right—oh how very right—they were.

Framing this temptation as an instance of anonymity breaking highlights the spiritual significance that anonymity assumed in the forties and thereafter. In telling this story, he made it clear that the leader was no exception when it came to anonymity. Moreover, in renouncing the desire for recognition of his role in founding the movement and producing the movement's central text, he highlighted the spiritual meaning of anonymity as a counterweight to the alcoholics' self-destructive desire for power, fame, and wealth. Anonymity was the spiritual foundation of the Twelve Traditions because it exemplified the spirit of humility and sacrifice that led AAs to sacrifice not only alcohol but also the relentless quest for power, fame, and wealth in order to survive as individuals and to make sacrifices for the common welfare of the group to preserve AA. "Just as sacrifice meant survival for the individual, so did sacrifice mean unity and survival for the group and for A.A.'s entire fellowship" (*AACOA*, 287–88).

MR. ANONYMOUS

The principle of anonymity not only served as a spiritual check on potentially destructive desires for fame, fortune, and power, it also led Wilson into the paradoxical role of "Mr. AA," the symbolic head and unacknowledged leader of a democratic and leaderless fellowship. From the outset, AA eschewed the language of governance. Bill and Dr. Bob were cofounders of AA, not its spiritual leaders. Nonetheless, there was a concept of "real leadership . . . notwithstanding the apparent lack of it," grounded in Tradition Two. As the commentary on Tradition Two explained, the ideal role of "the deposed founder" of a group was that of the "elder statesman . . . who sees the wisdom of the group's decision, who holds no resentment over his reduced status, whose judgment, fortified by considerable experience, is sound, and who is willing to sit quietly on the sidelines patiently awaiting developments" (*12&12*, 134–35).

Although Bill undoubtedly aspired to the "elder statesman" role, he was also for all practical purposes the "designer" of AA. Not only was he the first of the two cofounders, the primary author of the Big Book, and the author and promoter of the Twelve Traditions, he was also, in collaboration with others, the first author of *Twelve Steps and Twelve Traditions* and *Alcoholics Anonymous Comes of Age* (Wing 1998, 56–57). Although the books were all published anonymously, Bill's leadership role, indeed, his organizational genius, was widely acknowledged during his lifetime by those within and beyond the organization (Wing 1998, 53–63). Given the nature of the organiza-

FIGURE 5.2. Bill Wilson in his writing studio, "Wit's End," at Stepping Stones, Katonah, New York, 2 December 1951. Courtesy of the Stepping Stones Foundation Archives.

tion he did so much to create, he was logically enough obliged to decline a request to be included in *Who's Who* and Yale's offer of an honorary degree. As he explained to Wheeler Sammons Jr. in 1951:

Now, as I guess you are aware, one of our traditional cornerstones is this: Alcoholics Anonymous does not publicize its leadership by name, picture or extensive personal description. This tradition, strictly binding on me, enjoins us to place principles before personalities. Such is the scope and reach of our anonymity. To us it has immense spiritual significance, it is probably the greatest protective device against exploitation and big-shotism that AA will ever have. Now here am I, the symbol and guardian of that tradition which I have done so much to uphold. Were you in my place, what would you say to such an honor as is now proffered by "Who's Who"? (WGW to Wheeler Sammons Jr., 6 February 1951, GSOA)

Although he characterized himself to Sammons as "the symbol and guardian" of AA's traditions, he was clearly more than that. Still, as chief designer of an organization that viewed anonymity as its spiritual foundation, he could not without contradiction receive credit for his design. Even if the characterization of Wilson as the "symbolic" head of a leaderless organization was somewhat misleading, it was, nonetheless, congruent with the aspirations of the organization and a necessary fiction during the several decades it took to create a self-perpetuating "leaderless" organization.

As Matthew Raphael (2000) has cogently argued, playing the role of Mr. Anonymous made him "a man of two personalities," divided between Mr. AA, the symbol of the whole, and his alter ego, Bill Wilson. The demands of his symbolic role were particularly acute in the forties, when they undoubtedly exacerbated his struggles with depression and led him, as he became more aware of his own individual needs in the late forties, to begin seeing a therapist. He explained what he was learning from his therapist to a friend (Fitzgerald 1995, 44):

Her thesis is that my position in AA has become quite inconsistent with my needs as an individual. Highly satisfactory to live one's life for others, it cannot be anything but disastrous to live one's life for others as those others think it should be lived. One has, for better or worse, to choose his own life. The extent to which the AA movement and individuals in it determine my choices is really astonishing. Things which are primary to me (even for the good of AA) are unfulfilled. I'm constantly diverted to secondary or even useless activities by AAs whose demands seem to them primary, but are not really so. So we have the person of Mr. Anonymous in conflict with Bill Wilson. To me, this is more than an interesting speculation—it's homely good sense.

He did not spell out the things that were primary for him here, but I suspect he was referring to his interests in mysticism and psychical research, which he found both personally compelling and potentially good for AA.

The paradoxes surrounding Bill's interest in these and other potentially controversial spiritual topics paralleled those surrounding his leadership.

Just as the Traditions required him to remain anonymous at the level of the public media, they also required him to avoid endorsements (Tradition Six) and taking sides on potentially controversial matters (Tradition Ten). Moreover, maintaining the Twelve Steps as a generically "spiritual" and religiously nonaligned path required him to make a rigorous distinction between publicly articulating AA's understanding of its generically spiritual "way of life" and his personal spiritual interests and views. Without that distinction, AA's way of life could easily have become another new religious movement with Bill Wilson as its prophet and spiritual leader. In order to maintain the distinction, Wilson and the AA leadership tried to keep his personal views out of the limelight (Kurtz 1991, 136, 358n2) and, at the same time, worked to undercut the tendency of the membership to idealize or denigrate him in the manner of a true or false prophet.

The fine line that he had to walk in this regard is evident in his relationship with the Catholic Church, where he simultaneously found himself suppressing his personal enthusiasm for Catholicism in order to avoid the appearance of aligning AA with the church and at the same time making it clear to concerned Catholic leaders that AA was not a heretical new religious movement. In letters written in mid-1957, we see him walking both sides of this fence. In a letter to Joe dated 8 October 1957 (GSOA), he gave his symbolic role in AA as one of the reasons he didn't join the church.

> Theoretically [he wrote] I have the same right to form other associations, as any other A.A. does. But in quite a practical sense I am hogtied by the A.A. Tradition of which I am a symbol. This is very emphatic about alliances and endorsements for Alcoholics Anonymous. Since I happen to be a symbol for the whole, this tradition bears down upon me with very special force. If I said publicly that I chewed Beeman's Pepsin gum, it would surely be construed as an A.A. endorsement.

Just a few months earlier, however, he was thanking Fr. John Ford for his careful reading of *AACOA* "from the theological point of view" and assuring Ford of his desire to "avoid every possibility of theological dispute which might result in a justification for declaring Alcoholics Anonymous a heresy" (WGW to Ford, 14 May 1957, GSOA).

With regard to heresy, Ford seems to have been worried that Bill's story, as recounted more fully than before in *AACOA*, might suggest that AA was a new religion launched in response to God's divine intervention at Towns Hospital. Bill hastened to reassure Ford that he viewed his experience at Towns as a "conversion experience" and that he could make no judgment as to whether or not it was "a miraculous and calculated intervention of God." He did allow, however, that it might be "natural for many people to assume, on account of the large reach and power of A.A. today, that God did make a very special intervention in my case" and that "in [that] connection, embarrassing things [were] already happening." Thus, he said:

> People are trying to put me on a pedestal where I don't belong. Serious-minded students are beginning to say that A.A. is about the biggest things since the time of Christ. At our Cleveland Convention in 1950 we had three speakers, two of them Catholics, one an Episcopalian. One guy compared Smith and me to Moses and Elijah; another comparison was with Jesus, and still a third gent got up and seriously implied that the A.A. book was a cut or two better than the Bible! I have seldom been more worried or embarrassed.

In response to Ford's concerns, Bill indicated that he had downplayed his role by stressing the point that "nobody invented Alcoholics Anonymous" in the opening pages of the book and emphasizing that "God's leaven had to work through a great many people . . . to make A.A. possible" (WGW to Fr. John C. Ford, SJ, 14 May 1957, GSOA). In *AACOA*, he returned to this point, indicating that "[a]s a society we must never become so vain as to suppose that we have been the authors and inventors of a new religion. We will humbly reflect that each of A.A.'s principles, *every one of them*, has been borrowed from ancient sources. We shall remember that we are laymen, holding ourselves in readiness to co-operate with all men of good will, whatever their creed or nationality" (*AACOA*, 231–32; emphasis in original). Finally, Bill added a footnote to the final version of the manuscript, which repeated the point yet again:

> Speaking for Dr. Bob and myself I would like to say that there has never been the slightest intent, on his part or mine, of trying to found a new religious denomination. Dr. Bob held certain religious convictions, and so do I. This is, of course, the personal privilege of every A.A. member. Nothing, however, could be so unfortunate for A.A.'s future as an attempt to incorporate any of our personal theological views into A.A. teaching, practice, or tradition. Were Dr. Bob still with us, I am positive he would agree that we could never be too emphatic about this matter. (*AACOA*, 232n1; see also Wing 1998, 75–76)

In this footnote, Bill acknowledged the crucial role that the distinction between the public Mr. AA and the private Bill Wilson played not only in developing and maintaining the democratic, leaderless structure of the organization but also in protecting the claim that AA was a spiritual way of life and not a new religion.

Maintaining this split took its toll on Bill Wilson personally and obscured his personal theological views, which I will consider in chapter 6. I will argue that, while AA embodied a tacit perennialism in its structure and organization that could be overridden by various theological perspectives, Bill Wilson was an explicit perennialist with Catholic proclivities who viewed his own unusual experiences—spiritualist, mystical, and drug-induced—as different ways of entering into the "unseen Reality."

Seeking

AA historians cautiously acknowledged Wilson's personal interests in spiritualism, parapsychology, Catholicism, mysticism, and LSD in its official history (*PIO*; *Dr. Bob*). They quote his close friend, Tom Powers,[1] who indicated that Bill's interest in spiritualism "was not at all divorced from A.A." and that "Bill never did anything that was not in some way connected with A.A. and with his own spiritual growth" (*PIO*, 280). Despite these clues, historians have not done a very good job of showing how these interests were connected. Matthew Raphael has done the most to integrate these interests into a larger account of his life, arguing that "all of them arose directly from Bill's quest for spiritual enlightenment, a quest that was intertwined at first with his search for relief from depression and later for an end to 'neurosis,' understood in the broadest sense as any human conflict" (Raphael 2000, 158). While Bill's quest was certainly intertwined with his struggle with depression, I don't think it originated there, but rather with his sudden experience, which he interpreted in light of his earlier experience of presence at Winchester Cathedral (Thomsen 1999, 83–84).

Bill pursued his quest in conversation with a handful of close spiritual companions—his wife, Lois; Bob and Anne Smith; Fr. Edward Dowling; his neighbor and fellow AA, Tom Powers; and authors Gerald Heard and Aldous Huxley. Lois, Bob, and Anne were all involved with the Oxford Group; Dowling was a Catholic priest and a member of the Society of Jesus; Powers was the founder of All Addicts Anonymous, an alternative to AA; and Heard and Huxley were writers well known for their eclectic interests in mysticism and drugs. Although Bill's tendency to focus rather obsessively on his interest du jour might tempt us to think of these relationships in isolation and his interests as "phases," doing so does not do him justice. His spiritual companions knew of one another; many of them interacted and others met through Bill. More crucially, they all shared an experiential orientation, a spiritual open-mindedness, and a tendency toward perennialism that was

---

[1] Thomas Powers's son-in-law indicated that using Powers's full name posthumously (versus using "Tom P.") would be in keeping with Powers's wishes (e-mail, 23 December 2015).

implicit in AA and expressly articulated in Aldous Huxley's *The Perennial Philosophy* (1944) and Tom Powers's *First Questions in the Life of the Spirit* (1959).

Rather than disconnected phases, Bill's interests and spiritual friendships make more sense if we view them as interconnected layers and cast each layer in light of the concerns that drove it. Viewed this way, we can consider Bill's interest in spiritualism, psychic phenomena, and LSD as reflecting his radical empiricism, his interest in what he considered to be the facts of experience (the existence of an unseen world and life after death) as they related to the great reality that he glimpsed at the cathedral and that opened up for him at Towns. His interest in Catholicism reflected his need for additional guidance on the path, a spiritual ideal (St. Francis), and methods of evaluating what he discovered empirically (discernment). His interest in the ideas advanced by Heard and Huxley with respect to psychic phenomena, spiritual practice, and mysticism reflected his need for synthesis and integration (a pluralistic perennialism).

Although his public talks allowed AAs to interpret his sudden experience as a release from the desire to drink and as a conventional conversion experience, other less public evidence suggests that Bill interpreted his sudden experience as an opening into "the great reality" or "the fourth dimension of existence" beginning in the thirties and that this "reality" or "dimension" was far more open-ended and far less conventional than most AAs suspected. This opening initiated a process of psychospiritual investigation that led him into spiritualism beginning in the thirties, Catholicism in the forties, and drug-based mysticism in the fifties. Bill's personal spiritual journey makes the most sense, in other words, if the God of his sudden experience is viewed as an opening into an unseen realm that generated a sense of calling, triggered unusual abilities, and launched him on a personal odyssey that is more like other figures in this book than we might have suspected.

SPIRITUAL EXPLORATION

It is within this generous and rather vague conception of God as a presence opening into a "great reality" or "fourth dimension" that we can situate Bill's eclectic spiritual explorations, beginning in the thirties with his interests in the guidance practices of the Oxford Group, spiritualism, and psychic phenomena, and continuing into the fifties with his interest in psychical research and his involvement in early LSD experiments. Although many would want to make a sharp distinction between evangelical-style "guidance" and spiritualist practices, there is considerable evidence to suggest that the founders of AA (and Al-Anon) viewed them as compatible if not overlapping practices. Bill sought something similar from both: a sense of direction for his life in this world and experiential evidence that life extends beyond death into an unseen world beyond this one. In pursuit of these ends, Bill developed an ability to communicate with suprahuman entities that was similar in many respects to that of Joseph Smith and Helen Schucman (the subject of the next case study), albeit less fully elaborated.

As discussed in chapter 4, Oxford Group guidance practices were centrally concerned with discerning God's presence and direction. Bill had a sense of being "guided" in the wake of his experience at Towns Hospital, which led him to break with the "group guidance" he received from his Oxford Group team. He participated in "quiet time" with the Smiths during his three months in Akron in 1935. The Smith's daughter Sue, who also participated, recalled that they began with a reading, followed by a prayer, "then we'd be quiet. Finally, everybody would share what they got, or didn't get. This lasted for at least a half-hour and sometimes went as long as an hour" (Dick B. 1998, 54–55). In her journal from this period, Anne Smith indicated that she viewed "guidance" as the structuring principle of the Bible. "The Bible," she said, "is *guidance written down* . . . . 'God spoke,' to . . . the prophets, to the Apostles. Paul was constantly guided by the Holy Spirit. Jesus was in constant touch with the Father. The Acts of the Apostles is called the Book of the Holy Spirit. . . . Modern theologians rule these things out of the Bible, because they don't realize that they still happen" (Dick B. 1998, 57; emphasis in original).

Although Anne stressed that Oxford-style guidance involved "normal thoughts" that "come with a sense of urgency enough for action," the line between the Oxford Group practice of sitting quietly "with a pad and pencil and put[ting] down anything that came into your mind" (Dick B. 1998, 55, 58–59) and the spiritualist practice of automatic writing could get blurry. *God Calling, by Two Listeners*, a popular Oxford Group devotional book originally published in the thirties, offered daily meditations that "two listeners" claimed to have received from God by means of Oxford-style guidance. One of the "two listeners" described her "persistent desire [after reading A. J. Russell's *For Sinners Only*, another Oxford staple] to see whether [she] could get guidance such as [Russell] reported, through sharing a quiet time with the friend with whom I was then living" (Russell 1945, 9). Although her results were "entirely negative," her friend's were not. "From the first, beautiful messages were given to her by our Lord Himself, and every day from then these messages have never failed us" (ibid., 9–10). Although the first "listener" stressed that "[they] were not in any way psychic or advanced in spiritual growth, . . . just very ordinary human beings" (ibid., 10), some evangelical Christians have since condemned *God Calling*, which has remained a Christian best seller down to the present, as "spiritistic literature" obtained "by the occult practice of automatic writing" (Gruss 1984).

We know that Bill, Anne, and Bob did not share these concerns. Indeed, according to AA historians, the letters Bill wrote to Lois during his summer

Oxford Group & The Vineyard?

with the Smiths in 1935 contain "references to séances and other psychic events" (*PIO*, 275). The AA-sponsored biography of Dr. Bob confirms that "Doc shared [an interest in unusual experiences] with Bill Wilson and a number of other early A.A. members" (*Dr. Bob*, 311). Unlike Bill, however, Dr. Bob "never had the flash of light—the spiritual experience" (*PIO*, 307). According to his son, Smitty, he was looking for "a spiritual revelation, which could come suddenly to some people . . . He hoped it would be revealed to him in that way" (*PIO*, 308–9). In search of it, he spent "an hour every day on some religious subject. . . . He read about every religion . . . not only the Christian religion. . . . He was even interested in people who claimed to have extrasensory perception and other forms of spiritual insight. . . . He felt that in far distant centuries, the science of the mind would be so developed as to make possible contact between the living and the dead" (*PIO*, 309, 311).

Some of the old-timers interviewed by AA historians recalled "a fellow named Roland J.," who seems to have been at the center of spiritualist activity among a subset of the AAs in Akron and Cleveland. According to John and Elgie R., "Doc would talk for hours to . . . Roland J., 'who believed in anything that came down the pike when it came to spiritualism'" (*Dr. Bob*, 311). Clarence S. concurred, adding, "A lot of us [in Cleveland] believed in the spiritual thing . . . We'd go to Roland's on a Sunday night. He'd call in the spirits." But Clarence said, "It got spooky after a while—beyond what we should be monkeying with. Doc backed off, too.'" AAs in Akron and Cleveland apparently started to feel that the practices were dangerous. After a while, Sue Smith recalled, "Dad got to feel he was being criticized, and he was. They didn't approve. But I think what really got them was that they weren't included" (*Dr. Bob*, 311).

Bill and Father Dowling discussed psychic phenomena at length in their early letters in response to Bill's interest. In a letter dated 6 January 194(2), Dowling indicated that he had made some "casual inquires" after they talked and was surprised to learn of the "prevalence of the phenomena" (quoted in Fitzgerald 1995, 23). Dowling reported that he had surfaced three Catholic authors who had written on the subject—J. Godfrey Raupert, Johan Liljencrants, and Herbert Thurston—all of whom rejected spiritualist claims, which had been condemned by the church, and offered varying explanations of the psychic phenomena that spiritualists claimed to have demonstrated. Raupert, as Dowling noted, took the more negative view, attributing spiritualist claims to "diabolical agency," while Liljencrants thought that most of the phenomena could be accounted for in terms of psychology and other natural causes (Liljencrants 1918, 268–70). Bill read Liljencrants's book "with intense interest and concern," but he questioned whether all the phenomena could be explained in terms of fraud or psychology (3 February 1942, WGW to Dowling, GSOA; 18 February 1942, Dowling to WGW, GSOA).

Although Bill was attentive to concerns raised by the Catholic writers, this did not inhibit his investigations. Indeed, at some point, perhaps while he was in Akron in 1935 or perhaps earlier, Bill came to believe that he had psychic abilities and, within months of meeting Dowling, Bill and Lois moved to their own home in Bedford Hills where they set aside a downstairs room—nicknamed the "spook room"—for séances (*PIO*, 275; Raphael 2000, 159; Borchert 2005, 313). In a letter dated 19 January 1943, Bill thanked Bob for two books that he and Lois had shared with their new "'spooking' friends," all of whom were "A.A. neighbors" (WGW to RH Smith, 19 January 1943, WGW Collection 102: Correspondence 1939–50, Box 9, Folder 7 [SSFA]). Lois's notes from a séance on 20 March 1943 indicate that there were eight "regulars." In addition to herself and Bill, the regulars were Ginny and Tom Powers, Ruth and Burr S., and Anne B. (cofounder with Lois of Al-Anon) and her husband, Devoe (Séance Book, 20 March 1943; see also Borchert 2005, 314; *PIO*, 278). In some of the sessions, such as the one on March 20, they used a Ouija board; in others, according to AA historians, "Bill would lie on the couch in the living room, semi-withdrawn, but not in a trance, and 'receive' messages, sometimes a word at a time, sometimes a letter at a time. Anne B., neighbor and 'spook' circle regular, would write the material on a pad" (*PIO*, 278). According to Lois, "Bill would lie down on the couch. He would 'get' these things. He kept doing it every week or so. Each time, certain people [meaning discarnates] would 'come in.' Sometimes, it would be new ones, and they'd carry on some story. There would be long sentences; word by word would come through" (*PIO*, 278–79).

In his later reflections on their spiritualist investigations, Tom Powers indicated that Bill and Bob viewed the séances as a possible way to help atheists get the spiritual component of AA. According to Powers,

> I was a problem to these people, because I was an atheist and an atheist is, by definition, a materialist. I mean, you can't be an atheist unless you're a materialist, and a materialist is, by definition, someone who does not believe in other worlds. Now these people, Bill and Dr. Bob, believed vigorously and aggressively. They were working away at the spiritualism; it was not just a hobby. And it related to A.A., because the big problem in A.A. is that for a materialist it's hard to buy the program. I had a hell of a time getting on the program. Couldn't get it through my head that there was any God, because God was a supernatural being. And there ain't any supernatural beings, and everybody knows there isn't. So the thing was not at all divorced from A.A. It was very serious for everybody. (Tom Powers, quoted in *PIO*, 280)

Although Powers perhaps stressed the antimaterialist aspect in light of his own atheism, he was clearly right to stress that these investigations were not

FIGURE 6.1. The entrance to the downstairs room at Stepping Stones in which the Wilsons and their friends held séances or, as they referred to them, "spook sessions" (Wing 1998, 83). © The Stepping Stones Foundation Archives.

just a hobby for Bill and Bob but tied directly to their commitment to AA. The central issue for Bill, as we will see, was finding evidence—"facts," he would have said—to show that there is an unseen world and that life extends beyond death.

Although this was the bottom line for Bill, there is considerably more we can draw from the surviving records of the séances at Stepping Stones if we look at who was involved and what they were doing, what the spirits were communicating, and what the regulars drew from the spirits' communica-

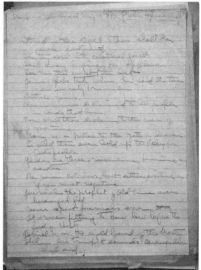

FIGURE 6.2. (*Left*) The notebook in which Bill and Lois Wilson and friends kept records of séances at their home at Stepping Stones. Handwritten on the cover are the words "Books" and "Spooks." (*Right*) A page of automatic writing that reads at the top: "Bill at the [Ouija] board May 14 '44 [Prebu—name of spirit] speaking." © The Stepping Stones Foundation Archives.

tions. With respect to the participants, it is important to note that they were the cofounders of AA (Bill and Dr. Bob) and Al-Anon (Lois and Anne B.) and their close AA friends. All seem to have been spiritually curious and open to experimentation. In his letter to Dr. Bob on January 19, Bill described the various abilities the regulars were developing.

> [Tom] P[.] writes automatically, throws the table about plenty and clairvoyantly saw a relative the other night. . . . Both Tom P[.] and Ruth S[.] border on trance. They are developing quite fast. We have been able to talk (through the table) to Lois' father and mother and uncle—as well as to relatives of the others. Communications seem fairly authentic. Lois, once very skeptical, is now sold. (WGW to Bob, 19 January 1943, WGW Collection 102: General Correspondence, 1939–50, Box 9, Folder 7, SSFA)

Although it is difficult to determine who is doing what in many of the surviving records, Bill's abilities are clearly evident. Two séances recount communications that Bill received from a control named "Helen Wheat," one of which is undated and the other dated March 30. He also received messages from "GER" on 20 March 1943, from "Euripedes" "on the [Ouija] board" on 11 February 1944, and communicated with a "Mr. Westinghouse" at Anne and Devoe's home in Chappaqua on 25 February 1945, probably also via the Ouija board. The long dialogue with Mr. Westinghouse, which is preserved in several copies, also included communications from "Euripedes," "Moody, the Evangelist," "Ignatius Lyola," and "Herecles" (Séance Book, n.d., SSFA; misspelled names in original).

The content of the communications varied, but many of them were dialogues between the regulars and various spirit controls. As Bill's letter to Dr. Bob indicates, some of these involved communication with or news of dead relatives while others inquired about the spirits' experiences in the other world. In a lengthy dialogue with Helen Wheat, the sitters asked a series of questions about her beliefs when living, her views on various spiritualist beliefs, and her interactions with God ("Have you ever seen God yes. Is God visible to you Yes. Is that God the Father Yes . . . Does God appear to you in human form Yes. Are there such things as great high dietys [sic] no Are there angels Yes Do you ever see them yes") (Séance Book, n.d., SSFA). In the dialogue with Mr. Westinghouse, Mr. Westinghouse grew impatient with the sitters' questions, cutting them off in order to expound at length on metaphysical truths related to "space and time" (ibid.). The tone and content of his communication is reminiscent of the revelations received by Joseph Smith and Helen Schucman from allegedly more elevated sources.

Sometimes the spirits' communications were more personal. On March 30, Helen Wheat informed Lois and Bill that Bill had been "Abraham Lincoln . . . in a previous incarnation" and that "there were 3 AAs in the White Brotherhood [a pantheon of theosophical "masters" most of them discarnate], Bill, Doc Smith & Devoe B[.]" (ibid.). As their references to "spooking" indicates, they took these revelations with a grain of salt. When their AA friend Fitz was in the hospital, Bill wrote Bob, letting him know that "friends across the vale are unanimous that he has cancer probably in the region of the aorta and predict that the doctors won't spot it—do you think that possible? They also say that he will go over presently and they have made him a White Brother in anticipation" (27 July 1943, WGW Collection 102: General Correspondence, 1939–50, Box 9, Folder 6, SSFA). Updating Bob a month later, Bill indicated that Fitz was recovering and cautioned him "not to take our friends across the line too seriously. They can, and have at times, dished out some really malicious misinformation. The low-grade ones I mean. At first you cannot be absolutely positive which is which" (23 August 1943, WGW Collection 102: General Correspondence, 1939–50, Box 9, Folder 6, SSFA).

Two other communications, one from Helen Wheat and the other from "Euripedes," strike me as particularly revealing, because they are specifically addressed to Bill, speak to him regarding his life mission, and offer him guidance and direction. Helen's communiqué instructed Bill to "stop smoking," because he was "being prepared as a chanel [*sic*] for important things."

> You must believe us when we say that you are destined for tremendous development. Please, please, Bill, do this and do not fail us. So much now depends upon your attitude and action. You are a link in a strong chain and you must not be the weakest point. (WGW Collection 101.7: WGW's Automatic Writings, n.d., SSFA)

This development was apparently to proceed along spiritual as opposed to psychic lines, drawing on the "common denominators of all religions" and in doing so offer hope to the world. Communicating through the Ouija board on 11 February 1944, Euripedes stressed somewhat different, yet compatible, themes (WGW Collection 101.7: WGW's Automatic Writings, Box 7, Folder 6, SSFA). He indicated to Bill that "A.A. [was] but the start" of his "mission." This larger mission involved bending "the levers of faith & reason . . . to the simple truth that God is all." When this truth is seen, Euripedes said, "it will encompass faith & science." Euripedes instructed Bill to "Hold firm to [his] convictions that our world [the spirit world] interlocks with yours & that the proofs of this will be completed to the satisfaction of all mankind during your earthly lifetime." He concluded by admonishing Bill to exercise patience in converting those who were skeptical. "[W]hen dealing with psychic matters you do not seem to realize that your listeners are not under the same compulsion that your alcoholic people are. A listener to your psychic discourses will not die if he smiles & turns away."

These messages indicate quite clearly that these two spirits were coaching Bill and offering him guidance relative to his destiny and mission in life. Much as the Lord admonished Joseph Smith for his mistakes, so, too, Helen Wheat was telling Wilson to give up smoking and Euripedes was advising him on how to deal with skeptics. Moreover, both Helen Wheat and Euripedes had a spiritual agenda that Wilson was—in their view—positioned to promote. Helen Wheat's vision for Bill confirmed the direction AAs had taken with the Twelve Steps and encouraged him to draw from the "common denominators of all religions," something he continued to do and that would be particularly evident in *Twelve Steps and Twelve Traditions*. Euripedes's vision for Bill was not incompatible with Helen Wheat's but was more expansive. It extended beyond AA and involved reconciling "faith & reason" based on the "simple truth that God is all" and the conviction that (1) the spirit world "interlocks" with the everyday world and (2) that there would be "proof" of this during Bill's lifetime. This, as we will see, is very much the agenda that Bill hoped to promote in the late fifties, when he sought to give up his role as Mr. AA and pursue his own personal interests.

An undated, handwritten page elaborates on Euripedes's vision, indicating that the reconciliation of faith and reason involves both "bringing reason to Rome & faith to France" and informing Bill that two of his AA connections were in a position to help with this (WGW Collection 101.7: WGW Psychic Phenomena, Box 7, Folder 3, SSFA). This unnamed spirit, referring back to an earlier communication, addressed itself—it appears—to Bill, saying: "[Y]ou have discovered two bridges, one bringing reason to Rome, the other faith to France. Dr. Tiebout the scientist whose great faith is proclaiming God to the psychiatric world. The other bridge is of course Father D[.] who even before he had met you was all ready inspired to bring reason to his fellow priests."

Dr. Harry M. Tiebout was a well-known friend of AA and the first psychiatrist who sought to understand how the spiritual dimension of AA worked. His paper attributing AA's success to the emotional force of religion was published in the *American Journal of Psychiatry* in January 1944 (Tiebout 1944). If "France" was a reference to psychiatry's antireligious origins in Paris under Charcot, then Tiebout was definitely extolling the value of bringing "faith to France." Although the reference to Father D. is more obscure, we have two clues to his identity. In another message, Euripedes, who indicated that he "often visit[ed] the Chicago AA group" and listened in on the gossip there, passed on the news that "[p]oor Father D[.] has been much intoxicated of late."[2] In October 1944, Bill wrote Father Dowling and described the visit of "Brother D[.]" to Stepping Stones. Since the "Brother" and the "Father" have the same last name in the archival records, D. was apparently a friend of Fr. Ed Dowling and a member of the Chicago AA group. As Bill recounted to Dowling, "Brother D[.] saw something of our neighbors, especially Tom P[.], ... [who] has come all the way from belligerent skepticism to the [presen]t where he now most seriously thinks of the church again." At first, Bill hesitated to talk to D. about psychic phenomena due to the "Church party line," but in the end, Bill reported, "there was so much discussion of things Catholic and those phenomena that no one bothered to sleep much" (WGW to Edward Dowling, 16 March 1944, GSOA). Bringing "reason to Rome" thus likely meant incorporating the evidence ostensibly derived from psychical research into Catholicism. As we will see, this double-sided vision of uniting faith and science by spiritualizing psychiatry and rationalizing Catholicism goes a long way toward integrating Bill's disparate enthusiasms.

In a letter to Clem L. four years later, Bill indicated that the realization that he had psychic abilities initially left him with the feeling that he was someone special, much as he felt after his sudden experience at Towns Hos-

---

[2] This message was appended to the communication with Mr. Westinghouse, Sunday, 25 February 1945, at Devoe and Anne B.'s home in Chappaqua, New York.

pital. He told Clem that he went through "the same process [of reassessment] with the psychic phenomena business" as he had with his experience at Towns.

> I am no longer impressed, to any degree, just because I happen to be a little psychic sensitive. A psychic sensitive is apparently a guy who has red hair instead of black. It does not necessarily have a thing to do with the quality of the person. Actually, the world is full of these sensitives. Only most of them don't know it. The only thing surely worth while out of the psychic experiences is the conviction that there is no death. Knowing myself as a poor filter for these impressions, I take every one of them, when they propose to go into detail, with about a tablespoon of salt. (WGW to Clem L., 8 April 1948, GSOA)

It's understandable that the spirits' sense of Bill's outsized mission might have left him feeling he was someone special. But reassessing his abilities relative to others did not involve a denial of the conviction "that there is no death," which was central to the vision that Euripedes promoted. When other AAs wrote to tell him of their psychic experiences over the years, he continued to stress these core convictions. When Charles S. described an "extraordinary psychic experience" in 1957, Bill told him that he got "many such reports" and was "satisfied that many of these occurrences are absolutely genuine." Indeed, he added, "I have experienced some of them myself, and am utterly convinced that life goes on beyond the undertaker and that we are in touch with the unseen around us" (WGW to Charles S., 27 February 1957, GSOA). Bill felt that psychic experiences, both his own and those reported by others, established that there is an unseen world and that life extends beyond death. This conviction, however, also lay at the heart of his sudden experience at Towns and his interest in Catholicism.

CATHOLIC DISCERNMENT

Bill Wilson's interest in Catholicism has puzzled many and seems initially to have also puzzled him. Growing up in rural turn-of-the-century Vermont, where an interest in spiritualism was less remarkable than an interest in Catholicism, it was easy to absorb the usual Protestant suspicions of Catholics (Cheever 2004, 41). In talking to Catholic audiences, he acknowledged that in AA's earliest years he still carried the "uneasy feeling [from his childhood] that Catholicism might be a superstition of the Irish" (Bill W. 1954; see also Fitzpatrick 2012, 87). The shift in his attitude came as a result of his connection with St. Francis as a spiritual exemplar, a prayer attributed to St. Francis that he adopted as a central spiritual practice, and his relationship with Fr. Ed Dowling as his spiritual sponsor. The appeal of Catholicism, in other words, lay in its offer of an ideal that went beyond sobriety, a practice that helped him focus on that ideal, and a spiritual sponsor who could help him discern the path toward that ideal. The Oxford Group, which embraced Jesus as a spiritual exemplar and used "checking" as a process of discernment, did provide resources of this nature, but the Catholic tradition offered a more populated unseen realm than even the most experientially oriented Protestant traditions, and a correspondingly richer and more developed set of resources for navigating it.

Apart from his correspondence, Bill spoke most expansively about Catholicism in two talks that he gave to largely Catholic audiences, the first at LeMoyne College in 1954 and the second at St. Thomas Hospital in Akron in 1965. In the latter talk, given in honor of Sister Ignatia's many decades of work with alcoholics, Bill described "Father Ed [Dowling] and Sister [Ignatia] [as] the channels through which [he] learned the meaning of the church." But he attributes his initial shift in attitude not to Father Ed or Sister Ignatia but to St. Francis (Fitzpatrick 2012, 89). He made the connection to St. Francis, he said, prior to writing the Big Book, apparently in the context of his time in Akron with Bob and Anne. After recounting how Anne Smith's readings from the Bible during their quiet time revived childhood memories of "a few sessions at Congregational Sunday school," he continues:

> I think the beginning of my appreciation [for Catholicism] was made when I first contacted one of the greats of this wondrous church. He came to me across the centuries through the words of a biography written, I think, by a non-Catholic. And at length my eyes fell upon this prayer, which says, "This, Bill, is all that you or anyone could possibly aspire to." Just like the newcomer who comes into AA saying of his sponsor, "This guy practices what he preaches"—so did I look upon Francis. . . . The [big] book was done after this experience, and, as we know, the ideas that went into it stemmed from many sources. But always there was centered in my mind this man of poverty, this man of wisdom, this man of love almost beyond compare. (ibid.)

For Bill, St. Francis was an exemplar of poverty, wisdom, and love, and meditation on the prayer attributed to him served to remind him of his highest aspirations.[3]

Bill compared his connection to St. Francis to the AA who is attracted to a sponsor because the "guy practices what he preaches" and linked this connection to his movement "out of the kindergarten and into the first-grade

---

[3] On the role of this prayer in Bill's spiritual life, see Fitzgerald (1995, 39). The prayer, which opens "Lord, make me a channel of thy peace—that where there is hatred, I may bring love—that where there is wrong, I may bring the spirit of forgiveness" (12&12, 99), though attributed to St. Francis, was actually of much more recent vintage (see Renoux, 2001).

experience." These are telling analogies. The first suggests Bill's need for a sponsor—for a spiritual guide. This is reinforced by his grade school analogy. Bill often referred to this life as a "spiritual kindergarten," which suggests that movement "into the first-grade" represented a step into a larger spiritual world. In his talk at St. Thomas Hospital, Bill positioned his discovery of St. Francis—his virtual sponsor—as the second of three formative experiences, after his "sudden illumination" at Towns Hospital and prior to his meeting with Fr. Ed Dowling, his living sponsor (Fitzpatrick 2012, 87–88).

When Dowling read *Alcoholics Anonymous* shortly after it was published, the parallels between the Twelve Steps and the Spiritual Exercises, developed by the Society of Jesus's founder St. Ignatius of Loyola, struck him and other members of the Jesuit House in St. Louis. Inspired by the parallels, Dowling wrote a piece on AA for the Jesuit magazine, the *Queen's Work*, which he shared with Bill. He then decided to visit unannounced—late, on a bitter, sleeting night in November 1940—at the AA clubhouse in New York where Bill and Lois were still living. As Bill told the story, he initially thought Dowling was another drunk looking for a safe haven in the storm. Instead, it turned out to be another key event in Bill's spiritual journey.

What transpired is hard to say. According to some biographers, they had a long, involved spiritual conversation in which Bill unburdened his heart, working through Step Five ("Admitted to God, to ourselves, and to another human being the exact nature of our wrongs") for the first time (Thomsen 1999, 275–78; Kurtz 1991, 98). When he described their meeting in his talk at St. Thomas Hospital, Bill said he mostly listened. Regardless of how much Bill actually revealed of his personal journey that night, Father Ed took on the role of Bill's spiritual sponsor, and their correspondence provides ample evidence that they discussed spiritual issues close to Bill's heart until Ed's death in 1960. As Bill's secretary and his and Lois's close friend, Nell Wing (1998, 120) said, "overestimating the role Father Ed played as Bill's spiritual sponsor is impossible."

Still, as should already be clear, Bill's relationship with Father Ed did not supersede his interest in spiritualism and psychic phenomena. Insofar as his relationship with Father Ed focused on discernment, Catholicism added a means of assessing his empirical investigations of the unseen realm. Ironically, however, Catholicism was not only layered onto his investigations as a means of discernment, it also infused them. In light of his empirical investigations, Bill could not make a straightforward distinction between Catholicism, spiritualism, and psychic phenomena, first, because the unseen realm that he and his friends explored in their séances was populated with numerous discarnate Catholics, including St. Francis, and, second, because, according to Bill, psychic phenomena confirmed the factual basis of "90% of the Catholic party line" (WGW to Dowling, 16 March 1944, GSOA).

Discarnate Catholics: AA historians offered two firsthand accounts of sé-ances, both of which involved Catholic figures. In the first, Bill described a Ouija board session in which he said, "The [O]uija board got moving in earnest—it was a strange mélange of Aristotle, St. Francis, diverse archangels with odd names, deceased friends—some in purgatory and others doing nicely, thank you! There were malign and mischievous ones of all descrip-tions, telling of vices quite beyond my ken, even as former alcoholics. Then, the seemingly virtuous entities would elbow them out with messages of comfort, information, advice—and sometimes just sheer nonsense" (Séance Book, n.d., SSFA; also quoted in *PIO*, 278). In the second account, Lois described a session where Bill was lying on the couch and would "get these things." Usually, she said, he got things word by word, but in this case it came letter by letter. Lois thought what came through looked like Latin, so Bill showed it to Dick Richardson, who confirmed that it was "perfectly good, though difficult [Latin]" and that, based on the content, it looked "like the beginning of . . . an allegorical account of the founding of the Christian church in Italy" (*PIO*, 279).

Although these stories blend Catholicism and spiritualism, they seem rather incidental to AA. We have a much clearer and more graphic descrip-tion of the role that a discarnate Catholic saint played in the writing of *Twelve Steps and Twelve Traditions*. In a 17 July 1952 (GSOA) letter to Dowl-ing, Bill wrote:

> I have good help [with writing], of that I am certain. Both over here and over there. One turned up the other day calling himself Boniface. Said he was a Benedictine missionary and English. Had been a man of learning, knew missionary work and a lot about structures. I think he said all this more modestly but that was the gist of it. I'd never heard of this gentleman but he checked out pretty well in the Encyclopedia. If this one is who he says he is—of course there is no certain way of knowing—would this be illicit in your book?

Dowling wrote back that the missionary sounded like "Boniface . . . the Apostle of Germany" (24 July 1952, GSOA). With regard to whether their communications were "licit," he hedged, saying, "I still feel, like Macbeth, that these folks tell us truth in small matters in order to fool us in larger. I supposed that is my lazy orthodoxy." He also encouraged Bill to take a look at the "Two Standards Meditation" in the Spiritual Exercises that Bill had asked him to send a few weeks earlier (see also, Fitzgerald 1995, 55–61).

Their discussion of the value of communications with discarnates over the next few weeks illustrates the candor of their exchanges and the nature of their differences. In his allusion to Macbeth and his reference to the Two Standards Meditation, Dowling situated discarnate voices in the context of the Ignatian choice between the Two Standards of Christ and Lucifer. In the meditation, Lucifer is depicted as calling up "innumerable demons . . . ordering them to lay traps for people and to bind them with chains." The demonic forces tempt people to riches, honors, and unbounded pride, while Christ calls people to spiritual poverty, "insults and contempt" rather than worldly fame, and humility rather than pride. Wilson, as we have seen, was well aware of the temptations of riches, honors, and pride.

Writing back (8 August 1952, GSOA), Bill said he was "pretty well convinced that Ignatius rightly portrays the general situation," but, he said, he got stuck on "the Church's deductions from the general situation." He wasn't convinced that things were nearly as clear-cut as Dowling seemed to think. He noted that it is perfectly proper for a Catholic to pray to a saint for assistance, but "if an entity purporting to be Ignatius seems to place specific thoughts or inspiration in my mind, or if I think I have heard him, or seen him, then the whole business becomes highly suspect." He conceded, though, that "great caution is certainly indicated [with respect to such claims], . . . [b]ecause . . . the latitude for flim-flam is so great."

The problem, as Bill intuited, was that any claims to have seen, heard, or received inspiration from a suprahuman entity could easily become a claim to having received (new) revelation. The Catholic Church, then and now, sees itself as the guardian of Truth, fully revealed in Christ, such that there could not be any authentic new revelation. Thus, while the Spiritual Exercises presupposed a lively unseen world populated not only with good and bad spirits in service to the ultimate powers of Christ and the devil, but also an entire panoply of (discarnate) saints open to the petitions of the living, the Society of Jesus was an arm of the church, and its discernment processes were embedded within the framework of church teachings. This meant that while spiritualists and Catholics both presumed the presence of a rich unseen world, the official Catholic view of how Catholics might properly interact with discarnate entities was far more constrained.

Bill found the logic of these constraints unconvincing. As he explained to Dowling (8 August 1952), "I cannot be fully persuaded that unless I communicate only with the Saints of the Church and under the strictest of Church Auspices, I must write off all other communications from deceased people as the certain work of the Devil. It doesn't seem reasonable to think that the Devil's agents have such direct and wide open access to us when other well-disposed discarnates including the Saints themselves cannot get through. That is, in any direct way. . . . I don't see why the aperture should be so large in the direction of the Devil and so small in the direction of all the good folks who have gone ahead of us." Assuming that a wide range of discarnates of varying dispositions might seek to communicate, Bill asked why the same "prudent discrimination and good morality . . . necessary when we deal with people in the flesh" shouldn't "be the rule with discarnates, too?" He added, though, that he offered these thoughts more in the spirit of "speculation than argument, for the spook business is no longer any burning issue so far as I am concerned." While he still sometimes experienced "intrusion[s] such as the one [he] described in the case of the purported Boniface," he was for the most part "quietly detached from the subject" by the early fifties. Reports of "fresh phenomena around A.A." aroused his interest, but for the most part, he simply "retain[ed] the feeling that help does come from across the line but precisely how, [he] could no longer venture to say."

Facts: The bottom line for Bill was that spiritualist phenomena not only established the fact of another world but also confirmed—as he put it—"90% of the Catholic party line." In the wake of Father D.'s visit in 1944, Bill recounted his and Father D.'s discussion of why he hadn't joined the Catholic Church to Father Ed. In a letter dated 16 March 1944 (GSOA), Bill wrote, "I explained that I felt very close to the church partly [due to] my association with Catholics, especially you, partly from [an] unaccountable urge to the Church and partly from the [asto]nishing confirmation of 90% of the Catholic party line which [has] come thru observation of the phenomena." "Naturally," Bill continued, "he wanted to know what about the 10%," which Bill told him "mostly [had] to do with matters of authority and questions of who [is] damned etc."

Father Ed and Bill returned to this theme three years later when discussing infallibility. In a letter dated 1 October 1947 (GSOA), Father Ed argued that the idea of infallibility rested on "an intervention by a Power greater than ourselves," along the lines of the "superhuman intervention" that Bill witnessed at Towns. Bill replied that he did "believe in Intervention," but only in those interventions that were "confirmed evidentially by experience—the Resurrection and return, the healing miracles, spiritual experiences themselves, and the like" (15 October 1947, GSOA). In a letter to Clem L. a year later, in which he downplayed the significance of his psychic experiences, he nonetheless affirmed that "[t]aken in the aggregate, though, the sum total of my psychic experiences do seem to point strongly in the direction of Catholicism" (8 April 1948, GSOA). Moreover, he added, "I doubt if I could now be considering Catholicism if I had not had them. But again, that's anybody's guess." In the early sixties, when he was no longer considering Catholicism, he continued to stress the importance of distinguishing between "pure abstractions and those tentative conclusions which we support by facts." Writing to Colin R. on 28 August 1962 (GSOA), he indicated that "my feeling for immortality is not only founded on faith; I believe it to be founded on some pretty hard facts." Based on his own "psychic experience" and what he had observed "among others," he said, he was "convinced on evidence that human consciousness survives the undertaker."

For him, he said, "this sort of evidence has been helpful," but ever careful not to impose his personal views, he immediately added, "I would be the first to admit that many people are averse to such inquiries, finding them nothing but confusing. Therefore I am sure that each individual has to choose for himself. And, as you remarked, the choice in A.A. is very wide indeed."

PERENNIALIST INTEGRATION

On 29 August 1956, Bill Wilson took LSD for the first time under the auspices of researchers at UCLA. His friends Tom Powers and Gerald Heard took notes. Bill and Tom both took LSD on other occasions in Los Angeles and with a small group in New York (*PIO*, 371). If we were considering Bill's personal spiritual development as a series of phases, we could devote this third section to his experiments with LSD. It makes more sense, I am arguing, to view Bill's interest in LSD as continuous with his empirical interests in spiritualism, psychic research, and mysticism, which he shared with Dr. Bob and Tom, and to recognize that the timing of his decision to investigate LSD wasn't linked to a fundamental shift in interests but to his growing freedom to explore his personal interests as AA "came of age." Viewed in terms of interconnected layers rather than phases, the distinctive feature of this third layer is not his interest in LSD but the drive for synthesis and integration, which lay at the heart of AA's latent perennialism and his own personal beliefs.

The synthetic impulse first surfaced, according to Bill (W. 1945), after reading Dr. Alexis Carrel's *Man, the Unknown* (Harper, 1935) while working on the Big Book. While Carrel's book awakened Bill's sense of himself as a synthesizer, the synthetic process was aided and abetted by a circle of intellectual companions, including Tom Powers, who became an important collaborator after Dr. Bob's death in 1950; the writer, Gerald Heard; and Heard's close friend, Aldous Huxley. All four were writers, although Heard's and Huxley's writings were, of course, far better known. They were all spiritual seekers (Falby 2008, 62–73) intent on both exploring and synthesizing what they learned of other worlds and unseen realms. Eugene Exman, the religion editor at Harper and Brothers, was a mutual friend and collaborator (Hedstrom 2012, 80–114). He not only shared their interests but made Harper and Brothers the leading publisher of books on spiritual topics, including many of Huxley's books and most of Heard's (1941, 1949), as well as AA's *Twelve Steps and Twelve Traditions* and Powers's *First Questions on the Life of the Spirit* (1959).

Although their spiritual journeys differed, they shared the metaphysical conviction that lay at the center of Huxley's best-selling *Perennial Philosophy*: the conviction that there is "a divine Reality substantial to the world of things and lives and minds; the psychology that finds in the soul something similar to, or even identical with, divine Reality; the ethic that places man's final end in the knowledge of the immanent and transcendent Ground of all being" (1945, vii). They also shared the view, again expressed by Huxley, that "the nature of this one Reality is such that it cannot be directly and immediately apprehended except by those who have chosen to fulfill certain conditions, making themselves loving, pure in heart, and poor in spirit" (ibid., viii). In more psychological terms, the central claim was that the individuals could only experience the connection between the "eternal Self" deep within and "the divine Reality," if the "personal ego" was sidelined or, in AA terms, was "deflated at depth."

Although we don't know exactly when Bill first encountered the ideas of Heard and Huxley, we do know that he visited Heard at his religious retreat center in Trabuco Canyon, when he and Lois were in California in 1944 (Lattin 2012, 140; Wing 1998, 124) and then at least twice more before Heard sold the property to the Vedanta Society in 1949. The extensive correspondence between Wilson and Heard dates from the late forties, and their letters and visits were interwoven with his letters and visits with Dowling. This means that Bill and Lois's first visit to Trabuco Canyon took place when the AA "regulars" were engaged in intensive spiritualist investigations and Bill was corresponding with Dowling about joining the Catholic Church.

The fact that Bill told Dowling of his "unaccountable urge to the Church" two months *after* he visited Heard's retreat center in January 1944 suggests the importance of viewing Bill's ambivalent relationship to the Catholic Church in light of the perennialism advocated by Heard, Huxley, and spirits, such as Helen Wheat and Euripedes (WGW to ED, 16 March 1944, GSOA). Although Bill was clearly aware that joining the church would appear as an endorsement and thus a violation of AA's sixth tradition, his personal feelings about the church were sufficiently mixed that joining was never a real possibility. While, on the one hand, Catholicism's "sound core of spirituality"—as exemplified in St. Francis and Dowling—drew Bill to the church, its claims to "rightness" and "infallibility" kept him from it. Cast in positive terms, it was Bill's perennialism, his belief that all the great religions, not just Catholicism, had a "sound core of spirituality" that kept him from joining the church. Three years later, he summed up his still-conflicted feelings in a letter to Dowling (3 September 1947, GSOA): "I'm more affected than ever by that sweet and powerful aura of the Church; that marvelous spiritual essence flowing down the centuries touches me as no other emanation does, but—when I look at the authoritative layout, despite all the arguments in its favor, I still can't warm up."

During the forties and fifties, Wilson actively pursued his interest in psychical phenomena with Powers, Heard, and Huxley. In October 1950, he wrote Heard a long letter detailing the psychic abilities of his sister, Dorothy

Strong, who, he said, had been channeling messages from Camille Flammarion, a deceased astronomer and spiritualist; Heard responded by suggesting that the foursome should get together for another séance (Lattin 2012, 197). In September 1952, Eugene Exman, who was on the board of the newly organized Wainwright House, invited Bill to participate in a seminar he was arranging "for people who might be called Gerald Heard's 'peers' to come together to have informal sessions on the general area of parapsychology. What we want to talk over is the relevance of this means of extrasensory evidence to the intellectual and spiritual life of our time." At Exman's suggestion, Bill invited J. B. Rhine, who ran the parapsychology laboratory at Duke University. Rhine was unable to attend, but Bill updated him on his interactions with Arthur Ford, who had given an impressive "demonstration of mediumship" at the Wilsons' house, and Eileen Garrett, the New York medium who had been willing to participate in controlled tests in Rhine's lab.[4]

Bill hoped that he could retire as Mr. AA and pursue his more personal interests once AA officially "came of age" at its Twentieth Anniversary Convention. Anticipating retirement and the opportunity to expand his mission—much as Euripedes had advised in the midforties—Bill discussed his options with Heard, who suggested he take up "psychic research of some sort." When he mentioned Heard's idea to Rhine, asking "what in heaven's name I could do about psychic research that isn't already being done," Rhine's response was discouraging. "I think the same shrewd realism is working in your hesitation to follow Mr. Heard's advice," he wrote.[5]

> The main fact to consider is that during the last few decades this field of parapsychology has undergone a very great change. It has become a subject of university research and today almost everything worth while is going on either in the universities or under direction from them. The kind of exploring Mr. Heard himself has done now and then, and which had a definite place in the origins of the field, has become more and more peripheral and incidental.[6]

While the older-style investigations of mediums conducted by the Society for Psychical Research had been displaced by controlled laboratory research in parapsychology, new research on the effects of hallucinogenic drugs in the midfifties offered an alternative means of contributing to research that

---

[4] Eugene Exman to WGW, n.d.; WGW to JB Rhine, 22 September 1952; WGW to JB Rhine, 16 October 1952; JBR to WGW, 13 November 1952, Parapsychology Laboratory Records, David M. Rubenstein Rare Book and Manuscript Library, Duke University; hereafter PLR-Duke.
[5] WGW to JB Rhine, 19 and 26 September 1955, PLR-Duke.
[6] Thanks to Philip Deslippe for help in acquiring these letters.

might foster personal spiritual transformation and offer alternative means of accessing the "great reality."

Initially Bill was hesitant, but events soon changed his mind. He and his friends "eagerly purchased" and read *The Doors of Perception*, Huxley's account of the mystical effects induced by mescaline, when the book first came out in 1954. But when Humphry Osmond, the Canadian psychiatrist who had given Huxley the mescaline, contacted Bill to let him know that he and his partner, psychiatrist Abram Hoffer, were using hallucinogens to treat alcoholism, Bill was wary (Wing 1998, 81–83, 124; *PIO*, 369). Positive results from Osmond's and Hoffer's research, along with Huxley's visit to New York in 1956, played a significant role in Bill's decision to experiment with LSD. When Huxley visited, Huxley and Heard were collaborating with Sidney Cohen, a clinical professor at the UCLA Medical Center, who was researching the effects of LSD (Novak 1997; Stevens 1987). In *The Doors of Perception* (1954) and *Heaven and Hell* (1956), Huxley interpreted mescaline and LSD as a means of inducing visionary experiences and entering into "Other Worlds" ([1956] 1990, 99).

Reading *Heaven and Hell* in the wake of Huxley's visit to New York, it looked to Bill as if the experimental research, his personal experience, and the integrative perennialist vision he had long been pursuing were all converging. As he wrote Heard afterward:

> Lois and I have most carefully read his recent "Heaven and Hell." It was one of the most integrating experiences we have known in a long time. We feel positive that he is on precisely the right track. It was astonishing to see how our own psychic experiences, and those of many friends, fitted into the frame of reference that he has drawn. We could almost substantiate every chapter, page and verse. When you see him, will you please tell him this? (1 May 1956; quoted in Lattin 2012, 197)

A few months later, Bill took LSD for the first time at the Los Angeles Veterans Administration Hospital, administered and supervised by Sidney Cohen. Heard and Powers took notes. Bill and Powers both later took LSD at the home of Cohen's associate, Betty Eisner, who was conducting research on the potential therapeutic benefits of LSD, and both were involved in a small group, which also included Exman, that met in people's homes in the New York area between 1958 and 1960 to explore the clinical and spiritual potential of LSD. Bill also induced Lois, Nell Wing, and Fr. Ed Dowling to try LSD at least once (*PIO*, 371; Wing 1998, 81–82; Novak 1997, 97).

It is not hard to see why Bill found reading Huxley's *Heaven and Hell* such an integrative experience. Huxley drew upon geographical metaphors to describe unusual "mental events," arguing that "such metaphors express very forcibly the essential otherness of the mind's far continents." Humans, he said, consist of "an Old World of personal consciousness and, beyond a dividing sea, a series of New Worlds . . . and across another, vaster ocean, at the antipodes of everyday consciousness, the world of Visionary Experience" ([1956] 1990, 84–85). Huxley distinguished between visionary and mystical experiences, locating the former within the realm of opposites, such as heaven and hell, and the latter beyond it. Visionary experiences allowed people to view the ultimate, nondual Ground or Reality from one of many vantage points (New Worlds) outside the ordinary world, including "heaven" and "hell" but not limited to them. Thus, at death, "a minority are capable of immediate union with the divine Ground, a few are capable of supporting the visionary bliss of heaven, a few find themselves in the visionary horrors of hell and are unable to escape; the great majority end up in the kind of world described by Swedenborg and the mediums" from which they may pass "to worlds of visionary bliss or the final enlightenment" (ibid., 139–40). Huxley's vision of multiple other worlds made room for a "posthumous state" of the kind encountered by spiritualists: "a heaven of blissful visionary experience," such as Bill experienced at Towns Hospital, and a hell of "appalling visionary experiences as is suffered here by schizophrenics[,] . . . some who take mescaline," and, of course, alcoholics. But there was also, Huxley said, "an experience, beyond time, of union with the divine Ground" (ibid., 140).

When Bill told Father Ford a year later (14 May 1957) that his Towns experience had convinced him "that God is my Father; that His grace is available to me; that life goes on beyond the grave; and that in His house there are many Mansions," I suspect that Bill interpreted the Christian metaphor of "many Mansions" in light of Huxley's integrative vision. For Bill, the idea of "many Mansions" most likely went well beyond the claim that there were many religious paths to God. It also signaled the presence of other "worlds" or "realms" that could encompass the range of experiences—spiritualist, psychic, visionary, mystical—that Bill and others he knew had experienced and, thus, the presence of multiple otherworldly vantage points from which to apprehend the "great reality."

Huxley's book not only served to integrate the various types of experiences Wilson had had into a unified cosmology, it also identified the core features of his Towns experience—the light and the mountain—as common features of visionary experiences more generally, whether evoked by ascetic practices or drugs (mescaline, LSD, or, perhaps, in Bill's case, belladonna). Thus, Huxley stressed that visionary accounts of "all the Other Worlds and Golden Ages" typically involved "preternatural light, color, and significance" ([1956] 1990, 99). Light, of course, was a central feature of his sudden experience, but Huxley also stressed the role of "transporting landscapes," particularly those that are very far or very near (ibid., 126–27), which likely evoked

Wilson's feeling of elevation and transport. In light of the resonance between Huxley's description and Bill's experience at Towns, it is perhaps not surprising that when Bill took LSD for the first time in Los Angeles a few months later, the experience strikingly resembled his earlier experience at Towns Hospital (Novak 1997, 97).

By late 1959, Eugene Exman and Tom Powers were growing disenchanted with their LSD experiments, and the New York group disbanded shortly thereafter. Some in AA were troubled when they learned of Bill's experimentation, and their response heightened his awareness of the difficulties inherent in stepping down as Mr. AA. He wrote a long letter to Sam Shoemaker discussing the difficulties involved when the "father symbol" of a movement attempts to step aside and what he would do if he were free to pursue his own interests. He devoted most of the letter to spelling out a vision much like the one Euripedes suggested in the midforties (December 1958, WGW to ED; June 1958, Shoemaker letter, *PIO*, 373–76).

> I have come to believe proof surely exists that life goes on; that if better strategy and modern instrumentation were applied to the survival problem, a proof could be made to the satisfaction of everybody. . . . I realize that both science and religion have a really vested interest in seeing that *survival is not proved.* They fear their conclusions might be upset. . . . Everything considered, I feel that full proof of survival would be one of the greatest events that could take place in the Western world today. . . . Easter would become a fact; people could then live in a universe that would make sense. (quoted in *PIO*, 373–74; emphasis in original)

Although when he wrote this in 1958, he still hoped that LSD research would provide a means of providing this proof, I am more struck by the continuity in his vision. Not only is it in accord with the spiritual path that AA charted between organized religion and organized medicine, it embraces Euripedes's vision for uniting faith and reason by proving that life survives death and captures the outcome in distinctively Christian terms: "Easter would become a fact." Nell Wing thought that Bill's "willingness—even eagerness— to step down as leader . . . [made him] absolutely unique among the charismatic leaders of great movements" (1998, 62–63). Bill's willingness to step down was fueled, I suspect, not only by his deep embrace of AA principles but also by his sense that there was more that he was called to do.

A Course in Miracles

Helen Schucman, like Joseph Smith and Bill Wilson, had a strikingly unusual experience—her "subway experience," as she called it—that she, like they, connected with the eventual emergence of an ability to connect with a realm beyond the everyday on a regular basis. In Schucman's case, she linked her subway experience with the later emergence of an internal Voice that she attributed to Jesus and the "scribing" of *A Course in Miracles* (ACIM). In this case, the result of the process was a self-study course and a loose network of students, supported by two official foundations (the Foundation for Inner Peace [FIP]), which publishes the Course in various translations, and the Foundation for *A Course in Miracles* [FACIM], which teaches the Course); several "unofficial" centers, one of which—the Miracle Distribution Center—keeps track of study groups around the world; and a number of independent teachers (Miller 2008, 205–8).

This loose network further illustrates the way in which particular experiences and constellations of collaborators give rise to social formations with specific characteristics. In this case, Helen Schucman and her key collaborators—William Thetford, Kenneth Wapnick, and Judith Skutch—coalesced, like the early Mormons, around the claim that the text she "scribed" at the behest of the "inner Voice" had revelatory import, illuminating a new spiritual path and leading in time to a radical revisioning of traditional Christianity. Yet ACIM—like AA—identified the feeling of "specialness" as the central problem that humans needed to overcome. This, plus Schucman's ambivalent relationship with the Voice and its teachings, undercut any efforts to view her as a "prophet," Jesus as "the Messiah," or Christianity as the one true path. Thus, ACIM, like AA, emphatically declares that it is not a religion and its scribe was not special, while positioning itself as avowedly "spiritual." In proclaiming itself as "one version of a universal curriculum," ACIM adopts an overtly perennialist stance that contrasts with AA's tacit perennialism. In expressing its teachings in "the language of traditional Christianity," which it reinterprets in light of its nondual thought system, ACIM, like the Book of Mormon, makes claims that many theologically informed creedal Christians view as heretical.

As with the Book of Mormon and the Big Book, those involved with the emergence of the Course prior to its publication did not view themselves as acting on their own but as discerning through a process of collective inner guidance how the Voice, who they believed had dictated the Course, would have them guide the Course's way into the wider world. Because the first edition of *A Course in Miracles* initially gave no indication of how it came to be, the transition from the scribing and editing process to the published product was even more sharply demarcated in the case of ACIM than it was with the Book of Mormon or the Big Book of AA. In contrast to the first edition of the Book of Mormon, which highlighted Joseph Smith's role as translator and the Nephite prophets as authors, and the Big Book, which attributed authorship to the anonymous first hundred members of AA, the initial printing of the first edition of ACIM recorded no author, had no preface, and said nothing about how it came into being. When, in response to requests, a pamphlet that explained "How It Came—What It Is—What It Says" was inserted in later printings of the first edition in 1977, it did not disclose the names of "the collaborators" who "recorded" the Course, because, it said, "the *Course* can and should stand on its own" (Schucman 1977, 4). It was, however, incorporated as a preface in subsequent editions with names of the "authors" and their institutional affiliation.

Key Collaborators

Dr. Helen (Cohn) Schucman (1909–81) was the daughter of wealthy New York parents, both half Jewish, but raised by devoutly Christian governesses and baptized at her own request at thirteen. In 1933, she married fellow New York University undergraduate Louis Schucman (1908–99), and for a number of years assisted her husband, a culturally Jewish New York bookseller, in his business before entering graduate school in clinical psychology at NYU (PhD, 1957). In 1958, William Thetford offered her a research position at Columbia University Medical School and later appointed her as chief psychologist at the associated Neurological Institute. Thetford and Schucman collaborated on numerous research papers and, between 1965–72, on scribing the Course. Schucman retired in 1975 and remained in New York City with her husband until her death in 1981. She had little involvement with the Course after 1976. Her husband, Louis, while aware of the Course, was not involved in its production.

Dr. William Thetford (1923–88) was born in Chicago to practicing Christian Science parents of modest financial means. His parents left the church after his older sister died when Bill was seven. A gifted student, Thetford attended DePauw University on a scholarship and earned his doctorate in

FIGURE 7.1. The key collaborators, 1976: Helen Schucman (*left*), Judith Skutch (*right*), Kenneth Wapnick (*left*), Bill Thetford (*right*). © Foundation for Inner Peace.

psychology at the University of Chicago (1949). He held a number of academic and government research positions prior to his appointment as associate (later full) professor of medical psychology at Columbia University Medical School and director of clinical psychology at Columbia-Presbyterian Hospital in New York City. In addition to research, teaching, and administrative duties, he coedited the *APA Journal of Abnormal Psychology* from 1965–71. After he retired from Columbia in 1978, he moved to Tiburon, California, with Judith and Robert Skutch and died there in 1988.

Dr. Kenneth Wapnick (1942–2013) was brought up in a Jewish home in Brooklyn but rejected religion as an adolescent. He developed an interest in mysticism in his twenties, completed a doctorate in clinical psychology (PhD, Adelphi University, 1968), and, influenced by the writings of Thomas Merton, was baptized in 1972 with the intention of becoming a monk. Shortly thereafter he met Thetford through Thetford's student Fr. Benedict Groeschel; Wapnick almost immediately became a core member of the ACIM team, helping with the editing of the Course and its movement into the world. With his second wife, Gloria (m. 1981), he created the Foundation for *A Course in Miracles* in 1983 to train teachers of the Course. He and his wife remained in the New York City area until 2001, when they moved their foundation to Temecula, California. Wapnick wrote numerous books on the Course, as well as *Absence from Felicity*, a biography of Schucman, before his death in 2013.

Judith (Rothstein) Skutch (Whitson) (b. 1931) grew up in an upper-middle-class Jewish family in Brooklyn, the daughter of an internationally promi-nent Jewish lay leader. Shortly after graduating from Hood College in 1951, she married and raised two children. In the late sixties, she took courses in parapsychology at the New School for Social Research and taught courses in parapsychology at New York University. In 1971 she and her second hus-band, Robert Skutch (m. 1966), established the Foundation for ParaSensory Investigation, which she directed, to fund research and conferences on the subject. She met Schucman and Thetford in 1975 and, like Wapnick, almost immediately became a core member of the team. In 1976, the team estab-lished the Foundation for Inner Peace in order to oversee the publication of the Course, with Judith Skutch as its first president and the others as board members. The Skutches moved to Tiburon, California, in 1978. They were divorced in 1981 and Judith married Dr. William (Whit) Whitson in 1984. Judith Skutch Whitson, Robert Skutch, William Whitson, and Judith's daughter, Tamara Morgan, are all current members of the foundation board.

SOURCES AND BEGINNINGS

As was the case with Smith and Wilson, we lack real-time sources for Schuc-man's initial "subway experience." Moreover, because ACIM downplayed Schucman's "specialness," as AA did Wilson's, her subway experience, while personally significant, did not function as a "prophetic call experience" in the way Smith's "first vision" did in Mormonism. In all the early accounts of ACIM's origins, the story begins not with her subway experience but with her colleague William Thetford's "there must be another way" speech in June 1965. Joining with Thetford in searching for a solution initiated a series of unusual experiences on Schucman's part over the next few months, lead-ing into to the emergence of the Voice and the scribing of the Course.

We have a comparatively rich set of sources for reconstructing the emer-gence of ACIM in the wake of Thetford's speech:

- *Absence from Felicity* (1st ed. 1991 [2nd ed. 1999]; hereafter *AFF*), Kenneth Wapnick's biography of Schucman, written from primary sources and firsthand knowledge from the point of view of a Course insider;
- letters from Schucman to Thetford during the period in which the Voice was emerging (extensively quoted in *AFF*);

- a journal that Thetford kept for a time while they were scribing the *Course* (extensively quoted in *AFF*);
- transcriptions of Schucman's notebooks (copyright by Kenneth Wapnick and unavailable to researchers, apart from copies "illegally" posted on the Internet);[1]
- an early typed version of the Course (nicknamed the "Urtext") that contains "special messages" for Schucman and Thetford (copyright held by FACIM and unavailable to researchers, apart from copies "illegally" posted on the Internet);
- authorized and unauthorized versions of the published Course, including the Hugh Lynn Cayce version, the Criswell version, and the three editions published by FIP;
- retrospective autobiographies from both Schucman (1975; referred to as HS in text) and Thetford (1983; referred to as WT in text;), available on the FIP website;
- early interviews with Schucman (1976), Skutch (1977) and Thetford (1984), as well as other early articles published in *New Realities Magazine*, all available on the FIP website;
- *Journey Without Distance* (1984a; hereafter *JWD*), Robert Skutch's account of the emergence of the Course, written with the support of Judith Skutch, William Thetford, and Kenneth Wapnick;
- *A Still, Small Voice: A Practical Guide on Reported Revelations* (1993), a later dissenting interpretation of events from Fr. Benedict Groeschel, a student of Thetford's and one of the first people with whom Thetford shared portions of the Course, written from a Catholic theological perspective;
- later interviews with the people involved at this early stage, some in the FIP archives and some done by other authors and quoted in their books (see, for example, Howe 2009 and Vahle 2009).

---

[1] There are copyright issues surrounding some of the primary materials. A court case brought by Penguin Books for the Foundation for Inner Peace and the Foundation for *A Course in Miracles* against the New Church of Full Endeavor and the Endeavor Academy in 1996, and settled in 2003, placed the "Criswell edition" of the Course in the public domain in the United States (see *Penguin Books v New Christian Church*, No. 96 Civ. 4126). Earlier versions, including the typed version that Helen Schucman and Bill Thetford shared with Hugh Lynn Cayce (the HLC version) and the "Unpublished Writings of Helen Schucman" (hereafter Notes) and A Course in Miracles Manuscripts (hereafter Urtext) that Kenneth Wapnick copyrighted and deposited at the Library of Congress in 1990, were illegally copied and made available on the Internet (see Wapnick, n.d.). Because the Library of Congress currently has no record of these holdings, I worked from the Internet versions of the Notes and Urtext in reconstructing the initial months of scribing the Course. Most of the material I cite, using Thompson's (2008) citation system, is included without specific citations in Wapnick's *Absence from Felicity*; quotations from other portions of the Notes and Urtext have been kept to a minimum in accordance with fair use practices, specifically, "quotation of short passages in a scholarly or technical work, for illustration or clarification of the author's observations."

The nature of the sources allows us to focus on the interplay between individual abilities and small group interactions under three broad headings: "Emergence," on the emergence of the Voice (chapter 7); "Teaching(s)," which focuses on the teachings of the Course and the Voice as the teacher of Schucman and Thetford during the initial phases of scribing the Course (chapter 8); and "Roles," on the roles that they played in the process during the periods in which the Course was scribed, edited, and published (chapter 9).

Emergence

In 1975, with Kenneth Wapnick's encouragement, Helen Schucman prepared an autobiography that now exists in "eight and a half—mostly similar—versions." Part 1 of the autobiography was taken from a graduate school paper that she wrote long before she began scribing *A Course in Miracles*, but the remainder was written after it was scribed. According to Wapnick,

> It was mutually understood by us that her unpublished autobiography was hardly a true and accurate account of her life, being rather an over stylized, literary rendering—her public stance—that did not truly reflect the deeper level of Helen's feelings and experiences. Our one attempt to correct the inaccuracies and edit out the distortions, while an improvement in some places, proved in many others to be even worse than the original. Recounting certain events in her life—especially those of a religious nature, and even more specifically, those events surrounding *A Course in Miracles*—aroused tremendous anxiety in Helen, and her discomfort directly led to an almost fierce over-editing that affected the faithfulness of her life's retelling. It was out of this context, therefore, that I said to Helen that I would write her story, as well as the related events—inner and outer—that preceded, accompanied, and followed her taking down the Course. Helen agreed that this was a good idea. (*AFF*, 1–2)

Wapnick's biography of Schucman is a remarkable source in its own right, simultaneously a scholarly biography that handles its primary source material with critical sophistication and transparency and an insider's interpretation of Schucman's life from the point of view of the Course (*AFF*, 15). As Wapnick indicates in his preface, Helen's ambivalent feelings about the Course, as well as her and Thetford's inability to realize its teachings in their own relationship, resulted in accounts of Schucman and her relation to the Course, even prior to her death, that they felt were distorted. Wapnick wrote the biography to explain what Schucman herself was unable to explain: her ambivalent relationship with God and Jesus, the two sides to her personality, and her relationship with Thetford.

Although Wapnick acknowledged that Helen's "ambivalence toward her parents and organized religion . . . provid[e] a goldmine for a psychologist seeking to find psychodynamic causes for her inner experience," he viewed her ambivalence as "reflective of [the] deeper God-ego conflict" that lies at the heart of the Course's teachings. Thus, Wapnick interpreted the "ultimate origins of [Helen's] conflict . . . [as] born on a raging battlefield of a trans-temporal mind far greater than its tiny expression we call Helen Schucman" (*AFF*, 3). Wapnick's biography is therefore not only a biography but also a spiritual interpretation of Schucman and the Course that seeks to make sense of the unusual relationship between the Course and its scribe. In Wap-nick's hands, as Olav Hammer observes, "the story of Schucman and the others involved in the early days of A Course in Miracles can in itself be made to serve as an illustration of the basic principles of the Course" (2001, 449). This reading, as Hammer points out, can be inverted, such that from an outside perspective, her metaphysics can be read as a projection of her own internal division (ibid., 449). In Part 2, I will read all three case studies as attempts to resolve personal or familial dilemmas in ways that others also found compelling and in turn gave rise to new formations. In that sense, they were highly successful "projections" that enlisted others and were widely embraced. Here, I will simply argue that, while Wapnick interpreted Schucman's life in light of the metaphysics of the Course, we can reread the evidence to reconstruct a more dynamic process that forged long-standing tensions and tendencies into a deeply divided self.

BEGINNINGS

The three-part pamphlet describing "How It [the Course] Came—What It Is—What It Says" (Schucman 1977) was a joint production of Schucman and the Voice. According to the version that now forms the preface to *A Course in Miracles* (FIP 3rd, vii), Schucman wrote the first two sections her-self; the third was received through "inner dictation." In "How It Came," which quotes portions of her earlier autobiography, Schucman began the story of the Course with "the sudden decision of two people [Schucman and Thetford] to join in a common goal." She said that who they were did not matter. The crucial thing was that God was able to act through them despite the fact that "their lives were hardly in accord with anything that the Course advocates." They were, she wrote, "anything but spiritual" and "their rela-tionship with each other was difficult and often strained." They were in-vested in "the values of the world," for example, "personal and professional acceptance and status." At the time, in other words, they were pursuing what

FIGURE 7.2. William Thetford and Helen Schucman in New York City, 1965.
© Foundation for Inner Peace.

the Course refers to as "specialness," that is, "the idea of sin made real" (FIP
3rd T-24.II.3:1) and "always at the cost of peace" (FIP 3rd T-24.II.2.1). It was
in this context of discord and dissension that, Schucman wrote, "[t]he head
of my department [Thetford] unexpectedly announced that he was tired of
the angry and aggressive feelings our attitudes reflected, and concluded that
'there must be another way.' As if on cue, I agreed to help him find it. Apparently this Course is the other way."

Although we do not have a real-time account of this June 1965 conversation between Thetford and Schucman, both they and Wapnick characterize
them as temperamentally very different, their relationship as very interdependent and at the same time turbulent and filled with animosity (HS,
26–27; WT, 14). Wapnick, who got to know them both well some seven
years later, described their relationship, which he viewed as essentially unchanged, in the wake of scribing the Course. Generally, he wrote, "they
would argue throughout the day, and then in the evening would often spend
another hour or so on the phone going over their mutual grievances, each of
them desperately convinced of the correctness of his and her position. Constantly critical of each other, their discussions were seemingly endless" (AFF,
80–81). At the same time, he said, their "hostility . . . existed, paradoxically,
in the context of a mutual trust and support that defied rational psychological explanation" (AFF, 80).

Theirs was, in short, a highly enmeshed relationship that Thetford and
others who knew them both thought was fueled in part by sexual tensions.
According to Wapnick, "[a]t first Helen had felt attracted to Bill. . . . Bill's
lack of sexual interest in her [as a gay man] was perceived by Helen as ef-

fectively thwarting her desire to control him sexually" (*AFF*, 81). Thetford later alludes to this dynamic as well, stating that he played multiple roles for Helen. "I was her boss, her fantasy love object, her savior in terms of this material [the Course], and I was expected to do everything that had to be done at all times. I was a substitute for her husband, her brother, and her father. I was supposed to make up for her feelings about her father, and what he didn't do in her life. I don't know why I accepted this. It was a very complicated relationship. At the same time I felt a lot of emotional dependency on Helen, although I was clearly the person in charge. . . . In our relationship we became so mutually interdependent that it was very difficult for either one of us to function in any other way" (WT, 24–25).

Carol Howe, who became close friends with Thetford after he moved to California, highlights Thetford's role as an unrequited "fantasy love object" for Schucman, but notes that Schucman's "obsession with Bill" did not preclude genuine devotion to her husband (2009, 70). Schucman's feelings, which came out in numerous contexts, became particularly intense when Thetford spent time on Long Island during the summer. According to Wapnick, "Helen felt that Bill used the [beach] house in part as a way of avoiding her, and she resented it very much. She was able to persuade Bill and his friends to allow Louis [her husband] and her to come out, which they did fairly often" (*AFF*, 121). According to Howe, "[when] Bill and a number of his close friends rented a house . . . on Fire Island, an area known for its gay community, Helen insisted they rent a place with a room for her and Louis as well" (2009, 70). When he later purchased his summer place in Watermill, Long Island, with a married couple, "Helen actually paid for a room and bath to be added to the house for her and her husband."

Helen's letters to Bill at Watermill in the summer of 1965, a few months after his speech about finding a better way, provide real-time illustrations of the dynamic between them. In them, Helen discussed her resentment, admitting forthrightly that she "hated Watermill, probably above all places on the face of this earth" (*AFF*, 128). Hoping to change, she reflected on her upcoming visit, writing Bill that "Watermill will represent a rather severe test," because she had invested it with a great deal of symbolic significance, which she had come to feel was not justified (*AFF*, 128). She continued:

> However much rationalization I may have applied to this most disastrous state of affairs [i.e., hating Watermill], it remains my responsibility to undo a symbol of so much evil. . . . I am quite afraid of Watermill, because I think it's a real threat to me. . . . I have really prayed that I will not misunderstand things [on her upcoming visit], and see them wrong. . . . I hope that by the time I leave Watermill this time, I will do so with thanks and a sincere blessing for the house and every-

FIGURE 7.3. Bill Thetford and friends on the porch of his summer house, Watermill, Long Island, New York, July 1959. © Foundation for Inner Peace.

body there. I don't know if I can really make this, but I hope, at least, I will make a very genuine effort. (quoted in *AFF*, 129–30)

Wapnick commented that, although "she did make the attempt," she didn't succeed. "[Y]ears afterwards she was still unable to speak of Watermill without bitterness and anger towards Bill" (*AFF*, 130–31).

We will revisit their complicated relationship in this and subsequent chapters on ACIM and consider Schucman's motivations more fully in chapter 12; for now I want to return to the way they cast the beginning of the story. Two features are worth noting. First, despite the difficulties in their relationship, all their accounts—Helen, Bill, and Ken—found something mysterious and meaningful in their coming together. This will be a recurrent theme; although their relationship was very difficult, they shared a deep spiritual connection. Second, the usual insider accounts of Bill's "there must be another way" speech depict the speech as a response to the tensions between them and within their department, and consistently portray Helen and Bill—to quote Helen—as "anything but spiritual." Wapnick's *Absence from Felicity* is in large part devoted to offering a more complex reading of Helen's conflicted relationship with God. Here I want to offer a more complex interpretation of Thetford, which I think has been obscured partly by matters of definition and partly by a desire to see both Helen and Bill as unprepared for what unfolded.[1] Although scholars have noticed various parallels and potential influences, such as Christian Science, New Thought, and the writings of Carl Rodgers and Edgar Cayce (Hammer 2001, 448–49), Bill's retrospective account of the emergence of the Course offers evidence to suggest that his reading of Hugh Lynn Cayce's book about his father, Edgar, a month before his "impassioned speech" gave him (1) a sense that there might be a better way and (2) a way to go about finding it.

Looking back, Thetford claims that his "spiritual journey" began the day he made his "impassioned speech to Helen . . . and when she agreed to help find it [a better way]." Much depends, however, on where we locate the beginnings and how we define "spiritual." Thus, although Bill said his "spiritual journey" began with his speech, he also said that he was in a transitional period in which he was starting to question whether his focus on "professional achievement and recognition" was as "important or significant" as he'd been assuming, and he was becoming more open to "spiritual direction." In addition, although he said he "didn't have any spiritual interests at the time," he mentioned that he read Hugh Lynn Cayce's book *Venture Inward* (1964) the month before his impassioned speech.[2] He said that this was an unusual choice on his part, and he remembered having the following reaction:

> I remember thinking it didn't seem to me that Hugh Lynn Cayce was making this story up, although it was obviously preposterous by ordinary standards. I believed in telepathy anyway, as I had had my own experiences with that. Yet I had a feeling that all these improbable things he said about his father, Edgar Cayce the noted psychic, were true. If they were, I would have to think about this whole thing differently and open my mind to other possibilities. Hugh Lynn's accounts of major healings at a distance, paranormal experiences, and the possibility that the "Lost Continent of Atlantis" once really existed, any of that, if true, could permeate other aspects of my thinking. . . . I knew that if I accepted any of this . . . then I would have to . . . change an awful lot. Yet I wasn't sure at all how much of this was true, but I

---

[1] Thus, for example, in an early interview, Judith Skutch said: "It was important for me that neither of these two people had the background or interest in spiritual literature or psychical experiences that might have prepared them for this" (1977, 7).

[2] Despite Helen's claim that Bill did not come across Hugh Lynn Cayce's book about his father until after the third series of visions began (HS, 35; *AFF*, 103–4), Bill's detailed recollection of reading the book prior to his passionate speech suggests that either Bill did not tell her about the book until later or that Helen rearranged her autobiography for narrative effect, as Wapnick indicated she was wont to do.

was also aware that I might need to find out. So in 1965 I arranged a trip for Helen and me to do just that. We went down to Virginia Beach to visit the Association for Research and Enlightenment (ARE), the organization established to preserve and study Edgar Cayce's life and readings. Helen was impressed with Hugh Lynn Cayce and the people there. I always felt that that trip gave her permission to do what she did. (WT, 15)

There are a number of significant details here. First, Bill indicated that he believed in telepathy because he had had his own experiences with it. Although Bill described himself as an "agnostic" and lacking in "spiritual interests" at the time of his impassioned speech (see also Thetford interview, 1984, part 2), he apparently did not view his belief in and experiences with telepathy as spiritual. These experiences, however, clearly shaped his response to reading Hugh Lynn Cayce's book and suggest why he may have been drawn to the book in the first place.

Second, although some might view Bill's statement "that 'there must be a better way'" simply as a response to frustration, I think his outburst was infused by a hope that emerged in response to reading Cayce's book, which claimed that "venturing inward" would provide "spiritual and psychological insight" and thus was a means of finding a "better way" (Cayce 1964, 203). Since Bill's reading of the book left him with a feeling that the improbable claims discussed in the book were true, I think a Cayce-inspired feeling that there could be a better way infused his frustrated outburst and, in the wake of Helen's positive response, shaped how he guided their search.

Third, in retrospect, Bill highlighted two events in September 1965—a trip to Virginia Beach to visit Hugh Lynn Cayce and the paranormal events surrounding a trip to Mayo Clinic—as pivotal. He referred to the Virginia Beach trip as giving Helen "permission to do what she did" and, in an interview in 1984, to the Mayo Clinic trip as "crystalliz[ing] the whole new direction that we would take" (Thetford 1984, part 1). Both—in Bill's post hoc reading of events—served to confirm that Helen's "extraordinary experiences" over the summer were evidence of paranormal abilities. These details suggest that Bill's interest in and previous experiences of the paranormal triggered (1) his call for another way, (2) his framing of Helen's unusual experiences over the summer, and (3) their visit to Virginia Beach to see Hugh Lynn Cayce in September, after the Voice emerged but before it began to dictate the Course.

Helen's unusual experiences over the summer, however, did not simply arise spontaneously in response to their "joining," but arose in the context of meditation practices that Hugh Lynn Cayce specifically recommended and that Bill suggested they adopt. These practices, which Hugh Lynn Cayce recommended "as the safest and surest way to the higher levels of the unconscious" (1964, 217), involved a daily discipline of "stilling and focusing consciousness so that higher areas of the unconscious [could be] unlocked" (ibid., 202). As developed and taught at ARE conferences in Virginia Beach after Edgar Cayce's death in 1945, the practices were much like other mantra- or affirmation-based practices that taught meditators to focus their attention on an affirmation and return to the affirmation whenever the mind was distracted. In its goal of accessing the higher self or the Divine within through a "boundless unconscious," the practice was clearly in keeping with the metaphysical tradition shaped by New Thought, psychical research, and the psychologically informed perennialism that also shaped Bill Wilson.

Echoing words that would frame the emergence of the Course, Cayce wrote that "[t]hrough meditation the 'inner self,' 'the higher self,' 'the oversoul,' 'the Divine within,' is awakened and the energy and power from it pours into the stream of daily activity, providing guidance and a strengthening of the will to choose the 'better way' " (1964, 203). Moreover, according to Cayce, the endpoint of the practice was "the point of stillness." This point of stillness was associated with "light," which could vary from a tiny point of light to "a warm, enveloping, penetrating flow of light." At this point, in which "consciousness . . . can be moved to the light[, he said,] . . . there will be a knowing, an awareness, which cannot be described, for the meaning is different for every man." Symbolically, Cayce associated this movement into the light with Jesus's parable of the prodigal son, framing it in Christian terms, such that "the prodigal son of man's consciousness which has been lost in matter proclaims at this point, 'I will return to my Father' " (ibid., 207).

Helen indicates in her autobiography that "Bill was convinced [that meditation] would be helpful to us, but . . . I did not understand [it] and found [it] vaguely frightening. Bill, however, was reading books on the subject, and I listened to his eager accounts with some irritation. I did not feel that our agreement to try a new approach to problems justified entering into 'crackpot' areas . . . like ESP, flying saucers, spirits from another world, and Indian mysticism" (quoted in *AFF*, 86–87). At his urging, however, she overcame her "considerable resistance" and agreed that they would both meditate "for a few minutes . . . when we woke up, and before going to sleep at night. It was during these times [she continued] that the first picture sequence began" (HS, quoted in *AFF*, 86–87). In other words, it was in the context of these meditation practices that the mental "picture sequences," which will be discussed in the next section, started to emerge and develop into the Voice. If Thetford hadn't read Cayce's *Venture Inward*, he might well have expressed his frustration in an impassioned outburst and might even have expressed a desire to find another way, but he would not—I am suggesting—have had an inner feeling that there actually was another way and that venturing inward was the means of discovering it.

Thetford's and Schucman's retrospective autobiographies thus provide evidence to indicate that the beginnings of the Course were profoundly shaped by Thetford's sense (1) that there was another way, specifically, an "inward way"; (2) that this inward way could provide spiritual and psychological insight ("a better way") based on psychic discoveries; (3) that these psychic discoveries could be most safely accessed by means of daily meditation practices that quieted the conscious mind and led to an experience of light; and (4) that the experience of light would be linked to "a knowing, an awareness" associated with a "return to [the] Father."

THE EMERGENCE OF THE VOICE

Schucman's undated letters, which were most likely written during the summer between Thetford's speech in June and the scribing of the Course in October 1965, provide real-time evidence of the emergence of the Voice and can be supplemented with her 1975 autobiography, which, as Wapnick indicated, was a stylized retrospective rendering of the events of this period. Because the letters are not dated and the autobiography describes her unusual experiences during this period thematically, we cannot reconstruct a precise chronology of events. In his biography, Wapnick included extensive excerpts from Helen's letters, which he sequenced based on internal evidence (*AFF*, 119, 191). The nine surviving letters, which are all highly introspective, make frequent references to phone conversations between Bill and Helen after work and while they were on vacation. They offer Helen's reflections on herself, Bill, and others, as well as the interactions between herself and Bill (Letters 1, 2, 3, 5, 6, 8, 9); they recount significant dreams (Letter 3) and mental "picture sequences" that came to her during the day, often while she was meditating (Letters 4, 5, 6); and they refer to communications between her and a capitalized other, variously designated as "It" or an "Authority" giving "Orders" (Letters 6, 7, 8).

Although Wapnick's and my analysis of the emergence of the Voice are compatible in a number of respects, we part company at key points. First, although Wapnick excerpted and discussed the real-time evidence, he presupposed the existence of Jesus and viewed the process as one in which Helen progressively allowed an ever-present Voice to speak. He claimed that Helen had a lifelong relationship with Jesus, "whether or not she chose to accept the fact" (*AFF*, 45). He did so based on Helen's long-standing attraction to religion, particularly Catholicism; her deeply ambivalent feelings about her attraction; and their shared devotional relationship with Jesus in the period after the Course was scribed. In light of his reading of Helen, Wapnick interpolates "Jesus" (in square brackets) into some of the primary sources from this period at points where Helen refers simply to a nonspecific, capitalized entity. At the same time, and in seeming contradiction,

Wapnick highlights ideas that she discussed in her own voice that were more fully developed later by the Voice of the Course, perhaps in an effort to counteract the idea that Helen was spiritually insensitive (*AFF*, 191–92). Rather than assume that "Jesus" was present all along, I interpret the Voice as an emergent phenomenon. In the initial stages of the process, I interpret Helen's references to capitalized entities as indications of what she was willing to say to Bill at any given point in time and then, once another voice begins to speak through Helen (in its own voice, as it were), I analyze the way it characterizes itself. Even though in time the Voice clearly self-identified as Jesus, Helen and Bill often referred to it simply as the Voice.[3] I will generally refer to it with whatever term seems most appropriate to the context.

Second, Wapnick and I differ in our metaphysics. Wapnick, in keeping with the nondual metaphysics of the Course, understands the divisions within Helen as exemplifying the division of the self into an illusory ego-self convinced of the reality of the material world and a higher self that recognizes that it is an eternal aspect of the oneness that is God's Son, an emanation of a loving God, which is all that is real. Our ordinary (false) selves are a developmental product of ultimately illusory mind-brain processes, but our true Selves (our higher selves) are an unchangeable, timeless part of God. Since the brain, evolution, and time are all illusory from the point of view of the Course, the naturalistic explanation I will develop more fully in Part 2, which presupposes the finite, time-bound reality of human evolution, breaks with the epistemology of the Course.

As in the previous case studies, I argue that we can understand the Voice as emerging in the context of the interaction between Helen and Bill and more specifically in the context of the practices they initiated as a means of finding a better way in the wake of Bill's speech. These interactions between Helen and Bill elaborated tensions and tendencies within Helen that had previously surfaced primarily in dreams and seemingly spontaneous experiences and refined them into two distinct alternating selves, an "ego self" and a "higher self," the latter capable of "channeling" Jesus, understood in the context of the American metaphysical tradition, as the Christ within us all. The metaphysical notion of the "Christ within" posited an integral connection between the higher self and Christ, which makes it impossible to make

---

[3] Accordingly, Wapnick writes, "Bill never did get over his discomfort with the person of Jesus, and preferred to speak of him as 'J.C.,' the Holy Spirit as 'the H.S.,' or more often than not he simply used the more impersonal term 'Guidance'" (*AFF*, 442n100). According to Judith Skutch Whitson, "Helen and Bill were both 'embarrassed' by the fact that people would not understand the Source, especially since they felt they were not referring to the 'historical Jesus' but rather to that spirit representing unconditional love and forgiveness. Bill always called it the Voice when speaking to me when he was seriously discussing the Course. He sometimes would indeed jokingly use the short hand 'J.C.' when he was in a playful mood" (e-mail communication, 13 October 2014).

a sharp distinction between Helen's higher self and Christ (or God's Son in the terms of the Course). Wapnick acknowledged this when he indicated that Schucman was not simply "a blank channel through whom Jesus dictated," but, "when identifying with her healed mind [her higher self], she was the Voice of Wisdom" (*AFF*, 177).

We can track the emergence of the Voice, first, by exploring Helen's visualization abilities as they emerged in the context of meditation and then by analyzing the content of this inner process in the context of Helen and Bill's relationship.

Visualization Abilities: Before she introduced the series of visions she experienced that summer in her autobiography, Helen paused to explain her ability to see "very clear mental pictures" when she closed her eyes:

> They were so much a part of my own awareness that I thought they happened to everyone. The pictures could be of anything. . . . Sometimes I would recognize part of a picture as related to something I had actually seen, but even then there were details I know had not been there originally. Most of the pictures did not seem to be associated with anything. A few other images I identified as my own imaginary pictures of how someone I was going to see would look, or what a place I was going to visit would look like. Pictures of this kind rarely turned out to be accurate, but they still rose to mind in connection with the people or places originally giving rise to them. The pictures were particularly sharp just before I fell asleep, but I often became aware of distinct visual images during the day even when my eyes were open, while I talked with someone else and even when I was by myself. In fact, the pictures seemed almost to represent the words or thoughts as corresponding symbols at a different but related level of consciousness. They could come at virtually any time. They did not interrupt or even disturb my overt activities in any way. It was as if there were a constant mental activity going on in the background that could be brought to the foreground at any time I chose to notice it. (quoted in *AFF*, 85–86)

Helen noted that her mental pictures changed during the summer.

> For years the pictures had been motionless and exclusively black and white, appearing much like a series of "stills," often without any obvious relationship or progression. As our "adventure in cooperation" continued, however, the pictures began to take on color and motion, and soon afterwards frequently appeared in meaningful sequences. So, too, did my dreams, which often continued with themes begun before

I fell asleep or with images from dreams of the preceding night. (quoted in *AFF*, 86)

After recounting the "three more or less distinct sequential lines of fantasy and dream images" in her autobiography (HS, 28), Helen indicated that "Bill was very much interested in these picture series," but that her husband Louis was not. As a consequence, she provided Bill with "a running account of the episodes as they occurred" and made a point of not sharing them with her husband (HS, 35).

If we turn to the letters, we have evidence of how these changes unfolded in real time. In Letter 3, Helen commented parenthetically that "the funniest things come to me in meditation," adding that "it worries me a little, but I guess it's all right" (*AFF*, 135). In Letter 4, she told Bill, "I don't have visions, but sometimes pictures come to me. They used to be perfectly still, but they seem to include much more action now. Also, they have come to be much more associated with me, instead of a kind of nameless person, or place, or thing suspended in motionlessness" (*AFF*, 141). She then recounted a picture sequence that "crossed [her] mind while [she] was meditating," at the same time, reminding him (Bill) that meditation was "a thing [he] very much want[ed] [her] to do."

Also in Letter 4, Helen indicated her sense that some of the picture sequences were "just for [her], but others are imperatively for both of [them]" and indicated the means she was using to distinguish them. "The rule (for now)," she said, "seems to be that anything that has to do with light, sight, or brightness is also for you" (*AFF*, 141). In describing the picture sequences and the rule, she tacitly suggested some sort of intentionality behind their emergence. The picture sequences were not simply random events triggered by focusing attention on her mental images; instead they were more like communications that she was supposed to convey to the right people based on the "light rule." Nor did she associate the light rule with Cayce's book, though he indicated that the "venture inward" culminated in the merging of consciousness with the light; rather, she stated the rule as if it, like the images, had been communicated to her from elsewhere.

In light of this evidence, I would suggest the following interaction between Schucman's visualization abilities and the practices introduced by Thetford:

(1) In the wake of his passionate speech, Bill convinced Helen to start meditating. As she says in Letter 4, "It annoyed [her] to death at first, but it's gotten to be very restful" (*AFF*, 141).
(2) At some point, perhaps in the context of meditation, the motionless, black-and-white mental images that had appeared to her all her life as background mental activity began to take on color and motion and ap-

pear in meaningful sequences (*AFF*, 86). These picture sequences could appear in dreams, on the border between sleeping and waking, or during the day, most often while meditating.

(3) Since Bill was very much interested in the picture sequences, Helen provided him with a running account of what was unfolding internally—at work, over the phone, and through letters when one of them was out of town. Much of what transpired over the summer appears not to have been recorded, although in Letter 3, Helen indicated that Bill had encouraged her to write down one of her dreams and, after their trip to ARE in Virginia Beach in September, Bill convinced her to begin keeping a "sort of diary" of her experiences, which has since been lost (*AFF*, 167).

(4) Helen received the impression that not all the picture sequences were "intended" for Bill, along with a sense of how to tell the difference based on whether the sequences had anything to do with "light, sight, or brightness."

The process was clearly highly interactive. Bill precipitated it with his passionate speech and structured it around meditation. Helen reluctantly took up meditation, which led to an increased focus on and shifts in the nature of her mental imagery. Encouraged by Bill, Helen provided him with a running account of developments, which seemed to come to her as if from elsewhere, and which they then reflected on to discern their meaning. As the images proliferated, Helen began to distinguish between those that were personal and those that were "intended" for them both and thus "responses" to their quest for "another way." This marked the beginning of a discernment process.

Thematic Content: If we turn to the content of the picture sequences as recounted in the letters, we can see how key themes that link Cayce, Helen's past, and the Course were integrated during the process of emergence. Analyzing the contents chronologically, we can identify a developmental process that unfolded in the following steps: dreamlike meditations, Voice-like reflections, the emergence of an "other," and an explicit "coming out" of the Voice. Although there is no evidence of a direct connection, the steps are similar to those that Carl Jung deliberately employed to generate and enter into dialogue with "anima figures," which he claimed were generated by the unconscious. As he understood it, his method of active imagination relied on the image-producing function of the psyche and allowed opposing positions within the psyche to enter into dialogue (Jung 1997).

Dreamlike Meditations: Letter 4 (*AFF*, 141), in which she described a picture sequence that came to her while meditating, offers a good illustration of the initial stage. The "wreath meditation," as we can call it, centered on the theme "Thy will be done." She said that she didn't pick the themes in advance, but rather "the idea of the right one seems to come just before I lie down," which suggests that these themes functioned much like the affirmations recommended by Cayce. In response to the theme, a picture then came to mind that was "quite clear and very bright" and initiated a dreamlike sequence.

We can tease apart her description of the image sequence from her attempts to interpret it (*AFF*, 141):

> REFLECTION: I did not see quite the beginning. I came in at the point where I was kneeling in an almost Japanese kowtow,—I think that's right, although it was Siamese in *The King and I*. Come to think of it, that last is a very good association. Perhaps this is the next chapter of Heaven and Helen. Anyway . . .
>
> IMAGE: I was kneeling, with my head and arms touching the ground, and a very bright light in front of me. It had no shape, and it did not quite touch me. In my hand was a laurel wreath . . .
>
> REFLECTION: a symbol of victory to the Romans and most older cultures, I *think*. I am missing something here, but let it go. This one is short. The idea seemed to be that the wreath should not be mine, but belongs to the light.
>
> IMAGE: I think it [the wreath] went into the light and burned up. There is a missing link here, because the transition is missing. Something happened, and the wreath disappeared.
>
> REFLECTION: I think the idea is that victory is not made by us, but it is made for us. It embarrasses me very much to have written this, but since it is also for you I thought I should, I am afraid you'll laugh, but remember I did try.

As was the case with Bill Wilson's sudden experience and Joseph Smith's first vision, we have an experience of light that is embedded in an image—in this case an image of kneeling before the light with a wreath, then something happened and the wreath was no longer present. Helen filled in two significant details that she consciously inferred from the image: (1) that the wreath was not hers but belonged to the light and (2) that it went into the light and burned up. Beyond that, she provides a series of associations (i.e., the wreath with the Roman symbol of victory, kneeling with kowtowing and *The King and I*, and the next chapter of "Heaven and Helen") and reflections (victory is not made by us, but it is made for us). The whole experience—the images, the filling in, the associations, and reflections—is what we would expect in reflecting on a dream, and Helen acknowledged that her image pictures/visions were dreamlike.

In this dreamlike sequence, we see elements from the Cayce structure: (1) meditation culminates in an experience of light (Helen bows before the light), (2) consciousness moves into the light (Helen moves the wreath into the light), and (3) moving consciousness into the light gives rise to a "knowing awareness" that Cayce associates with the Father (Helen knows that victory is not made by us). Reflecting on the sequence, Helen wondered if this was the next chapter in "Heaven and Helen," the name she associated with the paper she wrote in graduate school about her (failed) religious quest. Clearly, the implied question was: Has the quest now resumed? Is this knowing awareness another glimpse of heaven?

The next morning (Letter 5), she thought not. In light of Letter 5, it appears that she read what she had written in Letter 4 to Bill over the phone the night before, most likely struggling with the implied questions. Bill encouraged her to say a prayer, which she did. But although the picture sequence (or "vision" as she calls it in Letter 5) "briefly . . . seemed real," she was soon assailed by doubts. "A lot of horrible things" crossed her mind, which she wrote down and then tore up (Letter 5, *AFF*, 142–43).

Helen's doubts were triggered, she wrote Bill, by a skeptical thought. "It began," she said, "when I thought it was really quite odd that, what with all the strange things happening to me, I don't really believe anything is happening. You do, but I don't. That's very peculiar. I bet if I asked people whether they thought it was noteworthy or not, chances are they'd say yes. Not me. You yes. Jonathan yes [her name for her husband Louis] (though he doesn't know yet what's really happening). Me no."

She continued (referring back to what she had read to Bill over the phone the evening before):

And then, after a short period of conviction (that word I think should be noted), I thought, no . . . People get fooled so easily. . . . I thought I was sure, but I wasn't. A rather savage doubting set in, and I suddenly realized I could probably account for a lot of the things that happened in other ways quite within normal chance variation, and how could I ever be so silly as to fall for all this?

As Wapnick commented, this letter reflects "the same doubts Helen expressed in her autobiographical account of this time period." "And yet," Wapnick added, "another part of Helen did believe, or at the very least, trusted enough in what was happening to allow the experiences to continue" (*AFF*, 143). Indeed, in the midst of the doubts that morning, she found herself saying: "sort of without intention and it's gone now—'I am a channel,' which seemed to mean something at the time. But the channel got clogged up, so it doesn't always work except when things get through the intervening mass. It's not open yet" (Letter 5, *AFF*, 142–43). At this point, she seemed to be vacillating, as she herself noted, between seeing deep meaning and significance in the picture sequences—signs that her earlier religious quest was resuming—and chalking the patterns up to chance.

Helen's Voice-like Reflections: In the next section of Letter 5, Helen reflected on imbalances in her own and Bill's personalities and on their relationship in her own voice, which nonetheless sounded to Wapnick much "like the voice of Jesus, imparting the same tone of gentle wisdom that is so characteristic of *A Course in Miracles*, and yet . . . predates the Course's scribing" (*AFF*, 146). In terms of content, Helen's reflections merged themes from Cayce (balance, light) with ideas drawn from their professional research (personality assessment, statistical cluster analysis, syndrome analysis). This passage thus reveals a blend of Course-like themes in a Course-like voice that at this point Helen was still experiencing as her own.

In terms of content, Helen compared people to lights, writing:

> I think people get together in little clusters of lights for a time, while that cluster serves best in the syndrome analysis. But the nodes change, and their meaning changes as they do. Lots of times the clusters remain together for a long time, until the balance is stabilized and all the lights shine equally. . . . I think you and I belong in the same cluster for quite some time. We have a special balance problem at the moment . . . The weighting system has been poor, and that has obscured the real meaning of the data. (Letter 5, *AFF*, 144)

Along with dreams, meditation, and light, balance is an important theme in Cayce's discussion of the "safer doorways to the unconscious" (1964, 175–80). The language of "clusters" referred to the statistical method of cluster analysis that Thetford and Schucman used in their research. Syndrome analysis referred to an analytical method used in clinical psychology, which they drew upon in conjunction with the Personality Assessment System (PAS) to analyze the role of personality in susceptibility to certain illnesses, that is, conversion hysteria, migraines, ulcerative colitis, and so on (Saunders and Schucman 1962).

The PAS, which was the primary focus of their research, analyzed personality structure in terms of three major dimensions: Externalizer-Internalizer, Regulated-Flexible, and Role Adaptive-Role Uniform (Schucman and Thetford 1968, 232–35; Howe 2009, 41–62). In Letter 5, Helen referred to relabeling an additional personality dimension, which as far as I can tell was not a formal aspect of the PAS, from "passive-aggressive" to "receptive-creative." She then analyzed their negative associations with receptivity and creativity and the problems these associations had created for each of them: Bill's difficulties with teaching and her inability to "listen to

God." Because she associated "receptivity [with] death," she said, she had "closed the channels" of communication with God (Letter 5, *AFF*, 145). She was unable, she said, to change "much yet, because I am still afraid to open the channel and redefine both extremes. Bill, this dimension *has* to be straightened out. The lights in the cluster are all off-balance" (Letter 5, *AFF*, 146; emphasis in original).

Although the blending of Cayce, their personality research, and concerns regarding personal transformation foreshadows the form that the Course would take, this passage also tells us something crucial about what Helen could and could not do. Specifically, it illustrates Helen's ability to analyze their personalities and their difficulties interacting from a detached point of view that is similar in tone and sophistication to the Voice that will later emerge. We can call it Helen's "protovoice." At the same time, she was quite clear that she was not yet able to do what she saw needed to be done. At this point and, it will turn out, in the long run, she was able to see a problem but unable to make the changes needed to solve it, much as she was able to see that she had turned Watermill into a symbol of evil but was unable to undo it. It was this discrepancy between seeing and doing that I think led to a dissociation between a wise God-aligned Voice and Helen-who-was-unable-to-change in accord with the teachings of the Voice.

Thinking of Helen as both an insightful "seer" and a resistant "doer" provides a way to think about the process of emergence. Thus, although this tension was undoubtedly present in Helen prior to Bill's impassioned speech, their decision to search for a better way provided a context in which the "seer's" abilities were valued, cultivated, and expanded. But this expansion generated increasing resistance from the skeptical "doer." Letters 4 and 5, which gave intimations of an "other" but did not actively engage it, illustrate the extent to which the "seer" and "doer" could coexist uneasily within Helen's conscious sense of herself. Her collaborators—Thetford, Wapnick, and Skutch—later describe her as flipping between two sides of her personality, which they characterized as very wise, on the one hand, and highly neurotic, on the other (see, e.g., quotes in Vahle 2009, 123–24). They associated her wisdom with her council as a therapist, the occasions in which she would explain the Course to others, her identification with an ancient priestess figure, and her devotion to Jesus. They saw her neurotic side in her conflictual relationships and her anger, skepticism, and inability to change.

I want to suggest, however, that the "seer" side of Helen was capable of more than therapeutic insights, skillful interpretation of the Course, and devotion to idealized figures. Over the summer, with Bill's active encouragement, the seer side of Helen developed the ability to envision and dictate the Course. But doing so required her to adopt an idealized vantage point, which she symbolized initially in terms of the priestess-who-merged-with-the-light and later as the voice of Jesus. From this vantage point, she could

[handwritten margin note: Author denies her true experience? ✗]

see in a more expanded sense, but she could not contain the one who saw in this way within her already rather divided sense of self. It was, I am hypothesizing, the internal pressure to see in this more expanded sense that began to manifest as an unnamed other in Letter 6 and an unnamed capitalized Other in Letter 7.

The Emergence of an Other: In Letter 6, Helen offered more wise-sounding insights into Bill's personality and the internal conflicts he had brought to their mutual impasse. Her reflections contain two references to an unnamed other, whom Wapnick retrospectively identified as Jesus. In the first passage, Helen described a picture that came to her before she went to sleep, in which a light ray emanated from a single very bright star to Bill's forehead. Helen then wrote: "I did ask for an explanation [from Jesus] of this, and I believe we both need it" (Letter 6, *AFF* 147; "Jesus" inserted by Wapnick). If we do not interpolate Jesus into the text, Helen's real-time action seems simply to have asked an unnamed other, perhaps in prayer, to offer an interpretation of the mental picture. After an elaborate discussion of the meaning of the image in relation to Bill's "star-crossed" life history, she wrote:

> It is my own responsibility (and this was told me [by Jesus] very sternly, too) to see to it that you understand, realize, and fully accept the *fact* that you are not star-crossed any more. None of that matters now. The only reason why I was asked (and even urged) to write this is because you *must* learn that the past is helpful only as it contributes to the learning conditions in which you function in the present to create the future. And make no mistake—you *do* create it. (Letter 6, *AFF* 150; emphasis in original; "Jesus" inserted by Wapnick)

Here we have Helen trying to help Bill with an issue that, as Wapnick points out, the Voice will attempt to help Bill to resolve in much the same fashion during the scribing of the Course. At this point, though, Helen was offering advice to Bill based on the picture image that had come to her, the interpretation she had requested and received from an unnamed other, and stern instructions from the unnamed other to relay the information to Bill. Assuming that, at the time, Helen either did not know or at least did not want to say (even to Bill) that the unnamed other was Jesus, this letter represents a next step in the emergence of the other with capabilities beyond those that Helen was willing to claim for herself. It was the unnamed other who provided the interpretation and insisted that she relay it to Bill.

In Letter 7, she returned to the stern instructions issued by the unnamed other in Letter 6, but heightened the sense of otherness by capitalizing her references to it. Thus, Letter 7 opens:

I am not sure I want to write this, but I have an idea I am obeying an Order. These Orders are rather stern, and the main feeling I get is that I wouldn't dare to disobey them. This is the 2nd one, the 1st one being given on Thurs. morning [i.e., in Letter 6] when I was so convinced that I *must* be sure you know you are fully released and perfectly free. I seem to wake up with certain very definite Instructions from a compelling Authority who is definitely *not* fooling. (*AFF*, 151; emphasis in original)

The Authority gave orders through Helen for both Helen and Bill, instructing them on how to balance their relationship. Bill was instructed to take "charge of anything that [had] to do with Timing" and Helen was to "follow [his] directions in that dimension." In light of the capitalization of Timing, the reference seems to be to the timing of decisions with respect to finding another way. Helen reported "the choice of progress versus stasis seems to remain a problem. You will gain as you choose to go forward and I will gain as I choose to follow you right" (*AFF*, 151–52).

The paragraphs that follow (*AFF*, 153) reveal interesting separations of and shifts in voice, as Helen attempted to relay the instructions of the Authority, which include the Authority telling her to quit giving Bill advice and to let him take the lead. At one point, she paused "to take a minute or so out and say a prayer about this," in effect, to check on the guidance she felt she was receiving, much as Anne Smith encouraged early AAs to do in Akron. Struggling to figure out what she was supposed to convey, she wrote: "Things got a little gentler. It says 'Open your heart to the gift of God and follow it.' I'll try, but I have *to be* careful. I think it's safe to go on. You are entitled to an explanation of course, the word 'explanation' was impertinent of me. The word should have been 'clarification,' and it does *not* come from me. (It's not *for* me, either)" (emphasis in original). Here we see "It" guiding Helen to distinguish between herself and It. "She" chose the word "explanation." "It" corrected her and replaced "explanation" with "clarification." Helen had a clear sense that the "It" and its choice of words were separate from her and that the message, at that point, was directed toward Bill and not her. Moreover, at two points in this letter, she wrote "It says," followed by a phrase in quotations, indicating that "It" was in some sense "speaking" to her.

In Letter 8, Helen's sense of being under orders expanded. She said she was "not used to being in the army (maybe it's really the army of the Lord) and I have had a rather rough time this weekend. A Top Sergeant (who says that's the right term to use . . .) has literally been issuing orders which, though they have not been punitive, have been *very* stern. . . . Writing this is one of them, and this is one of the very few I resent to some extent. I *will* try though" (emphasis in original). The orders over the weekend apparently had to do mostly with taking a less domineering role with respect to her husband. The orders came in different ways. The first that day came as a "definite conviction" upon waking. Later in the morning the reason for the order simply "came to [her]." But at lunch, she specifically "asked" if she had to be "quite this 'subservient'" and "the answer was stern and quick, 'Only until you're safe. I have use for you'" (*AFF*, 155–56). At this point, in other words, she was not only receiving impressions or "orders" but was also entering into an internal dialogue with the Top Sergeant.

The letters take us to the end of the summer. In later accounts, Bill and Helen describe two important events that took place in September: their attempt to confirm the seemingly paranormal images that came to Helen in conjunction with their visit to Mayo Clinic in Rochester, Minnesota, and their trip to Virginia Beach to visit Hugh Lynn Cayce. Bill viewed the events surrounding their visit to Mayo Clinic as "a very central part of the preparation" for scribing the Course (WT, 17). In the 1984 interview conducted by James Bolen (editor of *Psychic Magazine*, later renamed *New Realities*), he recounted that Helen visualized an image of a church in so much detail shortly before they left that she was convinced that they would "somehow . . . see [the] church from the airplane window as we were about to land in Rochester" (Thetford 1984, part 1). She was so upset when no church was visible that Bill suggested they hire a taxi and search the Rochester area. Twenty-seven churches later, there was still nothing remotely resembling the image Helen had seen. Then, as they were leaving, Bill picked up a booklet on the history of Mayo Clinic in which he found "a picture of Helen's old church, exactly as she had described it with all the turrets and towers. It was even a Lutheran church." It had been razed to build Mayo Clinic. In response to this discovery, Bill said to Helen: "[Y]ou really weren't out of your mind after all. Your church was there but it's no longer around. When you thought you were looking down on it as from an airplane, you were really looking back through time" (Thetford 1984, part 1). In her autobiography, Helen recalled exclaiming, "So that's why I was looking down on it [the church] . . . It was because it's in the past." At which point, she said, "a chill went over [her] and [she] did not want to talk about the church any more" (quoted in *AFF*, 109). The seemingly paranormal events surrounding the Mayo Clinic visit, coupled with the trip to Virginia Beach to meet with Hugh Lynn Cayce shortly thereafter, heightened their confidence in viewing the emerging voice as more than a split-off aspect of Helen's personality and allowed it to develop more fully, although Helen indicated that as "Bill's interest in [the Cayce documentation] deepened [her] own anxiety grew" (HS, quoted in *AFF*, 114).

The Voice Comes Out: After their return from Virginia Beach, Helen began keeping "a sort of diary" at Bill's urging. The diary flowed, quite literally, into the first of the Course notebooks. In it, she recorded "her own thoughts, as well as messages from Jesus (or her internal Voice as she sometimes preferred to think of him)" (*AFF*, 167). According to Wapnick,

> The notebook in which these thoughts and messages were contained unfortunately is gone, if indeed there even were a separate notebook. All that remain from this "pre-Course" period of writing are an entry that was written on three separate sheets of paper, and several pages written on the three days immediately prior to the beginning of the scribing. These pages are contained in the same notebook as the opening pages of the Course. (*AFF*, 167n42)

This diary provides a window on the transitional period in which the Voice came into its own as a more fully realized entity with a plan and began explicitly identifying with "Jesus." In these diary pages, Schucman not only distinguished between her own thoughts and prayers and those of the Voice but also entered into dialogues with it.

Wapnick quotes passages from the entries that demonstrate these complex shifts in voice. In one such passage from October 20, the Voice spoke at length in the first person to Helen about Bill's difficulty in responding to its (the Voice's) communications, the way Helen undermined Bill's responses, and specified things Helen should tell Bill, for example, not to overevaluate her as a person. Helen then summarized what the Voice had said in a few sentences, which she addressed directly to Bill in her own voice. Most of the next entry was addressed to Bill in Helen's voice. In it, she recounted her own reflections on an interaction between herself, the Voice, and Bill the previous evening, but when her account shifted to the present, the Voice told Helen to ask Bill to help her get over "being mean about it." Helen then added, in her own voice, that "at the moment [she had] serious doubts about everything" (*AFF*, 178–79).

In these entries written just prior to the emergence of the Course, Helen for the first time referred to the voice as "Christ." The Voice itself talked about God and indicated that a New Testament passage had been mistranslated (*AFF*, 168–70), which suggests that the Voice was identifying as Jesus. The Voice finally came out, as it were, with a reference to "My crucifixion," which he assured Helen was done of his own "perfectly free will," in the context of explaining to her that "[she] cannot lose [her] crown." If she were to throw it away, the Voice told her, "I may have to keep it for you again, but that will always be because you threw it away." This appears to be an allusion to the dream in which Helen bowed to the light and her wreath disappeared into it. This fusion of the dream in which Helen expressed her devotion to the light with the voice of the crucified one may well have been precipitated by the visit to ARE and Cayce's explicit metaphysical Christianity (Johnson 1998).

The "coming out" of the Voice in the wake of the visit with Hugh Lynn Cayce, coupled with Helen's statement to Bill "that she had the feeling she was 'about to do something very unexpected'" (*AFF*, 167), suggests to me that this was the point at which the idea of the Course emerged. If we do not assume that the Voice came from a source beyond Helen, but instead that the Voice and the idea for the Course emerged from within Helen, however split-off it may have been from her ordinary consciousness, then there are reasons to suggest that this was a plausible point at which the idea of dictating a course may have occurred to the "Voice."

(1) According to Bill, the trip to see Hugh Lynn Cayce gave Helen permission to do what she did. According to Helen, as "Bill's interest [in the Cayce material] deepened [her] own anxiety grew." This suggests, on the one hand, a deepening of the split between Helen, who was becoming more uneasy, and the Voice, who was feeling increasingly free to view everything from an idealized vantage point and, on the other, greater ability on Helen's part to allow the Voice to speak despite—or even due to—the widening gulf between them.

(2) Wapnick's interpolations aside, it is only in the wake of the trip to Virginia Beach that the Voice identified with the crucifixion and wove together key themes from the summer, such as Helen's dream of the wreath, with explicitly Christian themes. While Helen had a long-standing attraction to Catholicism, her deepened exposure to Cayce's metaphysical brand of Christianity seems to have facilitated the Voice's self-identification as Jesus. The impending death of Dave, a friend and a colleague at the Neurological Institute, I would suggest, then triggered the integration of their search for a better way with a fuller range of New Testament themes, including miracles, death, and resurrection, thus expanding the Voice's sense of the problem to be solved from something relatively personal to something universal, if not cosmic.

(3) The day before the Voice told Helen to start taking notes, Helen wrote out a lengthy prayer for her friend Dave in her diary that presaged key themes in the Course. Wapnick identified four themes: joining with another, joining with Jesus, the role of the miracle, and "the power of the mind . . . over the brain" (*AFF*, 176–77). Although the first three themes are compatible with Cayce's metaphysical Christianity, Helen's insistence "that the brain is *not* the seat of life . . . God is" (*AFF*, 177), which the Voice had stressed just previously (*AFF*, 170), was not characteristic of Cayce and signals how the Course would break with Cayce's metaphysics. Given that this long prayer was in Helen's voice, this passage led Wapnick to observe that she was "more than just a blank channel through whom Jesus dictated *A Course in Miracles*. In her own right, when identifying with her healed mind, she was the Voice of Wisdom"

(*AFF*, 177). The presence of these themes suggests that the core ideas—
the big picture—was already present at this point.[4]

(4) We can also note the prominence of another theme that Wapnick did
not mention: teaching. In her prayer, Helen repeatedly stressed the need
for Dave to teach others about miracles and that brain is not mind:
"Harry needs a miracle to teach him . . . He can learn this if you are
willing to stay and teach him . . . Silver has the whole Neurological Institute watching you. But they all think life is brain. Help them,
Dave—you are a teacher." I am hypothesizing that Helen's sense that
these central points needed to be *taught* triggered the idea of a course
and led Helen's seer persona to envision how they could be presented as
such. With this new idea, the Voice was, so to speak, off and running,
and able to announce the next day: "this is a course in miracles, please
take notes" (*AFF*, 180).

This hypothesis presupposes not only that the Voice was a dissociated
part of Helen, but that as such it had the ability to envision and dictate a
complex text such as the Course. This is a crucial issue, which will be taken
up in Part 2, when we compare the scribing of the Course with the translating of the Book of Mormon. Here we will continue to focus on the interactive process through which the Course emerged.

---

[4] Although he did not think that the content of the Course was Helen's "at least not the Helen
the world knew or the person she consciously identified with. . . . [yet] Helen knew what the published
Course ought to be. One could make recommendations, and Bill and I did from time to time, but
Helen had the finished form already in her head" (Wapnick n.d., 9–10; emphasis added).

CHAPTER 8

Teaching(s)

Helen "scribed" the words of the Voice in notebooks, beginning with the one in which she had written entries for October 18–21. She then read her shorthand version to Bill, who transcribed (or typed) it. As already noted, there are a number of extant versions of the Course, including the original notebooks, an early typed version known as the Urtext, the version shared with Hugh Lynn Cayce (HLC), and the version published by the Foundation for Inner Peace (FIP). References to the Notes and Urtext use the citation system given in Doug Thompson's collated edition of the Urtext Manuscripts (*"A Course in Miracles" Urtext Manuscripts: Complete Seven Volume Combined Edition* [2008]).[1] Since Thompson's claim that the original dictation is in the public domain is disputed by FACIM, I have kept direct quotes from the Notes and Urtext that are not already cited in *Absence from Felicity* (*AFF*) to a bare minimum.

In the pamphlet that became the preface to the second and third FIP editions, Helen states that "only a few minor changes [were] made [in the inner dictation that she took down in a shorthand notebook]." Although this is more or less accurate relative to the dictation as a whole, the original portions of the dictation, as both Schucman and Wapnick acknowledge, were heavily edited both in terms of arrangement and content, due to the large amount of more personal material they contained. If we take the Voice at face value as an emergent phenomenon, there is much that gets worked out in the opening months of scribing in terms of identity (who the Voice is), roles (what Bill and Helen are being asked to do), and the scribing process (how they are to do it). Above all, we see the Voice coming into its own, so to speak, and taking charge. The polished and consistent FIP version thus presents the teachings of ACIM as if Helen was simply a passive receiver of the dictation, while the Notes and Urtext depict a more complex interaction between Helen, Bill, and the Voice in the early months of scribing, thus

---

[1] According to the website of the Miracles in Action Press, a "newly forming" nonprofit is updating Thompson's 2008 edition, which will eventually be replaced with future editions of *A Course in Miracles* that incorporate Helen Schucman's shorthand notes with the Urtext Manuscripts. See http://www.miraclesinactionpress.org/ for additional information.

FIGURE 8.1. The notebooks in which Helen Schucman scribed *A Course in Miracles* (*above*) and a page from the notebooks (*left*). © Foundation for Inner Peace.

providing an invaluable window on the final stage of the process through which the Voice emerged into speech as a full-fledged teacher.[2]

If we analyze the types of material that appeared in the first few months of the scribed notes, we find considerable continuity with the material in the letters and the pre-Course "sort of diary" entries, along with a shift in the proportions as the process unfolds. Thus, during the initial period, the dictated material was a mix of dialogues, personal admonitions and instructions, general teachings, and scribal instructions and corrections, which gave way over time to the straight dictation of generalized teachings. During the first few weeks of scribing, the Voice made a distinction between the personal material and "the more generalizable quality which this course is aimed at" (Ur T1 B25i). This distinction between the personal and the general was formalized by mid-December, when the Voice said, "Nothing that relates to a SPECIFIC relationship belongs in the notes" (14 December 1965, Special Message; *AFF*, 283). As generalized teachings came to predominate during this transitional period, the Voice came into its own not only as an entity separate from Helen but as an author-teacher taking charge of the text it was producing.

The more personal material, which Helen and Bill referred to as "special messages," maintained the interactive quality of the earliest dictation, and the Voice reminded them in December "if you ask the Holy Spirit for SPECIFIC guidance in a SPECIFIC situation, He will give it to you very specifically." The setting apart of "special messages" therefore signaled the development of a guidance process alongside the emerging text, which functioned much as the early "revelations" did for Smith and his collaborators in the context of translating the Book of Mormon. As with the Book of Mormon, I focus here on the Voice as it presents itself and its teachings and defer consideration of how we might account for it in terms other than its own until part 2.

THE VOICE OF THE COURSE

What then can we say about the Voice of the Course? In the letters, Helen refers to It as an Authority, but It is not named. In the "sort of diary," the Voice speaks directly, identifies itself as the one who was crucified, and corrects a statement attributed to Jesus in the New Testament (*AFF*, 168–69). Early in the Notes, the Voice makes self-referential statements that paraphrase Jesus's statements in the New Testament (e.g., Notes 4:70–71) and refers to its role in the Atonement (Notes 4:69; see FIP 3rd T-1.III.1:1). Although this strongly suggests that the Voice identifies as Jesus, we learn much more about its self-understanding as the Course unfolds. By chapter

---

[2] See Wapnick (n.d.) and Perry (2004) for a discussion of the versions and their differences.

5, it is clear not only that the Voice is that of Jesus, but that he is a human being like other human beings and at the same time a model of "right thinking." The Holy Spirit is the "right mind" of Jesus. Thinking in one's right mind is "Christ-thinking." Since everyone is invited to join Jesus in Christ-thinking, Jesus is not *the* Christ in any exclusive sense. Although Jesus is the Voice of the Course, there are also references in the Course to the "voice of the Holy Spirit" and "the two voices within you." As one of God's Sons, Jesus, like all other humans, had to learn to hear the voice of the Holy Spirit, to listen only to the Holy Spirit, and in doing so to restore the integrity of his mind (see FIP 3rd T-5.I-II, which parallels the Urtext closely).

So, we can ask, what sort of Jesus is this? The Jesus of the Course is not the Jesus officially embraced by the Eastern Orthodox, Catholic, and most Protestant churches. Their understanding of Jesus goes back to the intense debates over the nature of Christ in the fourth century that resulted in the adoption of the Nicene Creed as revised at Constantinople in 381. There are, however, other traditions that also call themselves Christian that reject or ignore the fourth-century creeds and claim to base their understanding of Jesus on the New Testament alone or on the Bible plus later revelations. These "noncreedal" traditions include some forms of Protestantism (e.g., some Baptists, Quakers, the Disciples of Christ), the Christian metaphysical traditions (e.g., Christian Science, New Thought, Unity, and Church of Religious Science), and Mormonism.

In the early stages of the dictation, the Voice compared its teachings to those of two important Christian metaphysical teachers: Edgar Cayce (Ur T3 C36–37) and Mary Baker Eddy (Ur T2 A11), the founder of Christian Science. Exploring the similarities and differences between them allows us to situate the Course in relation to Jesus as he was understood by the metaphysical tradition that emerged in the nineteenth century and was elaborated over the course of the twentieth (Albanese 2007). The Jesus of the Course shares many features in common with Jesus as understood by Edgar Cayce, whose view, in turn, reflected many of the key features of the broader metaphysical tradition. Beginning with the Transcendentalists, these include an understanding of Jesus as a moral exemplar, miracles as reflective of an inner transformation, and a Neoplatonic understanding of reality that grounds the real in the ideal (Albanese 2007, 160, 163, 165). Beginning in the mid-nineteenth century, the metaphysical tradition made a clear distinction between Christ as a metaphysical principle and Jesus as a historical figure, an elder brother, and a way-shower (ibid., 288, 310, 432); soon it began to focus on mental healing or mind cure and typically referred to teachers, students, and lessons rather than preachers, converts, and sermons (ibid., 432). As Albanese indicates, however, the broader metaphysical tradition tended to "fudge" its idealism, uncertain whether to view the material world as spiritually infused or, more consistently, as illusory (see 167, 301, 307–9,

184 | CHAPTER 8

311). This was the primary point of contention between Mary Baker Eddy, the founder of Christian Science, and Phineas Quimby, with whom she studied, and between Eddy and the New Thought side of the metaphysical tradition more generally (Gottschalk 2006). It was also the primary criticism that the Voice raised with respect to Edgar Cayce. Thus, although ACIM's Jesus has some very positive things to say about Cayce in the Urtext, he notes that Cayce—like many in the metaphysical healing tradition—erred in "endow[ing] the physical with nonphysical properties" (Ur T3 C29; see also Ur T3 C36–37).

REALITY AND UNREALITY

Although there are differences at the level of purpose and practice, both scholars and students of the Course have noted "many striking parallels [between ACIM and Christian Science] at the metaphysical level."[3] It turns out that the Jesus of the Course did, too. In fact, in the Urtext (T2 A11) he singles out Mary Baker Eddy and Christian Science for having understood the Fall—or, as the Voice renames it, the Separation—correctly. Both ACIM and Christian Science are centrally concerned with the problem of theodicy, that is, with how a loving God could have created a world in which there was so much suffering, and both respond to the problem by claiming that God did not create the material world and that the material world, however real it might seem, is actually unreal.

This insistence on the ultimate nonreality of the material world allows both ACIM and Christian Science to adopt a consistent nondualistic metaphysics, which then leads both to view the atonement and the resurrection in nonmaterial terms. Both ACIM and Christian Science reject the idea of the atonement as a onetime event resulting from Jesus's sacrificial death on the cross. Thus, in *Science and Health* (1910, 22:5–7), Mary Baker Eddy forthrightly states that the traditional theological understanding of the atonement is "unnatural" and "man-made." We see something similar in the Course, where the Atonement, which began with the Separation (FIP 3rd C-6.2:4), is established not by Jesus's crucifixion but by his resurrection, which "demonstrated that nothing can destroy truth" (FIP 3rd T-3.I.1:2 and 7:6). The resurrection—like the crucifixion and the atonement—is not a onetime event. Jesus's crucifixion and resurrection model the process of awakening and rebirth and hence the dynamic between the ego's fear and God's love. The crucifixion, according to the Course, "demonstrate[s] that

---

[3] See, for example, Hammer (2001, 444–45) and Gallagher (2014). The quote is from FACIM Outreach Questions for 30 June 2004 at http://www.facimoutreach.org/qa/questions/questions90.htm. See also Rev. Tony Ponticello, "Isn't ACIM very similar to Unity, Christian Science, or Religious Science?" (2008) at http://www.miracles-course.org/joomla/index.php.

the most outrageous assault, as judged by the ego, does not matter" (FIP 3rd T-6.1.7:1–2 and T-6.1.9:1).

Although the Voice recognized the continuity between its teachings and Mary Baker Eddy's, Schucman and Thetford seemed unaware of the similarities, even though both were exposed to Christian Science when growing up. In her autobiography, Schucman described how, as an adolescent, her mother tried to help her with a weight problem by sending her to "the most wonderful Christian Science practitioner who, she [her mother] said, had shown her the light."

> My mother gave me a book on Christian Science to read first. Unfortunately it did not make much impression on me one way or the other, and I went to the practitioner more in the spirit of hope than of faith. The practitioner gave me a lot of arguments with the glibness born of frequent repetition, but I could not help thinking that by her way of argument you could prove just about anything. I realized very soon that I was up against the same old problem. You have to believe first and then find proof for what you believe. There was no point in going through all that again. (HS, 17)

Thetford was exposed to Christian Science at a younger age, having attended "Christian Science Sunday School until age seven, when my sister died suddenly and my parents lost all interest in religion." Although Schucman apparently had little interest in exploring the sources of the Course's teachings, Thetford did. Yet in trying to understand the Course, he was convinced "it was not the thought system I had grown up with" (WT, 19) and embarked on a wide-ranging quest to see if he could find parallels in other traditions (WT, 26–27).

Although the Course shares its understanding of Jesus as a way-shower and its insistence on awakening to truth through the transformation of the mind with the wider metaphysical tradition, and shares its consistent non-dual metaphysics with Christian Science, its psychology (post-Freudian) and its pedagogical format (text, workbook, and manual) are more developed than in Christian Science. The sharpest difference between the Course and Christian Science, however, lies in the Course's emphasis on "changing one's mind within the context of interpersonal relationships" (Wapnick 2009, 584). Thus, although both Christian Science and the Course—again, like the metaphysical tradition more generally—are concerned with healing, Christian Science focuses on healing individuals, while the Course focuses on healing relationships. This last difference flows directly from the problem the Course was intended to solve—the difficulties in Helen and Bill's relationship.

TEACHING HELEN (AND BILL)

The earliest portions of the Notes and the Urtext not only provide evidence for connections between ACIM and the American metaphysical tradition but also highlight the Course's relational emphasis, which Jesus models in his efforts to teach Helen and Bill how to apply the teachings in their own lives. During the first few months of scribing, Jesus repeatedly called Helen to her "real Self," trying to get her to see it. In late October or early November,[4] he reminded her that she was "a child of light," urged her to "forget the interval of darkness," and called her to be what she once was and "must be again." Because he (Jesus) had forgiven her, he said, "all hurt and hate you have ever experienced is cancelled" Ur T 1 B 16a-N7; Notes 4:45–46). This, he explained, is the meaning of the atonement:

> The purpose of the Atonement is to restore everything TO you. You HAD everything when you were created, just as everyone did. Having been restored to your original state, you naturally become part of the Atonement yourself. . . . Listen to my voice, Learn to undo the error, and DO something to correct it. (Notes 4:94–95; Ur T 1 B 23g–i; see FIP 3rd T-1.III.1:4–6)

Then, even more directly: "YOU are the work of God, and His Work is wholly lovable and wholly loving. This is how a man MUST think of himself in his heart, because this is what he IS" (Notes 4:99–100; Ur T 1 B24c; FIP 3rd T-1.III.2:3–4). This last message finally got to Helen. She wrote:

> The impact of this was incredibly intense—like a great burst of unexpected clarity. It was briefly so compelling that it seemed as though there was nothing else at all. The while [whole] world just disappeared. When it faded out there was no after effect, except a dim sense of wonder which also faded out, though a trifle slower. I was told to write nothing else that evening but we'd pick up the course again in the morning. It was also explained that that kind of experience is at the Revelation level, which is different but not by any means out of accord. (Ur T 1 B 24d-N3 [Notes 4:101–2])

The next day, the Voice launched into an explanation of revelation.

According to the Voice, "Revelations . . . represent the original form of communication between God and His souls . . . Revelation is PURELY a love experience" (Notes 4:105–6; Ur T1 B 24h-i; see FIP 3rd T-1.II.1). As a result, "Revelation is intensely personal, and is actually not translatable into

---

[4] The first date in the Urtext is 13 November 1965, at Ur T2 B 41.

conscious content at all. That is why any attempt to describe it in words is usually incomprehensible" (Notes 4:110: Ur T1 B25e; see FIP 3rd T-1.II.2:1–3). Miracles and Revelation, the Voice explained, intervene in the tug-of-war between fear and love, but where miracles release from fear and unite souls directly with each other, "Revelation induces a state in which fear has ALREADY BEEN abolished" and "unites Souls directly with God" (Ur T 1 B 24j-k; Ur T 1 B 25b).

Jesus not only applied this last point to Helen's experience of the night before, noting that her "Revelation occurred specifically after [she] had engaged at the visionary level in a process of DENYING fear" (Ur T1 B 25d), but seemed to allude to experiences of intense love that she had had in the past as well, thus incorporating them into the teachings of the Course. Such experiences undoubtedly included Helen's "subway experience," which she characterized as her "own most religious experience" in Letter 9 (AFF, 159). In the more elaborated version in her autobiography, she recounted that she was sitting on the subway, angry with Louis for insisting that they take the train and disgusted by the sounds of coughing and sneezing, the dirt, the smells, and the noise, when, feeling nauseous, she closed her eyes and "a stunning thing happened."

> It was a[s] though a blinding light blazed up behind my eyes and filled my mind entirely. Without opening my eyes, I seemed to see a figure of myself walking directly into the light. She seemed to know exactly what she was doing. It was, in fact, as if the situation was completely familiar to her. For a moment she paused and knelt down, touching the ground with elbows, wrists and forehead in what looked like an Eastern expression of deep reverence. Then she got up, walked to the side, and knelt again, this time resting her head as if leaning against a giant knee. The outline of a huge arm seemed to reach around her and she disappeared. The light grew even brighter and I felt the most indescribably intense love streaming from it to me. It was so powerful that I literally gasped and opened my eyes. I saw the light an instant longer, during which I loved everyone on the train with that same incurable intensity. The[n] the light faded and the old picture of dirt and ugliness returned. The contrast was truly shocking. (HS, 23–24)

In her autobiography, Helen indicated that she "felt something like the 'subway experience' [during the summer before she began scribing the Course] . . . , although with much less intensity. It generally took place in a crowd of people, for whom I would feel a brief but powerful affinity." So, for example, sitting in the darkness in a theater with Bill and her husband, she said: "I was suddenly aware of an intense inner light that began in my chest, growing increasingly strong and encompassing until it seemed to radiate throughout the whole theater and include everyone in it. My awareness of the light and the peace and joy that accompanied it lasted for some ten minutes. It was so strong that I could hardly believe no one else noticed it" (HS, quoted in *AFF*, 115).

The themes of light, love, and kneeling in this account of her subway experience are reminiscent of her "wreath" meditation, and kneeling is a prominent theme in her priestess visions, which she recounted in her autobiography but doesn't mention in her letters. Later references suggest that, during the summer, she and Bill interpreted the priestess in these visions as manifestations of Helen's higher Self and scenes from (one of) Helen's past lives (*AFF*, 87–93). There are several references to the "Priestess" in the Notes and Urtext. In one passage (Ur T1 B 410), the Voice describes the role of the "Priestess" in the past (i.e., to experience revelations and work miracles) in much the same terms that he was using to describe the "Sons of God" in the Course. A dialogue passage in the Notes (Notes 5:46–47, quoted in footnote at Ur T1 B41ac) between the Voice and Helen concludes with the cryptic line, "It was originally 'sister' not 'Priestess.'" It is as if in teaching Helen, the Voice alluded to her past experiences and deliberately suggested how they might be reinterpreted in light of the teachings of the Course. From the perspective of the Course, these would be considered shifts in content but not in form, such that the central teaching remained constant, even though the images or symbols through which it was conveyed shifted. Thus, from the perspective of the Course, these changes don't matter much. Relative to the overall argument of this book, however, they illustrate the way that Helen's dreamlike visions were being reframed by the Voice in the language of the Course and thus integrated into its thought system.

The Compromise

At the outset of the scribing process, it appears that the Voice hoped that Helen and Bill would not only scribe the notes but study them, allow the teachings to transform their relationship, and then demonstrate, if not actually promote, the teachings more widely. Thus, the Urtext version of chapter 3, scribed in late October 1965, opened with an exasperated Voice explaining to his wayward students that he expected them to read and study the notes, not just scribe them.

> This course is a MIND-TRAINING course. Good students assign study periods for themselves. However, since this obvious step has not occurred to you, and since we are cooperating in this, I will make the obvious assignment now. B is better at understanding the need to study the notes than you are, but neither of you realizes that many of the problems you keep being faced with may ALREADY have been

solved there. YOU do not think of the notes in this way at all. B DOES from time to time, but he generally says, "It's probably in the notes," and DOESN'T look it up. He believes that, although he read them over, they cannot REALLY help him until they are complete. (Ur T3 A1-A2, see also FIP 3rd T1.VII.4–5; *AFF*, 251–52)

Besides the fact that Helen and Bill were not studying and learning from the notes, the Voice was also frustrated by the inordinate amount of time the three of them—Helen, Bill, and the Voice—were devoting to analyzing Helen and Bill's inept personal interactions. The Voice was clearly more invested in producing the Course than in serving as Bill and Helen's personal coach. After a long stretch of notes in which the Voice tried to show them how they could have been more "miracle-minded" in their interactions (see *AFF*, 253–58), the Voice asked them to "consider all the time that we had to waste today. AND all the notes that could have been devoted to a better purpose than undoing the waste, and thus creating further waste. There IS a better use for time, too. I would have liked to have spent some time on corrections of the past notes, as an important step before reviewing them" (Ur T3 A36 [2 November 1965]; *AFF*, 257).

The Voice's desire to get on with dictating and correcting the notes and its distinction between personal and "more generalizable" material, which it asked them to separate out (Ur T1 iB25i; also Special Messages, 14 December 1965), suggests that the Voice was dictating the Course's teachings for more than just Helen and Bill. On several occasions, the Voice alluded to the larger mission it had in mind. Thus, on 26 December 1965, the Voice stated: "We have another journey to undertake, and I hope that, if both of you will read these notes carefully, they will help to prepare you to undertake it" (Ur T4 A10). Not long thereafter, it told them: "You are not at peace, because you are not fulfilling your function. God gave you a very lofty responsibility which you are not meeting. You KNOW this, and you are afraid. But your egos have chosen to be afraid INSTEAD of meeting it" (Ur T4 B25). Then, the Voice stated directly:

> Your mission is very simple. You have been chosen to live so as to demonstrate that You are NOT an ego. I repeat that I do not choose God's channels wrongly. The Holy One shares my trust and always approves my Atonement decisions, because my will is never out of accord with His. . . . Your gratitude to each OTHER is the only gift I want. I will bring it to God for you, knowing that to know your brother IS to know God. (Ur T4 G14–15; *AFF*, 277)

The Voice clearly had an expansive agenda that entailed Helen and Bill scribing, studying, and demonstrating the mind-training potential of the Course.

Helen wasn't prepared to do this, however. As she recounts in her autobiography (HS, 43), she needed Bill's "constant encouragement" simply to overcome her "virtually constant panic states" and continue to scribe the text. Bill was very much aware of his role in the process, indicating in his autobiography that despite Helen's anxieties, "I felt very strongly that Helen could do this, and I know that without my constant support and encouragement, she would not have continued" (WT, 23). Helen's way of dealing with her anxieties was to focus on the process and, as much as possible, ignore the content. According to Bill (WT, 22; see also Skutch 1984, 61), Helen told him early on that he was "responsible for what it says" and that she was responsible only for its grammatical style and purity. Helen, Bill added, "split herself off, really, in that way [from the content of the Course]." In an attempt to help her overcome her anxieties, Bill suggested they show the material they had transcribed to Hugh Lynn Cayce, with whom Bill had remained in phone contact since their visit the previous September. Helen resisted the idea of showing the manuscript to anyone, but "after weeks of reassuring her," she finally agreed it might be helpful (Skutch 1984, 62). According to Skutch, Hugh Lynn found the material "absolutely inspired" and "felt parts of it were quite similar to the more spiritual portions of his father's trance readings" (ibid., 64).

Although neither Bill's nor Hugh Lynn Cayce's efforts relieved Helen of her anxieties, both Bill and Helen felt they had "an assignment" or a "function" with respect to the Course to which they were committed. Thus, despite her panic, Helen said, "it no more occurred to Bill to just let the whole thing drop than it seriously occurred to me. In many ways we seemed to be fulfilling a joint assignment. We were both faced with wildly contradictory feelings, but we shared a sense of the importance of continuing" (HS, 43). Bill echoed Helen's sense of the importance of their task. "This was not something minor. . . . It was something that we were joined in doing. In fact, we shared the feeling of being joined in a common purpose, unlike some of our other activities, like writing papers or doing projects at the Medical Center" (WT, 23). Although they didn't know what it would turn out to be or how long it would take, they "shared a feeling of excitement" and the sense, in Bill's words, that "somehow we had found our function."

Nonetheless, and this is my point, Helen's—and perhaps also Bill's—view of their function seems to have been more narrowly conceived than the "mission" the Voice was envisioning. Insider accounts discuss the marked change in the dictation several months into the process, but they do not comment on the disjunction between the Voice's expansive vision and the more narrowly conceived "assignment" Helen and Bill agreed to carry out. Wapnick noted that the dictation became "increasingly flowing and more objective, reading more like a lecture than a dialogue" by about chapter 5 of the published edition of *A Course in Miracles*. He explained this by compar-

FIGURE 8.2. Bill Thetford seated at the typewriter he used to transcribe *A Course in Miracles* as Schucman dictated from her shorthand notes. © Foundation for Inner Peace.

ing Helen to "an unused faucet, which when it is first turned on runs rusty water," and after a while runs clear (*AFF*, 180). Robert Rosenthal, an early student of the Course, suggests that the transition occurred "because Helen and the Voice had found their groove. She was no longer fearful. She no longer got in the way, even if she couldn't embrace the material whole-heartedly" (Rosenthal 2014).[5]

In light of the disjunction between the Voice's expansive aims and Helen's expressed anxieties, I think the shift occurred because Helen and the Voice

[5] Dr. Robert Rosenthal was introduced to the Course by Judy Skutch (his college roommate's mother) in December 1975 and lived in the Skutch's New York home throughout June 1976 when the first hardbound edition of *A Course in Miracles* was published. He knew both Helen and Bill, and was a close friend of Bill's until his death. He joined the board of FIP in 1992 and was elected in 2014 to its executive committee in anticipation of taking on a future leadership role.

worked out a compromise. The Voice wanted to dictate the Course efficiently, expected Helen and Bill to study it, and hoped, through them, to offer its teachings to a wider audience. This prospect left Helen feeling incredibly anxious. She wanted to keep the Course a secret, limited for the most part to herself and Bill, and resisted change. The Voice's attempts to teach Helen and Bill were taking a lot of time, slowing the dictation process, and producing little lasting change. Practically, if not consciously, I think that Helen agreed to take down the Voice's dictation efficiently, *as long as she didn't have to pay attention to the content*. Channeling without having to think about the material reduced her anxiety and allowed her to channel more efficiently. An implicit compromise of this sort fits with Helen's later oft-repeated, half-joking statement that she agreed to take down the Course, but she never said she'd practice it (Skutch 1982, 1), as well as with Thetford's later observation that "[t]he same process of dissociation that enabled Helen to take down the Course, also made it virtually impossible for her to learn it" (*AFF*, 371).

Helen's circumscribed view of her "function" placed Bill in a bind. In his autobiography, he described the frustration he felt in the face of her inability to discuss the content of the Course and thus their inability to work together to understand it. "We did talk about it," he wrote, "but what I regarded as a challenge to change, she regarded as a threat, and seemed determined to hold on to her positions. So it was hard not to have anyone to talk with about this, as Helen wanted to keep it our secret, something not to be shared or discussed with others, at least not yet. Nevertheless, I at least needed a confidant who shared our interests, someone trustworthy and willing to abide by a vow of silence and with a background capable of appreciating the material" (WT, 23). By the end of September 1966, Bill had found a confidant in Cal Hatcher, a colleague in the department. In his journal, Bill indicated that he began meeting with Cal every morning to review the previous day's notes (from Bill's journal, 28 September 1966, quoted in *AFF*, 309–10). He concluded this journal entry—his last—on an upbeat note: "I feel very encouraged that we [he and Helen] are making considerable progress now, and much more than either one of us recognizes. Helen is beginning to see that there are really only two emotions, love and fear. . . . As we continue to see this clearly and with conviction, we should have no problems with the course, which is very explicit on this point."

His optimism, however, proved unwarranted, and he continued to reach out to others for support and encouragement. In 1969, Bill reached out to the well-known psychic Eileen Garrett, who agreed to meet with them. As he had with Hugh Lynn Cayce, Bill convinced a reluctant Helen to accompany him. Helen was, he said, "in a panic about the whole idea and said, 'I don't want to see any medium.' . . . It seemed all very threatening to Helen, who was very frightened of the idea of losing control and of dissociated states. . . . I dragged Helen down there somehow" (WT, 29; Howe 2009, 266–67). According to Bill, Garrett confirmed both the value of the material and his efforts to study the Course; he left "reassured that the woman who was considered the greatest living psychic really felt that you had to work with the material, and that it came from such a high source" (WT, 30). About a year later, during the fall of 1970, Bill and Helen reached out again to Hugh Lynn Cayce, sending him a copy of the text portion of the Course and soliciting his feedback.[6] According to Bill, "Eileen Garrett and Hugh Lynn Cayce were two very important people from the beginning of this process. They gave me a lot of support" (WT, 30).

At the same time that he was reaching out to prominent psychics for support and encouragement, Bill also began reading widely in the world's religions and spiritualities in an effort to place the Course's teachings in a broader, comparative perspective. In his reading, he was particularly struck by the similarities between the Course and the Hindu Vedanta (and later often referred to the Course as the "Christian Vedanta"), but also noted similarities between the Course and "the teachings of Unity Church," Huxley's perennial philosophy, Joel Goldsmith's *Parenthesis in Eternity*, the Cayce material, and Gina Cerminara's *Many Mansions* (with an introduction by Hugh Lynn Cayce), "which was about reincarnation." Toward the end of the scribing process, he became interested in spiritual healing and found particular meaning in a visit to the English psychic Ronald Beesley (misspelled in Bill's text as "Beasley"), who pronounced his and Helen's auras as "remarkably similar," and attended a live performance by the evangelical preacher Kathryn Kuhlman, whom both he and Helen felt demonstrated "tremendous spiritual power" (WT 30, 32).[7] Then, too, in the fall of 1970, while they were still scribing the "Workbook for Students," Bill set up a special internship for Fr. Benedict Groeschel, a Capuchin friar who was working on his doctorate at Teacher's College at Columbia, whom he supervised for the next two years. Bill and Ben discovered their common interest in mysticism when Bill made a reference to St. John of the Cross in class, and, after getting to know him better, Father Ben became the fourth person (and first non-Cayce-related person) with whom he and Helen shared the Course, which, as Bill noted, "was an unusual thing to do in those days" (WT, 31).

Helen, for her part, did not study the Course with Cal Hatcher and interacted with Hugh Lynn Cayce and Eileen Garrett at Bill's insistence. Although she warmed somewhat to Cayce and Garrett, she resolutely refused to align herself with them and identify as "a psychic." Based on her self-

---

[6] *Penguin Books v New Christian Church*, No. 96 Civ. 4126.

[7] On Ronald Beesley (1903–79), see Centre of New Directions, http://www.lightcoloursound.com/about/.

characterization in the preface to the Course, we might be tempted to assume that her resistance stemmed primarily from her scientific rationalism, yet the situation was much more complicated than that. Between scribing the "Workbook for Students" and the "Manual for Teachers," she wrote an account of the priestess visions that she had had during the summer of 1965, commenting in 1971, that "the priestess still turns up from time to time, but I have never been able to identify completely with her yet. Whenever I see her, though, I am strongly impelled to try. Perhaps I will succeed when Bill and I have finally worked out our relationship once and for all" (*AFF*, 88). Wapnick interpreted this as an indication that Helen consciously viewed herself as divided between "the priestess and her ego self," adding that her "seeming inability to unite with this innocence in herself [symbolized by the priestess] reflected the inability in her lifetime consciously to forgive Bill, except for rare moments" (*AFF*, 88). During this same period, Helen began to write poetry. The first poems reflected the teachings of the Course, but they did so, she said, in her own "inspired" voice, not in the Voice of the Course (Schucman [1982] 2008, xx). In contrast to Bill's wide-ranging exploration of diverse religions and spiritualities, Helen's devotional poetry consistently referred to God the Father, God's Son, and Christ (ibid., 3–39).

The Voice, for its part, aligned with the metaphysical tradition that shaped Cayce, but did so critically, opting for a more rigorous distinction between spirit as real and matter as illusion, along the lines of Christian Science, and rejecting the less rigorous position adopted by Cayce and the New Thought side of the metaphysical tradition. With the removal of the material they deemed more "personal," the Voice's explicit engagement with Edgar Cayce and Mary Baker Eddy disappeared from view and the Voice taught as Jesus, who, although critical of misinterpretations of his life and teachings, spoke the truth directly to his readers.

Down the road, students of the Course's teachings, picking up on its claim that it was "but one version of the universal curriculum . . . [all of which] lead to God in the end" (FIP 3rd, preface, ix), would continue Bill's efforts to compare and contrast the teachings of the Course with other religious and spiritual paths. Some, such as Frances Vaughan and Roger Walsh, would follow Bill's interpretive lead, viewing the Course as "a contemporary version of the 'perennial wisdom,' that common core of wisdom at the heart of the great religions" (1988, 9). Others, such as Kenneth Wapnick (1989; Wapnick and Clarke 1995), following Helen's lead, would stress the similarities between the Course, Platonic philosophy, and Christian Gnosticism, and therefore view it as a radical critique of traditional Christianity.

CHAPTER 9

Roles

The compromise between Helen and the Voice that allowed the scribing of the Course to proceed blocked resolution of Helen and Bill's relationship difficulties and deferred any consideration of what they were to do with the Course once it was scribed. When they finished scribing the main text (and before they knew there was more to come), it was Bill, as we might expect, who raised the question (*JWD*, 73). Helen agreed to consult the Voice, who, she reported, said "they were to do nothing" at that point. Although Helen was relieved, Bill was left somewhat confused, viewing it as unlikely that the lengthy manuscript was intended for them alone, yet sure that the uninterrupted, run-on text would appeal to a very limited readership as it stood (ibid.). Bill later returned to the question, feeling that they needed to do something to make the material more readable. This time, when Helen again asked for guidance, they received an affirmative answer, which they then implemented by inserting subheadings at natural breaks in the text (ibid., 78). By the time the final part of the Course was completed in September 1972, subheadings had been inserted in much of the text and Bill had convinced Helen to let him show the material to four people—Cal Hatcher, Eileen Garrett, Hugh Lynn Cayce, and Fr. Benedict Groeschel—but, according to Skutch (ibid., 85), Helen was so resistant to further sharing of the material that Bill finally locked it away, awaiting "whatever the future was to hold."

At this point the Voice's goal of producing a "generalizable" text had reached an impasse, stalled by Helen's resistance. If we set aside the question of the Voice's origins and simply consider the Voice as it presented itself through Helen, that is, as an active intentional agent who wanted to make its teachings available to a wider audience, it is easy enough to view the Voice as working strategically to circumvent Helen's reluctance to publicize the Course. Viewed from the inside, it looks as if the Voice, faced with Helen's resistance and the continuing antagonism between Helen and Bill, first brought Kenneth Wapnick into the inner core of the process through Fr. Benedict Groeschel, thus initiating the editing of the Course (1973–76) and then, working through Bill, drew Judith Skutch into the inner circle to spearhead the publication and dissemination of the Course (1975–78).

We can only get so far in our attempt to understand the complex dynamics that unfolded during this crucial period, however, if we refer simply to Bill, Helen, and the Voice. To get a clearer sense, we need a more complex way to think about "Helen." Thus, while recognizing that much of the time Helen made a very sharp distinction between herself and the Voice, there were also times, as we saw in her 1965 letters, when Helen presented *herself* to others in a very Voice-like way. As the split between "the Voice" and "Helen" deepened, the Voice-like aspect of Helen tended to appear as a sudden shift in personality. Those who knew Helen well, and some students of the Course who had met her only a few times, commented on this. Willis Harmon, for example, recalled "discussing the Course with Helen, who still felt somewhat ambivalent about it, and seemed somehow not fully able to adapt its insight into her own life. Suddenly [he wrote] she seemed to transform into another person—not visually so much, as in terms of personality. For a minute or two, for a few sentences, this 'other' Helen spoke of the real meaning of the Course with an authenticity and deep wisdom that left me awestruck. Then, as if by another flick of an inner switch, she was the ordinary Helen again" (*JWD*, foreword). It was this wise "other" Helen who identified with the priestess and claimed inspired authorship of her poetry.

From an insider perspective, the "other" Helen was Helen's higher God-identified self (*AFF*, 3), which she expressed in her inspired devotional poetry, and which she manifested occasionally in sudden shifts in personality. But Helen's "ordinary self," which insiders would call her ego self, had numerous aspects that shifted relative to her various roles and relationships. In this regard, she *was* quite ordinary; everyone presents different aspects of themselves in different roles and relationships. Nonetheless, her so-called ordinary self was—as I think most insiders would agree—more neurotic and compartmentalized than most. To understand the unfolding dynamics, we can't just consider "Helen," even the "ordinary Helen," as a singular self but must consider how different sides of her personality allowed her to relate to people in different ways.

In what follows, I will argue that Bill, Ken, and Judy saw all these sides of Helen but connected to them in different ways. As we have seen, Bill and Helen's relationship was painfully complex and enmeshed. Ken's and Judy's relationships with Helen, while still complicated, were less complex and much less volatile. All four of them were deeply committed to the Course and to the Voice-led process of inner direction. When Helen and Bill were focused on the Course, their relationship was at its most harmonious, and differences in perspective between the foursome were relatively subtle. Although Bill and Helen had a close professional relationship as colleagues and

collaborators, which they did not have with Ken or Judy, the most significant differences in their relationships were at the personal level. Bill referred
to the many roles he played for Helen as "boss, fantasy love object, her savior
in terms of [the Course] . . . [and] as a substitute for her husband, her
brother, and her father." Ken and Judy, by way of contrast, were the "son"
and "daughter" that Helen had never had. At a personal, psychological level,
the Course team took on family roles with Bill and Helen as the "parents"
and Ken and Judy as the "son" and "daughter." Ken and Judy witnessed the
painful, seemingly endless fights between Helen and Bill, but had good—albeit different—relationships with them both. Ken was closer to and more
spiritually akin to Helen; Judy was closer to and more spiritually akin to Bill.
When Robert and Judy Skutch decided to move to California, it empowered
Bill to leave New York and facilitated a "separation" between him and Helen
in the wake of his retirement from Columbia. Kenneth Wapnick remained
in New York with Helen and Louis Schucman.

In the next two sections, I explore the shifting dynamics as first Wapnick,
then Skutch, joined the inner circle. In the next section, I also discuss
the role played by Fr. Benedict Groeschel, who I think was more a part of
the inner circle for a time than either he or insiders tend to acknowledge, at
least in retrospect. Regardless of how we assess the level of his involvement,
an analysis of his role allows us to surface an aspect of Helen that we have
not yet considered—her long-standing attraction to and fascination with
Catholicism.

Editing the Course (1972–75)

During the period (1972–75) in which Kenneth Wapnick and Helen Schucman edited the Course, the dynamics unfolded on multiple levels. At the
level of the Course, the Voice moved the process forward by bringing Ken
in to work with Helen on the editing, and assume the Voice-guided role that
Bill had had with Helen while scribing the Course. At the level of spirituality, we will see that Ken, Helen, and Bill bonded most closely in their shared
exploration of Helen's psychic intuitions regarding a cave in Israel; Ken and
Helen bonded in their shared devotion to the Jesus of the Course, which
Bill, who tended toward a more generic perennialism, did not share; and
Father Ben and Helen bonded, I will argue, in a shared appreciation of traditional Catholic devotion to Mary, which Ken did not share. Perhaps most
surprisingly they all came together—albeit with different theological views
and levels of comfort—in weekly Masses that Father Ben celebrated for the
four of them in Helen's office. Finally, at the level of personal dynamics, the
intense "mother-son" connection between Helen and Ken left Bill feeling
displaced and longing—at multiple levels—for someone to join them to
complete the process.

The final editing of the Course by Helen and Ken prior to its official publication in 1976 has been the focus of much controversy among followers of the Course (*AFF*, 347–55; Howe 2009, 109–10). Those who believe that the Course was dictated verbatim by Jesus worry that Ken unduly influenced Helen during the editing process and as a result obscured the original words of Jesus, despite the fact that the substantial differences are limited to the first five chapters. Ken addressed their concerns directly, commenting:

> Anyone who knew Helen would clearly recognize the absurdity of this idea. No one, including Jesus, could ever get her to do anything she did not want to do. To think that I could have had an influence on Helen is most strange. Indeed, we were very close and she respected me—I was like her spiritual son—but in no way could that be taken to mean that something I might suggest would be seen as gospel, *unless she believed it to be true and checked it first with Jesus.* (Wapnick n.d.; emphasis added)

As this quote stresses, the editing process undertaken by Ken and Helen during this period was guided by the Voice of the Course, just as the scribing process had been. The Voice, in other words, was in charge of the process of moving the teachings out into the world, as the Voice had been envisioning from the outset.

Superficially, the substitution of Ken for Bill was a matter of aptitude for the task, since Bill didn't much like editing, but as Ken's self-description reveals, he and Helen became very close, and their relationship—as spiritual mother and son—was far different from Helen and Bill's. Not only was their mother-son relationship much less fraught than Bill and Helen's, but Helen and Ken bonded in large part due to their mutual devotion to the Jesus of the Course, which Bill, devoted as he was to the Course, did not share. Ken and Helen's relationship allowed the editing process to move forward despite Helen's "almost legendary anxiety" (*AFF*, 348). Just as Bill supported Helen through the scribing process, Ken, according to Judy, "walked her through the editing of the manuscript. He didn't do the editing—he instigated the editing. Helen needed to have her hand held" (quoted in Vahle 2009, 83).

Kenneth Wapnick: Benedict Groeschel introduced Bill and Helen to Kenneth Wapnick, a clinical psychologist who had recently been baptized by a priest in Groeschel's religious order in November 1972, just two months after Bill and Helen finished scribing the "Manual for Teachers," and just days before Ken was scheduled to fly to Israel for a year. As Ken tells the story (*AFF*, 5–6), he was raised in a Jewish home, attended a Jewish school through the eighth grade, but declared himself an agnostic at age thirteen. Later in life he had some unusual experiences, which he did not consider spiritual at the time, but which led to an interest in mysticism and a doctoral dissertation in clinical psychology at Adelphi University in the late sixties that focused on St. Teresa of Avila (Wapnick and Wapnick 1998). By 1970, he had a sense of God's presence in his life, and then, in 1972, after reading a number of books by Thomas Merton, he started attending Mass and arranged to visit the Abbey of Our Lady of Gethsemani, where Merton was a monk. He was so caught up in the life of the monastery that "[he] decided that God wanted [him] to become a Catholic" (Wapnick 1983, 5). In September 1972, he was baptized and confirmed as a Catholic with the intention of entering the monastery after the requisite one-year waiting period, which he decided to spend in monasteries in Israel.

Meanwhile, Ken had come to Groeschel's attention through Bill, who shared an article of Ken's on "Mysticism and Schizophrenia," which argued, contrary to the prevailing views in psychiatry, that "schizophrenics were not mystics, and mystics were not schizophrenics" (*AFF*, 6). When the chaplain who had baptized Ken mentioned to Groeschel that he had done so, Father Ben indicated that he was anxious to meet him. They met in October and, according to Ken, "became very good friends" (Wapnick and Wapnick 1998). Some weeks later, Father Ben arranged for Ken to meet Helen and Bill at Bill's apartment in November 1972.

Three experiences were crucial to Ken's involvement with the Course: the first connected him to Helen, the second to the Course, and the third to Jesus. The first took place at Father Ben's apartment, where he stayed the night after he met Helen and Bill. According to Ken, Father Ben offered to share "Helen's book" with him that night, but Ken did not feel ready to look at it. Unable to sleep, he recalled a dream involving a spiritual teacher, whom he associated with Helen, thus recognizing "in Helen the powerful presence of a spiritual authority." This connection with Helen then led to the second experience, his return to the States from Israel in May 1973, in response to an inner sense that he needed to read the manuscript. Doing so, he recalled, changed the direction of his life: "it did not take me very long to realize that *A Course in Miracles* was my life's work, Helen and Bill were my spiritual family, and that I was not to become a monk but to remain in New York with them instead" (*AFF*, 78–79, 323; quote on 79). The third experience, which occurred when he visited the abbey to tell the monks of his change in direction, linked his own inner voice, which he previously identified with God, with the Jesus of the Course (*AFF*, 323–25). This experience brought his inner sense of presence into alignment with the Jesus of the Course and, in effect, with Helen's inner voice. It therefore established the vantage point from which he reread his own previous experiences of presence and Helen's earlier descriptions of her inner life, and provided the basis upon which he could insert "Jesus" into the earlier sources, confident that, whatever Helen may have written, it was Jesus who was actually speaking.

Marian Devotion: At the spiritual level, Helen and Ken's shared devotion to the Jesus of the Course was just one piece of the "Helen puzzle." Although Kenneth Wapnick was baptized as a Catholic, he was, as Helen "pointed out to [him], a very funny Christian" (*AFF*, 323). As his experience at Gethsemani indicates, Ken fairly quickly adopted the Course's heterodox view of Christianity, while most likely allowing Father Ben to maintain the impression that he (Ken) still considered himself Catholic, when Ken did not, at least in any orthodox sense. Ironically, Helen, or, more precisely, an aspect of Helen, was deeply attached to traditional Catholic practices, such as attending Mass, saying novenas, and reciting the rosary.

Although Helen, like her husband Louis, is often characterized as Jewish and/or agnostic, she had a lifelong fascination with Catholicism. Both her parents were "half Jewish," meaning each had one Jewish parent, but her father was uninvolved religiously and her mother, according to Ken, "bitterly resented her Jewish roots and spent most of her adult years as a spiritual seeker," including periods of interest in both Theosophy and Christian Science. Helen's initial connection to Catholicism came through a devoutly Catholic governess, who cared for her as a young child (*AFF*, 23). She described her on-again off-again relationship with God in her autobiography, including her experience when visiting Lourdes with her family at age twelve and her Protestant baptism at thirteen with the encouragement of their housekeeper, a devout Baptist.

Helen's fascination with Catholicism waxed and waned over the course of her life, but it never disappeared. She dropped into Catholic churches, sometimes to pray to the Virgin Mary, other times to hear Mass. Her visits apparently intensified when she needed something (*AFF*, 28, 36). Looking back, Ken wrote: "Helen went to church very frequently in her life, and during certain periods would attend daily Mass, perform Novenas (a series of nine daily rosary recitations for a specific prayer intention), and often recite the rosary. She even carried in her purse a 'pocket rosary,' which allowed her to say the rosary while walking, riding a bus or taxi, even if Louis were present, for no one could see the activity of her hands within her pocket: another of Helen's secrets that she held from the world" (*AFF*, 407; see also 410). Ken also indicated that, in "[k]eeping with her psychological identification as a Catholic, Helen held an exalted opinion of priests and nuns, magically believing that they were more spiritually advanced than others simply by virtue of their vocations" (*AFF*, 409), an attitude that most likely drew her to Father Ben.

Ken's description of Helen as turning to traditional Catholic practices—the Mass, novenas, and the rosary—when she was feeling particularly anxious suggests to me that Helen may have reached out to Father Ben during this period, sharing her more traditionally Catholic-sounding side with him, *as a means of counterbalancing her Course-focused relationship with Ken*, and thus maintaining the divisions within herself. In contrast to her Course-oriented devotion, which was Jesus-centered, her traditional Catholic devotions centered on Mary. According to Ken, Helen's attraction to Mary was lifelong and unambivalent. "While Helen was never shy about sharing her angry feelings towards Jesus or even God," he wrote, "I never once heard her say anything negative about Mary" (*AFF*, 410). According to Helen, her attraction to Mary dated back to her childhood, when she saw "a statue of a lovely lady," while accompanying her governess to church. A young Catholic friend taught her how to pray the rosary and encouraged her to pray to "the Blessed Virgin, who was very kind and would listen to practically anyone," including little girls who were not Catholic (HS, 7). A side of Helen, I am suggesting, was devoted to Mary in the traditional Catholic sense of an intercessor, a kind maternal figure, who "would listen to practically anyone"— even Helen—and hence someone she could turn to when she felt anxious and alone.

Although Ken did not share Helen's "Catholic mentality of venerating Mary," there was, however, a deeper, less orthodox level at which he not only joined but actively encouraged a connection to Mary, interpreted in light of the Course. Thus, he explained:

> During the scribing of *A Course in Miracles*, Jesus made occasional references to Mary, comparing Helen to her in terms of function— Mary's bringing forth the person of Jesus, Helen's bringing forth his message through *A Course in Miracles*—with intimations of the same degree of holiness. . . . There were thus intimations . . . that Helen shared the same inner radiance and purity as did Mary, and likewise, that Helen was as intimately one with Jesus as was Mary. And so we can say that the figure of Mary, the mother of Jesus, would not only be comparable but identical in *content* to the ancient priestess of Helen's vision. (*AFF*, 411)

Although this analogy between Helen and Mary as "mothers" of Jesus wasn't developed in the Course itself, it was implied in one of Helen's poems ("Mother of the World") and apparently also came out in more direct communications with the Voice. In connecting Helen with Mary and the ancient priestess, the analogy reinterpreted Mary as it did Jesus, not as a savior or, in Mary's case, as an intercessor (who could relieve her of her anxieties), but as a brother/sister/mother already eternally loved by God. But just as Helen was not often in touch with the priestess side of herself, so, too, I suspect, she had difficulty internalizing her Marian role as the "mother" of the Course and continued to turn to Mary in traditional Catholic intercessory fashion, especially when she felt anxious. When Groeschel later stated that he felt that Helen's "devotion to the Blessed Virgin Mary was genuine"

(1993, 77), it was likely because Helen felt more comfortable sharing the conventionally Catholic side of her devotion to Mary with him than she did with Ken, who did not share it. Conversely, Groeschel's later sense, that her devotion to Mary was "uncompromised" by the heterodoxy of the Course, suggests that Schucman did not share the Voice's analogy between herself as the ancient priestess and Mary as mother of Jesus with Groeschel.

Helen and Ken most certainly discussed the analogy with Bill. Indeed, Ken's devotion to Helen as the "Mary" who brought forth the Jesus of the Course particularly rankled Bill, who related the way the analogy infused their relationship—and sidelined him—with obvious annoyance:

> Helen was susceptible to all this attention and massive devotion from Ken. It was amazing; she now had the word of Jesus and the whole thing—this was it. Ken thought Helen was sort of the Mother of God, the Virgin Mary. Helen thought Ken was one of the world's greatest saints of all time. She would say things like, "I can't think of any saint in history who was as beatific as Ken." So I would have lunch with the Virgin Mary and the world's greatest saint. Of course, I was the world's greatest sinner; I was the terrible guilty party. I'm not sure why I was guilty. That was more obscure. But someone had to be guilty, so I was it. Probably one thing was that I was not being loving enough with Helen; I wasn't impressed by the fact that she was the Mother of God. This sort of thing went on for quite a while and I was both relieved and annoyed by it all. (WT, 33)

Bill, who shared neither Helen and Ken's devotion to the Jesus of the Course nor Ken's unambivalent devotion to Helen, was not impressed by the Marian analogy. His simultaneous relief and annoyance, however, reflected his ambivalent feelings regarding the shift in his relationship with Helen. The intense, conflict-ridden dyad between Helen and Bill was now a triad, and Bill was in many ways the odd man out.

Father Ben did little to fill in the void. Bill was Father Ben's teacher, supervisor, and therapist. They shared an interest in psychology and spirituality, but of the four, their actual spiritual inclinations were the least compatible. Father Ben was not only a student but also a Catholic priest, who wanted "to open the doors of the Church to [his] two friends [Helen and Bill] . . . [believing] that with what was going on in their lives, they would be helped by a good dose of Christian theology" (Groeschel 1993, 78). Looking back, Groeschel thought that this hope was more realistic with respect to Helen than Bill. Helen, in his view, was more ambivalent about the Course than Bill, without whom, he believed—probably rightly—it would never have been published (ibid., 79). He also viewed Helen as more open to orthodox Christianity. "Bill remained essentially unrelated to any kind of orthodox Christian teaching. It seems to me now that at the time Helen had faith and that Bill did not." In retrospect, Groeschel said, "I don't think he [Bill] ever actually was a believing Christian," though, he added, "I must say that he honestly tried to follow the teachings of this Course" (ibid., 78). Groeschel summed up his relationship with Bill, saying: "Although he was most kind to me, I always felt that he was not entirely capable of the honest, open sharing that is necessary for a friendship" (ibid.). Bill would have un-doubtedly agreed that without his support the Course would never have been scribed, much less published, and that, while he was not "any kind of orthodox Christian," he was "honestly trying to follow the teachings of [the] Course." Given that Groeschel seems to have come to this conclusion belat-edly, Bill may not have been entirely forthcoming with him with respect to their spiritual differences at the time. As to the lack of honest, open sharing, this again was most likely true, but, given that Thetford was Groeschel's supervisor and therapist, a closeted gay man, and inclined toward the more esoteric and metaphysical spiritual traditions, it is hardly surprising that he did not fully reveal himself to a Catholic priest, who was hoping to bring him into the Catholic fold.

With no one to fall back on, the growing spiritual intimacy between Ken and Helen left Bill feeling displaced. Referring to this period, Carol Howe, who knew Bill well after he moved to California, wrote that, despite their difficulties, "they [Bill and Helen] were extremely codependent and genu-inely and deeply cared for one another; introducing a third party into the mix was more than a little unsettling for Bill. Ken's services were badly needed and truly appreciated, but they came at a price from his [Bill's] per-spective" (2009, 102). Based on her later knowledge of Bill, Howe speculated that "Helen and Ken's apparent mutual adoration, which developed right away, was the perfect setup to trigger within Bill a deep sense of rejection and betrayal" (ibid.). Recalling this period, Thetford said: "It was a difficult triangle when the three of us were together. After some exposure to all of this [during the ten weeks Ken was in New York], I told him I couldn't stand it and I thought there was a lot of spiritual grandiosity going on. I didn't think that was the spirit of the *Course* and I was fed up with it. Ken went back to Israel in June, but not before extracting a promise from Helen that she would come to Israel in August and bring him back" (WT, 33).

Initially, Ken was not particularly attuned to the effect that his arrival was having on Bill and Helen's relationship, though he "observed that [Helen and Bill] were caught up in a horrific relationship that was clearly far, far beneath the spiritual stature present in both of them" (*AFF*, 326). Swept up "in the aura of *A Course in Miracles*," Ken at first dismissed "the incongruity of the two scribes fighting together like children" when they weren't focused on the Course (*AFF*, 323, 326). Ken's return to Israel, coupled with "the cave episode," a new Course-related development that the three of them all found engrossing, diffused the tensions between them and deepened their bond with one another in relation to the Course.

The Cave in Israel: The "cave episode," as I have been calling it, deepened the bonds between them by drawing them more deeply into a shared interpretive frame and in doing so illustrates how seemingly "psychic" intuitions were reinterpreted when their evident meaning was disconfirmed. In this case, Helen's intuitions were triggered by Ken's mention of a cave that he had been helping to excavate in Israel. According to Ken, Helen immediately " 'tuned in,' and began to describe in remarkably accurate detail the physical characteristics of the cave," stating that "she felt there was something of great value in that left-hand corner. This topic grew to become almost an obsession, especially as Helen felt that the 'something' could very well have been the chalice of the Last Supper." The sense that there was something significant buried in the cave excited them all and predictably filled Helen with anxiety (*AFF*, 330–31). She vacillated between wanting to find something, trying to let go of the need to find something, speculation as to what Ken would find, and then, finally, asking Bill "what we were supposed to do if there's nothing in the cave" (July 31, *AFF*, 334).

These real-time exchanges reveal not only her anxieties but the uncertainty that is typically present in the meaning-making process. Bill, in response to Helen's question, offered a classic rejoinder that illustrates how commitment can grow even in the event that prophecy—so to speak—fails.[1] He reminded Helen of the last time that they were sure prophecy had failed, that is, when Helen had a vision of a church that she was sure they would see when they visited Mayo Clinic in September 1965 (*AFF*, 108–9). The church, Bill reminded Helen, "wasn't there any more, either, but there was no question that the image and the place all meant something even more important. I guess the idea is not to allow the luxury of disappointment to come in. *I'm sure that we can always ask what the lesson is, and there has to be an answer whatever comes out in fact*" (July 31, *AFF*, 334; emphasis added).

In the end, they decided that the meaning of Helen's intuitions had little to do with the cave but rather with Qumran, a site that Bill insisted they visit after he, Helen, and Louis joined Ken in Israel (*AFF*, 343). The result, as Ken described it, "was totally unexpected."

> [A]s with the Mayo Clinic episode years before . . . the strange events of the summer finally received their explanation. . . . As we stood on

---

[1] Here I am alluding to Festinger, Riecken, and Schachter ([1956] 2008) and the long line of research that has stemmed from their claim that, even when "prophecy fails," believers find ways to interpret the "failure" so that in their eyes it didn't. For discussions of subsequent research, see Hood, Hill, and Spilka (2009, 221–26) and Tumminia and Swatos (2011).

the site of the ancient community, we looked across the roped-off area to a series of caves, including the one where the scrolls were found in cylinders not unlike what Bill thought might be in "my" cave. At some point Helen burst into tears, and told us that the cave in front of her was the exact cave she had seen in her vision of the "God is" scroll. She then exclaimed that she was standing on the holiest place on earth.

Later, when Helen, Bill, and Ken discussed the events of that "rather emotional morning," they fit all the pieces together. "It occurred to all of us," Wapnick wrote, "that it was this cave at Qumran, and what it represented for Helen [her burial in the cemetery in Qumran in a past life], that was the true object of what had so preoccupied us during the summer. The preoccupation had been displaced to the cave at the monastery" (*AFF*, 343). This new insight not only disconnected Helen's vision from a Catholic monastery and reassociated it with a site that the metaphysical tradition associated with Jesus's origins (Johnson 1998, 69–70), it also confirmed the association that Ken and Helen were making between Mary and Helen and reaffirmed Bill's (and Helen's intermittent) belief in reincarnation. Even though they never figured out where either the chalice or the scroll were buried, these new insights made for a highly satisfying conclusion. The lesson in this case, as with the Mayo Clinic experience, was that the (true) meaning of events emerged when they "trust[ed] with no concern for the outcome" (*AFF*, 344).

Tensions: In the wake of their return from Israel, Ken began to realize that "the situation was hardly the spiritual Camelot I thought I had wandered into" (*AFF*, 10; see also 344–45, 357–61) and began to face the incongruity of Helen and Bill's inability to apply the Course in their lives. Although he held out hope that they would be able to forgive each other, the failure of the Course to transform their relationship raised the core issue that he would later seek to address in *Absence from Felicity*.

Nonetheless, we learn that, in the midst of this "complex hotbed of pain and hatred" (*AFF*, 10), Ken, Helen, Bill, and Father Ben together experienced a "peaceful time of intimate sharing" in Masses that Father Ben began celebrating for the four of them weekly in Helen's office. Thus, according to Ken:

> During one period of our friendship, [Ken writes] Michael [Father Ben] would pick Bill up once a week at his apartment early in the morning, drive to the Medical Center, where Helen and I would meet them. Michael would then say Mass in Helen's office for the four of us. While Bill was the least comfortable with religious rituals of any kind, let alone a Catholic Mass, he, along with Helen and me, enjoyed this peaceful time of intimate sharing. . . . Every once in a while we would

gather in my apartment for Mass, and then a light supper (for which Louis usually joined us—*after* Mass)." (*AFF*, 408)

Nor were these ordinary Masses. Instead of the standard lectionary readings, Father Ben allowed Ken to substitute a reading from the Course for the "epistle" reading, that is, the traditional reading from the letters of St. Paul, and to select a Gospel reading "following the same theme found in the Course reading" (*AFF*, 408). These were, in other words, Course-inflected Masses.

In terms of group dynamics, Father Ben, Ken, Helen, and Bill, here as in other spiritual matters, most likely glossed over their differences and stressed what they shared, thus allowing them to partake of the Eucharist while interpreting it differently. Looking back, Wapnick recalled that they joined with Father Ben's "obvious sincerity and devotion to God," but not with his belief that "the bread and wine literally became the body and blood of Jesus. . . . Helen used to joke with Michael [Father Ben] about this and say, 'After all, Mike [Father Ben], bread is bread' " (*AFF*, 408–9). Whether Helen, who also attended Mass at Catholic churches and kept rosaries hidden in her purse so she could pray in secret, *always* thought about the consecrated bread that way is—I think—an open question.

Within this family-like small group, the interconnections were complex and ultimately unstable. The increasingly close relationship between Helen and Ken, both spiritually and practically, in terms of the editing process did not include either Bill or Father Ben as fully. As the incompatibilities between the Course and Catholicism became more evident, Father Ben distanced himself, although he stayed in touch with Helen until her death in 1981. The other three stayed together, but Bill struggled. As Bill recounts in his autobiography:

> We got back from Israel in the fall of 1973, just before the Yom Kippur War. Ken and Helen were continuing their "special relationship," which seemed to be going full blast. . . . I remember feeling alone, feeling that Helen and Ken had their own special thing now. I felt very isolated, but obviously had to keep going. There was no gratification anywhere. I just wanted to get through this stuff and find the people who could take it over. (WT, 35)

The editing process, which—like the scribing—was much prolonged due to Helen's anxieties and ambivalence about the Course, was not completed until well into 1975. It was at that point that Bill wrote, "[a]s if on cue, . . . and apparently in response to my need to find people to take things over, Judy Skutch arrived on the scene in May of 1975" (WT, 35).

Publishing and Disseminating the Course (1975–78)

Judith Skutch: Like Kenneth Wapnick, Judith (Rothstein) Skutch grew up in a Jewish family, but otherwise they were drawn to the Course in very different ways, which, I will argue, shaped the way they understood the Voice and thus, in subtle ways, how they presented the Course to a wider audience. In her earliest account, Skutch stressed an unusual experience that occurred when she was thirteen, the unusual—apparently paranormal—abilities of her daughter Tamara, her subsequent involvement with parapsychological research, and feelings of depression and emptiness triggered by the sense that something was missing in their scientific approach to the paranormal. In *Journey Without Distance* (*JWD*), her then husband Robert Skutch (1984a, 93–94) sketched details with regard to her family, which, looking back, Skutch Whitson now views as crucial in interpreting her understanding of the Course (Skutch Whitson, November 2014).

The unusual experience, which Skutch later described as "a spontaneous transcendent or mystical experience," took place when she was given nitrous oxide for dental surgery at the age of thirteen. Fighting the feeling that she was losing herself as she went under the anesthetic, she felt as if her consciousness was being forced through the apex of a triangle, a movement that she equated with death. When she could no longer fight it, she "felt [herself] catapulted through the barrier of pain and into total peace" (*JWD*, 95). At that point, she said:

> There was no perception, just a feeling of beautiful, distilled absolute light. But I was not a body; I was seeing without eyes. I had an awareness of a total reality that far transcends the senses. An overwhelming feeling of well-being encompassed me, and in that place we call "knowing" I was one with the universe—with all living souls and with God. (*JWD*, 95)

Without a framework to interpret the experience, she set it aside until it resurfaced, first in relation to her daughter Tamara's unusual "sense of attunement to the world around her in a way that went far beyond the five senses," and then later in dreams just prior to her discovery of the Course (*JWD*, 96s, 102). Incidents of apparent telepathy and precognition led Judy to conclude that her daughter had the ability to extend "her consciousness beyond the parameters of her body . . . [in a way that] somehow allowed her a far greater connectedness with people than I had originally thought possible" (*JWD*, 99).

When a family friend gave her Jess Stearn's book on Edgar Cayce (*Edgar Cayce: The Sleeping Prophet*) in 1966, both she and her husband, Bob, became intrigued, and Judy decided to investigate the scientific research on the paranormal. She took courses at the New School for Social Research and attended programs offered by the American Society for Psychical Research and the New York branch of the Association for Research and Enlightenment (ARE). She developed friendships with leading academic investigators, including Stanley Krippner, Montague Ullman, Ian Stevenson, and Lawrence LeShan. In 1971, she and her husband decided to create a nonprofit foundation—the Foundation for ParaSensory Investigation—to help support research on parapsychology (*JWD*, 99). From 1971–75, Judy worked closely with researchers at the Dream Laboratory at Maimonides Hospital helping to raise money to launch projects they thought were promising. For four years, she taught courses on Experimental Parapsychology and Healing at NYU's School of Continuing Education and organized conferences there on related topics. Extroverted and enthusiastic, she was a popular speaker in a variety of venues, helped to found and then joined the board of the Institute of Noetic Sciences in Northern California, and began doctoral studies at the Humanistic Psychology Institute in San Francisco (*JWD*, 101).

It was in this whirlwind of activity that she began to feel as if something was missing and to have dreams that reminded her of her experience as a thirteen-year-old. Through a series of seemingly synchronous events, she wound up visiting a numerologist, who told her "that within a year [she] would publish one of the most important spiritual documents known to humanity" (*JWD*, 104). The next morning a friend, Dr. Douglas Dean of the Newark College of Engineering, who—it turned out—had just met Thetford at a conference that Skutch had organized, called to ask her to join them for lunch. At his insistence, he and Judy met with Bill and Helen a few days later. In a meeting on 29 May 1975 that has now become the stuff of ACIM legend, Judy blurted out to Helen—seemingly apropos of nothing— "you hear an inner voice, don't you?" This precipitated a move to Helen and Bill's private offices and a two-hour visit in which Helen and Bill recounted "the story of the past ten years" (*JWD*, 106). Judy immediately became an integral member of the ACIM team, meeting almost daily with Helen, Bill, and Ken to study and discuss the Course (*JWD*, 109).

Events unfolded quickly in the wake of their initial meeting. Within days, Judy left on a planned trip to California to meet with Dr. Eleanor Criswell, the founding director of the Humanistic Psychology Institute (now Saybrook University), under whom she intended to write her doctoral dissertation. With Helen and Bill's approval, Judy shared a Xerox copy of the manuscript with both Criswell and her friend James Bolen, the editor of what was then called the *Psychic Magazine*. Eleanor Criswell suggested publishing a reduced-size offset version of the manuscript. Judy, Helen, and Bill consulted the Voice and received an affirmative response. The interest among her friends in the Bay Area was so great that Judy encouraged Helen, Bill, and Ken to join her while she was visiting in California. Bill and Helen agreed to come, meeting with more than five hundred people over the course of a four-week visit (*JWD*, 109–10, 112). Helen continued to express her feelings of ambivalence during this period. That fall, after nine weeks of scribing the "Clarification of Terms" (later added to the "Manual for Teachers"), she complained that the Course was interfering too much with her life and announced that she chose "no longer . . . to *write* it . . . [or] read it either." When Ken, in response, threw her scribing notebook in the trash, however, she panicked and retrieved it (*JWD*, 103–14).

Robert Skutch's account, published three years after Helen's death, highlights the role of guidance throughout this process. Two "special messages" from December 1975 provide real-time documentation. In the first, dated 15 December 1975, the Voice cautioned them, saying: "Between now and the end of December some very important & necessary changes will take place. One of them is factual and the others are shifts in attitudes. Until these have been accomplished it would be pointless to try to force through a plan." Then, on 31 December 1975, the Voice told them: "This year you will set up a place which will be the home of the course; a place where it will grow from infancy into a helper of the world." In February 1976, a plan emerged, when, in response to a number of feelers from people interested in publishing the Course, they again consulted the Voice. Helen received the answer that it was "to be published by those who have only the Course as their focus." Helen and Bill interpreted this to mean Judy's Foundation for ParaSensory Investigation, which held the copyright to the Criswell offset edition (*JWD*, 117–18).

Two crucial naming decisions were made as the Course was making its public debut. In the wake of the decision to have Judy's foundation publish the Course, Helen indicated that she "felt strongly that . . . the Foundation's name should be changed. 'Parasensory Investigation,' she said, 'is misleading and inappropriate to the focus of the Course.'" The others agreed and sought guidance on a new name, which ultimately came to Helen as the "Foundation for Inner Peace" (*JWD*, 119–20). A similar naming issue arose the following August, in the immediate wake of the publication of the first edition, when James Bolen wanted to publish an article on the Course in the *Psychic Magazine*. Again, the foursome asked the Voice for guidance. "The answer was very clear, and Helen expressed it most concisely. 'I heard that the Course is not to be associated in any way with anything psychic,' she said. 'Its thrust is spiritual, metaphysical and psychological, and should not be confused with the psychic'" (*JWD*, 123). Shortly thereafter Bill suggested *New Realities* as an alternative name for the publication, which Bolen, who had already been looking for a more comprehensive name, willingly accepted (WT, 38; *AFF*, 369; *JWD*, 125). Thus, formally and officially, *A Course*

A Course in Miracles ○ Saul Bellow-Mystical Laureate
Powers of Mind ○ The Buddha & Nuclear Physics
Interview: Judith R. Skutch 'cosmic catalyst'

Vol.1 No.1 $1.50

New Realities

you are entitled to miracles . . .

FIGURE 9.1. *A Course in Miracles* went public in the April 1977 issue of *New Realities Magazine.* (Cover art: Jean Shinoda Bolen, MD © James Bolen. Used with permission.)

in Miracles was positioned as spiritual, metaphysical, and psychological, but *not psychic.*

Terminology: From the metaperspective of this book, all these terms—spiritual, metaphysical, psychological, and psychic (as well as mystical, paranormal, magical, and occult)—are complex cultural concepts that do not uniquely specify a particular type of experience. This point is not foreign to the Course. In the "Clarification of Terms," which was dictated just prior to these two naming decisions, the Voice stated: "A universal theology is impossible, but a universal experience is not only possible but necessary. It is this experience toward which the course is directed. Here alone consistency becomes possible because here alone uncertainty ends" (FIP 3rd C-Intro.2:5–7). I interpret this to mean that the Course can direct people to-

The Course is concerned with universal experiences

ward a particular type of experience, which it claims is universal and accessible to everyone, but it cannot uniquely specify the experience conceptually because "all terms are potentially controversial" (FIP 3rd C-Intro.2:1).

Nonetheless, the ACIM team, like early AAs and Mormons, used their guidance processes to select the terms that they felt best characterized their spiritual path, and in doing so tacitly positioned or framed their path in relation to others. As we have seen many times over, Helen was personally very sensitive to terminology and did not want to be associated with anything labeled psychic or paranormal, even though she had experiences and held beliefs that could easily be perceived as such, based on how the words were used at the time. The Voice clearly supported her in this as it guided the Course into the public realm.

Judging from the content of the Course itself, however, the Voice's views were more complex than Helen's statement that the Course's thrust was "spiritual, metaphysical, and psychological and . . . not . . . psychic" would suggest. Of the terms listed, the Course uses "spiritual, psychotherapy, and psychotherapist," but does not refer to "metaphysical, mystical, or paranormal." It also makes repeated references to "magic" and "magical," and a few references to "psychic" (Wapnick 1997). In the thought system of the Course, "spiritual" and "psychotherapeutic" are positive terms, "magic" is negative, and "psychic powers"—like "reincarnation"—can go either way. Although "spiritual" carries a positive valence, the Course more commonly uses "real," "reality," "truth," and "true" to refer to what it values and "illusion" and "ego" to refer to what it does not (ibid.). "Magic" is an illusory power that the equally illusory ego ascribes to itself (FIP 3rd T-4.II.9:1), but the "Manual for Teachers" advises teachers to tread carefully with respect to pupil's "magical thoughts," because attacking such beliefs simply "strengthens fear, and makes the magic seem quite real to both [student and teacher]" (FIP 3rd M-17.1:1–3).

Reincarnation and psychic powers are also explicitly addressed in the "Manual for Teachers" in light of the overall teachings of the Course. From the point of view of the Course, both can be considered true when properly understood, but neither reflects the ultimate goal of the Course—"the glorious surprise of remembering Who [one] is [as God's always loved Son]" (FIP 3rd M-25.1:5, see also M-18 and M-24). Contrary to the impression given by Helen's emphatic statement that the Course is "not psychic," the Course affirms that "there are many 'psychic' powers that are clearly in line with this course [and that] communication is not limited to the small range of channels the world recognizes" (FIP 3rd M-25.2:1–2). If there were not a wider range of channels of communication, it goes on to explain, it would not be possible to directly "experience . . . the Holy Spirit, Whose Presence is always there and Whose Voice is available but for the hearing. . . . [Anyone] who transcends these limits in any way is merely becoming more natural.

He is doing nothing special, and there is no magic in his accomplishments" (FIP 3rd M-25.2:5–8). At the same time, these powers can be misused by the ego in service of illusory ends (FIP 3rd M-25.3–6). The Course thus acknowledges that it is premised on the existence of "psychic powers," if these are understood simply as channels of communication beyond the five senses, since without such channels no one would be able to access the Voice of the Holy Spirit. At the same time, it reframes such powers as a means to an end rather than as an end in themselves and recognizes that they can also be misused in an effort to achieve illusory ends.

Reframing Experiences: The Course's discussion of psychic powers allows us to consider how Bill and Judy, as well as others who came to the Course through an interest in and experiences of psychic powers, reframed their experiences in light of the Course, much as the Voice reframed Helen's priestess visions and Ken reframed his inner voice as the Jesus of the Course. I was initially quite puzzled by the relationship between psychic phenomena and the Course, given the explicit rejection of psychic terminology, on the one hand, and extensive evidence of the importance of psychic phenomena in the emergence of the Course, on the other. As we have seen, Bill viewed his and Helen's Mayo Clinic experience and their visit to Virginia Beach as turning points that convinced him that Helen was not simply highly imaginative (or crazy) but had (psychic) access to something real. After Judy joined the group, she, Helen, and Bill, and—to a lesser extent—Ken continued to discuss and explore past lives, reincarnation, and other related themes. Visits to psychics continued during this period (WT, 40), including a visit with Ena Twigg, a prominent British psychic, when they were in London in 1977 (Skutch Whitson 2014; see also *AFF*, 442; Howe 2009, 86–91, 267–68). Moreover, in her 1977 interview, Skutch indicated that many of her friends immediately saw a connection between parapsychology and the Course. When she "showed the fifty principles of miracles . . . to my friends in parapsychology," she said, "the general reaction was, 'Of course. A perfect description of psychic phenomena'" (Skutch 1977). There is a sense, in other words, in which the connection with the Voice and the scribing of the Course was premised on a belief in the possibility of psychic connections to past events.

The key to understanding this seemingly simultaneous embrace and repudiation of psychic phenomena lies in recognizing that the thought system of ACIM *reframes* psychic phenomena as expanded channels of communication; it does not eliminate such experiences. Indeed, it relies upon them, recognizing that such experiences can be (and are) named in a variety of ways and used toward positive and negative ends. Working out this puzzle led to a more adequate interpretation of the way that Judy Skutch reframed her past experience in light of her involvement with the Course. In my ini-

FIGURE 9.2. Visiting the medium Ena Twigg and her husband, Harry, in London, 1977. *Front row*: Helen Schucman, Ena Twigg, Judith Skutch, and Harry Twigg. *Back row*: Bill Thetford, Jerry Jampolsky, and Kenneth Wapnick. © Foundation for Inner Peace.

tial draft of this chapter, I minimized the extent to which she reframed her experience in light of her stress on the importance of her experience in the dentist's office, her daughter's psychic abilities, and her involvement in parapsychological research in her early accounts, all of which seemed to highlight the congruence between the Course, the psychic, and the paranormal. Robert Rosenthal, who knew her at the time, however, stressed in a personal communication, "Judy's interest in parapsychology immediately and rather completely gave way to her commitment to the Course, a commitment that she sensed was to be lifelong" (November 2014). Judy's 1977 interview supports Rosenthal's observation. Not only did Judy say that Bill and Helen told her that the Voice had predicted her arrival, but the Voice "also indicated that that woman [i.e., Judy] was now ready for her own spiritual education." This, Judy said in the interview, "was truth to my ears. My path was made clear. I just knew it was my life's work. The change of the foundation's name was a reflection of this realization" (Skutch 1977).

Skutch Whitson herself responded to my initial analysis by reframing her involvement with parapsychological research as "a beginning of [her] commitment to the idea of expanded consciousness," which she supported with a fuller description of her religious background and her relationship with her father, Samuel Rothstein, a lawyer and a prominent Jewish lay leader, who served as the president of the United Synagogues of America, a national organization of conservative synagogues, and a founding member of the World Council of Synagogues. As she summed up her understanding of her earlier experience:

I was brought up with my father's passion for God, which permeated our household, and my Hebrew training was much more extensive than Ken's. My early mystical experiences fit in with that passion, but I did not see them as limited to my born religion. So you could say, I was indeed on a "Search for God." While at graduate school at Columbia University, I also audited courses at the Jewish Theological Seminary and had the excitement of learning from the Jewish mystic Abraham Joshua Heschel. (Skutch Whitson 2014)

This new information did not strike me as simply post hoc reframing of her early experiences but as highlighting aspects of her life that she took for granted at the time she was telling the story of how she became involved with the Course in 1977. Responding to Skutch Whitson on 18 November 2014, I wrote: "It looks to me like you are saying that you were somewhat of a perennialist from an early age—that you felt your mystical experience(s) went beyond Judaism (not limited to your born religion), [and] that your parapsychology explorations were linked to an interest in expanded consciousness—in other words, that there was a congruence throughout." She replied via e-mail on the same day: "I never thought of it in exactly that way, but I would say you are absolutely right."

Her account of how she explained her involvement with the Course to her father in 1976 also highlights their perennialist views. Thus, she recounted:

One day, during proofreading the manuscript, I read [aloud] portions of what he thought was the Course to him and he really did not want to hear [it]. But I had actually read a couple of paragraphs from *God in Search of Man* by my father's hero, Abraham Heschel. When I told him, he was truly moved. I then read a paragraph from the Course that had the almost identical concept. He thought about it, then said, "He was a great mystic." I concurred and explained, "that is what I am studying, that is my goal." I could tell he was moved almost to tears as he rose, patted me on the head, and replied, "A mystical life is a very hard thing to attain." I felt as if he had bestowed a blessing on me instead of a judgment. From that moment on (1976), I felt his acceptance and pride in what I was doing. (Skutch Whitson 2014)

Although she was not focusing explicitly on the perennialism of the Course, it is implicit in her and her father's acknowledgment of the similarities between the two readings, which they clearly thought of in terms of a mysticism that transcended any one particular path.

This suggests subtle but important differences in the way that Judith Skutch and Kenneth Wapnick connected their past experiences with the teachings of the Course, which paralleled the differences we have seen between Thetford and Schucman. Skutch connected most deeply to the Course through its resonance with a series of experiences, most notably, the feeling of oneness with the universe that she first experienced at thirteen, which resonated closely with Bill's reluctance to "talk in very specific Biblical terms" and his sense that the ultimate reference of the Course "was beyond conceptualization" (WT, 46–47). Wapnick connected most deeply to the Course through his personal experience of the Jesus of the Course when he visited the Abbey of Our Lady of Gethsemani, an experience that resonated closely with Schucman's devotion to the Jesus of the Course. This difference, I will suggest, played a role in how they each presented the Course.

Group Dynamics: Judy's arrival and, more specifically, Bill's role in recognizing Judy as the one who would move the process forward, signaled another shift in the group dynamics. In the 1977 *New Realities* interview, Judy indicated that Helen and Bill had told her they were not surprised by her arrival or her immediate affinity for the Course, because, she said, "[t]he 'inner voice' had . . . predicted that 'a woman would come along who would know what to do with it,' and they had been instructed to hand the manuscript over to her" (Skutch 1977; see also Schucman 1976). Looking back now, however, Skutch Whitson stresses that "Bill was the leader in this phase. . . . Bill had felt strongly that the Course was not for them alone. Helen was not happy with this idea. . . . He persisted by 'recognizing me' as the one who would continue the effort. He felt I would know what to do" (Skutch Whitson 2014). That Bill would have taken the lead in moving the Course toward publication makes sense in light of his long-standing sense that the Course was intended for a wider audience.

Bill received guidance that encouraged him to take a more prominent role through Paul Solomon, a well-known psychic, who did a reading for Bill in spring 1976 at the Skutch's apartment in New York.[2] According to Carol Howe, Bill specifically queried Solomon about his "function" in relation to the Course. Solomon, who channeled a voice that referred to itself as the Source, told Bill "[he] did not yet understand his relationship to the *Course*" and that "Bill would be unable to take his next step related to the Course until he understood and owned his full participation in its conception and birth" (Howe 2009, 86–87). His role, Solomon said, was crucial. He was the father to Helen's mother; the priest to Helen's priestess. Solomon's reading, which seems to have given Bill access to a Voice-like Source independent of Helen, indicated that he not only bore responsibility for the "birth and growth and maturity" of the Course, but also that his "responsi-

---

[2] On Solomon, see the Paul Solomon Foundation webpage at http://www.paulsolomon.com/index.html.

bility end[ed] not with the introduction of this [the Course] to the world, but with its maturity and application, the responsibility of learning from it, using it, not controlling how it shall be used but rather experiencing that which is given to experience. Go out to the people on your own and express, assist, share ideas, be a part of the Source of the material, and demonstrate its growth" (Solomon reading, quoted in Howe 2009, 87). Thus, the reading not only encouraged Bill to think of himself as a full participant in the conception and birth of the Course, it also introduced the idea that he might "go out to the people *on [his] own*" (my emphasis), which I take to mean, *independent of Helen*. This, as far as I know, was a new thought.

In discussing Bill's role, Solomon's reading drew heavily on the family metaphor, not only referring to Bill and Helen as priest and priestess, but also as father and mother (of the Course) and indicating that they had been married in a previous life (Howe 2009, 88). He also referred to "the channel [i.e., Helen] . . . [and] others that are as a part of the family even in this time" (ibid., 87). We have seen that Helen and Ken thought of their relationship in mother-son terms, and it is clear that Judy took on a "daughter" role, particularly in relation to Helen, who liked Judy to call her "Mama" (ibid., 119). This evidence suggests that Judy's arrival marked a shift in the "family" dynamics, such that Bill gradually took on more leadership than he had in the past and, in light of Judy's close ties to both Helen and Bill, that Ken, as the oldest "child" may have felt a bit displaced by his new younger "sister." Taking the family metaphor a step further, the reading also introduced the idea of a "marital separation." We need to take these underlying dynamics into account as we look at the way the Course entered the world and how different "family members" viewed the way the process unfolded.

Publicizing the Course: In a special message dated 25 January 1978, the Voice announced, "it is through Judy that I will speak" and then followed up on 24 February 1978 with a clear directive regarding the Foundation for Inner Peace. "The foundation has a limited function in the life of the Course. Its purpose is to publish, distribute and discuss the material, and the steps followed in meeting this aim should be carefully checked with the Author. He knows how He wants these functions carried out and how this part of the program should be handled." The message continued, however, stressing that "[t]hese steps are preparatory to the real function for which the Course was given" and indicating that they each had "appointed roles" for which "each has been very carefully chosen, and there have been no accidents nor accidental meetings." From the perspective of Helen, Bill, and Judy, this was all clear enough. The Voice had brought Judy into the picture so that she could take charge of disseminating the Course, publishing it under the auspices of her renamed foundation.

Ken, however, viewed things differently. As Wapnick later recalled, "in the early years of our association [prior to Judy's arrival] Helen, Bill, and I spoke of one day living together and having a school or center where *A Course in Miracles* would be taught. In fact, Helen had seen in her mind a large country house near water, which she thought would be such a place. On a symbolic level Helen saw this center as a white temple with a gold cross atop it, representing the person and message of Jesus" (*AFF*, 366). He credited the deterioration of Helen and Bill's relationship with their inability to realize this vision and Judy's arrival as allowing Bill and Helen to step back. "It was almost as if with Judy's coming, Helen (and Bill to a lesser extent) abdicated responsibility for the Course's life in the world" (*AFF*, 365). Looking back in 2008, Wapnick felt some regret. "I think it was unfortunate that they abdicated all responsibility for the Course. They gave it to Judy to take to the world and basically withdrew from any kind of leadership or authority. If they hadn't, the Course would have gone a different way. Although nothing is better nor worse, there are alternate scripts and I think there was clearly a script for Helen, Bill, and myself to have more of a sense of responsibility for shepherding the Course" (Wapnick interview, 2008; quoted in Howe 2009, 116). "In the absence of Helen's supervision and guidance at the beginning of its public life, the Course has thus developed in a much less focused direction than it would have otherwise gone. Judy, I believe, represented an alternate 'plan' for the Course's growth in the world, and one which involved its becoming quite popular, with approximately 700,000 sets sold as of September 1991" (*AFF*, 365).

Ken also made the somewhat surprising statement that Helen and Bill, despite their extensive consultations with the Voice, had completed their assignment "without asking Jesus first" (*AFF*, 367). He explained:

> I am referring not to the concrete decision to have Judy and the Foundation for Inner Peace publish the Course, but to the inner and not always conscious decision that, for all intents and purposes, they completed their involvement with the external life of the Course. Helen's and Bill's inability to forgive each other, let alone identify with *A Course in Miracles*, made such a leadership role impossible. And this despite repeated assurances from Jesus of the important roles they each would play, above and beyond the scribing of the Course. (ibid.)

Whether Helen and Bill's decision regarding their "function" reflected an unwillingness to consult with Jesus on the matter, as Ken felt, or was simply a reassertion of the bargain Helen had insisted on from the outset is a matter of interpretation. Based on the evidence that the Voice envisioned a larger role for Helen and Bill *from the start*, I suspect that Helen was simply reasserting her original conditions for efficiently scribing the Course.

Skutch Whitson offered a more prosaic perspective on the failure of the vision of living together, which, she said, they continued to discuss after she joined the group. In contrast to Wapnick, her sense of why it did not come to pass rests not so much on Bill and Helen's relationship (that is, on ACIM "family" dynamics), as it did on the wishes of Louis Schucman and Bob Skutch, neither of whom, she said, wanted anything to do with the idea. Not only were they opposed to a common living arrangement, but Louis Schucman was committed to living in New York City and Bob Skutch wanted to move elsewhere. According to Skutch Whitson, when their views became evident, "We realized it was not to be and that is when, having already abruptly sold our apartment in New York, Bob [and] I moved to California and Bill followed us there" (Skutch Whitson 2014).

Wapnick's prominent role as a teacher of the Course and the role of *Absence from Felicity* in shaping an understanding of this period make it easy to forget that many of his insights came later and tend to eclipse the vision implicit in the path that was taken. If we try to reconstruct how things looked from Bill and Judy's point of view at the time, we can discern an alternate, although not necessarily incompatible, vision for presenting the Course. Thus, we know that from the outset, Bill had an interest in the paranormal, in meditation practices, and in understanding the Course in relation to various world religions, all interests that he shared with Judy and her circle of friends in California, including James Bolen, the editor of *New Realities*, psychiatrist Jerry Jampolsky, and psychologists Frances Vaughan and Roger Walsh.[3] Frances Vaughan recalled that "Bill and Ken were polarized at times, because they did not have the same interpretations of the Course on a number of points. For instance, Ken always emphasized that the source of the material was the historical Jesus; Bill thought of it more as the universal Christ-mind or consciousness that we all share" (quoted in Miller 1997, 49). Moreover, whereas Ken and Helen shared a common devotion to the Jesus of the Course and routinely referred to the ultimate reality as God, Bill and Judy often referred to the Voice and ultimate reality in more abstract terms, such as Mind and Source, which resonated more easily with other traditions that shared the Course's metaphysics but not (necessarily) its Christian vocabulary. While Ken was ultimately most comfortable viewing the Course in relation to the debates over orthodoxy and heresy within

[3] Dr. Gerald Jampolsky, a psychiatrist and early Course adopter, founded the Center for Attitudinal Healing in Tiburon in 1975. The first West Coast study group, which included Jampolsky, the Skutches, and Thetford, met in his home. They were joined shortly thereafter by Frances Vaughan, a clinical psychologist who joined the faculty of the Institute for Transpersonal Psychology in Palo Alto when it was established in 1975, and, when possible, her future husband, Roger Walsh, MD, PhD, who had just accepted a faculty position at UC Irvine, where he is currently professor of psychiatry, philosophy, and anthropology. Jampolsky, Vaughan, and Walsh have all published extensively on the Course.

the history of Christianity, specifically, as a heretical, precreedal Christian thought system with affinities to Plato and the Gnostics (see Wapnick 1989), Bill was more inclined to position the Course in relation to the world's religions, specifically, in relation to nondual forms of Hinduism, thus characterizing it as a form of "Christian Vedanta," without losing sight of its connections to modern metaphysical forms of Christianity.

Skutch's 1977 interview with James Bolen, which she notes was "vetted and corrected by Helen and Bill" (Skutch Whitson 2014), reflected this less Christian-sounding way of presenting the Course. Thus, while she acknowledged the Course's use of Christian terminology in the interview, she made little or no mention of Jesus, often used alternative terms for God (e.g., Source, love's presence, or "the one Self we all share"), and stressed its compatibility with other religious and spiritual frameworks. She characterized the Course as one of many paths whose "purpose is . . . to help us reach a state where we recognize our oneness with the All." When Bolen noted that all the Christian terminology made it sound like the Course might be "a new religion or cult," Skutch stressed that it wasn't "a religion . . . [and did] not require a commitment to religion." "The Course," she explained, "is actually opposed to the idea of introducing a new system, and just tries to encourage people to work within whatever their present framework is, with this as an additional dimension. . . . The emphasis is always on the Inner Teacher, speaking to each of us according to our understanding and our needs" (Skutch 1977).

Frances Vaughan and Roger Walsh, who joined the nine o'clock morning meetings at Jerry Jampolsky's home in Tiburon shortly after Bill, Judy, and Bob moved to California (Howe 2009, 143, 178–80), developed the implications of this emphasis more fully. In their publications on the Course, the first of which appeared in 1983, Walsh and Vaughan acknowledged the Course's Christian vocabulary, but stressed the idea that it embodied "the perennial wisdom found at the core of all the world's great religions." In contrast to Wapnick, who preferred not to translate the Course into other religious idioms, they stressed its translatability. "Some Buddhists have said that the Course echoes the words of the Buddha; yogis have remarked that it expresses the wisdom of Vedanta; and psychologists have found that it offers insights comparable to some of the best contemporary thinking about phenomena such as perception, belief, and identity" (Vaughan and Walsh 1983, 7–9; Miller 1997, 125–42; Howe 2009, 163–64).

CONCLUSION

In the end, the team's inability to live together led Ken to support the viable route, which he viewed as a definite "Plan B." Judy's appearance, the bond between Bill and Judy, and Bill's decision to move to the West Coast along with Judy and Bob Skutch precipitated a bicoastal solution, freed Bill to practice the Course independent of Helen, and may have triggered Helen's virtually complete retreat from the Course in the wake of Bill's departure. Ken remained in New York with Helen and Louis until Helen's death in 1981. He and his wife, Gloria, whom he married in 1981, created the Foundation for *A Course in Miracles* (FACIM) in New York in 1983, which evolved into the teaching arm of the Course. It was located in Ardsley, Crompond, and Roscoe, New York, in the eighties and nineties, before they finally relocated to Temecula, California, in 2001. As Helen's death neared and she retreated further and further from the Course, Helen and Ken interpreted her "physical and emotional deterioration" as a means of "get[ting] out of its [the Course's] way" (*AFF*, 370). Although Ken characterized Helen and Bill as "estranged from each other until the end" (*AFF*, 368), Judy and Bill each called Helen every evening as she had instructed them—Judy at four o'clock and Ken at seven—not to discuss the Course but simply to maintain their personal connection with her. Despite Helen's inability to embrace its teachings in her relationship with Bill, Ken devoted *Absence from Felicity* to interpreting her divided mind in light of the Course, a split that the peaceful expression on her face at her death led him to believe she finally overcame (*AFF*, 475–79).

Although Judy Skutch grew up in New York City and Bill Thetford in Chicago, their move to the West Coast—where many of Judy's friends and contacts devoted to exploring higher consciousness, parapsychology, and the "noetic sciences" were already located—seems entirely fitting. Their more perennialist approach to the Course was particularly well suited to West Coast audiences that were loosely affiliated with particular religious traditions, and in the early years of the Course, many prominent people interested in spiritual transformation weighed in with positive endorsements (see Van der Horst 1977).

Ken Wapnick, who was disposed to use more Christian-sounding language in discussing the Course, was operating in a very different environment. As a therapist with a clinical practice comprised mostly of Catholics in the New York Archdiocese, his earliest Course-related publication, titled "Christian Psychology in *A Course in Miracles*" (1978), while addressed to Christians generally, was specifically written for "a group of Roman Catholics—nuns, priests, and laypeople—that [he] was most involved with at the time" (Wapnick [1983] 1992 [4th ed.], xi–xii). Although in his earliest writings he attempted to build a bridge between traditional Christianity and the radical teachings of Jesus in the Course, he increasingly stressed the differences, comparing the Course with Platonic philosophy, Neoplatonism, and Christian Gnosticism (Wapnick 1989). In doing so, he situated the Course in relation to the history of Christianity and Western philosophy rather than world religions and spiritualities. As Patrick Miller (1997) points out in his history of the Course, these differences in emphasis echo down to the present.

Finally, in terms of organization, the Course has generated no official structures other than the Foundation for Inner Peace (FIP) and its officially related teaching arm, the Foundation for *A Course in Miracles* (FACIM). There are, however, numerous other unofficial teachers, centers, and newsletters (Miller 1997), as well as more than two thousand study groups in sixty-five countries as of 2014 (FIP website). In addition to the initial study groups in Skutch's apartment in New York City and at Jerry Jampolsky's home in Tiburon after Judy, Bob, and Bill moved to California, numerous study groups sprang up on the East and West Coasts in the wake of the publication of the Course. Paul Steinberg, a Long Island contractor who gave many talks on the Course in the early years, was personally responsible for starting many of these early groups, mostly on the East Coast. Beverly Hutchinson (now McNeff) and her brother, Richard, were involved with many of the earliest study groups in Southern California and founded the nonprofit Miracle Distribution Center (MDC) in 1978 to keep track of the groups and help new students find one. Although Helen used to say "no groups" and Ken Wapnick liked to point out that nowhere in the Course does it say "go ye and form study groups," people nonetheless wanted to study it with others (McNeff phone conversation, 15 October 2014). According to McNeff, when Paul Steinberg, who preferred traveling to running a center, started turning over the information he collected to the MDC, it became the central hub for study groups.

Although it has no legal relationship with FIP or FACIM, MDC's interactive global map of study groups is now prominently displayed on the FIP website, but because groups are not a formal part of the Course nor conceived as foundational, as they are with Alcoholics Anonymous, MDC and FIP simply keep track of groups without any attempt to regulate them. Still, in response to requests, MDC does provide "a format outline for study groups that we had found to be effective." In a manner that organizationally averse AAs would recognize, the center stresses that these are "merely suggestions and should not be construed as 'hard and fast rules,' only guidelines. In the end, only the Holy Spirit can truly guide you in what to do in your group and life."[4] The upshot is that ACIM is slightly more organized than Helen Schucman or Ken Wapnick might have envisioned but has nothing like the level of organization we see in Mormonism, and considerably less than we see even in Alcoholics Anonymous.

[4] See the Miracle Distribution Center website at http://www.miraclecenter.org/wp/study-group-outline/.

Creating Paths

Methodologically, this project is built on a stipulated point of analogy between the three groups, each of which had a founding figure who had unusual experiences of a presence or reality that—as we have seen—guided the emergence of a new spiritual path with associated scripture-like texts. In Part 2, I want to explain the emergence of these new spiritual paths, the alleged presences that guided the process, and the production of the scripture-like texts in naturalistic terms. Doing so requires us to account for three main things: (1) how people came to believe that a presence other than themselves was acting in their midst, (2) how this presence was able not only to guide, but especially in the case of the Book of Mormon and the Course, to produce complex texts, and (3) who or what the presences were and what motivated believers (but not skeptics) to credit them with revealing the texts and the paths.

In naturalistic terms, the emergence of these new paths involved the collective reinterpretation of a key figure as a vehicle of this presence, such that the presence was not only able to manifest itself to the emergent group, but to guide the emergence of the group, generate the key text, and call them to reorient their lives in a profound and deeply compelling way. Because the reinterpretation of the key figure took place collectively, it simultaneously gave voice to the presence and called the group itself into existence. Although we can (and will) consider group interactions and the individual abilities of the key figures independently in chapters 10 and 11, they are actually inseparable aspects of the process that constitutes a new group—in effect bootstrapping it into existence. The emergence of a new group in conjunction with new understandings of themselves was in turn fueled by motivations—aims, desires, and longings—conscious and unconscious, personal and collective, which will be the focus of chapter 12.

Collectively agreed-upon reconceptualizations of self were at the heart of the process. If we think of the non-ordinary presences as dissociated subjectivities who were motivated to envision a way forward for the group as a whole, we can view those who (initially) constituted and those who (later) joined the groups as people whose motives coincided with those of the perceived presences. The key to the groups' ultimate success lay in their ability to transform problems that were initially of limited concern—Joseph Smith's family's disagreements over religion and his own uncertainty as to which denomination was correct, Bill Wilson's problem drinking, and the relational difficulties between Helen Schucman and Bill Thetford and in their department—into paths that offered spiritual solutions to more generalized problems.

Making this case rests on two discrete steps: first, deepening the comparisons between the three groups in order to specify features to be explained more precisely and then expanding the range of comparisons in light of the specific feature(s) in order to see if we can explain these features in naturalistic terms. The first step involves justifying or making the case that the features mentioned above are indeed features that the three groups share in common despite their differences. Much of this work will be done in chapter 10, where we will compare the process of group formation in the three cases focusing on the emergence of the presences and the group guidance processes. Additional work will be done at the start of chapter 11, where I will justify a comparison of Smith as translator of the golden plates with Schucman as scribe of ACIM.

The second step involves bringing social scientific theories and experimental research to bear on the features we want to explain, while at the same time acknowledging their limits. This will begin toward the end of chapter 10 with the introduction of a social identity approach to creativity, which allows us to consider the role that groups play in stimulating and shaping the creative process, but it will have to be adapted and extended in order to characterize the shifts in self-conception that take place when groups attribute agency to a postulated presence rather than claiming it themselves. We will then expand this explanation in chapter 11 by considering individual abilities that facilitate these shifts in self-conception. In chapter 12 we will consider what motivates the postulated selves (human and suprahuman) to lead, form, or join a group. If we do not assume an everyday (folk) understanding of the self as unified, which recent research on self-agency would lead us to question, we can combine a less intuitive but more scientifically plausible understanding of the individual with the social identity approach to creativity to open up more possibilities for categorizing "selves"—including non-ordinary "selves"—and for attributing authorship and guidance within human groups (see Pacherie 2011 for an overview of research on self-agency).

CHAPTER 10

Groups

Having generated careful reconstructions of the process of emergence of these three groups, we are now in a position to compare and contrast the way the process unfolded with particular attention to the role that unusual experiences played in the process. What we find is that, although each of the key figures had a history of unusual experiences, their experiences were recast in light of what emerged and thus played very different roles in the group's respective narratives of their origins.

INTERACTIVE PROCESSES COMPARED

Initial Experiences: The differences between the three cases are particularly evident with respect to what they viewed as their initial experiences. Thus, Joseph Smith did not recount his first vision, which he most likely viewed initially as an evangelical-style conversion experience, until the early thirties when it took on an important role in recounting the origins of the restored church. Bill Wilson's cathedral experience, although he consistently viewed it as an experience of transcendent presence, was transformed into a warning of the dangers of drink for an AA audience. Helen Schucman's subway experience, although in her eyes her "most significant religious experience," played no part in the ACIM story at all.

Emergent Visions: In terms of the emergence of the three groups—viewed in real time—the most crucial development in each case was a vision of what could be, that is, a visionary *idea*, whether or not it was directly linked with a visionary *experience*. In Smith's case, the idea, conveyed to him by a personage in his 1823 dream-vision, was that there were records of ancient inhabitants that he was to recover buried nearby. In Wilson's case, it was the thought, which emerged in the wake of his sudden experience at Towns Hospital, that he could pass on to others what he had just experienced himself. In Schucman's case, the central idea, which was really Thetford's, was they could find a better way to resolve conflict by venturing inward.

Stabilizing the Vision: In each case, a period of instability and doubt ensued in which the idea was tested in a small group already known to the primary experiencers. The preexisting small group was involved in the appraisal of the idea and in generating a relatively stable interpretive frame. In each case, there were key moments of hesitation or doubt on the part of the experiencers, which suggested competing appraisals and possibilities for framing their unfolding vision.

In Smith's case, his hesitation the morning after his dream-vision, and his doubt when he was unable to recover the plates, suggest that he vacillated at first between interpreting the event as a "mere" dream rather than the appearance of an actual discarnate "personage." The response of Smith's immediate family to his dream-vision validated God as the source of the dream-vision and the personage as real; their eager interest in accounts of Smith's interactions with the personage affirmed his claim to have seen both the plates and the personage. Smith's inability to recover the plates led, I hypothesized, to the "chastisement by the angel" and his realization that he could make plates holding on—in faith—to the idea that the Lord could and would transform the homemade plates into ancient plates/records. This insight allowed him to reframe the plates as an object envisioned and made real through faith. The willingness of his family members to obey the command not to look at the plates directly affirmed the reality of the ancient plates and framed the concealed object that Smith presented to them as the recovered record of ancient inhabitants of the Americas.

In Wilson's case, he doubted his sanity in the wake of his sudden experience at Towns Hospital and immediately recounted his experience to Dr. Silkworth, who confirmed both his sanity and the value of the experience. Lois Wilson reinforced Silkworth's appraisal with her sense that he was fundamentally changed, Ebby T. by bringing him a copy of James's *Varieties of Religious Experience*, and the Oxford Group by confirming his appraisal of the experience in religious terms. It was this experience—verified by those close to him—that Wilson initially tried to pass on to others. The failure of his "testimony" to change others led Silkworth to question Wilson's approach and Wilson to doubt the authenticity of his experience when faced with the temptation to drink at the Mayflower Hotel in Akron. His insight at the hotel led him to reappraise his experience and to the realization that "mutuality" rather than "testimony" was the key to adding links to the chain.

Schucman, unlike the other two, was chronically doubtful and required constant feedback, encouragement, and support from Thetford. Her vacillation between explaining her sense of "knowing awareness" as "a glimpse of Heaven" or "normal chance variation" in summer 1965 exemplifies the competing possibilities. According to Thetford (1984, 1), their experience at Mayo Clinic, "as much as anything . . . crystallized the whole new direction that we would take." The core issue had to do with the appraisal of Schucman's images, whether they were the product of her imagination or perceptions grounded in reality. As Thetford indicated, his discovery of the picture of the church that had been razed to build Mayo Clinic helped convince him that Schucman wasn't "out of [her] mind after all," but was "looking back through time." Similar feedback from Hugh Lynn Cayce when they visited Virginia Beach, as well as later confirmations from the medium Eileen Garrett, played an important role in stabilizing Bill's interpretation of events and thus his ability to support Helen in the scribing process.

Incorporating Outsiders: In each case, there was a crucial transition as the first outsiders were incorporated into the preexisting small group. With Smith, the key additions were Martin Harris, Oliver Cowdery, and David Whitmer; with AA, the breakthrough addition was Dr. Bob, followed by Bill D., Hank P., and Fitz; with ACIM, the key additions were Kenneth Wapnick and Judith Skutch. Incorporating these new members was a rocky process. In the Mormon case, convincing Martin and Lucy Harris led to the transcribing of characters, the visit to Anthon, the loss of the first 116 pages, and the first real-time recorded revelation. Even with the addition of Dr. Bob, adding members to the chain was an iffy process for Bill Wilson. The loss of Ebby and Hank P., coupled with success in Akron and Cleveland, shifted the narrative away from Ebby and Bill to Bill and Bob. The addition of Kenneth Wapnick and then Judy Skutch to the ACIM team seems in retrospect to have proceeded more smoothly, but just as there were other possible first followers, such as Lucy Harris and Joseph Knight in the Mormon case and Hank P. and Fitz in the AA case, so too we can think of Cal Hatcher and Fr. Benedict Groeschel as potential first followers of ACIM, who were sympathetic but never fully incorporated as members of the inner circle.

In each case, their incorporation was premised on the acceptance of a core set of beliefs about what was emerging. In the Mormon case, incorporation was predicated on belief in the existence of ancient records recovered by Smith and his God-given gifts of translation and continuing revelation through the power of the Holy Spirit. In the case of AA, it was premised on the acceptance of a spiritual awakening grounded in mutual need as a basis for recovery. In the case of ACIM, it was premised on the belief that Schucman, with the help of Thetford, was the means through which the Voice was revealing a new spiritual thought system and continuing to guide them.

Skeptics: In each case, there were some who were involved at this early stage who were skeptical and thus echoed, rather than assuaged, the internal doubts of the key figures. In the case of Mormonism, Lucy Harris and Emma Smith's relatives in Harmony doubted and questioned. In the case of AA, Wilson's Oxford Group team questioned his claims regarding guidance, and the New York alcoholics evinced skepticism regarding his sudden experience at Towns. In the case of ACIM, Fr. Benedict Groeschel (1993) viewed the Course as mystical poetry but not revelation, and Louis Schucman (n.d.) viewed the Course as a product of Helen's intuitive and creative abilities.

Going Public: The addition of a (reasonably) stable set of first followers to the preexisting group was a precondition for movement into the public sphere and, in each case, fed directly into the publication of the group's scripture-like texts. In the Mormon case, Harris and Cowdery were directly involved in the translation process, which was completed in the Whitmer home. Harris, Cowdery, and Whitmer were the three witnesses who, in accord with the Lord's revelations to Smith (D&C 5, 17), were allowed to see the golden plates in a vision, and whose testimony to their existence was published along with the Book of Mormon (*JSP*, D1:378–82). In the case of AA, the addition of Dr. Bob and Bill D. established the first durable links in the chain, gave AA its official founding date, and within three years led to the collective decision to recount what they had learned in book form. They made the decision to publish in Dr. Bob's living room in Akron, and the book's content was edited by the AAs meeting in New York and in Ohio. Although Schucman and Thetford were able to complete the scribing of the Course together, it was not clear what was to be done with it once it was completed. The addition of Wapnick and Skutch allowed the editing and publication of the Course to move forward and made it clear that the scribed Course was intended for a wider audience, as the Voice indicated from the outset.

In each case, going public required the collaborators to characterize themselves as a group and their newly published text as a text. They had to name themselves or embrace what others called them—as Mormons, anonymous alcoholics, and students of the Course—and position their group relative to others. Smith and his followers constituted themselves as a church, albeit a restored church, headed by a prophet who had revealed new scripture; the anonymous alcoholics characterized themselves as a spiritual fellowship and mutual aid society that complemented but did not compete with the religious or medical "establishments"; and the Course's initial students presented it to the public as a self-study thought system that was spiritual, metaphysical, and psychological, but not religious, paranormal, or cultlike.

Recounting Origins: In discussing origin stories, we have had to distinguish between the core beliefs that constituted the groups as groups and the accounts they offered for the origins of their group as they went public with their new scripture-like texts. In each case there was a proto-origin story embedded in the new books. The Book of Mormon told the story of records kept by ancient inhabitants of the Americas on metal plates, "sealed up and hid," and now recovered and translated by Joseph Smith "by the gift of God." The Big Book gave the personal stories of Bill W. and Dr. Bob pride of place but recounted what was to become the official AA story as the meeting of two anonymous "friends" in an unnamed city in 1935. The Course initially offered no explanation of its proximate origins and left readers to infer its ultimate origins based on the self-identification of the voice of the text as God's Son. Hence, the two groups that made the strongest claims for the non-ordinary origins of their key texts were the least forthcoming as to their texts' proximate origins. AA, which made much weaker claims with respect to its ultimate origins, was much more forthcoming regarding its proximate origins.

In each case, however, each group offered fuller accounts of their proximate origins over time. Joseph Smith began recounting the proximate origins of the new revelation in talks to early Mormons and began writing his first history in 1832. His 1839 history, portions of which were later canonized in the "Pearl of Great Price," became the official origin account and the one best known to believers. Within two years of the publication of the Big Book, the outlines of the official AA story were in place. Bill W. recounted it over the course of the forties and it was published in the preface to the second edition of the Big Book and *Alcoholics Anonymous Comes of Age* (1955). In response to requests from early students, Helen Schucman and the Voice generated the three-part pamphlet that explained "How It Came—What It Is—What It Says" that was included as an insert with the first edition of the Course and became its preface in the second and third editions. The identities of Schucman and Thetford were not revealed, however, until after Schucman's death in 1981, at which point Thetford offered a fuller account of the Course's proximate origins in an interview (1984) and Robert Skutch offered the first extended account in *Journey Without Distance* (1984a).

GUIDANCE PROCEDURES

The groups' attribution of authorship not to individuals but to ancient Nephites via the Holy Spirit, an anonymous group guided by a Higher Power, and the Voice of God's Son distinguished the new texts from works of fiction and the emerging spiritual paths from dramatic performances. Indeed, belief in these presences and their ability to relate to them was what constituted them as separate groups and set them apart from their contemporary critics. These appraisals were consolidated in their official origin accounts, which then provided, in each case, a succinct statement of who they were, what their message was, and how they had received it. But, as these origin accounts attest, the emergent groups did more than simply communicate with these presences; they allowed themselves to be guided by them. In all three cases, having gained access to what they believed was a non-ordinary agent or power, they developed agreed-upon "guidance procedures" that allowed (respectively) the Lord (Mormonism), a Higher Power (AA), or the Voice of the Course (ACIM) to guide the emergence of the new path. The emergence of these guidance procedures shifted the ultimate responsibility for the emergence of the groups—and their authority structures—from themselves to a suprahuman presence and, in so doing, stabilized the group and the emergent path, providing a source of authority and a court of appeal in the face of difficulties.

All three groups developed these guidance procedures in the early stages of their emergence. In each case, we can identify three important steps: (1) establishing the *presence* of the source or entity, (2) formalizing *a means of communicating* with it, and (3) developing *criteria* for identifying authentic communications. The way that each group resolved these issues had far-reaching consequences. It not only constituted the group as a group in relation to the non-ordinary presence, it also determined the authority structure within the emergent formation and the final shape of the group's origin account. In naturalistic terms, we can view these guidance procedures as a means of tuning in to the needs of the emergent group and directing the formation process in light of the group's emergent aims.

Mormonism: In the case of early Mormonism, the presence of the Lord and other personages was known through Smith. Communications came initially via his visionary experiences and/or his seer stone. During the translation process, Oliver Cowdery hoped that he, too, might be allowed to translate, and he received a revelation via Smith indicating that he would be allowed to do so (Revelation, April 1829-B, *JSP*, D1:44–47 [D&C 8]), but when he was unsuccessful, the Lord explained that he had not proceeded properly (Revelation, April 1829-D, *JSP*, D1:48–50 [D&C 9]). During the translation process and thereafter, Smith typically requested revelations in response to inquiries, that is, through the "ask and receive" method discussed in chapter 3. After 1830, he typically requested revelations without the use of a seer stone or other object (*JSP*, D1:xxxiii).

David Whitmer later ascribed great significance to this shift from seer stone to the "mouthpiece" method, as he called it, claiming that authentic revelations to Smith came via his seer stone for the purpose of translating the Book of Mormon and thus ended when the plates were translated and Smith gave his seer stone to Cowdery in 1830. According to Whitmer, when "Joseph gave the stone to Oliver Cowdery and told me as well as the rest that he was through with it, . . . [h]e told us that we would all have to depend on the Holy Ghost hereafter to be guided into truth and obtain the will of the Lord" (*EMD* 5:199–200). Based on his understanding of the proper method and intended purpose of revelations to Smith, Whitmer challenged the 6 April 1830 "mouthpiece" revelation to Smith (today's D&C 21:1–5) that established him as " 'Prophet, Seer and Revelator' to the church" and disputed the claim "that the church should receive his [Smith's] words as if from God's own mouth" (*EMD* 5:201).

There were others in the wake of the founding of the new church in April 1830 that did not assume that Smith was the *only* legitimate channel for new revelation. According to Ezra Booth, "Cowdery's desires for this work [of receiving revelation] were so keen" that it felt to Cowdery like "a burning fire [was] shut up in [his] bones" (Booth, Letter 8, quoted in Howe [1834] 2015, 303 [apparently quoting from a revelation to Cowdery; see 303n59]). Subsequent revelations, however, stressed that Smith *alone* was appointed to receive revelations for the church. In a revelation to Oliver Cowdery (via Smith) in September 1830 (Revelation, September 1830-B, *JSP*, D1:183–86 [D&C 28]), the Lord explained that Smith alone was "appointed to Receive commandments & Revelations in this Church." Likening Smith to Moses and Cowdery to Aaron, the Lord explicitly instructed Cowdery to obey the revelations that he (the Lord) was giving to Smith as he had previously given them to Moses.

At about the same time, Hiram Page, one of the eight witnesses, claimed to have taken dictation from the Lord through his seer stone. According to Booth, Page saw writing appear on a smooth stone, which he transcribed. The result, Booth said, "bore striking marks of a Mormonite revelation, and was received as an authentic document by most of the Mormonites, till Smith, by his superior sagacity, discovered it to be a Satanic fraud" (Letter 13, quoted in Howe [1834] 2015). Thus, in the September 1830 revelation, the Lord instructed Cowdery to tell Page privately that "those things which he hath written from that Stone are not of me & that Satan deceiveth him" (Revelation, September 1830-B, *JSP*, D1:183–86 [D&C 28]). Sixteen months later, in February 1831, a Mrs. Hubble also claimed to receive revelations. According to John Whitmer, "[she] professed to be a prophetess of the Lord, and professed to have many revelations, and knew that the Book of mormon was true; and that she should become a teacher in the Church of Christ" (*JSP*, D2:257). Both Whitmer and Booth indicate that a number of the Ohio Mormons believed her. In order that the "saints might not be deceived," the Lord, according to Whitmer, offered a revelation through Smith upon his arrival in Ohio later that month. It reiterated "that there is none other appointed unto you to receive commandments & Revelations" except Joseph Smith (Booth, Letter 8, quoted in Howe [1834] 2015; Revelation, February 1831-A, *JSP*, D2:256–60 [D&C 43]).

There was also a seemingly more democratic aspect to the guidance process, which was spelled out in the September 1830 revelation. Thus, just prior to leaving—as instructed—on a mission to convert the "Lamanites," the

Lord instructed Cowdery to attend a forthcoming conference at which "my servent [sic] Joseph shall be appointed to rule the conference by the voice of it." The Lord laid out the ground rules for such conferences, specifying that everything "must be done in order & by Common consent in the Church by the prayer of faith & thou shalt settle all these things according to the Covenants of the Church" (Revelation, September 1830-B, *JSP*, D1:186 [D&C 28]). In specifying that nothing should be done "contrary to the Church Articles & Covenants," the Lord placed continuing revelation to Smith and his appointed successors at the heart of the governance process. The conference could *consent* to revelation for the church as a whole but they were not authorized to dissent. Ezra Booth, an early convert, summed up the situation in September 1831, shortly after leaving the church. "Every thing in the church is done by commandment [i.e., revelation]: and yet it is said to be done by the voice of the church. For instance, Smith gets a commandment that he shall be the 'head of the church,' or that he 'shall rule the Conference' . . . For this the members of the church must vote, or they will be cast off for revelling [rebelling] against the commandments of the Lord" (Booth, Letter 2, quoted in Howe [1834] 2015, 263–64; on Booth, see Staker 2009, 296–305).

Alcoholics Anonymous: In the case of AA, Bill Wilson experienced a sense of divine presence on many occasions, beginning when he served in World War I, but he embraced the idea of guidance in the context of Oxford Group meetings in the wake of his sudden experience in Towns Hospital. Lois Wilson described what the meetings were like.

> The Oxford Group, as we knew it back in the early months of 1935, worked in teams of six to a dozen, sitting quietly together like a Quaker meeting and listening for the guidance of God for each one. Bill belonged to a team for a while, but I didn't. The rest of the team would get guidance for him to work with such and such a person in order to "bring him to God." Bill usually had different guidance and felt no identity with the person they selected. He became a bit annoyed at being told what to do. He knew he could be far more useful working with alcoholics, with whom he could identify. He had been helped because Ebby was a fellow alcoholic and understood his problem. Therefore Bill began to invite all the alcoholics he ran into to meet with him at Stewart's Cafeteria after the Oxford Group meeting or to come to him at our home in Brooklyn. (*LR* 1987, 93–94)

John Ryder, who knew Bill during this period, recalled that "the '[Oxford] group' proper disowned Bill when he proceeded *on his guidance* to create a special group for AA's. At that time, if you were associated with the 'group,' your guidance seemed to be of questionable worth unless okayed by Sam Shoemaker or Frankie Buchman or one of their accredited representatives" (quoted in *PIO*, 174; emphasis added).

Guidance was also central to the Oxford Group practice in Akron. Henrietta Seuberling relied on guidance in responding to Wilson's call from the Mayflower Hotel (*PIO*, 137) and, as we have seen, guidance was at the heart of Bob and Anne Smith's daily "quiet time." Participation in the Smith's family-based quiet time likely reinforced the importance of seeking guidance but did so free of the interpretive constraints on guidance in the Oxford Group team meetings in New York. The summer Wilson spent with the Smiths in Akron provided a context in which they adapted the Oxford Group guidance practices to the needs of the emerging work with alcoholics.

In adapting Oxford Group practices, Wilson retained the Oxford Group sense that guidance needed to be "checked" by others, but transferred that power from the Oxford Group leadership to the special meetings for alcoholics (*PIO*, 171–72). In doing so, the guidance process was shifted from a movement focused on Christian conversion to a movement focused on recovery from alcoholism, but guidance was still rooted in the local group. Thus, when Dr. Silkworth offered Wilson a paid position at Towns Hospital in 1936, he initially felt "guided" to accept. Neither Lois Wilson nor the Tuesday evening meeting of alcoholics, however, confirmed this, arguing that the message of recovery had to be passed on solely out of love for the alcoholic and not for money (*PIO*, 177). Bill conceded and, in doing so, the group laid the groundwork for Tradition Eight, which states that AA should "remain forever nonprofessional."

Similarly, in 1937, upon realizing that more than forty alcoholics had stayed sober as a result of the program, Wilson wanted to expand their outreach through paid missionaries, special hospitals, and a book that would tell their story to the world. Bob Smith had doubts, so they called a meeting of the Akron members to get their feedback (*PIO*, 178–80). Here, too, the group objected to all but the book idea, narrowly approving it by one vote (*PIO*, 180). Wilson's embrace of the guidance of the group, at the expense of what he felt as an individual, located authority in the local group and laid the foundation for Tradition Two, which grounds "ultimate authority" not in a designated individual (a seer, prophet, oracle, or channel) but in "a loving God as He may express Himself *in our group conscience*" (emphasis added).

The Twelve Traditions emerged through the same process writ large, that is, through a back-and-forth between Wilson and AA members through the *Grapevine*, AA's newly inaugurated newsletter, letters to individual AAs, and then the vote of the membership at the AA Convention in 1950 (Kurtz 1991, 254–55). Although innovations were submitted to representatives of the group at both Mormon conferences and AA conventions, the notion of collective guidance in AA, with its base in the local group, differed sharply from the notion of prophetic guidance in Mormonism. The openness to guidance extended beyond AA proper to include outside groups with whom AA wanted to maintain good working relations. Thus, as we have seen, Wilson sent the final drafts of the Big Book, *Twelve and Twelve*, and *Alcoholics Anonymous Comes of Age* to a wide range of interested parties in the religious and medical world to solicit their input. Doing so dramatically cut down on negative feedback from potentially competing groups and allowed AA to position itself as compatible with them.

The role of the group in the guidance process set limits on individual guidance, but individual guidance was still an expected part of the process. Thus, all AAs were expected to establish a relationship with a Higher Power (Step Three). To make sure that AAs did not take Bill Wilson's sudden experience as the singular method for establishing such a relationship, AA modified Step Twelve and added an appendix on "spiritual experience" to the second printing of the first edition. Step Eleven specified that prayer and meditation were the general means of accessing one's Higher Power, but the specifics were left open. Access to the means of communication was limited only at the point where it threatened the common welfare of the group (Tradition One), at which point, the ultimate authority for determining "group purpose" was vested in "a loving God as He may express Himself in our group conscience" (Tradition Two). This mechanism was extended from the local AA group to AA as a whole as represented at its international conferences. Ultimate authority in AA was therefore not vested in a leader—a prophet or a president—but in the Higher Power as it expressed itself through the group conscience.

A Course in Miracles: The pattern of Schucman's interaction with the Voice was similar in many ways to Joseph Smith's interaction with the Lord. Both had sudden visionary experiences prior to translating (Smith) or scribing (Schucman) a lengthy text and both received direct guidance (revelations in Smith's case and special messages in Schucman's) during and after the production of the texts. In both cases, they received direct guidance on matters ranging from the mundane to the cosmic. As we have seen, in the early stages of dictating the Course, the Voice encouraged Schucman and Thetford to ask for guidance in everyday activities from shopping for clothing to catching cabs. This practice continued after Wapnick and Skutch joined the team. Indeed, Wapnick indicated that, "[a]fter we met Judy, this practice of asking for specifics continued, and if anything, seemed to increase with all the practical decisions that needed resolution" (*AFF*, 442).

In an interview with David Hammond in August 1976, a year after Judy's arrival, Helen offered a detailed description of their guidance practices. When Hammond asked whether Helen "continue[d] to hear the voice," she responded (Schucman 1976):

SCHUCMAN: Oh, no, I could ask what to do about something, particularly if the three of us (Helen, Bill Thetford and Ken Wapnick) were together. And we can ask, and we can get an answer . . . generally get the same answer. If we don't, we sort of feel somebody is off a little bit and we'll try again. But we generally do. . . .

HAMMOND: So you do hear now and then . . .

SCHUCMAN: I hear whenever I ask.

HAMMOND: In other words, at this point now it's really a matter of asking?

SCHUCMAN: Well now it's a little more a question of personal guidance as to what to do. We didn't know whether we were supposed to come here, for example, so we asked about that.

When it was just Schucman and Thetford, Schucman put questions to the Voice for both of them, much as Smith inquired of the Lord for himself and others. After Kenneth Wapnick arrived, asking took place primarily when Helen, Bill, and Ken were together and thus became a group process, which in time incorporated Judy as well. In the group context, everyone "asked" and, Schucman indicated, everyone got answers. On some occasions, as we saw in chapter 9, not everyone received an answer. Regardless, the group worked together to discern what the Voice was communicating, based largely on whether the responses they received were congruent or if someone seemed to be "off a little bit."

Different emphases with respect to individual guidance began to emerge in the late seventies. Although the Voice had encouraged Bill and Helen to ask "the Holy Spirit for *specific* guidance" in specific situations, which was still their practice when Ken joined them, Wapnick later confessed to feeling uncomfortable with this. Even at the time, he said, their practice started to seem "so *magical*" insofar as it presupposed an illusory separation between humans and God (*AFF*, 442; emphasis added). In the "The Song of Prayer," a supplement to the Course that Schucman scribed in 1977, the Voice distinguished between levels of prayer—a lower form that involves "asking" and a higher wordless form of "true prayer." In his later writings, Wapnick stressed this distinction, downplaying the role of specific guidance as an artifact of the illusion of separation (*AFF*, 283, 442, 453, 461).

In all three groups, early guidance practices involved making inquiries and receiving answers, and each group distinguished between individual and group guidance. In the Mormon case, everyone had access to personal guidance, as long as it did not conflict with guidance from higher up in the church; Smith alone, however, had access to guidance for the church as a whole. Similarly, in the case of AA, everyone had access to personal guidance from their Higher Power, as long as it did not threaten the welfare of the group; if it did, a loving God as expressed through the conscience of the group took precedence. Because ACIM adopted a limited form of organization, there was no formal understanding of the relationship between individual and group guidance as in the Mormon churches and AA. During the emergence phase of ACIM's history (1973–78), personal guidance fed into the small group guidance process. Although group guidance is still presumably integral to the procedures of the two official foundations (FIP and FACIM), it does not extend beyond them in any official sense since there is no structure to embody it, as there is in the Mormon churches (LDS and Communities of Christ) and in AA.

The form that guidance procedures took in each of these groups not only constituted the groups as groups in relation to suprahuman sources, they generated authority structures within each group. In doing so, suprahuman sources supplied core elements of each group's origin account, determining whether there was a singular person (a prophet) to whom revelation was given, as in the case of Mormonism, or an (anonymous) group to whom guidance was given, as in the case of AA. There is a sense in which, I think, ACIM could have gone either way. Had Schucman been able to embrace the Course in practice, heal her relationship with Thetford, and teach the Course publicly, she might have taken on more "prophet-like" characteristics. She and the other ACIM collaborators clearly did not want the Course to become "a cult" with a "guru-type" leader, so she turned her desire for anonymity into a means of focusing attention on the Course. Her collaborators waited until after her death to publicly name her and Thetford in their accounts of ACIM's origins.

From a naturalistic point of view, these guidance procedures are also highly instructive. Although insiders viewed them as a means of obtaining suprahuman input, we can view them as a means of tuning in to the needs of the emergent group and directing the process in light of the group's emergent aims. In each of the cases, the situation at hand—whether rival claims to revelation, new ideas for how to move forward, or uncertainty as to role or direction—led to questions that initiated requests for guidance. Norms for determining who could access the presumed presences and for determining what answers were authentic varied from group to group and developed over time within each group. Disagreements over these norms led to splits within the groups. Bill Wilson rejected the guidance of his Oxford Group team to start meetings for alcoholics based on his own sense of guidance. Oliver Cowdery and John Whitmer broke with Joseph Smith—at least for a time—over guidance practices. Kenneth Wapnick voiced concerns about the ACIM team's guidance practices, but did so without challenging the special message that FIP was to assume responsibility for publishing the Course, so did not generate a break within the group.

Guidance emerged from and was grounded in group processes. Faith in Smith and his gifts, which his family possessed starting at least with the Moroni visitation, was central to the recovery of the plates and then to the incorporation of outsiders into the translation process. During the translation process, Smith's collaborators' belief in his divinely appointed role was reinforced by the dictation of a text that not only justified their belief but also laid out the basic parameters (new scripture, a restored church) within which the guidance process operated. Many of the disputes over who had access to revelation took place within that basic set of parameters and thus led to splits within Mormonism rather than defections from it. Still, there were numerous defections, such as Ezra Booth's, in which defectors broke with the basic belief in the Book of Mormon as new revelation. Revelation through Smith had the potential to take surprising turns and, as the most authoritarian of the three guidance processes, provided little room for dissent. Followers were either drawn deeper into the system or forced out.

With the more communal forms of guidance, group processes provided a basis for collective discernment. AA emerged out of the Oxford Groups and continued to have small groups as its foundation. AA meetings, which relied on the Big Book, acquired a common sense of "what worked" that was passed on through the stories recounted in the Big Book and in AA meetings. The Twelve Traditions, which codified group norms, emerged out of and reflected group practice. After Skutch joined the ACIM team, the team began meeting daily to study the Course together. In the process, they acquired a shared sense of the Voice of the Course and its teachings and laid a foundation for discerning the Voice's guidance.

CREATIVE PATHS

New research on creativity, which examines the role that groups play in the creative process, allows us to consider the role of the group in the emergence of new spiritual paths. In contrast to most research on creativity, which treats the creative individual in isolation from those who judge their creative efforts, the social identity approach to creativity points out that in many cases creators and evaluators are linked in an identity-based relationship in which creators identify with and create for groups that "stimulate, appreciate and respond constructively to their creativity" (Haslam et al. 2013, 385). This line of research pays careful attention to the way that people categorize themselves (*self-categorization*), recognizing that we can easily shift between thinking of ourselves as individuals (*self-identity*) or members of groups (*social identity*). Haslam et al. found that when an individual's personal identity is salient, their creations are more likely to be idiosyncratic and guided by personal preferences. When their social identity is salient, "individuals' self-perceptions, evaluations, and actions are informed more by the shared attributes that define their social group membership and less by their unique individuating characteristics" (2013, 385–86).

In each of our three cases, we can identify the transformations of self-categorization and identity that were involved. In early Mormonism, Smith's identity shifted from that of a local seer seeking treasure to the prophet, seer, and revelator of new scripture and founder of a restored church. His followers became saints and baptized members of the new church. In Alcoholics Anonymous, Bill Wilson's identity shifted from a person who thought he could manage his own problems to an alcoholic—"an ordinary drunk"—dependent for his recovery on his fellow alcoholics and a Higher Power as expressed in the conscience of the local group. AAs viewed Dr. Bob as a cofounder along with Bill (and not Ebby T. or Hank P.) because Bill and Dr. Bob stayed sober in the context of the movement they helped to create. In theory, they had no followers, just fellow alcoholics likewise dependent for their recovery on one another and their Higher Power as they understood "Him" and as expressed through the group conscience. Likewise, students of the Course viewed Helen Schucman and Bill Thetford as collaborators, but while Thetford became a student of the Course once he moved to California, Schucman knew the Course but was reluctant to practice it. From a social identity perspective, Schucman identified as a scribe of the Course—referring to it on occasion as "my book"—but not, for the most part, as a practitioner. Although Thetford did identify as a student of the Course and played an important role in its initial publication, he was reluctant to take a leading role in its dissemination and interpretation. Both gladly turned the "management" of the Course—publishing and teaching—over to Judith Skutch and Kenneth Wapnick.

Although a social identity approach to creativity stresses the role of "self-categorization" of both individuals and groups in the creative process, it provides little help in understanding individuals or groups who view suprahuman creators as the primary or ultimate source of the emergent group and its new texts. Moreover, while the social identity approach views the evaluative role of the group, that is, the "beliefs, values, and norms that define the group's shared meaning," as integral to the creative process (Haslam et al. 2013, 392), the groups we have been considering ascribed these beliefs, values, and norms to suprahuman presences from which they continually sought guidance. Each of the groups therefore conceived the creative process as an interaction between humans, some of whom were perceived to have distinctive abilities (or "gifts"), and a presence that guided the emerging group in a manner that transformed particular problems (religious conflict, alcoholism, relational difficulties) into spiritual paths with broad appeal. Although we can still think about individual abilities and emergent groups in relation to social identity and self-categorization, we need to recognize the presence of selves that the groups distinguish from the humans who mediate them.

We can allow for the presence of such selves in the creative process by expanding the options for self-categorization. In a social identity approach, self-categorization operates at three different levels of abstraction: personal, group, and species. At each level, the self is categorized in contrast with others: the individual is contrasted with other individuals within a group at the most basic level, the group is contrasted with other groups at the midlevel, and humans are contrasted with other species at the highest level of abstraction (Turner and Oakes 1986, in Postmes 2010, 229). Individual differences in religiosity can be considered at the level of personal self-categorizations. At the group level, religious affiliation is typically considered alongside class, race, nationality, and occupation. Religious affiliation is only relevant, however, once a group exists. The chief difficulty in this case lies at the top level of abstraction, where the theory contrasts human beings only with other species. To conceptualize spiritual innovation within a social identity framework, we have to add postulated suprahuman selves to this uppermost level of self-categorization, so that people have the option of categorizing themselves, not only in relation to other species but also in relation to believed-in presences, such as deities, angels, and higher powers, which they view as other than themselves.

We could view this expansion at the level of human self-categorization simply as a matter of belief, which, when professed by a group, serves to establish its group identity as religious or spiritual. In these cases, however, we are dealing with something more. Each of the groups claimed that suprahuman entities were actively involved in the creative process. This means that we have to ask not only how people came to *believe in* such entities but how they came to view them *as present and acting in their midst.* We can think about this at the level of individual self-categorization insofar as key figures—in this case, Smith, Wilson, and Schucman—played a distinctive role in mediating a first-person voice that they claimed was not their own. But—and this is a central claim of the book and of social identity theory— their personal self-concept as mediator of something more than themselves cannot account for the formation of a new group around a newly revealed spiritual path. If an emergent group does not accept the presence of the suprahuman entities, no group will form and no path will emerge. Indeed, without group recognition, the individual claimant is likely to be perceived as eccentric, if not crazy. This means that the group itself is constituted in its own self-conception through its recognition of the presence of one or more suprahuman entities *conveyed by and at the same time distinct from* the humans who mediate them. It is at the group level that the "social-categorical self is a medium or channel for social-psychological interaction and a mechanism for the mutual emergence of irreducible social and psychological forms" (Turner and Oakes 2010, 237).

CHAPTER II

Selves

While recognizing that Smith, Wilson, and Schucman created within and for emergent small groups that viewed them as mediating the suprahuman presences for the group as a whole, they nonetheless brought unusual experiences and abilities to the process that were selectively appropriated by their respective groups. As we have seen, the differences in the spiritual paths they helped to create obscured the similarities between them at the level of personal experience. Mormonism heightened Smith's unusual abilities by designating him as prophet, seer, and revelator, while AA and ACIM downplayed Wilson's and Schucman's in keeping with the principle of anonymity in AA and devaluation of specialness in ACIM.

When it comes to the groups' key texts, there are other crucial differences. Although some AAs view the Big Book as inspired by a power greater than themselves, AAs who embrace this view would acknowledge that the Higher Power worked through everyday collaborative processes. In doing so, they are ascribing spiritual meaning to an ordinary process. Although there is definite evidence that Bill Wilson felt St. Boniface assisted him in the drafting of *Twelve Steps and Twelve Traditions*, the book is officially authored by Anonymous, and the evidence of Boniface's aid is buried in the AA archives. AA does not officially attribute authorship to Bill Wilson, much less to Bill Wilson aided by the spirit of St. Boniface.

Joseph Smith and Helen Schucman made different claims when it came to the production of the Book of Mormon and *A Course in Miracles*. Joseph Smith claimed to translate the Book of Mormon from ancient gold plates inscribed in Reformed Egyptian, and Helen Schucman claimed to scribe words dictated by the voice of Jesus. Moreover, those who assisted them in the translating and scribing processes did so based on the sense that Smith and Schucman produced complex texts that they could not have produced on their own. In chapter 10 we focused on the role that the collaborators played in cocreating the roles of translator and scribe and hence the social identities of Smith and Schucman as mediators of selves that were not thought to be their own. In order to identify underlying processes that allowed them to generate "selves" that seemed as if they were "other" both to themselves and their collaborators, we need to reconstruct *what it was like* to "translate" in Smith's case and "scribe" in Schucman's case based on the evidence supplied by them and those who observed them firsthand. Before launching into these reconstructions, we need to justify the comparison. Why compare someone who claimed to translate ancient records with someone who claimed to scribe the words of Jesus?

COMPARING SMITH AND SCHUCMAN

On the surface, translating an ancient record by the gift and power of God sounds rather different from scribing the voice of Jesus. Smith is usually thought to have seen things in his seer stone; Schucman usually referred to hearing a voice. Smith dictated what he saw to scribes; Schucman scribed what she heard in shorthand and then dictated the shorthand to a colleague, who typed it. Still, there are significant similarities in the complexity of the texts, the means of production, and the claims made by followers.

The Complexity of the Text: Both the Book of Mormon and *A Course in Miracles* are lengthy and complex. The 1830 edition of the Book of Mormon was 588 pages; *A Course in Miracles* includes the text (669 pages), a workbook (448 pages), a manual for teachers (92 pages), and two supplements (46 pages). The Book of Mormon was transcribed intermittently over the course of eleven months, but most of the transcription took place between 5 April 1829 and 30 June 1829. Schucman transcribed the three main ACIM texts over the course of seven years, beginning in October 1965 and ending in September 1972, with a break of about seven months between the text and the workbook and about a year between the workbook and the manual.

In terms of genre, the Book of Mormon reflects the complex composite structure of the Hebrew Bible, with its multiple books, authors, and points of view. As Hardy indicates, "it is first and foremost a narrative, offered to us by specific, named narrators. . . . The heterogeneous materials in the Book of Mormon . . . are all represented as the work of the three primary editor/historians" (2010, xv). It reflects the language and cadence of the King James Version and makes use of chiasmus, a rhetorical device found in portions of the Bible, in which clauses are inverted to create a parallel structure. *A Course in Miracles*, by way of contrast, is a complex, philosophically oriented teaching text with a workbook for students and a manual for teachers. In terms of genre, it is didactic rather than narrative, although much of it is composed in blank verse and iambic pentameter and is thus quite poetic (Wapnick, n.d., 9).

Means of Production: Although both texts were edited, we have portions of the original transcription of the Book of Mormon and the entire set of

Schucman's shorthand notebooks, both of which have features (e.g., lack of punctuation and headings) that are characteristic of oral composition or stream-of-consciousness writing. Based on corrections in the original text of the Book of Mormon, Royal Skousen (1998, 25) found evidence to support the claim that it was dictated orally and that the scribes had difficulty keeping up with Smith. He also found indications that Smith could recognize breaks in the text (chapters) but didn't know if the breaks signaled a new chapter or a new book, from which he infers that Smith didn't know in advance what the text was going to say or how it would be organized. Like Smith, Schucman did not feel as if the words were her own. The words came quickly, and she couldn't anticipate them ahead of time. As she wrote in her autobiography: "I would feel it coming on almost daily, and sometimes more than once a day. . . . I wrote in shorthand in a notebook that I soon began to carry around with me, just in case" (*AFF*, 182). Moreover, she continued, "I never knew when I started a sentence how it would end, and the ideas came so rapidly that I had trouble keeping up with them even in the system of shorthand symbols and abbreviations I had developed during many years of taking class notes and recording therapy sessions" (*AFF*, 182).

In responding to Scott Dunn's (2002) essay comparing the Book of Mormon with the fiction channeled by Pearl Curran, Rees (2006, 10), who is LDS, accepted the following similarities: "Joseph receiving information from some source outside himself, seeing words in the seer stone (or in his mind's eye), dictating a sort of stream-of-consciousness narrative, being able to pick up dictation/translation after interruptions and delays with no break in the narrative flow, producing a large body of material over a short period of time, and leaving the final text essentially unrevised—all of these have similarities to the producers of some automatically written texts." Schucman also received information that seemed to come from outside herself, scribed a stream-of-consciousness narrative in shorthand, picked up scribing after interruptions and delays with no break in the narrative flow, produced a large body of material, and left the final text, beyond the first five chapters of the published Course, only lightly revised (*AFF*, 180).

Claims Made by Followers: Followers of both Smith and Schucman argue that the texts are too complex for them to have created them, given their individual limitations. Smith's followers stress his ignorance. Emma Smith noted that he "could neither write nor dictate a coherent and well worded letter, let alone . . . a book like the Book of M[ormon]" (1879, *EMD* 1:539). We have seen how, in the wake of Harris's visit to the linguists, Harris interpreted the experts' inability to recognize the characters as evidence that the Lord was making use of the "foolish . . . to confound the wise." According to Eber Howe, a contemporary critic, "The extreme ignorance and apparent stupidity of this modern prophet, were, by his early followers, looked upon as his greatest merit, and as furnishing the most incontestable proof of his divine mission" ([1834] 2015, 19; *EMD* 3:303).

In light of her doctorate and academic career, Schucman's followers did not stress her ignorance, but rather her intense skepticism and her inability to embrace the teachings of the Course. In her 1977 interview, Skutch stressed the importance (for her) of Helen and Bill's lack of preparation. "It was important for me that neither of these two people had the background or interest in spiritual literature or psychical experiences that might have prepared them for this." Looking back, Thetford wrote, "As I read the material, I recognized that Helen's ego self in no way could have written what I was reading. It was totally alien to her background, to her interests, and to her mode of conceptualizing abstract ideas. There was simply no way that the ego part of Helen could have done this" (WT, 19). Kenneth Wapnick paints a more complex picture, stressing that "the form of the Course is from Helen" (n.d., 9), though in his view the content was not. In terms of form, Wapnick gave Helen credit for its idiomatic American English; its poetic, Elizabethan manner of speech; its underlying Platonic philosophy and Freudian ego psychology; its logical structure; and its curricular format.

Both Smith and Schucman were steeped in the genres of their respective texts. Smith was immersed in the King James Version of the Bible; Schucman was a philosophy major in college and loved Plato and Shakespeare (*AFF*, 33–34). Schucman also knew the Bible very well, quoting from it "almost as readily as she could from Shakespeare" (*AFF*, 407). She was a psychologist trained in Freudian psychology, who did research on ego development, and an educator. She also, according to Wapnick, had "one of the most logical minds I have ever seen" (n.d.). At the same time, insider accounts acknowledge factors that they do not stress, such as Smith's storytelling abilities and Schucman's lifelong attraction to Catholicism and her exposure to the American metaphysical traditions, including Christian Science. Moreover, insiders intimately bound up in the process recount details that prepared Smith to translate and Schucman to scribe. Lucy Smith thus indicates that her son had many conversations with an angelic personage who recounted what was written on the plates before the translation began, and Wapnick, as we have seen, pointed out how much Schucman sounded at times like the Voice in letters she wrote to Thetford months before the Voice instructed her to "take notes" (*AFF*, 180).

If—as I am arguing—we are dealing with individuals with unusual abilities, this broadly conceived set of similarities doesn't take us deep enough. We need to be able to specify their abilities much more precisely if we want to try to explain them. To get at this, we need to reconstruct, as best we can, what it was like for Smith to translate the Book of Mormon and Schucman to scribe *A Course in Miracles*. LDS scholars have given a great deal of thought to this question, but have been unable to arrive at a consensus. Dan

Peterson (2002, 2005) and Royal Skousen (1998), both conservative LDS scholars, have laid out a range of evidence, which I take as the starting point for this reconstruction.[1]

SMITH'S EXPERIENCE OF TRANSLATING THE GOLDEN PLATES

Most scholars (LDS and non-LDS) acknowledge that the translation of the Book of Mormon was not translation in the usual sense, since he did not look at the plates while translating (*JSP*, D1:xxix–xxxii). Many LDS scholars assume that ancient golden plates were present in an ordinary material sense during the translation process, though some have wondered why they needed to be present if Smith didn't need to look at them (see, e.g., Ricks 1993; Van Wagoner and Walker 1982, 53). As Givens (2002, 12, 42, 177–78; see also Flake 2007, 501) indicates, the presence of ancient plates, while not necessary for the translation, grounded the Book of Mormon in artifactual reality, established that there was something to translate, and created an ostensibly firm boundary between the Book of Mormon as translated scripture and channeled or fictional works. It has also led to much speculation by contemporaries and later LDS scholars on the relationship between the process and the ancient plates.

LDS scholars, generally assuming that Smith in some sense translated actual ancient records, are divided with respect to the degree of divine control exerted over the dictation of the text (Skousen 1998, 24). Skousen outlines three positions: loose control, in which ideas were revealed to Smith, who then put them into his own words; tight control, in which Smith saw specific words in English and read them off to a scribe, such that the accuracy depended on the care taken by Smith and his scribe; and ironclad control, in which case nothing, including the misspelling of common words, could be chalked up to human error. While LDS scholars today tend to adopt variations on the first two positions, Skousen (1998, 24) quotes passages to suggest that scribes and eyewitness observers (e.g., Joseph Knight Sr.

---

[1] Peterson (2005) offers the following list of facts we shouldn't overlook in offering alternative explanations: Smith dictated a lengthy and complex book orally to scribes in a short period of time; the scribes could see Smith; he didn't make use of books or manuscripts or the golden plates, which were obscured, but looked at a stone buried in a hat to block out the light. Also, according to the scribes, Smith couldn't translate if he had unresolved emotional issues (e.g., between himself and Emma); he couldn't translate with the "fake" stone Martin Harris gave him; he could see the spelling of names; and there were parts of the text he didn't understand and words he couldn't pronounce. Emma Smith and others said they did not believe Joseph Smith was capable of dictating the Book of Mormon off the top of his head (Peterson 2005, xv; *EMD* 1:542). Drawing from the scribes' descriptions, Mark Ashurst-McGee (personal communication) would add the back-and-forth process of dictation and checking of the translation (see Emma Smith 1856 [*EMD* 1:530–31], Harris 1870 [*EMD* 2:320–21], and Whitmer 1874 [*EMD* 5:15–16]).

[1833–47, *EMD* 4:17–18], Emma Smith [1856, *EMD* 1:530–31], Martin Harris [1881, *EMD* 2:320–21], and David Whitmer [1874, *EMD* 5:15–16]) held to the "ironclad" position.

We can recast these positions to highlight what they suggest regarding Smith's subjective experience. Skousen (1998, 23), who advocates the tight control position, argues that Smith saw specific words written out in English and read them off to the scribes. Peterson, adopting a similar position, argues that "Smith seems to have been reading from something . . . that was new and strange to him, and . . . that required a certain emotional or mental focus before it could be read" (2002). This theory, while faithful to the scribes' descriptions, makes Smith a reader of the text rather than a translator, which some believers find problematic. To get around this, those advocating the first position (e.g., Roberts 1992, 7–8; Ricks 1993, 205–6; Quinn 1998, 479n302; Flake 2007, 507) argue for a two-step process in which Smith received ideas, impressions, or images, which he then put into words (i.e., translated). Ricks, Quinn, and Flake all rely on Smith's revelation to Cowdery in which he was told that he "must study it out in [his] mind" (D&C 9:7–8) to argue for two steps. Quinn and Ricks do not dismiss the evidence that Smith saw words but argue that the English words appeared after he formulated a "translation" of the ideas or impressions he received (directly or indirectly) from the plates. Gardner offers the most recent version of this theory, drawing from research in psychology and neuroscience to propose that Smith received revelation in the form of prelanguage, which then appeared as "eidetic images," thus allowing him "to 'see' the words in English that he read to his scribes" (2011, 319).

Vogel (2004, 172–73) and Dunn (2002, 31) question the use of D&C 9 to understand Smith's experience, noting that D&C 9 was addressed to Oliver Cowdery, who was told in D&C 8 that he had two gifts, the gift of "revelation" and "the gift of working with the rod." Vogel and Dunn suggest that Cowdery translated using his divining rod rather than Smith's seer stone. Unlike a seer stone, a divining rod gives "yes/no" responses and therefore suggests a more interactive process in which Cowdery was expected to "study it out in his mind" and then check his results using his divining rod. Whether or not this was the case, we can't assume from this revelation to Cowdery that Smith himself was studying the translation out in his mind.

In claiming that Smith didn't attribute what he was dictating to "anyone . . . dictating to or communicating through him," but rather to "an actual tangible text from which his dictation was derived," Rees (2006, 12) articulates what he views as the chief difference between Smith's translation and a channeled text. Vogel, however, draws our attention to D&C 8, which highlights the role of the Holy Ghost in the process. Thus, in that April 1829 revelation, Cowdery was told:

I say unto you that as Shuredly as the Lord liveth . . . shall ye receive a knowledge of whatsoever things ye shall ask with an honest heart believeing that ye Shall receive, a knowledge concerning the engraveings of old Records which are ancient which contain those parts of my Scriptures which hath been spoken by the manifestation of my Spirit yea Behold I will tell you in your mind & in your heart by the Holy Ghost which Shall come upon you & which shall dwell in your heart now Behold this is the spirit of Revelation. (Revelation, April 1829-B, *JSP*, D1:45–46 [D&C 8]; misspellings are in the original)

In D&C 8, the gift of revelation and the gift of translation are not clearly distinguished, since the gift or spirit of revelation is "knowledge concerning the engraveings [*sic*] of old Records." Indeed, the original heading supplied by John Whitmer reads: "A Revelation to Oliver he being desirous to know whether the Lord would grant him the gift of Revelation & th[illegible letter] Translation." This early revelation, given shortly after Cowdery arrived to help with the translation, suggests (1) that the Lord, speaking through Smith, was not making a clear distinction between the gift of revelation and the gift of translation and (2) that the Holy Ghost was involved in the process. In this 1829 description, the role of the Holy Ghost in the translation-revelation process parallels the account offered by David and John Whitmers' pastor, the Reverend Diedrich Willers, in June 1830 (Quinn 1973, 320–21, 323). As translated from the German by Neal Chandler, it reads: "the Lord had appointed him to translate the same [golden plates] from ancient languages into English. . . . and that through the use of these spectacles he (Smith) was enabled to read these languages which he had never studied and that the Holy Ghost would give him the translation in English" (*EMD* 5:272–73). Smith's 1831 statement, that it was by the Spirit that revelations "were put into my heart," is similar as well (Minute Book 2, 12 November 1831, quoted in *JSP*, D1:xxxiii).

I draw the following from these discussions:

(1) The two-stage theory, which distinguishes between reading and translating, is premised on the belief that there was an original text in an ancient language. The two-stage theory also relies heavily on the directive to "study it out in his mind," which was addressed to Cowdery and may or may not have reflected Smith's experience.

(2) The one-stage theory and the second stage of most two-stage theories build on the descriptions provided by the scribes and other witnesses. Spelling out names is the best evidence that Smith visually saw words. Although the scribes provide firsthand *observations* of Smith's behavior, they do not have direct access to his subjective experience. Because the scribes were observers, they made inferences based on what they saw

(and what they believed). Evidence that Smith *sometimes* spelled words doesn't mean that he *always* saw words.

(3) Except for Vogel and Quinn, neither theory reflects on the role of the Holy Ghost in the process, as mentioned in D&C 8 and the Willers letter. Although D&C 8, like D&C 9, is addressed to Cowdery, the description of the role of the Holy Ghost in D&C 8 appears to be a general statement about the subjective experience of receiving revelation, which is specified as knowledge of the engravings on the ancient records. The Willers letter, written about a year later, corroborates the role of the Holy Ghost in the translation process. D&C 8, coming to us directly from the Lord via Smith (or from the recesses of Smith's mind) at the time when Smith and Cowdery were in the midst of producing the Book of Mormon, is the closest thing we have to a real-time subjective report. If we acknowledge the role of the Holy Ghost in the process, it suggests—contra Rees (2006, 12)—that there was in effect "someone dictating to or communicating through him." In terms of their subjective experience, this suggests that we need to compare what it was like for Smith to experience the Lord "tell[ing] [him] in [his] mind & in [his] heart by the Holy Ghost" and Schucman hearing the voice of Jesus.

SCHUCMAN'S EXPERIENCE IN SCRIBING *A COURSE IN MIRACLES*

Fortunately, while both Smith and Schucman were reluctant to discuss what the subjective process of translating and scribing was like, Schucman taped an interview with *New Realities Magazine*'s associate editor, David Hammond, in 1976 on the condition that it was not to be published or circulated. The tape was released on DVD by the Foundation for Inner Peace in 2006 with the understanding that Schucman's conditions applied only during her lifetime and is quoted here with the permission of Judith Skutch Whitson. Due to the probing questions of the interviewer, the interview is more revealing than any other surviving description of what the process was like.

> HAMMOND: Regarding the voice you heard in scribing *A Course in Miracles*, did it come from outside or from within?
> SCHUCMAN: There's nothing that I would call ordinary audition about this at all. It doesn't really . . . it's a curious thing that would be very difficult to explain. Somebody asked whether it was as though your hand was just moving. No, I wrote perfectly voluntarily in response to . . . I call it "a voice," but a voice has sounds . . . or sounds as though it has something to do with hearing. And I didn't hear anything. I think it's a sort of hearing that

you can't really describe. It doesn't have anything to do with ears, or waves hitting a drum or anything on that order. I don't really know. I think maybe I'm using the wrong word when I say "hear." I sort of recognized it. It was very rapid, I couldn't . . . if I didn't catch a phrase, I could sort of say, "Would you mind doing that again?"

HAMMOND: This was in your mind?

SCHUCMAN: This was strictly mental.

HAMMOND: Is it comparable to anything in terms of how we hear ourselves talk, or like you talk to yourself?

SCHUCMAN: It wasn't my voice. It couldn't have been because it talked about a whole area with which I am entirely unfamiliar.

HAMMOND: What about subvocalizing? When you're subvocalizing, you're hearing the words, you're actually hearing them.

SCHUCMAN: Oh, there's no subvocalization. It's a process I really would find impossible to explain. It's never happened to me before.

HAMMOND: You could hear the words clearly in your mind even though you didn't hear a sound?

SCHUCMAN: I knew that that was the word . . . I think "knew" may be a better word than "heard." I did not know consciously at the beginning of the sentence how it was going to end. And that puts me under a further handicap in terms of ordinary language. Because ordinarily, I think if you are going to say a sentence you know what it's going to be, you sort of get the Gestalt immediately. But I didn't. And it came very easily, very rapidly, very smoothly. I guess even painlessly, except that it annoyed me to death, but that's irrelevant. I guess "hear" isn't the right word. I could stop anything or pick it up anytime, and I did it in cabs and subways and anywhere, or sort of between phone calls. But you're raising a question I don't think I can answer.

HAMMOND: So a certain mechanism went on there, because you heard something you translated into the shorthand style . . .

SCHUCMAN: Yes, but I'm used to shorthand. I use it for group therapy sessions, so shorthand is quite familiar to me. It's really a matter of speed. I couldn't have kept up with it in ordinary writing.

HAMMOND: Oh, you couldn't . . .

SCHUCMAN: Oh no, it was very rapid. I needed the shorthand.

HAMMOND: What about automatic writing, a thing when pen takes over and writes for the person? The person doesn't have any control. Is that similar to what you are describing?

SCHUCMAN: No, that didn't happen at all. I could have stopped it at any time, and I frequently did. And I was very frequently interrupted, so that I would have to stop . . . I didn't lose awareness of where I was or what I was doing.

At a later point in the interview, Hammond asked Schucman about her desire to change words as she scribed the text. She said that she very quickly learned that doing so interfered with the internal consistency of the text, so she and Thetford went back and replaced the original words. The interview then resumed:

> HAMMOND: Did you remember the word or did you have to go back and just ask at the time?
> SCHUCMAN: [Although she usually remembered the word,] sometimes I wouldn't say more than two or three times—I didn't know. But I was aware that there was a goof-off in through there [a change introduced in the text], and I would feel the goof-off more than the right answer. And then, I would sort of look at a blackboard in my head and see it written, the word it should have been. And I would ask, "Can I see it on the blackboard?"
> HAMMOND: You would ask and also see it?
> SCHUCMAN: [T]hen I would be reading it. Because on the blackboard I would see it in letters.
> HAMMOND: Then it was a very visual thing in your mind.
> SCHUCMAN: Then it was visual. Ordinarily it wasn't. But I think that modality had to come in where I had kind of lost my way and then I really didn't know what the word should be.

AN ALTERNATIVE HYPOTHESIS

Based on a comparison between Smith and Schucman, I suggest the following:

(1) Although Schucman's experiences are typically characterized in terms of "hearing" and Smith's in terms of "seeing," the differences are not so pronounced when we get into the details. Helen says, "I think maybe I'm using the wrong word when I say 'hear.' I sort of recognized it. It was very rapid. . . . I knew that that was the word . . . I think 'knew' may be a better word than 'heard.'" Schucman's experience of "knowing" strikes me as a plausible description of what it might have been like to receive the Holy Ghost's "telling in your mind & in your heart." Schucman's description isn't quite hearing or seeing words, but it was more than receiving impressions or images. From her use of "knowing" and D&C 8's use of "telling," we might infer a flow of words that are consciously recognized (known), while at the same time arising outside

of consciousness as if "told to" the consciously aware self. To put it another way, they might have had a sense of meaning so immediate as to feel as if it were a word.[2]

(2) Like Schucman, Smith probably had a great deal of control over the flow of words, that is, he was able to stop and start the flow at will, picking up where he left off without prompts from the scribes, as long as he was in a good emotional state. This may have allowed him to pace his delivery to his scribes' ability to write, which was most likely slower than Schucman's shorthand. Helen said that scribing wasn't like automatic writing, if that meant "the person doesn't have any control." Her experience, she said, wasn't like that at all: "I could have stopped it at any time, and I frequently did. And I was very frequently interrupted, so that I would have to stop."

(3) Neither seems to have felt they were in a noticeably altered state of consciousness. Schucman specifically states, "I didn't lose awareness of where I was or what I was doing." I think they both may have been in a state of highly focused awareness.

(4) Smith, like Schucman, may have been able to shift from a "flow of words" modality into a visual modality in which he was able to see words spelled out. Schucman switched modes when she sensed she had made a mistake in scribing the text. She would "sort of look at a blackboard in [her] head and see it written." Ordinarily, she said, the process wasn't visual; it was a matter of "knowing" the words. Smith spelled out some proper names, and like Schucman, he may have had the ability to shift into a visual mode in order to "see" the spelling, when he was uncertain of what the word should be.

COMPARING SMITH, SCHUCMAN, AND HILGARD'S STORYTELLER

Based on this reconstruction, a naturalistic account would need to explain (1) the rapid flow of words that were "known" but seemed like they were not their own; (2) their ability to control the process, specifically to stop and start and shift modalities; and (3) their execution of a complex overall plan without evident planning. To move a step closer to an explanation, I want to introduce a third person with unusual abilities, a college student described by psychologist Ernest Hilgard, who, with his wife, Josephine, established and directed the Laboratory of Hypnosis Research at Stanford University for many years. The student in question showed up at their lab after having been hypnotized at a social gathering, during which time he recounted incidents from what he and others believed was a past life in Victo-

---

[2] Thanks to Kathleen Flake for this alternative formulation of what it might have been like.

rian England. He came to the laboratory, Hilgard writes, believing it was "a genuine reincarnation experience, but . . . willing to have it subjected to criticism" (1986, 51). After interviewing the student, the Hilgards learned that he had made "an intensive study of the British Royal family" many years earlier that he had subsequently forgotten. "Although the evidence is against the reincarnation interpretation," Hilgard writes, "it is interesting in its own right because it shows that memories may be captured without identification (as in source amnesia) and woven into a realistic story that is believed under hypnosis by the inventor of the story."

Although the student came to the lab because he had told the story "with such clarity and verisimilitude that he convinced those who heard him— himself as well—that it must have been a case of regression to a prior experience," his storytelling was, Hilgard indicates, "of a high order whether he was hypnotized or not" (1986, 196). In light of his ability to recount stories with such vividness that people felt they were accounts of actual experiences, Hilgard did some informal experiments in which he asked him to tell stories when hypnotized and when not. He transcribed part of the story the student told under hypnosis when Hilgard asked him to "transport [himself]" with his friends to explore "a newly discovered cave." Without hypnosis, he had him tell other stories, "such as the experiences of a coal miner in England during the early period of the industrial revolution, experiences with Indians on the western plains with a pioneer family, and the life of a stone cutter in medieval Italy" (ibid., 197).

All of the stories—whether under hypnosis or not—were told "so vividly" that Hilgard wanted to find out if there was a "difference between telling a story under hypnosis and in the waking state." The student's answer to this question, like Hammond's interview of Schucman, is highly revealing, and I quote the student's answer in full:

> In hypnosis, once I create the pattern, I don't have to take any more initiative; the story just unfolds. In fact once I start talking I know the main outlines of what is happening. For instance, I knew ahead of time that there would be another room outside of the cavern [in the newly discovered cave], and I knew I would go outside but I didn't know what it would look like until I walked through and was describing it. In the waking state it seems more fabricated. I don't *see* things that I describe in waking in the way I actually *see* them in hypnosis. I really saw everything today that I described. (Hilgard 1986, 198; emphasis in original)

When hypnotized, the student storyteller, like Smith and Schucman, experienced the event as it unfolded, as if it was actually occurring or, in Smith and Schucman's case, as if another entity was actually supplying the words.

This contrasted with what the student storyteller experienced without hypnosis, when, he said, he had more of a sense of making up the story.

In the course of his research, Hilgard discovered that he could tap into levels of mental activity that were not available to the consciousness of the hypnotized person. With specific follow-up inquiries, he was able to elicit reports from some highly hypnotizable individuals, which suggested an ability to dissociate executive and monitoring functions, that is, to separate the conscious (albeit hypnotized) acting part of the self from an observing part of the self of which the acting part was not aware. Hilgard used the metaphor of the "hidden observer" to refer to the monitoring function. After eliciting the information described above from the student storyteller, Hilgard followed up with a hidden observer inquiry, which "revealed that there was a part of him doing the planning, more like a stage director providing the promptings for the hypnotized part, the actor. The hidden part knew, for example, that the cavern was to have a beautiful room and that there would be a garden beyond. The hypnotized part did not know their *qualities* until *seeing* them. As he [the student] put it, 'The two parts worked together to form a story.' The hidden part also planned (and monitored) the length of the story" (Hilgard 1986, 198; emphasis in original).

There are some intriguing similarities between this student's abilities and those demonstrated by Smith and Schucman.

(1) Both the student and Smith recounted narratives of great vividness in two modes: the student in an ordinary and a hypnotized mode and Smith in an ordinary and a translating mode. Lucy Smith similarly attests to the vividness of Joseph's "recitals" in which he described the "ancient inhabitants of this continent" to his family after his initial discovery of the plates in 1823. According to Lucy (*EMD* 1:295–96), he described "their dress[,] their maner [*sic*] of traveling[,] the animals which they rode[,] The cities that were built by them[,] the structure of their buildings[,] with every particular of their mode of warfare[,] their religious worship—as particularly as though he had spent his life with them[.]" Accounts of neighbors from the early thirties refer to his "marvellous stories" (*EMD* 2:27, 60–61) and later accounts describe his "fertile imagination" (*EMD* 3:211) and ability to "utter the most palpable exaggeration or marvellous absurdity with the utmost apparent gravity" (*EMD* 3:93). Writing in 1834, Eber Howe concluded that "a natural genius, strong inventive powers of mind, a deep study, and an unusually correct estimate of the human passions and feelings" more than made up for any deficiencies in Smith's formal education ([1834] 2015, 20; *EMD* 3:303–4).

(2) There are indications that Smith and Schucman both absorbed information very quickly. C. C. Webb, who taught Smith English grammar

in Kirtland, said Smith "acquired knowledge very rapidly, and learned with special facility all the tricks of the scoundrels who worked in his company. He soon outgrew his teachers" (quoted in Persuitte 2000, 15). As a teenager, his mother described him "as "less inclined to the study of books than any child we had but much more given to reflection and deep study" (*EMD* 1:296). Wapnick describes Schucman's "phobia against reading" and "a writer's anxiety that bordered on the extreme" (*AFF*, 75). He attributes the fact that she not only got through graduate school but did so at the top of her class to "her tremendous learning skill" (*AFF*, 139), which he described as follows:

> Helen always had an extraordinary sense of logic (an ability utilized, for example, in the logical way that *A Course in Miracles* develops its argument). And so she was able to read a paragraph or two and deduce the basic argument of the book, or listen to a lecture and deduce the whole of the thought system of the course she was taking from just that small part. Similarly, as a psychologist, she could understand the totality of a person's ego system from just a few clues gleaned from a seemingly inconsequential statement. (*AFF*, 139)

From this three-way comparison, I draw the following possibilities. First, the context of translating and scribing may have cued a different approach to narrating a story in Smith's case or writing a philosophical "treatise" in Schucman's case, much as hypnosis triggered a different approach to story-telling for Hilgard's student. They most likely entered this mode with a sense of what was unfolding, but without specifics, much like the "pattern" from which the storyteller's story unfolded. This is supported by evidence that both Smith and Schucman had some knowledge of the contents of their respective books before they began translating or scribing. Both Joseph and Lucy Smith's accounts indicate that the angel had been telling Smith about the contents of the plates and that he had been recounting these stories to his family prior to recovering the plates. As Wapnick indicates, it is clear that Schucman was conveying ideas that would be central to the Course in the letters she wrote to Thetford in her own voice the summer before.

Second, even when they were not translating or scribing, both Smith and Schucman absorbed information quickly and, I suggest, had a marked ability to elaborate a big picture from minimal cues, each in accord with their own temperament and style. Thus, Smith elaborated in an imaginative storytelling mode that got him a mixed reputation among his neighbors and Schucman in a logical, systematic mode that stood her well in her graduate studies.

(handwritten margin note: explaining the revelations psychologically)

Third, in the context of translating and scribing, Smith and Schucman may have been able to split apart (dissociate) certain central control functions that are ordinarily integrated, for example, executive control (the sense of acting) from monitoring and planning, much as the storyteller was able to do under hypnosis (on this, see Hilgard 1986, 216–41). Were they able to do so, it would account for their knowing the words *as they appeared* but not before, much as the storyteller lacked awareness of what the scene in the cave would be like until he saw it. This sort of splitting would situate monitoring and planning outside of their conscious awareness, much as the monitoring and planning functions were split off for the storyteller. It would also automate it and thus take it out of the realm of conscious reflection.

THE ABILITIES OF HIGHLY HYPNOTIZABLE INDIVIDUALS

In comparing the abilities of Smith and Schucman to those of highly hypnotizable individuals (HHs), we need to understand what researchers mean by hypnosis and the distinction they make between hypnosis as "procedure" and hypnosis as "product." Thus, researchers commonly define hypnosis as a process (that is, a procedure) in which one person (the hypnotist) provides suggestions intended to effect changes in the experience or behavior of another (the subject) (Kirsch et al. 2011). Although the hypnotist provides suggestions that are intended to effect changes, the procedure does not guarantee that changes actually occur (Barnier and Nash 2008, 7–12; Heap, Brown, and Oakley 2004, 5–8). HHs are people who can most readily alter their perceptions in accord with the hypnotist's suggestions (that is, generate hypnosis-as-product). In the words of psychologist Auke Tellegen, they are people who have the ability to "represent suggested events and states imaginatively and enactively in such a manner that they are experienced as real" (quoted in Barnier and Nash, 8). In the terms I have been using, the "procedure" is a small-scale social interaction and the "product" is a change in experience or behavior, such that the subjects (and oftentimes others) experience the suggested events as real.

With these distinctions in mind, we can consider two preliminary questions. First, is an explicit hypnotic induction necessary in order to produce this change, and, second, does this change involve an obvious altered state of consciousness such as we commonly associate with being "in a trance" or being "hypnotized?" It turns out that the answer to both of these questions is "no." The most recent research indicates that the ability to produce such changes is based in part on an inherited ability to control and manipulate attentional processes in unusual ways (Egner and Raz 2007).[3] Hypnotic

---

[3] Researchers have known for a long time that neither hypnotizability nor suggestibility correlate with traditional measures of personality, including the Minnesota Multiphasic Personality Inventory,

induction procedures can help people focus their attentional abilities in relation to specific tasks, but they are not required, and HHs can use other methods to do so as well (Mazzoni et al. 2009; McGeown et al. 2012).

Although researchers have been debating for years whether hypnosis involves a special mental state or draws upon more mundane processes (for an overview, see Lynn et al. 2007; Mazzoni et al. 2013), the evidence that the hypnotic induction, which presumably triggers a distinctive hypnotic state, is not required to respond to suggestions indicates that an overt altered state of consciousness is not required either. This is not to say that HHs don't have unusual subjective experiences but rather to suggest that the subjective experience of an altered state, when present, reflects the interaction of a number of factors: the individual's ability to manipulate attentional processes, how individuals manipulate the processes in relation to a given task, and the sociocultural expectations surrounding the performance of the task. The descriptions of both Smith and Schucman switching rapidly between translating/scribing and everyday activities suggests that both had an ability to control and manipulate attentional processes in unusual ways. From observers' reports of Smith and Schucman's self-descriptions, both were apparently able to focus their attention on translating/scribing and maintain an awareness of where they were and what they were doing.

Although understanding the ability to respond to hypnotic suggestion in terms of cognitive control processes is a significant advance, control processes can be manipulated in many different ways, and there is corresponding variation among HHs, some of whom excel at some tasks and not at others. Researchers now recognize that they must account not only for different degrees of responsiveness (high and low hypnotizability), but also for individual variation among HHs. McConkey and Barnier (2004; see also

---

the Big Five Inventory, or the Eyzenk Personality Questionnaire. Correlations with pencil and paper tests for absorptive, imaginative, and/or dissociative abilities, however, have long been assumed. These, however, have also been called into question, and more recent research indicates that they correlate only in a subset of highly hypnotizable individuals (for reviews of these discussions, see Laurence, Beaulieu-Prévost, and du Chéné 2008, 235–39; Tasso and Pérez 2008; Barnier and McConkey 2004, 47–48). In light of these difficulties, researchers are now focusing on performance-based correlates (for reviews, see Egner and Raz 2007; Laurence, Beaulieu-Prévost, and du Chéné 2008, 239–44), primarily in cognitive systems related to attention and automaticity, that is, the ability to do something without thinking about it. These processes are sometimes grouped under the heading of "cognitive control," which can be defined as "the processes that underpin the flexible management of processing resources for optimal task performance" (Egner and Raz 2007, 31). Psychologists have traditionally measured the efficiency of cognitive control using selective attention tasks, such as the Stroop Task, which requires subjects to pay attention to one stimulus (the target), while ignoring another (a distractor). Usually people automatically pay attention to both, such that when the "distractor" conflicts with the "target," their response times are slower. Repeated studies have demonstrated that HHs can override this automatic response (Raz et al. 2002; MacLeod and Sheehan 2003; Lichtenberg 2004). Researchers are using neuroimaging to identify differences in the way that HHs process attention and genetic markers that are linked to those differences (Horton and Crawford 2004; Raz 2005).

McConkey, Glisky and Kihlstrom, 1989) push this even further, citing evidence that HHs not only employ a variety of different cognitive strategies but deploy them selectively in the context of different social interactions. Thus, variations in performance most likely reflect not only differences in underlying abilities but also strategic choices about which abilities to use depending on the nature of the task and the context in which it arises. As a result of this complexity, researchers are now investigating the abilities of HHs in a much more focused fashion using intrinsic approaches that explore the nature of hypnosis itself, and instrumental approaches that use the abilities of HHs to explore phenomena they are able to mimic (Cox and Barnier 2009; Oakley 2006; Oakley and Halligan 2013).

Although much of the research of the latter sort has used HHs to mimic clinical conditions in order to better understand causation and improve treatment, some of these studies ask HHs to do things that require abilities that Smith and Schucman most likely drew upon to produce complex texts. Three lines of research seem particularly relevant for understanding their abilities. In relation to a flow of words that seems to arise outside consciousness, we have evidence that HHs can dissociate thoughts while remaining consciously aware, such that the thoughts do not seem to be their own. We also have evidence that they can automate tasks over which they usually have control without practice. In relation to stopping and starting, we have evidence that hypnotic inductions cue shifts in cognitive control, an observation that suggests that other practices, such as seer stones and shorthand notebooks, might cue shifts in cognitive control in real-life contexts.

Dissociating Thoughts: Evidence of the ability of HHs to dissociate thought in response to suggestion comes from a team at King's College London who have produced a series of papers in which they used HHs to model a range of phenomena associated with dissociative disorders, but also with spirit possession, shamanism, and mediumship (Deeley 2003; Deeley et al. 2013, 2014; Walsh et al. 2014). In a study of automatic writing, researchers explicitly acknowledge and attempt to model what they refer to scientifically as "culturally sanctioned attributions of alien control of thought, speech, or movement by supernatural agents (such as spirits or deities), in which a human intermediary is often viewed as a vehicle through which a supernatural agent communicates or reveals information to a human audience" (Walsh et al. 2014, 25). They focus on automatic writing as "a prominent form of revelation," insofar as it is "attributed to an agent other than the usual conscious self, such as a deity, spirit, or subconscious self, occurring with or without conscious awareness." In light of the historical and cultural evidence that automatic writing takes a variety of forms, their studies distinguish between "the control and ownership of thoughts, or hand movement, either with or without a narrowing of awareness" (ibid., 25).

In the first of two studies (ibid., 26–27), they investigated whether participants could experience the suggested effects—thought insertion, alien control of movement, and presence or lack of awareness—selectively. To test this, twenty HHs, selected from a large pool of volunteers screened for suggestibility, were given a series of writing prompts while positioned in a mock fMRI scanner with a specially constructed writing frame. The participants, whose eyes were closed the entire time, were given a sentence stem via headphones, which they completed in the scanner under different conditions, including "thought insertion" ("you will have the experience that an engineer is inserting a sentence ending into your mind") and "alien control" ("you will have the experience that an engineer is controlling your hand movements as you write"). At the end of each trial, participants were asked to verbally rate their subjective experience of control, ownership, and awareness in relation to both the thought of the sentence ending and the movement of their hand when writing the sentence ending. Based on their subjective reports, the researchers demonstrated that HHs could produce "selective alterations in the control, ownership, and awareness of thought and motor components of [automatic] writing" in response to targeted suggestions. In the follow-up study using fMRI (Walsh et al. 2015), they found a reduction in the activity of the left supplementary motor area, which plays a key role in the control and ownership of both thought and movement, as well as task-specific changes associated with either thought or movement.

Automating Tasks: While there is a growing list of studies demonstrating HHs' ability to de-automate processes that are usually automatic, such as the Stroop Task (MacLeod and Sheehan 2003; MacLeod 2011; Raz et al. 2002, 2006, 2007), researchers have only recently sought to determine whether HHs can reverse the process and transform effortful processes into automatic ones. Humans do this all the time by practicing something until it becomes automatic; the interesting question is whether HHs can do so without practice. To test this, Amir Raz and collaborators (Lifshitz et al. 2012) adapted a well-documented visual task in which the direction of movement of lines is difficult to determine without "occluders"—superimposed shapes—that make the lines appear to be a shape whose movement is then easily recognized (see the demonstration at http://razlab.mcgill.ca/demomotrak.html). Rather than supplying the occluders, they asked subjects who scored high (HHs) and low (LHs, or low hypnotizable individuals) on measures of hypnotizability to visualize imaginary occluders. The HHs were able to perform the task with greater accuracy than the LHs. The ability of HHs to visualize imagined occluders allowed them to determine the movement of the lines more accurately, if not in this case more efficiently.

Although this is very preliminary evidence, it suggests that Smith and Schucman may have been able to both dissociate control over the flow of words and automate the process so that it flowed quickly and smoothly. Indeed, dissociating the flow of words so that they did not seem to be their own meant that they were not consciously reflecting on them as they dictated, as they would have if, in Smith's case, he was dictating a letter or if, in Schucman's, she was writing a paper. When consciously reflecting on writing, observers noted that they both were far less fluent and struggled to get it "right."

Both dream narratives and "confabulations"—defined as "fictive narrative[s] produced effortlessly, without insight as to . . . veracity"—provide evidence that most people can produce stories effortlessly (Pace-Schott 2013). In both dreams and confabulation, narrative production is experienced as nonvolitional and released from ordinary "reality processing." Although volitional and nonvolitional storytelling most likely draw on some overlapping brain networks, nonvolitional narratives, such as dreaming or confabulation, rarely produce "levels of organization equal to volitional narrative." In the case of Smith, Schucman, and the student storyteller, we have unusual cases where the level of organization of the nonvolitional story equals or, in the case of Smith and Schucman, exceeds what they would have been able to do volitionally. In terms of their abilities, this is what makes them stand out and why their followers have been inclined to attribute the texts they produced to a source beyond themselves.

Cueing Shifts in Cognitive Control: Research on HHs suggests that the hypnotic induction, which cues shifts in cognitive control, allows HHs to focus their attention in such a way as to make better use of their already exceptional imaginative skills and offers insights into how shifts in cognitive control, cued by the hypnotic induction, might enable unusual individuals to respond more effectively to specific suggestions, in this instance, to the suggestion to produce a well-organized nonvolitional narrative.

Although researchers have speculated on the relationship between the hypnotic induction and subsequent suggestions for specific changes in experience and behaviors for many years, recent studies using brain imaging (McGeown et al. 2009, 2012) indicate that the hypnotic induction elicits anticipatory changes in HHs that lead to heightened effects. Thus, McGeown et al. conclude that "the hypnotic induction may lead highly suggestible participants to focus attention on the anticipated suggestions, thereby allowing them to make better use of their imaginative skills" (2012, 115). In doing so, they apparently are able to "suspend spontaneous non-goal-directed, internally focused cognitive activity (e.g., daydreaming, self referential processing), in the absence of a task" (ibid., 101). These neuroimaging findings are congruent with earlier discussions in which it was suggested (Barnier and Mitchell 2005) that the hypnotic induction reshapes the hypnotic subject's context so that their attention is focused on a target goal and competing goals are inhibited. The hypnotic induction creates a "highly motivated, yet impoverished context, [in which] the suggested goal is highly activated and competing thoughts are reduced. In essence, although a response may be no less physically or cognitively demanding in hypnosis, there is perhaps less indecisiveness about whether or not to execute it. This indecision would, under normal circumstances, increase difficulty and perceived effort" (Barnier, Dienes, and Mitchell 2008, 159). With respect to producing a complex text, the reduction in competing thoughts would undercut the tendency to second-guess what was emerging, while increased decisiveness in relation to the suggested goal could well give the impression that the flow of words was not one's own.

Although neither Smith's translating nor Schucman's scribing was initiated through a formal hypnotic induction, Smith's seer stones and Schucman's stenographic notebooks most likely played a similar role in cueing a shift that focused their attention on the task of translating or scribing and inhibited competing activities. More specifically, focusing their attention on the seer stone in the hat or on the notebook most likely triggered the shifts in cognitive control processes that initiated the decisive flow of words that they then dictated or scribed.

Those who have proposed performance-based models of hypnotic responding have long stressed that subjects respond to hypnotic inductions on cue, which makes them more like actors than like people having sudden anomalous experiences (Spanos 1996; Lynn et al. 2008). This, of course, does not mean that HHs *are* acting, in the sense of consciously performing, but that they, like actors, are responsive to cues (Dienes and Perner 2007; Brown and Oakley 2004). This research indicates that HHs are not only able to manipulate attentional processes in unusual ways but that practices, such as the hypnotic induction, aid them in doing so. In the everyday world, these sorts of abilities, which may be cued by practices related to objects (e.g., seer stones and notebooks), are viewed as special or non-ordinary and oftentimes attributed to powers beyond the self.

Delusions

In seeking to explain Smith and Schucman's abilities, I deliberately began with research on hypnosis, which focuses on people with unusual abilities in the general population, in order to approach the question of whether Smith and Schucman were deluded in a new way. Research on delusions typically focuses on psychiatric disorders, such as schizophrenia, and, as a result, on people who seek clinical help. In that context, alien control and thought insertion are viewed as prime examples of delusional thinking. The research we have just reviewed, however, demonstrates that HHs can replicate these processes and highlights a crucial difference between those who seek clinical help and those who do not. Generally speaking, those who seek clinical help find their experiences distressing in ways that others do not. Their distress typically arises due to difficulties regulating or controlling their unusual experiences and, as a result, difficulty carrying out everyday tasks. HHs' ability to manipulate cognitive processes *in response to external cues*—an ability shared by Smith and Schucman—marks a key difference between them and those who seek clinical help.

A new approach to delusions, which explains dreams, imagination, and delusions in light of a common set of underlying cognitive mechanisms, has considerable potential to explain this difference if we extend it to include religious claims in the general population. In contrast to previous theories, which define delusions in terms of false beliefs, Gerrans (2014a) locates the source of delusions—along with dreams and imagination—in the mental processes associated with the "default mode network" (DMN), a "system that evolved to allow humans to simulate experiences in the absence of an eliciting stimulus." This "simulation system" allows humans to recall past experiences and imagine possible futures" (ibid., 67), and to bring those simulations to bear on the current situation. In the ordinary alert, waking state, we shift back and forth between simulations of past and future experiences and decisions that we need to make in the present. To facilitate this, the DMN is inversely correlated with and supervised by "decontextualized processing" systems, including various "reality monitoring" processes that reflect on the simulations in light of current input from the environment.

According to Gerrans, "delusions arise when *default cognitive processing, unsupervised* by *decontextualized processing, is monopolized by hypersalient information*" (2014a, xix; emphasis in original). When we dream, the default mode network is free to generate simulations in the absence of external input and with little oversight from high-level control systems (ibid., 68). In the case of delusions, which by definition occur when awake, the normal interaction between default and decontextualized processing is compromised in some way that leads to distress (ibid., 153). In contrast, HHs are able to manipulate the interaction between default and decontextualized processing, suspending certain aspects of decontextualized processes in response to external cues without distress.

Gerrans applies his theory to the experiences of alien control and thought insertion associated with schizophrenia. While his theory readily accommodates experiences of alien control, its extension from passive actions to passive thoughts proves more difficult. In reconceptualizing delusions as unsupervised default processing, Gerrans tried to explain why people *experience* thoughts as those of someone else, as opposed to simply *believing* they belong to others. Post hoc appraisals can explain the latter but not the former. If, however, we could think of passive thoughts—like passive movements—as "covert action(s) intimately connected with thought," then, Gerrans argues, passive thoughts could also be explained in terms of disruptions of predictive processing (ibid., 207). In chapter 12, I will suggest that research on motivation offers a way to understand thoughts that are ego-dystonic (seemingly not "mine") at the personal level in terms of competing, potential goal-directed *actions* at the subpersonal level. For the moment, however, it is enough to recognize that explaining the experience of inserted thoughts is not sufficient to explain the emergence of agents who interact with—indeed instruct and chastise—their hosts and dictate long, complex texts as well.

The comparison between HHs, the student storyteller, and Smith and Schucman breaks down at this point as well. The suprahuman entities with whom Smith and Schucman engaged had agency. They spoke in their own first-person voices and seemed to have a will of their own. The ability to stop and start by cueing shifts in cognitive control processes, to dissociate ownership and control of thought without loss of awareness, and to automate normally effortful processes only partly explains the abilities of Smith and Schucman. Compared to the Book of Mormon or *A Course in Miracles*, the thoughts dissociated and the tasks automated in the hypnosis experiments were very simple ones. Most crucially, the instructions in the thought insertion experiment suggest an impersonal process in which the engineer simply supplies words but does not address the subject directly, that is, as an agent speaking in first or second person. The comparison between Smith, Schucman, and the student storyteller breaks down when it comes to the matter of agency as well. The student storyteller spoke in his own voice throughout the recounting of the imagined cave adventure; it was not until Hilgard elicited the voice of the so-called hidden observer that the student storyteller spoke, so to speak, in a different voice.

ALTERNATE SELVES

In all three of our case studies, we saw important shifts in voice that we need to explain. In revising the original version of the Big Book, the authors shifted from a didactic, second-person voice that told the reader what they ought to do, while revealing little about themselves, to a first-person voice that explained what they had done, learned, and experienced. In doing so, the text took on and personified the voice of the fellowship as a whole. With Smith, we saw several shifts in voice. In his initial visionary experiences, he interacted in visions with a personage that he apparently saw and heard. Later he inquired of the Lord and received responses internally. Prior to recovering the plates, the personage he encountered in visions told Smith something of what was written on them. Following these encounters, Smith was able to recount stories of the ancient peoples of the Americas to his family *as if he had been there*, in other words, as if he had seen these things with his own eyes (in the first person). When translating, D&C 8 suggested that the Holy Ghost supplied the flow of words, but we know that the words themselves were the first-person accounts of the ancient Nephite narrators (Hardy 2010). Their first-person voice distanced Smith from the events, such that he was no longer there, but implied an ability to assume the point of view of the characters in his narrative. In the case of Schucman, we also saw several shifts in voice. Beginning the summer before and extending well beyond the scribing of the Course, Schucman could ask questions of the Voice, which she thought of as Jesus, and receive answers from him in his first-person voice, much as Smith "enquired of the Lord." Immediately prior to scribing the Course and continuing into the first several months of scribing, she actively engaged in internal dialogues with the Voice, which she recorded in the notes and then read aloud. After the inner dialogues largely ceased, the Voice continued to dictate in the first person as Jesus.

Smith and Schucman thus combined features of both the engineer and the hidden observer into a more complex scenario. Like the "engineer" who completed the sentence stems for the HHs, Smith and Schucman experienced a stream of words that seemed to come unbidden from someone other than themselves, but the flow of words they experienced were not just thoughts inserted *by* someone else but the thoughts *of* someone else: complex lectures recounted in the voice of Jesus in Schucman's case and complex stories recounted in the voices of ancient Nephites in Smith's case. Congruent with the idea of an ancient text composed by several narrators, the Holy Ghost supplied the flow of words of the first-person narrators, while the voice of Jesus communicated directly with Schucman. Although Smith may have interacted with a personage that he claimed was an ancient Nephite (i.e., Moroni) in visionary contexts, he did not interact with the Nephite narrators in the context of "translating," as Schucman did with the voice of Jesus in the early stages of the scribing process. Nonetheless, both apparently had internal access to a first-person flow of words that did not seem to be their own and that they did not experience themselves as planning or monitoring.

The shift to a first-person voice is a crucial step—actually, the key shift. If we can account for that, then we have a new agent speaking, presumably with some cognitive resources from which to draw, and much can flow from that. Although this is a more complex "suggestion" than that offered either to the HHs in the automatic writing research or to Hilgard's student storyteller, it is hardly unprecedented. People have access to voices that are not their own in a variety of contexts ranging from psychopathology (schizophrenia and dissociative disorders), pretend play and imaginary inner dialogues, fiction writing, drama, online games, spirit possession, and shamanism. In all these contexts, we have examples of alternate selves that take on a life of their own and generate more or less elaborate self-narratives, autobiographies, and, in some cases, complex works analogous to the Book of Mormon and ACIM.

Psychologist Mary Watkins discusses numerous instances in which people—mostly writers—experience "imaginal others" that seem to "have as much autonomy as the so-called real others [one] meet[s] in consensual space" (1986, 91–92). So, for example, she quotes novelist Enid Blyton, who had a method for allowing her characters to speak:

> I shut my eyes for a few moments, with my portable typewriter on my knee—I make my mind blank and wait—and then, as clearly as I would see real children, my characters stand before me in my mind's eye. I see them in detail—hair, eyes, feet, clothes, expressions . . . I don't know what anyone is going to say or do. I don't know what is going to happen. I am in the happy position of being able to write a story and read it for the first time, at one and the same moment . . . Sometimes a character makes a joke, a really funny one, that makes me laugh as I type it on my paper—and I think, "Well, I couldn't have thought of that myself in a hundred years!" And then I think, "Well, who *did* think of it, then?" (ibid., 96–97)

After offering a number of additional examples from luminaries such as Henry James, Flannery O'Connor, and Alice Walker, she notes that few within academic or clinical psychology have taken the nonpathological experience of autonomous imaginal others seriously, apart from Carl Jung, who actively engaged with imaginal figures and encouraged his patients to do so as well (ibid., 97–99).

If we return to the hypnosis analogy, we need to keep in mind that the flow of words, whether inserted by another party or conveyed in the first person, is a product of the "suggestion" regarding what is to occur, not of the "induction" or shift in attention that precedes the suggestion and its implementation. The induction cues the suspension of "spontaneous non-goal-directed, internally focused cognitive activity (e.g., daydreaming, self referential processing) in the absence of a task" (McGeown et al. 2012, 101). In other words, the induction suspends default cognitive processing (the activity of the DMN), which is what normally happens when we shift our focus to a task, but does so *in the absence of a task.* Thus, the induction *readies* the subject for the suggestion.

We can build on this to suggest how alternate first-person voices emerge. To do so, we need to expand our understanding of the DMN. As Gerrans explains (2014a, 75–87), the DMN not only generates simulations, it does so from the first-person point of view, which allows it to play a crucial role in elaborating our sense of self. The DMN is closely linked with our emotional and motivational systems (ibid., 79), which form the basis for our sense of

264 | CHAPTER II

self. The DMN is the source of our personal narratives, which it constructs in order to "make [our] experience intelligible in terms of [our] goals and motives" (Gerrans 2014b, 6). Left to its own devices, the DMN evaluates the narratives it generates based on their "*subjective adequacy* rather than [their] truth, accuracy, public acceptability, or verification" (Gerrans 2014a, 75; emphasis in original).

This means—to return to the hypnotic induction—that the "internally focused cognitive activity" that is suspended is the "self-referential processing" of the primary subject, in this case, Smith or Schucman. Shifting their attention to the seer stone or the notebook, I am hypothesizing, cued the suspension of their normal self-referential processing and readied them to focus their attention on the anticipated task. In Enid Blyton's case, she simply made her mind blank and waited. With Smith and Schucman, the anticipated task was dictating or scribing a flow of words from a first-person source (ancient Nephites via the Holy Ghost or the voice of Jesus). Blyton anticipated that her characters would come to life and start talking. Smith and Schucman were consciously responsible for the dictating and scribing. Blyton was consciously responsible for typing. In order to allow the other voices to flow, however, they had to suspend their own self-referential processing and allow another "self" to construct its own personal narrative using "their" default mode network. To continue the hypnosis analogy, the implicit suggestion that followed from the cueing of the dictation or scribing task was a suggestion to allow the "other" to speak in the first person. In terms of brain functions, I am hypothesizing that for these alternate first-person voices to emerge, Smith had to allow "himself" to be displaced as the self-referential center of the DMN and replaced by the Holy Ghost mediating the words of Nephite prophets; Schucman had to allow "herself" to be displaced by the voice of Jesus.[4]

As the reconstructions in Part 1 demonstrated, the abilities of both Smith and Schucman developed over time. Smith envisioned "treasure guardians" that kept him from recovering visualized treasures in his treasure-seeking days, interacted with an otherworldly personage in his dream-visions of 1823, and with angels and deities in his visionary experiences. He recounted narratives of these encounters to his family and practiced his storytelling skills on his more skeptical neighbors as well. Over time, he internalized these visualized others as he learned to recognize the Lord speaking in his mind in response to queries and the Holy Spirit putting a flow of words into his heart when he translated. He used his seer stone to make the transition from external to internalized "others," eventually accessing revelation without the aid of an object. In Schucman's case, the process began with

---

[4] Although, to bring AA back into the picture, Bill Wilson had to allow his voice to be displaced by the anonymous voice of "we alcoholics," this was a more ordinary process of shifting roles.

dreams that she elaborated in the context of her meditations and recounted to Thetford in response to their desire to find a better way. Over the course of several months, Schucman progressively distinguished between her own voice and that of another, who eventually emerged as the Voice of the Course.

Jung's instructions for entering into an active, imaginal dialogue sound very much like what Schucman did during the summer preceding the scribing of the Course and, in effect, describe how some people learn how to do this. Thus, Jung instructed a "Mr. O" to:

> [S]tart with any image, for instance with just that yellow mass in your dream. Contemplate it and carefully observe how the pictures begin to unfold or to change. Don't try to make it into something, just do nothing but observe what its spontaneous changes are. Any mental picture you contemplate in this way will sooner or later change through a spontaneous association that causes a slight alteration of the picture. . . . Hold fast to the one image you have chosen and wait until it changes by itself. Note all these changes and eventually step into the picture yourself, and if it is a speaking figure at all then say what you have to say to that figure and listen to what he or she has to say. (Jung 1997, 164; Watkins 1986, 101)

Although some scholars (e.g., Vogel 2004, xvi) have resisted the idea that Joseph Smith learned anything from using his seer stones to search for treasure, we can envision his seer stone as a means of focusing his attention on an object in which he visualized the "treasure" he was seeking, just as Jung advised Mr. O to focus on the "yellow mass" in his dream and Helen Schucman focused on the images that came to her while dreaming and awake. But, as Jung's instructions indicate, images can seem to change of their own accord if we stare at them intently. Smith may well have been watching for just such cues when using his seer stone to search for treasure, such that he interpreted spontaneous movements of the image as indicating either the direction he should move or the direction the imagined object was moving. Similarly, shifts in Schucman's imagery during meditation, such as, for example, when "something happened, and the wreath disappeared," set off a chain of associations: first, that the wreath went into the light and burned up, followed by the idea that "victory is not made by us, but it is made for us."

In the context of pretend play, inner-voice dialogues, fiction, drama, online games, and religious experience, the presence of alternate selves is often invited and roles forthrightly cultivated and skillfully managed. In most of these contexts, children and adults learn to cultivate and manage alternate selves through implicit learning processes that do not expect or require explicit reflection on the processes involved. In relation to these activities, people provide accounts of alternate selves that *seemed* very real to them, but neither they nor others find the seeming reality of their alternate selves problematic because they "know" that they created, enacted, or otherwise brought their characters to life and thus that they are not "real." In psychological terms, they are all adept at "reality monitoring." The difficulties arise when people claim that these alternate selves *are* real.[5] In the context of the psychological and clinical literature, such claims are often thought to involve deception or self-deception and thus, in the latter case, characterized as delusional. Since Joseph Smith was explicitly accused of deceiving his followers and Schucman could potentially be characterized in this way as well, we need to look at these lines of research carefully.

In the psychological literature, deception is understood to encompass avoiding, obfuscating, exaggerating, and casting doubt on the truth, in addition to outright lying, in relation to others. Self-deception directs these processes toward the self, such that "people favor welcome over unwelcome information in a manner that reflects their goals or motivations" (Von Hippel and Trivers 2011, 1). In Gerrans's terms, self-deception is the result of insufficiently supervised default cognitive processing, that is, insufficient "reality monitoring." Although the classic case of self-deception involves convincing oneself that a lie is true, discussions of truth, lies, and reality monitoring are more complicated in the real world than these definitions would suggest.

These discussions acknowledge that determining whether an individual's behavior is deceptive (or self-deceptive) may hinge on the individual's intent, which in many cases isn't clear and must be inferred. If we return to the trial in Lyons, New York, as discussed in chapter 1, the witnesses who testified against Smith claimed that he had disclosed to them personally that the box did not in fact contain ancient golden plates (i.e., that he was lying to them about its contents) and either told them directly or led them to believe that his aim was to deceive people in order to get their money. Martin Harris testified to his faith that there were ancient plates in the box, though he had never been allowed to see them, and that Smith was not motivated by financial gain. In chapter 2, I pointed out that there were other possibilities. It's possible that Smith created "homemade" plates that he believed the Lord could transform into "ancient golden plates," just as a Catholic priest initiates the Holy Spirit's transformation of a wafer into the body of Christ or the Book of Mormon recounts that the brother of Jared prepared stones that the Lord transformed into spheres of light.

---

[5] For nonpathological models of the self that make room for multiplicity in keeping with the approach taken here, see Hermans (2011) and Rovane (1998); more typically, however, multiplicity is associated with psychopathology (see, e.g., Radden 2011b).

In these alternative scenarios, the transformation is premised on "exceeding faith." If Smith created plates that looked like what he had seen in his visionary experiences (and believed, with his family's support, to be real), placed the homemade plates in a box believing (also in faith) that the Lord could transform them into ancient golden plates, and did all this for reasons that were high-minded (e.g., bringing forth new revelation) rather than nefarious (e.g., financial gain), then are we still talking about deception? If Smith genuinely believed that he was doing what the Lord was asking him to do (as Martin Harris believed), then we cannot call him deceptive. But, we can still ask, was he deceiving himself? As I indicated in chapter 2, I think that Smith himself struggled with doubt about the reality of the plates when he saw them (in a vision) but was unable to recover them. As he recounted the story of the recovery of the plates, he reinterpreted the moment of doubt as an assault by the "powers of darkness," thus casting it within an increasingly mythologized frame consistent with the larger story being told.

So what then do we make of these mythologized frames? Are they insufficiently monitored with respect to reality? Like traditional approaches to delusions based on "false beliefs . . . about external reality,"[6] Gerrans's approach to delusions rests on an understanding of reality, which he bases on a straightforward distinction between "subjectively adequate interpretations of experience" and "publicly available information" (2014a, 160). Religious claims, however, sharply challenge this simple distinction, opening up the vast space in which cultures and traditions generate an array of consensual "realities" that occupy the space between "subjectively adequate interpretations of experience" and "publicly available information." In real-world contexts, we have to ask (1) how public is public—does public mean accessible to everyone or at least one other person? And (2) what counts as information—does it have to be scientifically verifiable information or just information that convinces a few other people? Reality monitoring, in other words, is not just an individual process; it is a complex sociocultural process that typically goes under the heading of discernment.

In the cases we've been examining, the subjects monitored (and debated and assessed) the reality of their claims as their unusual experiences occurred. Smith likely considered the possibility that his dream-vision was just a dream. His family reinforced the reality of the personage based on their preexisting beliefs. Harris confirmed the reality of Smith's claims based on his own visions. Smith realized that it was not enough for him alone to "see" (or visualize) the plates; witnesses also had to see them as he did and testify to it publicly. Schucman and Thetford discussed the possibility that the

---

[6] According to the *Diagnostic and Statistical Manual*, a delusion is "a false belief based on [an] incorrect inference about external reality that is firmly sustained despite what almost everyone else believes and despite what constitutes incontrovertible and obvious proof or evidence to the contrary" (*DSM*-5 2013, 819).

emerging voice was a product of Helen's imagination. Schucman was never totally convinced that it was real, but Thetford (and at times Schucman) was convinced by the seemingly synchronous or paranormal events (e.g., at Mayo Clinic and in Israel) and by consultation with others (e.g., Hugh Lynn Cayce and Eileen Garrett). Bill Wilson assessed the reality of his unusual experience at Towns Hospital in light of the response of his wife and doctor and its ongoing effect on his life (he quit drinking). Bob and Anne Smith assessed the reality of the involvement of a Higher Power in Bob's recovery in light of their previous beliefs. All four sought further confirmation through investigation of spiritualist and psychic phenomena; Bill Wilson saw further confirmation in his drug-induced experiences. Although they all monitored their claims regarding the presence of suprahuman entities, none did so on the basis of publicly available information.

In defining delusions, the *Diagnostic and Statistical Manual of Mental Disorders* (*DSM*) recognizes the importance of social context, specifying that the "false beliefs" in question are not those "ordinarily accepted by other members of the person's culture or subculture (e.g. it is not an article of religious faith)." Philosophers have wrestled with this religious exception in an attempt to make a clear distinction between delusions and ordinary religious beliefs, but found no intrinsic grounds on which to do so (Radden 2011a, Bortolotti 2010). In a recent effort, Radden concluded, "to differentiate spiritual delusions from more ordinary spiritual convictions, it seems we must rely on aspects of context or accompanying symptoms rather than [features] of the delusions themselves" (2011a, 108). This means that in the absence of symptoms other than the allegedly delusory belief itself, the distinction between ordinary belief and delusion turns on context, that is, on whether the belief makes sense within the context of a culture or subculture. Whether we are conceiving of delusions as false beliefs or as the product of insufficiently supervised default cognitive processing, some sort of assessment of reality is involved.

Many claims regarding suprahuman entities are not publicly accessible. At the same time, however, people do not simply reject such claims on those grounds but assess them in light of cultural norms and expectations. From this perspective, the key issue is what others think of the claim. Notice, though, how the *DSM*'s exception for articles of religious faith is premised on preexisting claims already accepted by people. There is little room in this definition for novelty, for the possibility of new revelation. Once others agree on a shared interpretation, it makes more sense to speak of consensual realities, however contested. From this vantage point, whether or not individuals are deluded or facilitating the emergence of a new spiritual path or religious movement rests on whether or not they can get others to share their novel beliefs.

This brings us back to Jesse Smith's astute, albeit somewhat puzzling, observation that his nephew Joseph had "eyes to see things that are not, and then [had] the audacity to say they are." What exactly does it mean to say someone has eyes to see things that are not? Does it mean that the things do not exist, that they are imagined or made up, as Jesse Smith believed? Does it mean that there are things that do exist that are not visible to those who do not have the eyes to see them, as Joseph Smith's followers claimed? Or might it mean that he and others like him had eyes to see what *could be* and the audacity to give what he envisioned tangible form. If we view Smith, Schucman, and Wilson as skilled perceivers, we can view their unusual abilities as opening up possibilities present in a particular historical moment and the emergence of these spiritual paths as evidence of their ability to bring forth what they envisioned. Highlighting the role of skillful perception allows us to acknowledge that some people may perceive these possibilities through insights or inspirations that seem to come from beyond the self without dismissing them as self-deception or delusion (Dreyfus and Kelly 2011, 209).

In light of these possibilities, we can envision three broad reactions to unusual experiences. People might ignore or dismiss them and, if they do not recur, that may be the end of it. Whether they recur or not, people may reflect on them and bring them to the attention of others. If others consistently find the experiences worrisome and the experiencer and/or the experiences persist, the others are likely to seek culturally sanctioned assistance. In contexts where psychiatric help is sought, this may lead to a diagnosis of psychosis. Alternatively, at least some others may view the experiencer as gifted or insightful and the experiences in question as compelling. They may encourage the experiencers to engage them more fully, whether in service of deeper self-understanding, spiritual insight, or new revelation. The unusual abilities of Smith, Wilson, and Schucman did not and could not have led to the emergence of publicly recognized alternate selves on their own. It was only through the interactions between them and their earliest collaborators that the meaning of what they experienced was hammered out and developed into the social formations we see today. But given that the responses to Smith, Wilson, and Schucman were mixed, we still need to ask why some responded positively, while others did not.

CHAPTER 12

Motivation

In chapter 10, we discussed how each group established the presence of a suprahuman entity and a means of communicating with it. In chapter 11, we discussed the suprahuman entities as alternative selves, explored how such selves can emerge psychologically, and considered the range of claims made for them. In this chapter, we ask why some people participated in the process of group formation and others did not. This is a question about motivation. To fully explore the question of motivation, however, we must also ask what motivated the alternative selves we have been discussing—the Lord or Holy Spirit of Mormonism, the Higher Power of the AA group, and the Voice of ACIM. From a naturalistic perspective, this is an admittedly odd—but crucial—question that takes us to the heart of the phenomena we seek to understand.

In psychology, motivation refers to "factors that activate, direct, and sustain goal-directed behavior. . . . Motives are the 'whys' of behavior—the needs or wants that drive behavior and explain what we do. We don't actually observe a motive; rather, we infer that one exists based on the behavior we observe" (Nevid 2013). There are several things to notice about this basic understanding of motivation. First, it is goal-directed. However else they characterize themselves, each of the groups we have been considering views itself as a spiritual path. A "path" is a means to an *end*; it normally goes somewhere and thus points toward a goal. Second, a path is a *means* to an end; it may twist and turn and the goal may not always be in sight, but it is still presumably marked in some way, so that those on the path are able to follow it. Third, people follow a path for a *reason*; they have motives—implicit and explicit—for doing so that reflect the goal they want to attain. Reasons, however, are not necessarily "reasoned" in the sense of being thought out; typically, they are affective, that is, *emotion-laden* (Thagard 2006). Finally, people follow a particular path because they believe it will take them where they want to go. More often than not, I suggest, people who are open to or actively seeking a new path are less interested in reflecting on the historical, philosophical, or scientific evidence that might support or undermine the path's truth claims, but instead want to know if the path will "work" for them. They want to know if it will solve their problem, change what they find unsatisfactory, and guide them in a more promising direction. If they *experience* it as doing so, this then *confirms* for them that the path is true.

In discussing why some people participated in the process of group formation and others did not, we can distinguish between key collaborators who were present from the outset as a "founding team" and those who joined them as their "first followers."[1] We can also distinguish between founding teams that viewed themselves as modifying an existing path and those that claimed to mediate the emergence of entirely new paths. We can view all first followers and those founding teams that modified an existing path as converts and analyze the motives underlying their conversion. In the case of founding teams that claimed to mediate the emergence of new paths, we need to explain what motivated them to embrace a new goal. In all cases, we need to explain what motivated the alternative selves to guide the emergence of the group along a new or modified path.

In what follows, I argue that the alternate selves can be understood as *group-identified selves*, that is, as selves that were *motivated* to speak for the group as a whole and thus to guide the emergence of the group as a group. In that sense, they were the creators of the paths. In social identity terms, these group-identified selves—the Lord, the Higher Power, and the Voice—articulated the norms and values of the group and "chastised" individuals when their individual identities threatened the goals of the emerging group. Individuals were motivated to postulate or confirm the presence of a suprahuman entity and its role in guiding them when doing so promised to resolve deep-seated problems. In so doing, they became founding teams. Individuals were motivated to convert—becoming first followers—when their individual aims meshed with or could be positively transformed in light of the apparent goals of the postulated entity.

THEORIZING MOTIVATION

In referring to motivation, I am assuming that motives are best understood as explanations of goal-directed action and that individuals can pursue individual goals and act in concert with others to pursue collective goals. Research on goal-directed action over the past few decades has revealed that much, if not most, goal-directed action is initiated, directed, and sustained at an unconscious level. The realization of the extent to which this is the

---

[1] In what follows I will be considering the Smith family (Joseph, Emma, and Joseph's parents and siblings); Bill and Lois Wilson, along with Ebby T. and Dr. Silkworth; and Bill Thetford and Helen Schucman as founding teams, and Martin Harris, Oliver Cowdery, Robert and Anne Smith, and Kenneth Wapnick and Judith Skutch as first followers. I will be considering AA as modifying the existing Oxford Group path and the Mormon and ACIM founding teams as claiming to establish new paths.

case led social psychologists, such as Huang and Bargh (2014, 126), to consider goal-directed action in evolutionary terms, recognizing that the self-consciously intentional goal-directed actions that we pride ourselves on as humans emerged relatively late in evolutionary history. Since other animals are perfectly capable of goal-directed action in the absence of conscious self-reflection, Huang and Bargh suppose that they—and to a large extent humans as well—are guided by "some other, unconscious, less centralized system(s)" upon which conscious goal-directed action relies.

These shifts in understanding have led to the nonintuitive view of humans and other animals as comprised of behaviorally inferred "goals" that exist at multiple levels within an organism from the cellular to the organismic and that, at any given level, compete for priority, such that certain goals (or sets of compatible goals) are activated at any given point in time and therefore direct action at that level. This means that at the subpersonal level, "multiple conscious and unconscious goals operate, each steering the individual toward specific (and oftentimes conflicting) end-states" (Huang and Bargh 2014, 126). As organisms, we have evolved to manage these competing possibilities, but because each goal, when activated, "constrain[s] the individual's information processing and behavioral possibilities in a way that encourages achievement of the goal's end-state," the competition between goals for expression and dominance can and does give rise to "inconsistencies in individual behaviors" (ibid., 126–27). An evolutionary perspective thus radically upends our everyday sense of ourselves as unified "selves" in favor of a view of humans and other animals as comprised of multiple, mostly unconscious impulses directed to different ends that compete for attention and gain primacy in serial fashion (McCubbins and Turner 2012, 393–94).

To understand more clearly what this research on motivation can contribute to our understanding of the emergence of the three groups, it will help to understand what is new about this research. Whereas early twentieth-century behavioral and psychoanalytic theories of motivation focused on "drives," current researchers have largely abandoned this approach in favor of cognitive approaches to goal-directed action. "Cognitive," as used here, does not refer simply to higher mental processes but is used more broadly to refer to a language for describing how we process all the incoming information available to us from our bodies and the entire environment in which we are situated—social, built, and natural—in functional terms, that is, in terms of what we do with it.[2] Any psychological process can be described in

---

[2] There is a narrow and broader sense in which the term is used. As John Tooby and Leda Cosmides indicate: "Some researchers use it [cognitive] in a narrow sense, to refer to so-called 'higher mental' processes, such as reasoning, as distinct from other psychological processes, such as 'emotion' or 'motivation'; that is, to refer to a concept that corresponds more or less to the folk notion of reasoning while in a calm frame of mind. In contrast, we [Tooby and Cosmides] are using the word *cognitive*

cognitive or information-processing terms, whether conscious or unconscious. Although psychologists have traditionally considered cognition and motivation separately, evolutionary psychologists, such as Tooby and Cosmides, have adopted an integrated approach premised on the idea that "the brain evolved as a control system, designed to generate action" (2005, 51). From this perspective, they indicate, we would expect that "conceptual structure, motivation, and action [form] . . . a single integrated system."

We can use Gerrans's theory of delusions to develop an integrated model that links the discussion of groups, selves, and motives in Part 2. As indicated in chapter 11, the default mode network (DMN), which is the source of our personal narratives and elaborates our sense of self, is closely linked with our emotional and motivational systems. Moreover, as Gerrans explains, the DMN constructs personal narratives in order to "make [our] experience intelligible *in terms of* [our] goals and motives" (2014b, 6; emphasis added). If, as the motivation research indicates, we have multiple conscious and unconscious goals competing for priority, these goals can surface to consciousness within the DMN as impulses or forces "directing" us to act in ways that may not seem like "us." Faced with competing centers of motivated goal-directed action, in other words, the DMN constructs narratives to make sense of them and, in doing so, may personify them as selves, either our self or another self seemingly acting in and through us.

Because the mechanisms involved in producing actions are only indirectly related to those that produce a sense of agency, acting and the sense of acting are easily dissociated. As Pacherie indicates, "We sometimes have a sense of agency for actions we did not actually prefer or did not consciously intend, and conversely we may lack a sense of agency for actions we did consciously intend and actually performed" (2011, 443). We make inferences about who is acting based on internal and external cues. As hypnosis researchers have demonstrated, these cues can easily be manipulated (Wegner 2002; Aarts 2007; Dijksterhuis et al. 2008; Aarts, Custers, and Marien 2009). In light of this gap between our actions and sense of agency, some theories of self (e.g., Dennett 1992; Gazzaniga 1998; Carruthers 2007) stress the role of narrative and other high-level interpretive processes in rationalizing or explaining our shifts in direction to make them seem as coherent as possible. Under some circumstances, however, we do not opt for coherence and instead, both for conscious and unconscious reasons (motives), may heighten the discontinuities such that it appears to "us" and others that

---

in a different and more standard [cognitive science] sense. . . . We use . . . *cognitive* and *information-processing* to refer to a language or level of analysis that can be used to precisely describe any psychological process: reasoning, emotion, motivation, and motor control can all be described in cognitive terms, whether the processes that give rise to them are conscious or unconscious, simple or complex. In cognitive science, the term *mind* refers to an information-processing description of the *functioning* of an organism's brain" (1992, 65).

certain of "our" goal-directed actions are initiated, activated, and sustained by someone else.

Left to its own devices, as Gerrans (2014a, 75) indicates, the DMN evaluates the narratives it generates based on their subjective adequacy rather than their public acceptability. As indicated in chapter 11, reality monitoring in the everyday world is a complex sociocultural process in which multiple "publics" differ greatly in terms of the narratives they consider acceptable. The social identity approach to the self, which we have been using to theorize the creative process, allows us to specify "public acceptability" in relation to groups and, thus, to take a more nuanced, group-specific approach to "reality testing." It also allows us to analyze the interplay between subjective and more public assessments of adequacy and to predict that, when individuals shift from an individual (personal) identity to a social (group) identity, their narratives are likely to be guided by the norms and attributes of the social group rather than simply in terms of their personal preferences.

We can use this theoretical framework to consider the motivations of various types of collaborators in the process of group formation. We can begin with converts, understood here to include all first followers and founding teams that modified an existing path. In the theoretical terms we are using here, converts can be conceived in terms of an initial set of competing motivations and prior experiences that they bring to an existing or emergent path. Conversion involves adopting a new social identity, which includes a group narrative and norms, and reframing not only their own self-narrative, but also *reorganizing their goals and motivations* in light of those of the group. With founding teams that claim to mediate a new path, one or more individuals mediate the emergence of a new goal around which the team can coalesce. The new goal allows them to reframe their collective identity and reorganize their individual goals and motivations in light of the new goal. Finally, the emergence of suprahuman entities can be understood not only as a socially recognized alternative self mediated through shifts in the self-identify of one or more members of the group (a collectively agreed-upon subjectivity), as discussed in chapter 10, but also as a personification of the goals of the group motivated by the needs of the group as a whole (a motivated collective subjectivity).

MOTIVATED CONVERSIONS

New paths "worked" for converts because they solved a problem. They did so, I am arguing, by reorganizing the converts' motivational priorities. The deeper and more intractable the problem, the more profound the reorganization required to "solve" the problem and enable the new path to "work." Although we don't have a lot of information on the personal problem that Mormonism solved for early converts such as Martin Harris and Oliver

Cowdery, we do not have to search far to find the problem that motivated Bill Wilson's search for a new path.

Wilson's Conversion: Bill Wilson's explicit goal was to overcome his alcohol addiction, a goal that he shared with his wife, Lois, Dr. Silkworth, and Ebby T. In Akron, Dr. Bob was also seeking a path that would enable him to overcome his addiction, a goal that he shared with his wife, Anne, and others, such as Harriet Seuberling. Underlying motives included Lois's and Anne's fears for their husbands' lives, their marriages, and their livelihood. The alcoholics, moreover, had an underlying desire to keep drinking. Their covert goal of drinking was in direct competition with the overt goal of abstaining and, as the current literature describes it, repeatedly "hijacked the motivational system" (Huang and Bargh 2014, 126; Köpetz et al. 2013). In a recent study, Marien et al. (2012) provided evidence that alcoholism is a particularly obvious instance of the general ability of unconscious (experimentally primed or environmentally cued) goals to "hijack" executive control functions by drawing attentional resources away from goals the individual is consciously pursuing. The goal in these terms was to prevent this hijacking from taking place.

When it came to compulsive behaviors, Wilson had other behaviors related, for example, to smoking and women that apparently continued to "hijack" him. Indeed, Tom Powers was apparently motivated to found All Addicts Anonymous in the late sixties partly in reaction to Wilson's inability to deal with his other "addictions" (Cheever 2004, 231–32). Although Wilson's record was mixed when it came to compulsive behaviors, he was, as we have seen, well aware of his own desires for fame, fortune, and power, and frequently characterized himself as a "power-driver" (Wing 1998, 63) and quite consistently subordinated his personal interests and sense of "calling" to the needs of AA. Had he not done so, his initial feeling that he was someone special in the wake of his sudden experience at Towns Hospital, his similar feeling with regard to his psychic "sensitivities," and the messages from the spirit world regarding his larger mission and destiny might have led him to proclaim "new revelation" and thus to view himself as mediating the emergence of a new path with new goals. As it was, he went to great pains to stress that his sudden experience at Towns was a conversion experience, that he was in no position to judge whether it should be considered "a miraculous and calculated intervention of God," and that AA was not "a new religious denomination."

Given Wilson's emphasis on these points, I think AA is more accurately viewed as a modification of an existing (Oxford Group) path rather than a new path. Although Wilson broke with his Oxford Group team's guidance to found a group for alcoholics, we can view this as a "schism"—to use the old-fashioned term—that modified the goal, gradually shifting it from salvation to recovery, and pruned the path to make it more generic, without claiming to have produced something distinctively new. The stripping-down process created a path that was implicitly perennialist, but, as we have seen, AA deliberately did not embrace perennialism as a "theological" tenet in order to avoid competing with exclusivist traditions, even though Wilson did embrace perennialism personally. Had AA done so, it would have broken more decisively with its Oxford Group roots.

The tension between AA's tacit perennialism and Wilson's overt personal perennialism allows us to interpret his sudden experience at Towns Hospital on two levels. From an AA perspective, it was a sudden, personally transformative conversion experience; from Bill's personal perspective, as it developed over time, it was an experience of "Presence" that opened into a fourth dimension that convinced him that the spirit survives bodily death and that science and religion, as he understood them, could be reconciled. We can also view the historical emergence of AA in terms that are quite compatible with how AA views itself, such that Bill's sudden experience "converted" him to the Oxford Group path. His vision of passing the message through a chain of alcoholics did not bear fruit, however, until he modified his understanding of the path in the Mayflower Hotel and connected with Dr. Bob in Akron on the basis of mutual need rather than testimony.

So, viewed as a conversion experience, why did Wilson's sudden experience actually enable him to stop drinking? How and why did it work for him? In the case of Wilson and others who had relatively sudden and powerful transformative experiences, their narratives suggest that they quite suddenly (and unconsciously) associated mental representations (the goals of the path) with specific bodily sensations, perceptions, emotions, and memories to produce "an experience" that stood out. To be a transformative experience, however, the linkage had to reorganize the individual's conscious and unconscious goals, such that the new goal became the dominant goal and, when practiced and recalled, subordinated other goals to it.[3]

Based on the analysis of Wilson's experience in chapter 6, I think his sudden experience may have "worked" as a result of his immediate, most likely unconscious, association of his bodily sensations of light, elevation, and release with the image of the cleansing wind on a mountaintop. Regardless of how Wilson's bodily sensations were triggered—whether by belladonna, despair, prayer, or some other means—and regardless of whether he associated

---

[3] This builds on Boyer's (2013) cognitively oriented review of Luhrmann (2012), as well as a long history of research on the psychology of conversion, deconversion, and spiritual transformation (for overviews, see Paloutzian et al. 2013, Paloutzian 2014, Bulkeley 2014, and Streib 2014). Paloutzian et al. indicate that there is little evidence to suggest that conversion results in modifications at the level of basic traits or temperaments, but that "midlevel functions [such as] goals, purposes, and strivings, and aspects of the more overarching level of personality such as purpose, meaning, and worldview often become different after a religious conversion" (2013, 400–401).

the image and sensations consciously (and I doubt that he did), I think that the association of the wind on the mountaintop image and his bodily sensations likely drew its depth and transformative power from its resonance with the story of his alcoholic grandfather's sudden recovery experience atop Mount Aeolus. I suggest, in other words, that the unconscious connection of his bodily sensations with his grandfather's experience of sudden release from his desire for drink allowed Bill to reorganize his conscious and unconscious goals (to recover and not drink) *as his grandfather had done*. Because at some deep level he associated his bodily sensations with his grandfather's experience of transformation, I am hypothesizing, he was able to believe that the same thing *had happened to him*—that he had been transformed—and this was what was needed to produce an actual transformation of his motivational priorities and to generate a feeling of freedom and release. This feeling of release and internal transformation expressed itself in his physical demeanor in a way that was evident to Dr. Silkworth and Lois Wilson, who both acknowledged and affirmed the transformation.

In suggesting this, I do not mean to imply that his conversation with Ebby was unimportant; I simply do not think it was sufficient. In passing on the message of how "getting religion" had allowed him to stop drinking, Ebby primed both the idea of an evangelical-style sudden conversion experience and the idea of a message passed on from one alcoholic to another. Bill consciously connected his sudden experience with his conversation with Ebby and his vision of a chain of transmission from one alcoholic to another with the Oxford Group, but the transformative power of his sudden experience was rooted, I am suggesting, in a chain that went back through Ebby to his grandfather's sudden (evangelical) conversion experience.

Shortly after his sudden experience, if not immediately, Wilson integrated his feeling of presence and his glimpse of "a great reality" at Winchester Cathedral with his experience at Towns. Upon his release from Towns, he took all this with him into his Oxford Group "team" where he assimilated the Oxford Group's understanding of guidance with his sudden experience. In breaking with the guidance of the Oxford Group to follow his own inner guidance, he recast the Oxford Group mission, generating a "sectarian" split that redefined the nature of the group (from evangelicals to alcoholics) and the primary concern of the group's guiding presence (from conversion to recovery). This shift laid the foundation for Mr. Anonymous—the symbolic head and unacknowledged leader of a democratic and leaderless fellowship—whose authority rested on "a loving God as He may express Himself in our group conscience."

As Wilson was the first to admit, discerning how God was guiding the growing group of anonymous alcoholics involved much trial and error. Neither his sudden experience nor his break with the Oxford Group was sufficient to allow him to forge new links in the chain. As we have seen, he was not able to extend the chain to another alcoholic until he reconceptualized the nature of the links, emphasizing the alcoholics' need for one another rather than the need for a sudden experience of the sort that had transformed both him and his grandfather. The feeling of presence that he associated with Winchester Cathedral, and his sudden experience at Towns, although downplayed in his AA story, nonetheless remained an integral part of his personal story and spiritual quest.

The need to maintain the generic path of AA, while at the same time remaining true to his own more specific spiritual insights, led to the split between Mr. Anonymous and Bill Wilson, and the continuing tension between his role in AA and his sense of a broader calling. Indeed, Wilson's struggles with depression may well have arisen in part due to the tension between living his life for AA and living his own life. His early tendencies to view himself as specially gifted, either in light of his sudden experience or his psychic abilities, lessened as he recognized and in turn heightened the divide between himself (Bill Wilson) and Mr. AA. Mr. AA, Anonymous (as the author of AA literature), and the AA group conscience (as a vehicle for God as we understand Him) were all of a piece. All rested on anonymity as the spiritual foundation of AA, that is, on a willingness to place "principles [e.g., anonymity] before personalities" and thus to articulate and speak for the good of the group as a whole. Wilson consciously shifted between his individual identity as Bill Wilson and his collective identity as Mr. AA, but that should not prevent us from recognizing the two identities as motivated subjectivities—one that looked out for Bill personally and one that looked out for AA as a whole.

Other Converts: If we turn briefly to the accounts offered by Kenneth Wapnick and Judith Skutch as ACIM's first followers, and Gloria Wapnick as an early convert, we see a similar pattern of self-transformation, although each account turns on a somewhat different presenting problem. As we have seen, Kenneth Wapnick brought a history of unusual experiences, which he began to interpret as signs of God's presence in his life a few years prior to his discovery of the Course. His experience of connecting to the Course culminated in his identification of his "now . . . familiar inner voice, which [he had] always identified with God" with the Jesus of the Course. He described this intensely emotional experience, in which "[he] could not contain the tears that streamed down [his] face, nor the inner joy [he] felt," as "the central experience of [his] existence here on earth" (*AFF*, 324–25).

For Gloria Wapnick, who was a devout Catholic as a child, the teachings of the Course resolved issues of theodicy that were brought home for her during a year in Italy as a thirteen-year-old in the aftermath of World War II. Her exposure to the devastating effects of the war on people's lives led her to question God and to conclude "that if this world were the best that God could create, I wanted nothing more to do with Him" (Wapnick and Wapnick 1987/2006, xxiii). Twenty-three years later, in 1977, a psychic encouraged her to go to "Wainwright House," a spiritually oriented learning center in Rye, New York, where, the psychic said, "[she] would find what [she] had been looking for all [her] life." The workshop she attended was on the Course and, like Kenneth Wapnick and Judith Skutch, she was immediately drawn to the text. "For the first time in many years I could feel Jesus' presence. From the opening pages of the text I could almost hear his voice in the very words themselves. As I read Jesus' words explain that God did not create the world, it was as if 'lightning bolts' crashed through my head. 'Why hadn't I thought of that?' I kept thinking to myself. 'It is so simple; that's the answer.' Finally after twenty-three years, the puzzle in my mind was solved" (xxiii–xxiv). For Gloria Wapnick, the Course resolved the theodicy problem in a rational way and, at the same time, allowed her to again feel Jesus's presence.

Just prior to meeting Schucman and Thetford, Judith Skutch had begun to have physical symptoms (a peptic ulcer), feelings of depression, and "dreams that were a continuation of [her] earliest mystical experience." She described this period "as "the lowest point of [her] life." She had everything a person would normally want, yet she felt "a huge void inside as if I were splitting apart" (*JWD*, 102–3). Then, in a moment reminiscent of Bill Wilson's sudden experience, she writes:

> And then in an emotional breakdown, alone in my bedroom I began to weep, and without even knowing how or where the words came from, I let out a desperate, wrenching cry: "Won't someone up there please help me!" The words surprised me, for I had never used them before, or even had thoughts like them before. (quoted in *JWD*, 103)

Some days later, when Bill Thetford took out the black binders containing the Course manuscript, Skutch said, "I felt electrified. . . . When I finished reading [the] first passage [of the Course] a great sigh of relief welled up inside of me as I heard the inner voice proclaim, 'Here is your map home.' And I knew absolutely this was the answer to my call for help" (quoted in *JWD*, 107).

The subtle differences in their presenting problems, grounded in their past experiences, shaped the nature of their self-transformations and, as we have seen, shaped their interpretation of the Course. Thus, the Wapnicks' explicitly Jesus-related conversion experiences led them to characterize the Voice as the voice of Jesus and, in their interpretation of the Course, to stress the ways in which it broke with traditional Christianity. Judith Skutch's mystical, Source-oriented conversion, by way of contrast, led her to stress the perennialism inherent in the Course's claim to be but one version of a universal curriculum.

Down to the present, all three groups—Mormons, AAs, students of ACIM—stress the role of experience in authenticating the conversion process. Referring to the present, Richard Bushman writes: "Mormons collect the evidence and make the arguments but believe that in the last analysis faith is gained through life experiences, not through research and argumentation. . . . They don't believe because of their researches, they say, but because of the Spirit" (2008, 33). AA's Twelve Steps explicitly walk members through a process of identifying and relating to a Higher Power that results in a "spiritual awakening." Students of ACIM, like many attracted to New Age–style spiritualities, are especially attentive to "synchronicities," which are, in effect, meaningful connections between the teachings of ACIM and people's everyday experience. Thus, Robert Skutch indicated that for him, "one of the most interesting aspects of the story of *A Course in Miracles* is that the events give credence to the belief that nothing in life happens by chance. Although some readers may explain many of the events as coincidences, it is my feeling, after documenting the story, that there are no coincidences in life, and that lives that are meant to be joined for a significant purpose cannot avoid being so joined" (1984b, n.p.). In his article on the earliest ACIM students, Brian van der Horst writes, apropos of synchronicity, "it is in the *Course's* interface with people's lives that they generally find themselves drawn in, resonating and convinced of the *Course's* genuineness and efficacy" (Van der Horst 1977, 6).

Conversion and Deconversion: Ezra Booth, the Methodist minister who briefly converted to Mormonism in 1831, offers an insightful description of what it felt like to convert. Looking back, in the wake of his disillusionment and deconversion, he wrote:

> When I embraced Mormonism, I conscientiously believed it to be of God. The impressions of my mind were deep and powerful, and my feelings were excited to a degree to which I had been a stranger. *Like a ghost, it haunted me by night and by day, until I was mysteriously hurried, as it were, by a kind of necessity, into the vortex of delusion.* (Booth to Rev. Ira Eddy, September 1831, quoted in Howe [1834] 2015, 257; emphasis added)

Booth's description of his conversion highlights two crucial aspects of many deeply felt conversion experiences: first, his emotions were aroused beyond anything he had experienced previously and, second, the feelings activated a goal that took charge and, in doing so, constrained his behavioral possibilities in a way that encouraged his conversion. Third, we see a dramatic shift in his appraisal of the unconsciously activated goal. At the time of his conversion, he believed the powerful feelings that compelled him to act to be *of God*. In the wake of his deconversion, he characterized them as "*like* a ghost" that "mysteriously hurried [him], *as it were*, by a kind of necessity into the vortex of delusion."

He also noted an inability to reason about the "delusion" as one would about other things in a manner that Gerrans's theory would predict. Thus, he wrote:

> These men [who are in the thrall of a delusion] . . . will converse like other men [on other subjects]; but when their favorite system is brought into view, its inconsistencies and contradictions are resolved into inexplicable mystery; and this will not only apply to the delusions now under consideration, but in my view, to every delusion, from the highest to the lowest; and it matters not whether it carries the stamp of popularity or its opposite. (Booth to Rev. Ira Eddy, September 1831, quoted in Howe [1834] 2015, 276)

Booth's emotions were aroused, he indicated, by the miracles that seemed to be taking place among the early Mormons and the miraculous powers attributed to Smith. Once he converted, repeated disconfirmations led him to question their claims and ultimately to reject them as "delusional." Booth, in effect, tested the reality of Smith's claims and found them wanting, while those who remained accepted the contradictions as "mysteries" rather than disconfirmations.

Booth's account is remarkably congruent with Gerrans's theory of delusions, but, like it, downplays the role of group dynamics, and as a result applies the term selectively to those he sought to discredit. Thus, while he explained his temporary acceptance of Mormon claims regarding miracles and new revelation as delusional, he did not extend his analysis to the similarly mysterious and inexplicable claims that are foundational to Christianity more generally. Booth took the revelatory claims of Christianity for granted, I want to suggest, because they were widely shared in his cultural context. The basic Christian path "worked" for him and thus gave him no reason to question it.

In contrast to Booth, I contend that our questioning is always selective. Questions arise when the path we are on (spiritual or otherwise) doesn't "work" for some reason. The problems that arise are typically grounded in the contradictions that arise in everyday life experience—that is, when things do not go as we expect in ourselves, our relationships, or the world around us—rather than in abstract reasoning. Even the most abstract intellectual problems, however, only become "problems" for us when we are emotionally motivated to solve them. Potential converts are aroused to consider a new path when they find something lacking in their current path or conclude that others, who tell them their path is inadequate, may be right. Those who are satisfied with their current path and unconvinced by the claims of others have no reason (motive) to consider whether an alternative path would "work" for them. When challenged to adopt an alternative path, those who are satisfied typically respond with reasons for rejecting the alternative; they typically draw reasons from the teachings of their own path or offer a "debunking" explanation that they apply to the alternative path but not to their own (see Taves 1999).

CREATING A NEW PATH

Although as scholars we can argue that Mormonism and ACIM presupposed and built on preexisting paths and in that sense were not "new," neither group viewed their origins that way. Smith, Thetford, and Schucman all stressed their alienation from existing paths. They did not view themselves as "converts" to an existing path; they claimed to reveal fundamentally *new paths*. We can distinguish between founding teams, the members of which mediate the emergence of the path, and their first followers, who help them to develop it. Hence, in the case of early Mormonism, the Smith family (Joseph, Emma, and Joseph's parents and siblings) was a founding "team" that received a new revelation and materialized the golden plates; Martin Harris and Oliver Cowdery were first followers who aided in their translation. In the case of ACIM, Bill Thetford and Helen Schucman were a founding team that scribed the Course, and Kenneth Wapnick and Judith Skutch were first followers who helped to bring it into the world. In the first part of this chapter, we considered motivation as it relates to adopting an already existing goal and, in the case of AA, transforming it. Here we need to consider motivation as it relates to the emergence and legitimation of a new goal. Doing so allows us to think about the problems faced by the preexisting small group in terms of an array of potentially competing motives, and the path as a goal-directed attempt to resolve them, which met with challenges that they were able to overcome to a greater or lesser extent.

Initial Motives: In earlier chapters, we touched on what motivated both Joseph Smith and the ACIM collaborators to seek a new path, but now we need to consider this more closely, looking not only at the explicit motivations but also at what we can infer about implicit motivations.

Mormonism: In the case of Joseph Smith, Richard Bushman and Dan Vogel agree that if there was a personal motive for Joseph Smith's revelations, it was to resolve the religious difficulties within his own family (Bushman 2005,

27; Vogel 2004, 58). They portray the difficulties somewhat differently but agree that when differences surfaced, Joseph aligned himself with his father (Bushman 2005, 37). So while both Bushman and Vogel recognize that there were tensions all along, Bushman depicts Smith's motive as one of "satisfy[ing] his family's religious want [lack of church religion] and, above all, to meet the need of his oft-defeated, unmoored father" (ibid., 27). In saying this, Bushman acknowledges that Lucy was drawn to evangelicalism, which presupposed a need for conversion, while her more skeptical husband rejected it outright in favor of universalism, which did not (ibid., 23–27). Vogel emphasizes the heightening of tensions after Lucy and the three oldest Smith children—Hyrum, Samuel, and Sophronia—all joined the Palmyra Presbyterian Church in the wake of the 1824–25 revival and not long after the devastating loss of Joseph's brother Alvin (Vogel 2004, 44, 58). Although Joseph spent some time with the Methodists during this period (ibid., 59), neither he nor his father joined a church, and both shared a long-standing interest in treasure seeking. Based on Joseph's reputation as a local seer, Josiah Stowell enlisted Joseph and his father in a treasure-seeking partnership in 1825, thus further polarizing the family. While they were digging for treasure near his future in-laws' home in Harmony, Pennsylvania, the family lost the title to their farm, which they had not quite paid off, through the underhanded actions of a would-be buyer and, in 1826, Stowell's nephew, fearing Smith was defrauding his uncle, had him arrested and tried on charges of being "a disorderly person and an imposter" (ibid., 75–86). Thus, while reputation and financial stability were issues, the primary problem was the growing divide between his religiously skeptical, treasure-seeking father and his evangelical mother and siblings. In Smith's case, the most pronounced personal and public motives—overcoming religious conflict and dissension—were congruent and thus reinforced one another rather than generating conflicting goals.

ACIM: In the case of Helen Schucman and Bill Thetford, there is evidence to suggest that Schucman was committed to conflicting goals that she was never able to reconcile. As we have seen, the overt problem was the discord between Helen and Bill, and within their department, and their overt motive for joining together was to find "a better way." Helen and Bill's relationship was deeply enmeshed, however, and, as indicated in chapter 7, fueled in part by sexual tensions that arose due to Helen's romantic and sexual attraction to Bill, which he—as a gay man—did not reciprocate. Judy Skutch recounted a story to Carol Howe from their New York days that brought this to the surface. In the wake of an intense fight between Helen and Bill, Judy said, she "made the mistake" of asking Helen why she couldn't "be a little nicer to him." Helen, she said, "turned on [her]" and said: "You stupid, stupid child! Don't you know I would have followed him to the ends of the earth? I would have left everything, my work, my life, everything to be with him wherever he said, *and he didn't want me!*" (Howe 2009, 119; emphasis added). Helen, in other words, was deeply in love with a gay man who would inevitably be unavailable to her in the way she desired, and there was, in Judy's words, "all this furious, romantic rage and fantasy life, a lot of fantasy life, in her [Helen's] mind with Bill" (ibid., 119). The expressed problem was thus interpersonal conflict; the latent problem was Bill's romantic unavailability and Helen's feeling of being rejected.

These motives gave rise to contradictory goals. The Voice's goal was to have Helen and Bill present a solution to the expressed problem to the world. Helen's goal, to quote Judy, was to "keep him [Bill] tied to [her] for the rest of [her] life" (ibid.). Helen was willing to do anything to keep Bill but forgive him for not wanting her, because that would mean letting him go. Helen's dual motives for joining with Bill to find a better way could not be reconciled without subordinating one to the other, thus leading to the split between the goals of "the Voice" and the goals of "Helen." The dual aims led Helen to agree to scribe but not practice the Course, which allowed her to avoid forgiving Bill, and required the Voice to work around Helen's refusal by enlisting Ken and Judy's assistance in bringing the Course into the world. Bill's move to California, which left "Helen . . . so angry she wouldn't talk," ended the Course's usefulness as a means of tying Bill to her and may have helped precipitate the deep depression of her final years.

Some students of the Course might be troubled by Judy's story, but the incident obviously did not shake either Judy's or Carol Howe's commitment to the Course. If you believe, as the Voice said, that it picked Helen and Bill, not because they were special but because they were willing, their imperfections and Helen's perhaps questionable motives are of little import. The Course is what it is; the portions addressed to Helen and Bill were edited out because they were personal, and the developmental process through which the Course emerged is, in the eyes of many of its students, irrelevant. Teachers, such as the Wapnicks, want students and outsiders to engage the final version of the Course as a thought system in the form they believe the Voice of the Course intended.

I agree that Schucman's inability to practice the Course—although a tantalizing puzzle—is ultimately a side issue. The deeper issue has to do with the authorship of the Course and the underlying question of who creates and how. In contrast to the Course's self-understanding, my counterexplanation is based on a naturalistic outlook grounded in evolutionary biology that presupposes the reality of the material world, however fragile and impermanent, and a sense of the difficulty involved in healing wounds created by the absence of love in early childhood. In contrast to Groeschel, who located the beginnings of Helen's need for love—religious or otherwise—in her visit to Lourdes as a child, I locate it where she and her husband Louis did, in the nursery in which she was isolated as a child, cut off from contact with her parents and her older brother, interacting only with her governesses, both of whom were highly religious. When the Course refers to the eternal presence of God's love and to the perception of its "lack" as an illusion, I cannot help but think of Helen's description of her lonely childhood. "When I was a little girl I lived at one end of a big apartment with Miss Richardson . . . Everyone else lived at the other end . . . When we went out we always came straight back to our own part of the apartment. I very rarely even saw the rest of it. . . . Miss Richardson brought our meals to our sitting room and we ate there together" (HS, 6).

Louis Schucman came to a similar conclusion, pointing out that the Course was about love, "which she had yearned for all her life and hadn't gotten."

> And to be honest, I think that the love she was seeking, that was missing from her father, she didn't even totally find in our marriage. I'm being very honest here. We were very close, but she didn't get that hole filled up that her father had left in her. It's very difficult to have one substitute, especially later on. The Course is full of love and spiritual values, and I think that Helen refused to accept the fact that she had created them on her own. (n.d.)

I would therefore root Schucman's inability to implement the teachings of the Course in her relationship with Thetford in her inability to recover from this early absence of love, which she recapitulated in her unrequited and unrealistic romantic attachment to Thetford and attempted to maintain through their mutual creation of the Course. When the Course "failed" to maintain their relationship as it was, she abandoned it and fell into depression, unable—even with the help of the Voice—to experience the deeply ingrained feeling that she was unloved as illusory.

Emergent Goals: Conceiving of the individual as comprised of multiple goals—conscious and unconscious—each of which is "selfish" in the sense of "guiding judgments and behavior in the service of the current goal" allows us to consider the presences that guided Smith and Schucman as emerging in conjunction with the articulation of new goals (Huang and Bargh 2014, 133). If we define goals as "mental representations of desired end-states" (ibid., 124), we can ask when and how the new representations emerged.

Mormonism: In the case of the Smith family, the new representation referred to an object. Whether expressed in terms of "Plates . . . [containing] Records [of] the Promises of the Lord" (D&C 3), "hidden treasures of wisdom & knowledge, even divine revelation, which has lain in the bowels of the earth for thousands of years" (lost 1828 letter, cited by Jesse Smith, 17 June 1829, *EMD* 1:554), a "gold book" (Jesse Smith, 17 June 1829, *EMD* 1:554), or a "Gold Bible" (Abner Cole, *Reflector* [Palmyra, New York], 23 September 1829, *EMD* 2:226), the represented object linked the ideas of buried treasure and divine revelation. In doing so, it bridged the divide between his treasure-seeking father and evangelically oriented mother and offered a representation that potentially united the interests of both.

Although we do not have real-time evidence to confirm this, I find it entirely plausible to assume that Smith had a dream in September 1823 in which a "personage" presented him with this new representation. It is also congruent with Lucy Smith's statement that the family discussed the pluralism of the churches the evening before Smith had the dream. It would only point toward a solution of the family's religious differences, however, if they all found it compelling. All the family members' accounts of what transpired indicated that they immediately affirmed it. Their affirmation constituted the dream as more than "just" a dream, the personage as a goal-oriented entity separate from Smith, and the recovery of the ancient plates as a goal around which they all could unite under the guidance of the personage.

Vogel's (2004, 53–67) reconstruction of the events between the discovery of the plates in September 1823 and their recovery four years later suggests that the death of Joseph's brother Alvin two months after their discovery derailed the process for a significant period of time. According to Lucy Smith, Alvin was a mainstay of the family system and deeply committed to the idea of recovering the plates.

> Alvin [Lucy said] manifested, if such could be the case, greater zeal and anxiety in regard to the Record that had been shown to Joseph, than any of the rest of the family; in consequence of which we could not bear to hear anything said upon the subject. Whenever Joseph spoke of the Record, it would immediately bring Alvin to our minds, with all his zeal, and with all his kindness; and, when we looked to his place, and realized that he was gone from it . . . we all with one accord wept over our irretrievable loss. (1853, *EMD* 1:305–6)

In the midst of their grief, the goal of recovering the ancient record was too painful to contemplate. It was in this context that Lucy and Joseph's siblings were drawn to an alternative means of unifying the family, a revival preacher who wanted "to effect a union of the different churches, in order that all might be agreed" (*EMD* 1:306). When Lucy attempted to unite the family around this goal, Joseph and his father declined and some months later went with Josiah Stowell to dig for treasure in Pennsylvania (*EMD* 1:309), thus further polarizing, rather than uniting, the family.

In keeping with Vogel's suggestion (2004, 57), that Smith may not have attempted to recover the plates in either 1825 or 1826, that is, during this period of grief and polarization, I think it is possible that the goal of recovering the plates receded following Alvin's death and did not come to the fore again until 1827, when Joseph was severely chastised by the angel of the Lord for his negligence in recovering the plates (*EMD* 1:325). In other words, it's possible that the family as a whole lost its motivation for recovering the plates—due to their painful association with Alvin—and that it reemerged with renewed insistence in the voice of the angel, who not only indicated that the time had come to recover the plates but how Smith was to accomplish this. If the recovery of the plates and all that portended constituted the goal, then the angel was the personification of the motivation to realize the goal. As such, it guided judgments and behavior in service of the goal, which included chastising recalcitrant parts of Smith (oriented toward other goals) in order to either suppress them or bring them into line with this goal. In casting itself in terms of the promises of the Lord, the goal asserted its primacy relative to other lesser goals.

As I have argued, the entire process of materializing the plates—from their discovery to their recovery—was a collective process that involved the entire family. As such, it exemplified the ability of a joint goal to create a new group, recategorizing out-group members as in-group members (Sherif et al. 1961; Huang and Bargh 2014, 130), in this case, uniting the churched and unchurched in the Smith family around the goal of recovering buried *sacred* treasure. Over time, the motivator shifted from an angel of the Lord to the Lord himself, and the goal from recovery to translation to church-founding and proselytizing, but with the family-based materialization of the plates, the foundation was laid for others to join them.

ACIM: In the case of ACIM, the initial goal was to find a "better way." I have argued that Thetford's speech, voiced at a point of great frustration with the conflictual relations between him and Schucman and within the department, was primed by his reading of Hugh Lynn Cayce's *Venture Inward*, which explicitly suggested that "venturing inward" would lead to a "better way." Helen's willingness to join with Bill in searching for a better way united them in a common goal, which, as the motivation research would suggest, reduced the conflict between them when that goal was activated. Joining in this goal in turn activated mental processes that "encourage[d] achievement of the goal's end-state," including a mutual agreement to meditate, Helen's unusual experiences, and Bill's desire to find meaning in her experiences. In this supportive environment, the motivation to find a better way began to personify itself as a distinctive voice. The visits to Mayo Clinic and Virginia Beach in September 1965 heightened their sense that the voice was more than a split-off part of Helen, which made Helen more uneasy and further exacerbated the split between "her" and "the Voice." At some point, the goal of finding a better way gave rise to the idea of dictating a Course, thus giving specific content to the goal of finding a "better way." As I argued in chapter 7, I suspect that Helen's feeling that "she was 'about to do something very unexpected'" (*AFF*, 167) in the wake of the visit to Virginia Beach was triggered by the sense that a new, more elaborate goal was taking shape.

Higher Motives: As personified goals that chastised, prodded, and cajoled competing aspects of Smith and Schucman into cooperating with their respective agendas, the "angel" and the "Voice" promoted goals that served to unify their respective small group and—as the model would predict—overcome conflicts between individuals within the group, at least temporarily. The role that the discovery of the ancient plates played in uniting the Smith family while Alvin was alive was mirrored by their loss of motivation in the wake of his death. Their ability to rally around the goal again a few years later indicates a high level of congruence between the angel's goals and the family's. Because Helen's personal goals with respect to Bill were at odds with the Voice's goal of finding a better way, their relationship remained conflictual when they were not focused on the Course.

The model not only predicts that conscious or unconscious attention to a goal will constrain mental processing so as to facilitate the pursuit of the goal, but also that in some cases the active goal is powerful enough to reconfigure mental processes "to the point of making typically effortful processes efficient and automatic, if this is necessary for successful goal pursuit" (Huang and Bargh 2014, 131–32). This would seem to be another way to describe what some highly hypnotizable individuals are able to do when cued to a specific (goal-oriented) task and thus what I hypothesized that Smith and Schucman were able to do when translating the plates or scribing the course.

Huang and Bargh also discuss the question of self-deception in relation to this process, recognizing that "the capacity of active goals to operate and become completed independently from the individual's conscious desires can be seen as 'self-deceptive' insofar as the individual remains unaware—or inconsistently aware—of his or her motives" (2014, 132). Although some researchers (e.g., McKay and Dennett 2009; Von Hippel and Trivers 2011) have argued that self-deception could be an evolutionary and adaptive strategy insofar as it allows individuals to avoid "display[ing] subtle but telling cues of lying," Huang and Bargh offer another way to view this lack of awareness. Insofar as "human judgment and behavior were driven by goal processes before a central 'self' even evolved, many instances of 'self-deception' can be seen as a result of the autonomous nature of all goal pursuits. Both conscious and unconscious goals encourage single-minded pursuit of the end-state and are capable of producing effects that appear on the surface to be in the service of 'deceiving' the individual" (Huang and Bargh 2014, 132–33; see also Thagard 2006, 219–35).

The congruence between Smith's personal and expressed goals and the conflict between Schucman's goals accounts for their very different emotional reactions as the Lord and the Voice sought to generalize their respective paths. In both cases, generalizing the path entailed overcoming a major obstacle. In the Mormon case, the obstacle was convincing others of the reality of the ancient golden plates; in the ACIM case, it was getting around Schucman's unwillingness to practice the Course and her desire to keep Thetford trapped in a highly codependent relationship.

In Smith's case, his father's affirmation that the dream-vision was "of God" and his family's immediate validation of the idea set a process in motion that culminated in the entire family's baptism in the restored church. The generalizability of the transformative insight depended on others sharing a desire for new revelation and believing that Smith had recovered ancient golden plates and had been called by the Lord as seer and translator. Establishing the existence of the gold bible was the key challenge that had to be overcome in order to generalize the insight. Smith's joyous response to the testimony of the three witnesses and to his father's baptism provide a telling indication of an emotional arc that runs from his father's affirmation of his dream-vision in 1823, through the showing of the plates to the three witnesses in 1829, to his father's baptism in the restored church the following year. Highlighting the problem of pluralism in the revival context, rather than in Smith's family, explained the need for new revelation in a generalized framework that extended beyond the family to the culture at large.

In Schucman's case, the conflict between her personal motives and the Voice's set in motion a process that culminated in the breakup of the ACIM "family." As long as the ACIM family was living in New York, Schucman was able to support the Course's movement into the public arena. When the conflicting desires of Louis Schucman and Bob Skutch made this impossible, it triggered a geographical split within the ACIM family that Helen experienced as "abandonment" by Bill and resulted in her "abandonment" of the Course. In *Absence from Felicity*, Wapnick used the teachings of the Course to account for Helen's inability to practice it, thus interpreting her failure in a generalized framework that extended beyond her need to keep Bill close to her.

Conclusion

The distinctive feature of the groups examined in this book was not that they experienced unusual presences, whether in the context of seeing visions, hearing voices, or felt sensations. Such experiences are relatively common in the general population, especially in the wake of the death of a loved one (Aleman and Larøi 2008, 61–64). Nor did the groups' reliance on path metaphors set them apart from other social movements. What set them apart was their claim that a suprahuman presence guided the emergence of the path.

Insofar as an emergent path involves such a claim, the emergent group must establish procedures for recognizing the alleged presence. Although in some cases recognition alone may suffice, these groups went beyond recognition to give the suprahuman presence an active role in the emergence process. The development of procedures for recognizing and giving voice to these suprahuman entities played a crucial role in the emergence of these three paths, as *spiritual* paths. These guidance procedures, which took a different form in each group, not only marked the paths as spiritual, they provided a mechanism whereby the suprahuman presences could actively guide the group's emergence, whether as the active leader (in the case of ACIM), a consultant (in the case of AA), or something in between (in the case of Mormonism).

At the same time, procedures that regulated access to the suprahuman entity established an authority structure within the human group. Each group was structured differently, however. AA located access to the ultimate source of guidance in the group, ACIM in the core team, and Mormonism in a singular prophet. This did not mean that others could not receive inner guidance or revelation, but in each case individual guidance was subordinated to that of the group (in AA), the team (in ACIM), or the prophet (in Mormonism). Failure to subordinate individual guidance to that of the group resulted in schisms.

These guidance procedures emerged over time and, in each case, the procedures were specified more fully as first followers were added to the initial collaborators. Thus, D&C 3 was recorded in the wake of the loss of the 116 manuscript pages, which was an outgrowth of the attempt to incorporate Martin Harris as a first follower. Recording the revelation, I have argued, initiated a procedure that stabilized the emergence process. When Martin Harris returned to Harmony in March 1829 and wanted to see the plates, Smith had a formal procedure in place for receiving an answer (D&C 5). When Oliver Cowdery appeared and offered to assist, Smith had a procedure in place for determining his role (D&C 6, D&C 8–9), as well as the procedures they should adopt in response to the disappearance of the 116 pages (D&C 10). The revelation in September 1830 (D&C 28) played a crucial role in establishing Smith's authority as sole prophet relative to his key first followers (*JSP*, D1:183–86). AA followed the Oxford Group practice of rooting guidance in the small group, but transferred authority from the Oxford Group meetings to the "nameless alcoholics" meeting in New York and Akron. The practice of bringing crucial decisions to the group for guidance was eventually codified in the Twelve Traditions, particularly Tradition Two, supported by Traditions One and Twelve. In ACIM, the guidance procedures began to emerge as Schucman and Thetford "ventured inward" during the summer of 1965 and took more definite shape as the Voice itself encouraged them to request guidance on matters large and small in the early days of scribing the Course. It appears that Thetford typically sought guidance from the Voice through Schucman until Kenneth Wapnick joined the team, at which point the practice became more communal. After Judith Skutch joined them, we know from Schucman's detailed description that the process was a communal one in which each "asked," and answers were shared and discussed.

In each of these cases, the authority structure that emerged in conjunction with the guidance procedures fundamentally shaped the organizational form adopted by the groups. Although the organization of the restored church was elaborated over the course of Joseph Smith's lifetime, ultimate authority rested with Smith as the church's prophet, seer, and revelator. In the wake of his death, authority was constituted differently in the two largest Mormon churches—the LDS Church and the Reorganized LDS Church (now Communities of Christ), but the leader of both is understood as Smith's successor, serving as a president and prophet of the respective churches. In the case of AA, as we have seen, Bill Wilson not only took the lead in developing the Twelve Traditions, he pushed for the development of the representative conference structure that formally lodged authority in the conference, that is, in the groups through their representatives. The full development of the structure, which was not complete until 1967, not only transferred the informal authority vested in the cofounders to the conference, it also restructured the relationship between the membership and the trustees of the Alcoholic Foundation. In time, the original Alcoholic Foundation, which held formal legal responsibility for the movement, was restructured as the General Service Board of AA and the third arm of the AA threefold vision of Recovery (Twelve Steps), Unity (Twelve Traditions), and Service (Twelve Concepts). In ACIM, the joint guidance procedures of the four collaborators were incorporated into the Foundation for Inner Peace and Foundation for *A Course in Miracles*. Joint guidance was established through shared board membership. As a much younger group, ACIM is still in the process of determining the shape of the transition from the core team to the foundations that emerged from their collaboration.

Each of these suprahuman "presences" was motivated by an expansive vision and was intent on guiding the human collaborators toward a goal— a restored church, a fellowship of recovering alcoholics, and a metaphysical training program. Belief in these presences and their interest in guiding the group not only stabilized the process and structured the group, they also supported claims regarding the authorship of the key texts and the ultimate origins of the group. These claims generated a paradox at the heart of the creative process that is inherent in the concept of revelation as such. From a naturalistic point of view, we can view this paradox as constituted by a displacement of creative agency, such that the collaborators ascribed suprahuman authority to split-off aspect(s) of the self (or selves in the context of group guidance) that were motivated to think for the group as a whole. In so doing, they collectively sacralized an aspect of themselves and/or others that seemed *as if* it were not them, because it was motivated to think in terms of the group as a whole. Insofar as it spoke for the whole, we can think of it as a collectively produced subjectivity. The creative paradox thus lies in the fact that each group created a motivated subjectivity that thought in terms of the whole and assumed responsibility for guiding its emergence.

DURKHEIM

We can put what I have just been saying into conversation with Durkheim's *Elementary Forms of the Religious Life*. Although Durkheim analyzed a small-scale society that already existed and we have been looking at emergent groups in a complex society, many of the features that Durkheim identified as integral to the emergence of religion in its most elementary form are features of the emergence process that we have been analyzing. If we reread *Elementary Forms* as theorizing the formation of groups, including groups within large-scale societies, we can see key elements of Durkheim's theory at work in the processes we have described.

Consecrated Things: Each group consecrated things, including ideas, which set them apart from other things and gave them certain properties. In Durkheim's words: "When a belief is shared unanimously by a people, to touch it—that is, to deny or question it—is forbidden . . . The prohibition against critique is a prohibition like any other and proves that one is face to face with a sacred thing" (1995, 215). Smith and his followers consecrated the idea of ancient golden plates, AA consecrated the ideas of the group conscience and anonymity, and ACIM consecrated the idea of reality as nonmaterial.

Collective Representations: The consecrated ideas were collective representations insofar as they were collectively agreed-upon representations of some "thing," for example, an object, a practice, an idea, a person, and/or an aspect of a person.

Totems: Some of these collectively agreed-upon representations also functioned as "totems" in Durkheim's sense (1995, 208), that is, as simultaneous symbolic representations of the suprahuman power and of the particular group. In my words, a small group collectively agreed to represent an aspect of themselves (of their minds) as not-themselves precisely because it seemed to represent the spirit, conscience, or voice of and for the group. The Lord, especially in his later twofold manifestation as the Heavenly Father and Heavenly Son, had a "totemic" role in Mormonism; Mr. Anonymous and AA's Higher Power as expressed through the group conscience had a totemic role in AA; and the Voice in ACIM.

Thagard has discussed the various ways in which we might understand the common tendency to attribute mental states to social formations, such as Wall Street, the banks, or the market. He cautions against the idea of collective mental states, while at the same time seeking to provide "a theoretical explanation of the occasionally successful attribution of mental states to organizations" (2010, 272). In the three cases discussed here, however, we are not talking about a collective mental state but about a mental state (a subjectivity) that claims to speak to and for the group. The groups did not attribute mental states to an organization, but—I have argued—to mental states within themselves or a group member that the group viewed as another self.

Insofar as we view Durkheim's totem as simply a static symbol of the whole—analogous to the flag of a country or the mascot of a team—then it too has limits. The suprahuman entities that led these groups were not just symbols of the emerging group. In each case, the Lord, the Higher Power acting through the AA group, and the Voice were fully capable of chastising, correcting, and directing Smith, Wilson, and Schucman. It is this dynamic, goal-directed activity on the part of these entities that led me to conceive of them as unconscious or split-off motivations. The collective agreement to represent these motivations as suprahuman entities constituted the group as a group and the split-off motivations as active agents intent on guiding the human collaborators toward group-oriented goals.

Motivated, Collectively Agreed-Upon Subjectivities: A careful reading of Durkheim suggests that in conceiving of deities as "society" or "the group incarnated and personified" (1995, 212), Durkheim, too, viewed them as motivated, collectively agreed-upon subjectivities that could only achieve their ends by working through human individuals. "Precisely because society [a group] has its own specific nature that is different from our nature as individuals, it pursues ends that are also specifically its own; but because it can achieve those ends only by working through us, it categorically demands our cooperation" (ibid., 209). In each case, though, the motivated, collectively agreed-upon subjectivity had an idea or vision for the group—a social idea—that it was intent on achieving. In the case of Mormonism, the idea was born in Smith's dream-vision of golden plates in September 1823; in the case of AA, the idea of a chain of alcoholics was born in the wake of Bill Wilson's sudden experience in December 1934; and in the case of ACIM, the idea of venturing inward to find a better way was born in June 1965 and the idea of the Course itself in the wake of Schucman and Thetford's visit to Virginia Beach the following September.

In each case, as Durkheim recognized, the idea had to resonate with others in order for the vision to give rise to a collectively agreed-upon subjectivity (ibid., 209–10). In analyzing what happens when an orator feels inspired, Durkheim captured the dynamic nicely.

> Sometimes [the orator] even feels possessed by a moral force greater than he, of which he is only the interpreter. . . . This extraordinary surplus of forces is quite real and comes to him from the very group he is addressing. The feelings he arouses as he speaks return to him enlarged and amplified, reinforcing his own to the same degree. The passionate energies that he arouses reecho in turn within him, and they increase his dynamism. It is then no longer a mere individual who speaks but a group incarnated and personified. (ibid., 212)

But while we feel this dynamic, he said, its causes seem obscure. "It [the influence of society] . . . uses psychic mechanisms that are too complex, to be easily traced to the source. So long as scientific analysis has not yet taught him, man is well aware that he is acted upon but not by whom. . . . Thus he had to build out of nothing the idea of those powers with which he feels connected" (ibid., 211). Even though we now have a better scientific understanding of the psychological mechanisms involved, this does not eliminate the subjective feeling of being acted upon or the sense that something larger than ourselves may be at work.

Delusions: Durkheim is quite adamant that these collective subjectivities are not simply "inexplicable hallucinations" with no "foothold in reality."

The believer's mistake, according to Durkheim, "lies in taking literally the symbol that represents this being in the mind, or the outward appearance in which the imagination has dressed it up, not in the fact of its very existence. Beyond these forms, be they cruder or more refined, there is a concrete and living reality" (1995, 226–27). Although I agree with Durkheim that there is a concrete and living reality to these collective subjectivities, we need to translate carefully between the conclusions he drew in thinking about a small-scale society and emergent groups in a complex society. The emergent groups we have looked at here brought something into being. They created a motivated collective subjectivity that guided the emergence of a new spiritual path. The new spiritual paths didn't have to exist, but, like any new creation, once they existed they took on "a concrete and living reality." While I view the Lord of Mormonism, the Higher Power of AA, and the Voice of the Course as creations, they were—as I've been saying—motivated collective subjectivities that envisioned spiritual paths that can and do transform people toward particular ends (salvation, sobriety, reality). These goals must, of course, be evaluated. While people will continue to disagree regarding their validity and value, the power of the paths to transform is—in my view—quite apparent.

DISCUSSION OF METHODS

This discussion and the charts that follow are intended to explain and demonstrate the methods adopted in this book in more detail to help researchers, primarily graduate students and advanced undergraduates, who are interested in applying them elsewhere. As discussed in the introduction, the book presupposes that scholars can both analyze and reconstruct phenomena as they seemed from the point of view of historical or ethnographic subjects, and also attempt to explain the processes that produced the phenomena in naturalistic terms. The first is common practice in the humanities. The second is less so and thus will be the focus of this discussion.

In the book, I have used "explanation" in the sense that practicing scientists, particularly biologists, neuroscientists, and psychologists, generally use it, that is, as a statement of how a process "works" in terms of "mechanisms" (Craver and Tabary 2016). A mechanism explains the behavior of a phenomenon in terms of the interaction of parts, also referred to as components or building blocks. Thus, "[a] mechanism for a phenomenon consists of entities (or parts) whose activities and interactions are organized in such a way that they produce the phenomenon" (Glennan forthcoming). Craver (2007) provides a visual representation (see figure A.1) of the relationship between the phenomenon as a behavior (system S engaging in behavior ψ) and the mechanism as an explanation of how the components (X_1, X_2, X_3, each of which is a system in its own right engaging in its own behavior Φ_1, Φ_2, Φ_3) are interacting (arrows) to produce the behavior of interest. We can adapt his illustration to depict the phenomenon we set out to explain in this book (emergent groups [system S] following the guidance of a presence [behavior ψ]) and the components (unusual abilities [X_1], motives [X_2], and group identification [X_3]), which I hypothesized interacted (arrows) to produce the phenomenon.

Each component can in turn be viewed as a phenomenon to be explained in terms of the components that interact to produce it. Thus, chapter 11 focused on explaining unusual abilities (X_1) in light of HHs' ability to manipulate executive control processes in response to external cues. Chapter 12 focused on explaining how competing motives (X_2) could be elaborated within the default mode network (DMN) to give rise to alternative motivated subjectivities. Chapter 10 drew on social identity research to explain how identification with a group (X_3) heightens the salience of group norms

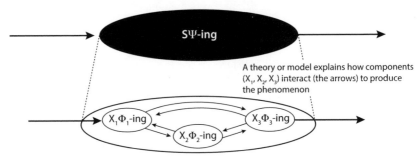

Phenomenon

to be explained (system S engaging in behavior Ψ):
the emergence of a "presence" guiding the emergence of a group

SΨ-ing

A theory or model explains how components
(X₁, X₂, X₃) interact (the arrows) to produce
the phenomenon

$X_1\Phi_1$-ing $X_3\Phi_3$-ing

$X_2\Phi_2$-ing

Small circles = components of system S,
X₁ = unusual abilities
X₂ = motives
X₃ = group identification

Mechanism

A mechanism consists of components or parts
(small circles, X₁, X₂ ...) that interact (arrows)
to produce behavior ψ.

FIGURE A.I. A visual representation of a single mechanism with three interacting components (adapted with permission from Craver [Oxford University Press, 2007, 7], figure 1.1).

and values. In chapters II and I2, I adapted Gerrans's theory of delusions to offer a theory of how these three components interact in everyday life to produce a presence that guides a group.

When we take our original components as phenomena to be explained and identify the components that interact to produce them, we are identifying a lower-level mechanism that is nested within a higher-level mechanism. When mechanisms are nested within mechanisms like Russian dolls, they are referred to as multilevel mechanisms. In the context of a multilevel explanation, "level" does not refer to disciplinary levels ranked according to their unit of analysis (e.g., physics, chemistry, biology, psychology, the social sciences, and the humanities) or to levels seen in nature ranked according to features, such as size and complexity (e.g., atoms, molecules, cells, organs, and organisms). Here "levels" refers to levels of mechanism, such that lower-level mechanisms are components of higher-level mechanisms. As Craver and Tabery make clear:

> [F]rom a mechanistic perspective, levels are not monolithic divides in the furniture of the universe . . . Rather, levels of mechanisms are defined locally within multilevel mechanisms: one item is at a lower level of mechanisms than another when the first item is a part of the second and when the first item is organized (spatially, temporally, and ac-

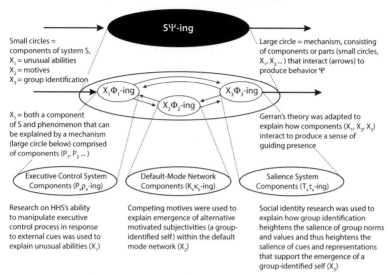

Phenomenon
to be explained (system S engaging in behavior Ψ):
The emergence of a "presence" guiding the emergence of a group

SΨ-ing

Small circles =
components of system S,
X_1 = unusual abilities
X_2 = motives
X_3 = group identification

$X_1\Phi_1$-ing $X_3\Phi_3$-ing
$X_2\Phi_2$-ing

Large circle = mechanism, consisting
of components or parts (small circles,
X_1, X_2 ...) that interact (arrows) to
produce behavior Ψ

X_1 = both a component
of S and phenomenon that can
be explained by a mechanism
(large circle below) comprised
of components (P_1, P_2 ...)

Gerran's theory was adapted to
explain how components (X_1, X_2, X_3)
interact to produce a sense of
guiding presence

Executive Control System
Components ($P_x$$\rho_x$-ing)

Default-Mode Network
Components ($K_x$$\kappa_x$-ing)

Salience System
Components ($T_x$$\tau_x$-ing)

Research on HHS's ability
to manipulate executive
control process in response
to external cues was used to
explain unusual abilities (X_1)

Competing motives were used to
explain emergence of alternative
motivated subjectivities (a group-
identified self) within the default
mode network (X_2)

Social identity research was used to
explain how group identification
heightens the salience of group norms
and values and thus heightens the
salience of cues and representations
that support the emergence of a
group-identified self (X_3)

FIGURE A.2. A visual representation of mechanisms within a mechanism
(adapted with permission from Craver [Oxford University Press, 2007, 194],
figure 5.8).

tively) with the other components such that together they realize the
second item. (2016, 20)

As illustrated in figure A.2, we can add another level of mechanisms to the
original diagram of the phenomenon explained in this book. Thus, each of
the components of system S (X_1, X_2, and X_3) will have its own mechanism
comprised of components that interact to produce it. So, for example, we
can explain X_1 in terms of executive control processes, X_2 in terms of the
default mode network, and X_3 in terms of the salience network. Each of the
components that make up X_1, X_2, and X_3 can be treated as phenomenon in
their own right with components that interact to produce their behavior and
so on down the multilevel stack.[1]

A mechanistic approach, understood in terms of levels of mechanisms,
allows us to understand the role that cognitive processes play in the formation of groups. Building on the research on self-identity that I drew on in

[1] Craver would characterize figure A.2 as a three-level mechanism, counting S, X, and P-K-T
each as a level of mechanisms.

chapter 10 (Tajfel 1974; Postmes and Branscombe 2010), Thagard elaborates on this key point:

> [T]he actions of groups result from the actions of individuals who think of themselves as members of groups. What makes a group a group is not the sort of physical bonding that makes a group of cells into an organ. Rather, social bonds are largely psychological and arise from the fact that individuals in the group have mental representations, such as concepts [implicit or explicit], that mark them as members of the group. The bonding process is not purely psychological, however, as it can also include various kinds of physical interactions that are social, linguistic, or both . . . These interactions tie people together into groups when they result in mental representations (affective as well as cognitive [and not necessarily conscious]) through which individuals come to envision themselves as part of a group. Without such envisioning the group cannot continue to function collectively. (2012, 36)

In my explanation of "guiding presences," social bonds play a crucial role. First, social bonds linked the preexisting small groups. Second, when individuals identified with the group via a mental representation (e.g., golden plates; we alcoholics; joining to search for a better way), group norms and values became more salient. Third, the ability of designated individuals to shift back and forth between an I-self (self-identity) and a we-self (social identity) was encouraged and validated by the groups and conceived as mediating a suprahuman presence (the Lord/angel/Holy Spirit in Mormonism, Mr. AA/Higher Power in AA, and the Voice in ACIM). Formulating sociological concepts (such as groups) in cognitive terms (as mental representations of groups) allows us to see the critical role that mental representations play in the process of group formation.

Although a mechanistic approach has been widely presupposed in practice in biology, the neurosciences, and psychology for some time, researchers have only more recently promoted it as an alternative to a range of issues in the philosophy of science (Craver and Tabery 2016) and as a basis for cognitively grounded social sciences (Sun 2012). Scholars in the humanities, familiar with and often wary of reductionistic approaches to explanation, are only beginning to explore the implications of the new mechanistic philosophy for explaining complex sociocultural phenomena. Influenced by these developments, I began developing what I call a "building-block approach" (BBA) for analyzing and explaining complex cultural phenomena, such as religious experience (Taves 2009, 2013, 2015). This approach, further refined in collaboration with Egil Asprem, is intended as a means of grounding historical research in the cognitive social sciences (see Taves and Asprem

2016; the Building Blocks of Human Experience (BBHE) website at bbhe .ucsb.edu). This book offers an example of how the BBA may be applied to complex cultural phenomena such as religion or, in this specific case, "revelation."

We refer to the research strategy at the heart of the BBA as "reverse engineering." Reverse engineering refers to the series of steps designed to take apart a complex system and analyze its constituent parts in order to (a) find out how it works and (b) trace how the parts have been assembled and labeled to generate specific formations. In what follows, I will retrace the steps as they unfolded in relation this particular project. We can specify them as (1) specifying the phenomenon of interest, (2) analyzing the phenomenon of interest (reconstructing the process of emergence), and (3) identifying components that interacted to generate the phenomenon and explaining how the components interacted to produce it.

1. Specifying a Phenomenon in Behavioral Terms

When I began this project I knew was interested is expanding my focus from "religious experience" to "revelation," a concept that is central to the Abrahamic traditions. "Revelation" as such, however, can't be explained in mechanistic terms, because it is a complex concept with multiple meanings and because it is not a behavior. Several substeps were required to redescribe it in a form that I could potentially explain.

1.1. Trace the development of "complex cultural concepts" (CCCs) to identify their different meanings and locate them in relation to "social formations." "Revelation" is a classic instance of a complex cultural concept, that is, an abstract noun with unstable, overlapping, culturally determined meanings that vary within and across social formations. A social formation is any social entity (organization, movement, network) that fixes terminology and meanings through shared discourse and practice. Examples of formations include traditions, political movements, social networks, and academic disciplines. Insofar as CCCs are built into formations, they typically take on specialized meanings within and for those formations.

Historians interested in the history of discourse and "genealogies" of concepts routinely trace their development and locate them in relation to various social formations, which is nothing new. We can use this kind of kind of analysis, however, to select from these different usages and refine those that are most relevant into descriptions of the processes we want to study. In the introduction, I distinguished three different ways the concept of revelation has been used in Western thought, that is, revelation as content, as type of knowledge, and as event, and indicated how they relate to various *social formations*. Thus, we typically find references to *revelation as content* within traditions of belief and practice that are premised on revelation as event, for example, Judaism, Christianity, Islam, and Mormonism. We typically find revelation as a *type of knowledge* in traditions of intellectual reflection, for example, in philosophical traditions of reflection on epistemology. Revelatory *events*, conceived as such, are foundational to the groups that claim access to revelation and are typically the central focus of their origin narratives.

1.2. Use basic concepts to characterize the phenomenon of interest. By basic concepts, we mean terms that are readily understood (and investigated) at subpersonal levels and, insofar as they are grounded in basic bodily processes, are more readily translated across times and cultures. Specific concepts will of necessity vary from project to project, depending on the researcher's question. The two basic concepts used to characterize the processes of interest in this book have been *events* and *paths*.

Clear characterization of the phenomenon is often helped by formulating it in the active voice to surface assumptions about who is doing what to whom by what means. To study the emergence of groups premised on "revelatory events," I reformulated *The Oxford English Dictionary*'s event-related definition—"the disclosure or communication of knowledge to man by a divine or supernatural agency"—in the active voice, that is, as knowledge *that some people claim* is disclosed by a suprahuman agent.

1.3. Use these more generic descriptions to identify cases for comparison. The three cases analyzed in this book were selected because (a) they each included a key figure or figures who acquired new knowledge that they attributed to a suprahuman source and (b) the knowledge led to the emergence of a new spiritual path. In two of the three cases (Mormonism and ACIM), the claim of new knowledge was embraced by the group and was central to the path that emerged. In the third case (AA and Bill Wilson), the group downplayed the claim, although it remained central to the figure in question and to the emergence of the path, if not an essential feature of the path itself.

2. ANALYZING THE PHENOMENON OF INTEREST

2.1. Identifying constituent parts. Having characterized the phenomenon of interest in more generic terms using basic concepts, we can identify constituent parts of the basic concepts and then bring that more refined understanding of parts into our analysis of our sources. In this case, since I identified "events attributed to suprahuman entities that lead to paths" as the phenomenon of interest and the point of comparison between my cases, I turned to the literature on event cognition and cognitive metaphor theory to better understand the appraisal processes associated with "events" and the transformation of events into "paths."

Paths: A path is a basic metaphor that involves a route from one place (a starting point) to another (a goal). Following a path is a form of goal-directed action. For an event to result in the emergence of a path, people have to appraise an event in such a way that it gives rise to goal-directed action. More specifically, people must frame the event or series of events as revealing a means of moving from a starting point (a problem) to a goal (a solution or endpoint). For a group to emerge, people have to agree on this framing. Established routes are typically marked in some way so that people can easily follow the path. In the emerging paths studied here, there were no established routes. The guides and guidance procedures emerged to help establish the route. Part 1 of this book reconstructed the process whereby small groups established the source of new knowledge and a means of obtaining guidance from it.

Events: Since this project focused on events in which new knowledge is conveyed, the event involved an action (conveying knowledge), a claim regarding how the knowledge was conveyed (the source of the knowledge), and a process whereby subjects made that determination, whether in the context of the event itself or after the fact (or some combination thereof). I used this basic schema, which was derived from research on appraisal processes (Taves 2009) and event cognition (see Taves and Asprem 2016), to analyze event narratives in order to reconstruct how people appraised events over time.

2.2. Reconstructing events. The confidence with which we can reconstruct events varies depending on the nature of the sources available to us. When we have relatively contemporaneous firsthand accounts of events, we may be able to reconstruct a plausible initial appraisal. If the accounts are sufficiently detailed, we may be able to break down an event narrative into sub-events, that is, a series of "happenings" within an overall event narrative. We can look to see if there was a tacit explanation of "why it happened" embedded in the subevent. Analytically, the goal is to see if we can tease apart the cues that the subject allegedly sensed or perceived ("what happened") from the causes or reasons they implicitly or explicitly gave for them ("why it happened"). Again depending on the nature of the sources, this distinction between "what happened" and "why it happened" may allow us to determine the extent to which unconscious appraisals were plausibly generated during the event itself. Thus, for example, when we have sources such as Schucman's letters, which offer close to real-time accounts of and reflections on her dreams, we can tease apart the narrative, as I did in chapter 7, distinguishing between the images that appeared and Schucman's post hoc reflections on the images. Initially, the images simply appeared as a series of "happenings" without any sense in the dream itself of why they were happening. Schucman reflected consciously on what they meant after the fact, often in dialogue with Thetford. After a while, Schucman began to implicitly ascribe otherness to a part of herself, asking "it" for an explanation of the images. In subsequent letters, she had the sense that she was "obeying an Order." This feeling suggests an ascription of authoritative agency to an alternative self in the context of the event itself.

Although immediate post hoc accounts such as these offer the best sources for reconstructing the interplay between what happened and appraisals of why it happened, multiple accounts of an event, when available, can also allow us to hypothesize about the subjects' initial appraisals. Thus, for example, I compared the various versions of Joseph Smith's 1820 and 1823 experiences (see chart 3) and Bill Wilson's sudden experience in 1934 (see chart 7) by dividing the event into subevents and interweaving the accounts so that we can compare the subevents. Depicting the analysis in charts allows us to see what subevents were added or deleted as the narrative was retold and analyze to what extent the narrator altered the way they described the subevents over time. When the description of "what happened" remains stable across accounts, this allows us to identify a plausible early representation of the sensory cues that comprised the experience. If some portion of the reasons the subject offers to explain the cues remains stable over time, this suggests that those reasons may have been closely connected to the initial unconscious appraisal of the event. Reasons that change over time likely represent the subject's more conscious reflections on the experience and can thus be analyzed in relation to the context in which the narrative was retold.

Reasons that change over time, which likely reflect the effect of new situations on memory (see Taves and Harper 2016), allow us to reconstruct the way the event was reinterpreted at various points in time. Each such recounting constitutes a new event with a new event context and reason for recounting the event. When a person recounts an event in a new time and/or place, the context implicitly or the subject explicitly provides a new frame for the event (Goffman 1974). In some cases, subjects link the event with other events to create a larger narrative, for example, a story, an autobiography, or an origin account. The larger narrative then frames the event and implicitly or explicitly offers a reason for recounting it. Groups typically recount narratives of their origins as means of constituting themselves as a group with a particular group identity. Thus, in chapter 3, I analyzed Smith's versions of his 1820 first vision experience in the context of recounting the history of the origins of the newly restored church in the 1830s. In chapter 4, I analyzed the changing role that Bill Wilson's sudden experience played in his narrative of the origins of AA. In chapter 9, I considered the small group interactions that led to the Course's publication and dissemination and shaped the way it was presented to the public.

3. Identifying Components and Explaining Interactions

In Part 2, I took up the task of identifying components that interacted to generate the phenomena (emergent groups guided by presences) and explaining how the components interacted to produce the phenomenon.

3.1. Identifying components. The comparative analysis of the emergence of the three paths in chapter 10 highlighted the centrality of guidance processes, refined the phenomenon that needed to be explained, and suggested a set of components that interacted to generate the phenomenon. As I worked on the chapters, I clarified the processes that needed to be explained and looked for research that might illuminate the mechanisms involved in producing each of the components. Ultimately, I devoted each of the three chapters in Part 2 to a component of the overall phenomenon: small group interactions in chapter 10, Smith's and Schucman's unusual abilities in chapter 11, and differences in motivation in chapter 12. In each chapter, I treated the behavior of the component as the phenomenon of interest and sought to explain how it worked. Thus, chapter 10 focused on how small groups could create a presence to guide them. Doing so required modifying the social identity approach to creativity to include a greater range of entities at the species level. Chapter 11 explained how Smith and Schucman, like HHs, may have been able to manipulate executive control mechanisms in order to shift from their ordinary self to another self. Chapter 12 explained how competing motives can—if elaborated—give rise to alternative subjectivities (group-identified selves) within the default mode network.

Explaining the abilities that enabled Smith and Schucman to dictate complex texts involved a lengthy series of steps that I constructed with considerable care. My goal was to demonstrate how we can compare diverse systems—the abilities of Smith and Schucman (S_1), the abilities of HHs (S_2), and the experiences of novelists (S_3)—that involve a common component (X_1) in order to identify a mechanism that produces the common component (X_1) without equating the systems (S_1, S_2, and S_3), all of which are comprised of other components in addition to X_1. Thus, after reconstructing Smith's and Schucman's experience when translating and scribing in order to get a clearer sense of what needed to be explained, I compared their reconstructed experience with the subjective experience of a single highly hypnotizable individual (the student storyteller) based on similarities that I perceived in their abilities. This three-way comparison of their abilities allowed me to propose a hypothesis to explain how Smith and Schucman were able to produce complex texts without knowing what was going to unfold or feeling as if they were authoring them. It was only then that I turned to experimental research on highly hypnotizable individuals (HHs) to see if there was experimental data that would support this hypothesis and also to accounts from authors and psychologists who deliberately sought to engage with imagined others.

3.2. Explaining how the components interact. Generating an explanation involves not only identifying the components and their mechanisms but also explaining how the components interact to generate the phenomenon. In this case, Gerrans's theory of delusions, underpinned by research in evolutionary psychology, provided a framework for integrating these lines of research. I would stress, however, that I did not start with Gerrans's theory, which I only discovered after the manuscript was drafted; I drew on it at the end, because it allowed me to relate components I had already identified.

In drawing on Gerrans, my goal was *not* to reframe the case studies as arising from delusions, but to explain how the components interacted to produce groups guided by a suprahuman presence. Gerrans's theory was easy to adapt because it explains delusions in terms of general cognitive mechanisms and compares how they interact to produce three different phenomena: delusions, dreams, and waking imaginings. Although he did not attempt to apply his general cognitive framework to cases in which people claim that what they experience is real and others agree with them, his theoretical definition of delusions specified points where different sorts of input could produce different effects. Thus, in theorizing that delusions arise when default cognitive processing (the DMN), unsupervised by decontextualized processing (reality monitoring), is monopolized by hypersalient information, both "unsupervised" and "monopolized" specify conditions that could be manipulated to produce different results. "Monopolized" points to issues related to salience and learning, while "unsupervised" points to the absence of reflective processing and, by extension, the absence of (positive) group interaction.

With respect to decontextualized processing, which Gerrans's theory suggests is integral to normal waking functioning, hypnosis research suggests that HHs can suspend decontextualized processing in response to cues, thus controlling the extent of reality monitoring in ways that clinical subjects typically cannot. The ability to control the interplay between these processes points to a crucial difference between those who experience distress and seek clinical help and those who do not. Research on unconscious motivation, agency, and self-agency suggests how the default mode network, with its ability to simulate self-related scenarios, could elaborate motivated subjectivities into an alternate group-identified self that could seek to guide the emerging group. The social identity research indicated how controlled shifts between individual and group self-identification could affect the appraisal process by increasing or decreasing the salience of group-based norms and priorities. Group identification increased the salience of cues and representations that supported the emergence of the group-identified self. When other people engaged directly with the alternate selves through collective guidance procedures, they enacted their appraisals and encouraged further elaboration.

The connection between the appraisal processes teased apart in Part 1, and the general theory developed through comparing the cases in Part 2, is realized most fully in chapter 12. There I drew on a multilevel approach to appraisal processes in order to explain sudden transformative experiences in terms of appraisals that most likely were unconsciously embedded in the experience itself and more gradual transformations in terms of appraisals generated through reflection, often in dialogue with others. Thus, in the case of Bill Wilson, I proposed that his sudden experience drew its depth and transformative power from an unconscious association between his bodily sensations and the story of his alcoholic grandfather's sudden recovery experience atop Mount Aeolus. In other instances, such as the emergence of the Voice of the Course or the development of Smith's first vision account, there was a much lengthier, more interactive process in which input from dreams and visions was appraised through reflection and interaction. In terms of the overall explanatory theory developed in Part 2, sudden experiences most likely reflect unconscious associations generated through default mode processing, while the more gradual processes involved interaction and metacognitive reflection on the unappraised images arising through default mode processing.

Summary of Steps

We can recapitulate the general steps as follows:

1. Specify the phenomenon of interest
    1.1. Trace the development of complex cultural concepts to identify their different meanings and locate them in relation to social formations.
    1.2. Use these more generic descriptions to identify cases for comparison.
2. Analyze the phenomenon of interest
    2.1. Figure out how best to analyze the emergence or development of the behavior, process, or event.
    2.2. Reconstruct how the behavior, process, or event unfolded.
3. Identify components and explain their interaction

3.1. Compare the process across cases to identify components, then treat each component as a phenomenon of interest and seek to explain how it is produced.

3.2. Identify, adapt, or generate a theory to explain how the components interact to produce the initial phenomenon of interest.

4. Ideally, you should now attempt to test your explanation. For more on this, see the BBHE website at bbhe.ucsb.edu.

FRAMING PROCESSES IN MULTILEVEL EXPLANATIONS

Those who are interested in bridging between the person-level focus of the humanities and social sciences and the subperson-level focus of psychology and the neurosciences need to be particularly attentive to framing processes, particularly those associated with their own discipline (McCubbins and Turner, 400–403). Group-based framing of events is an important component of explanations of person-level phenomena and one that is easily obscured if we, as scholars, are not careful to avoid descriptive reduction.

I can illustrate the problem and the benefits of avoiding it, using Dan Vogel's (2002) characterization of Joseph Smith's interaction with the three Mormon witnesses (i.e., Harris, Cowdery, and Whitmer) as a hypnotic induction. Since Smith formally and explicitly framed his interaction with the three men as "prayer," Vogel's redescription transformed it from a "prayer event" into a "hypnosis event," thus replacing Smith's framing of the event with his own. Descriptively, however, it is important to recognize each as a distinct event that is formally framed and initiated in its own way. In the hypnotic event, the interaction is initiated and framed *as hypnosis* by a hypnotist who performs a hypnotic induction. In the prayer event, the interaction is initiated and framed *as sacred* by an acknowledged seer through prayer. In both cases, the framing defines the event, focuses the subject's attention on the situation at hand, and (most likely) cues shifts in cognitive control. In contrast to the hypnotic induction, which contains general suggestions about the situation, the content of Smith's prayers with the witnesses most likely offered specific statements (or formal suggestions) about what is or would occur (i.e., an angel will appear and show you the plates).

Based on this more evenhanded setup, we can investigate to what extent the two interactions were produced by the interaction of common component processes, despite the differences in framing. In his analysis, Vogel noted that "each of the three witnesses had a history of visions" (2002, 93), which would indicate a greater than usual ability to incorporate and act on vision-related suggestions, much as I hypothesized in chapter 2 that Joseph Smith was unusually able to incorporate and act on his father's belief that his dream-vision in 1823 was "of God." As Vogel indicates, the relationship between Smith and the witnesses was also crucial. Hypnosis research would suggest that the ability to incorporate a suggestion depends not only on the subject's abilities, but also on the way the suggestion is framed and the relationship between those giving and receiving the suggestion (Lynn and Rhue 1991). Thus, people who "believe in" hypnosis are more responsive to hypnotic suggestions than those who do not. Correspondingly, those who believe in prayer are more likely to respond to events framed as prayers. The relationship between the suggester and the suggestee is equally crucial, such that people are more responsive when they receive a suggestion from a highly esteemed and trusted source, for example, from a trusted parent or friend, a researcher they consider an expert, or a religious leader they hold in high esteem (Schjødt et al. 2011; Sheehan, 1991).

Looking back some years later, Oliver Cowdery offered a very precise description of both the beliefs he held and the feelings he had for Smith while they were translating, in order to account—in a period of later doubt—for his conviction that they were translating plates, despite the fact that Smith was looking at a seer stone and there were no plates anywhere to be seen:

> I believed in both the Seer and the "Seer Stone," and what the First Elder announced as revelation from God, I accepted as such, and committed to paper with a glad mind and happy heart and swift pen; for I believed him to be the soul of honor and truth, a young man who would die before he would lie. . . . I felt a solemn awe around me, being deep in the faith, that the First Elder was a Seer and Prophet of God, giving the truth unsullied through "Urim and Thummim," dictated by the will of the Lord, and that he was persecuted for the sake of the truth which he loved. (1839, 8)

Cowdery carried these beliefs and feelings for Smith into the "witnessing event" in which Smith prayerfully suggested to his collaborators that an angel would appear to show them the plates.

Described more neutrally, we can say that the suggestion that an angel would appear was offered by Smith, whom they not only trusted ("believed to be the soul of honor and truth") but regarded as a seer, called by God, to translate an ancient record that promised that three witnesses would testify to the gold plates (2 Nephi 27:12) and through whom revelations (D&C 5, D&C 17) had already been given indicating that the plates would be shown to witnesses. In addition, D&C 17 confirmed that Harris, Cowdery, and Whitmer would see the plates and indicated that they would see them "as my servant Joseph Smith jr has seen them for it is by my power that he has seen them and it is because he had faith" (JSP, D1:84). The suggestion that they would see the plates in faith enabled three men, all of whom Vogel notes had visionary abilities, to see an angel and plates.

Finally, we can return to the truth question. If as D&C 17 indicates, Joseph Smith and the witnesses saw the plates by the power of God in faith, then the ancient record was, as I argued in chapter 2, a believed-in object, just as the angel of the Lord was a believed-in entity. Thus, from a naturalistic perspective, we can view interactions in the everyday world, such as prayers, as statements that are intended to change other people's perceptions of what is real and that in many cases actually do alter people's perceptions of reality. From a religious perspective, prayer can equally well be viewed as offering suggestions about reality (about "what is") intended to change subjects' perceptions so that subjects see what the suggester views as most real. Even if insiders and outsiders disagree as to whether angels appear or deities are responsive to inquiries, we can agree that visions can convey possibilities that those who believe in them can realize (live out) in this world. If we think of "suggestions" in everyday life as something like "testimonies," then hypnosis research demonstrates what insiders already know, that is, that convincing testimony to otherworldly realities is "faith promoting" in the sense that it allows people to experience otherworldly realities in this world.

CHART I

COMPARISON OF ACCOUNTS OF JOSEPH SMITH'S 1823 VISION

1832JS—Joseph Smith 1832 History, *EMD* 1:29–30
1835JS—Joseph Smith, Recital to Robert Matthews, *EMD* 1:44
1839JS—Joseph Smith 1839 History, *EMD* 1:63-66
1841WS—William Smith, *EMD* 1:478–79
1845LMS—Lucy Mack Smith, History, *EMD* 1:290–95
1853LMS—Lucy Mack Smith, History, *EMD* 1:290–95
1883WS—William Smith, *EMD* 1:496

Text	Visions	Told to tell someone?	Who does he tell? Where?	Then what?
1832JS	Three times at night and once the next day	No		Immediately went to the place (after the day vision)
1835JS	Three times at night and once the next day	Father in day-time vision	Tells father	Left and found place
1839JS	Three times at night and once the next day	Father in day-time vision	Tells father in field	Left field for place
1841WS	One time at night	No	Sent for his father and brother from field and then told whole family	He had other visions; the next day went to the place and brought them home
1845LMS	At night and once the next day	Told to tell his father in the vision at night; personage confronted him about not telling in daytime vision	Sent Alvin to get his father from the house; told father in the field	In the evening he told his whole family; no mention of going to the place

Text	Visions	Told to tell someone?	Who does he tell? Where?	Then what?
1853LMS	Inserts 1839JS	Same as 1845LMS	Sent Alvin to get father from house; told father in field	Soon after went to the place; told whole family that evening
1883WS	At night and one time the next day	Whole family in day vision	Asks Alvin and William to go to the house where he tells the whole family	Went to the hill (later that day?)

- All but one family account mentions appearances both at night and once the next day.
- All but one of the accounts that mention the daytime appearance explains that it had to do with telling about the night appearances.
- In the JS and LMS accounts, he is to tell his father; in the WS account, he is to tell his whole family. In the LMS account, he is first told to tell his father at night and then questioned about not doing so in the day appearance.
- The common theme is that JS fears that he/they will not believe what he has been told by the personage in the night appearance. He is commanded by the personage to tell either his father or his family about the messenger and the plates. In all cases, he is believed. In the JS accounts, he finds the place where the plates are located in the wake of the daytime vision. The LMS 1845 and WS accounts are not clear when he went to find the place.

Basic claim: JS recounted a dream-vision to father/family that he was afraid he/they would not believe, in which a personage appeared and told him about golden plates/treasure buried by ancient inhabitants. He did not go to find the plates until after he told him/them. JS then claims he found the plates but couldn't recover them. This launches a period of continuing visions in which contents of the plates were reported, and he recounted them to his family.

CHART 2

ACCOUNTS OF JOSEPH SMITH'S
DISCOVERY OF THE PLATES

1832JS—Joseph Smith, 1832 History, *EMD* 1:29*
1835JS—Joseph Smith, Recital to Robert Matthews, *EMD* 1:44–45
1839JS—Joseph Smith, 1839 History, *EMD* 1:66–67
1833WC—Willard Chase 1833, *EMD* 2:67 (recounting Joseph Smith Sr.'s narrative from
June 1827)

	Discovery	Doubt-Crisis-Struggle	Resolution
1832JS	I immediately went to the place and found where the plates was deposited as the angel of the Lord had commanded me and straightway made three attempts to get them	and then being exceedingly frightened I supposed it had been a dream of Vision but when I considered I knew that it was not	therefore I cried unto the Lord in the agony of my soul why can I not obtain them behold the angel appeared unto me again and said unto me you have not kept the commandments of the Lord which I gave unto you therefore you cannot now obtain them for the time is not yet fulfilled.
1835JS	I went and found the place, where the plates were, according to the direction of the Angel, also saw them [the plates], and the angel as before;	the powers of darkness strove hard against me.	I called on God, the Angel told me that the reason why I could not obtain the plates at this time was because I was under transgression.
1839JS	I went to the place where the messenger had told me the plates were deposited . . . I knew the place the instant that I arrived there. Under a stone of considerable size, lay the plates deposited in a stone box. [He described the box and its contents.]		I made an attempt to take them out but was forbidden by the messenger and was again informed that the time [for] bringing them forth had not yet arrived.

*Note that spelling and grammatical errors are in the original text.

	Discovery	Doubt-Crisis-Struggle	Resolution
1833WC	He repaired to the place of deposit and demanded the book . . . of gold; but fearing that some one might discover where he got it, he laid it down to place back the top stone [that had covered it], as he had found it; and turning round, to his surprise there was no book in sight. He again opened the box, and . . . saw the book, and attempted to take it out, but was hindered.	He [then] saw in the box something like a toad, which soon assumed the appearance of a man, and struck him on the side of his head.—Not being discouraged at trifles, he again stooped down and strove to take the book, when the spirit struck him again, knocked him three or four rods, and hurt him prodigiously.	After recovering from his fright, he enquired why he could not obtain the plates; to which the spirit made reply, because you have not obeyed your orders. He then enquired when he could have them, and was answered thus: come one year from this day, and bring with you your oldest brother, and you shall have them.

CHART 3

COMPARISON OF ACCOUNTS OF JOSEPH SMITH'S FIRST VISION

1832JS—Joseph Smith, "History," ca. summer 1832, *JSP*, H1:3–16.

1833A—Milo Andrus, 17 July 1853. Papers of George D. Watt. MS 4534 box 2 disk 1 May 1853–July 1853 images 231–56. Transcribed by LaJean Purcell Carruth, 3 October 2012; corrected October 2013.

1835C—Joseph Curtis, "Joseph Curtis Reminiscence and Diary, 1939 October–1881 March," MS 1654, 5–6, Church History Library, Salt Lake City, Utah.

1835JS—Joseph Smith, History, 1834–36, 9 November 1935, *JSP*, H1:115–19.

1839JS—Joseph Smith, History (ca. June 1839—ca. 1841), *JSP*, H1:205–35.

Light gray	material only in 1832JS
Dark gray	material only in later versions

UNINTENDED EXPERIENCE EVENT (WHAT HAPPENED)

1832JS	"my mind become exceedingly [*sic*] distressed"
1835JS	"being wrought up in my mind, respecting the subject of religion . . . perplexed in mind"
1835C	"he [JS] feeling anxiety to be religious his mind some what [*sic*] troubled"
1839JS	Felt "desire" and implicit distress

CAUSE EXPLANATION (WHY IT HAPPENED)

1832JS	"I [had] become convicted of my sins" in the context of "contentions and divi[si]ons"
1835JS	"looking at the different systems taught the children of men, I knew not who was right or who was wrong"
1835C	Because "a revival of some of the sec[t]s was going on [and] some of his father[']s family joined in"
1839JS	"I felt some desire to be united with [the Methodists]" but impossible to decide "who was right and who was wrong" ("desire" + inability to decide = implicit distress). *Context note:* "In the midst of this war of words, and tumult of opinions, I often said to myself, what is to be done? Who of all these parties are right? Or are they all wrong together? and if any one of them be right which is it? And how shall I know it?"

INTENDED BEHAVIOR EVENT (WHAT HE DID)

| 1832JS | "by searching the scriptures I found that mankind . . . apostatized from the true . . . faith and there was no . . . denomination that built on the gospel of Jesus Christ" |

REASON EXPLANATION (WHY HE DID IT)

| 1832JS | Implicitly to find a denomination where his sins could be forgiven |

UNINTENDED EXPERIENCE EVENT (WHAT HAPPENED)

1835JS	"under a realising sense that [the Lord] had said (if the bible be true) ask and you shall receive knock and it shall be opened seek and you shall find and again, if any man lack wisdom let him ask of God who giveth to all men libarally and upbradeth not[.]"
1835C	"this scriptures came to his mind which sayes if a man lack wisdom let him ask of god who giveth liberaly and upbradeth not[.]"
1839JS	"While I was laboring under . . . [these] difficulties . . . I was one day reading [James 1:5]. It seemed to enter with great force into . . . my heart." (No cause given)

INTENDED BEHAVIOR EVENT (WHAT HE DID)

| 1839JS | "reflected on it again and again" |

REASON EXPLANATION (WHY HE DID IT)

| 1839JS | "the teachers of religion of the different sects understood the same passage of Scripture so differently as [to] destroy all confidence in settling the question by an appeal to the Bible" |

INTENDED BEHAVIOR EVENT (WHAT HE DID)

| 1839JS | "I at last came to the determination to ask of God." |

REASON EXPLANATION (WHY HE DID IT)

| 1839 JS | "I must either remain in darkness and confusion or else I must do as James directs, that is, Ask of God." |

Intended behavior event (what he did)

1832JS	"I cried unto the Lord for mercy."
1835JS	"I retired to the silent grove and bow[e]d down before the Lord . . . and with a fixed determination to obtain it [information], I called upon the Lord for the first time."
1835C	"believing it he went with a determinati[on] to obtain to enquire of the lord himself"
1839JS	"I retired [to the woods] . . . kneeled down and began to offer up the desires of my heart to God."

Reason explanation (why he did it)

1832JS	"for there was none else to whom I could go to obtain mercy"
1835JS	"to obtain it [information]"
1835C	he "believed it" ("ask and you shall receive")
1839JS	"to ask of God"

Unintended experience event (what happened)

1835JS	"my toung seemed to be swolen in my mouth, so that I could not utter, I heard a noise behind me like some person walking towards me, I strove again to pray, but could not, the noise of walking seemed to draw nearer, I sprung up on my feet and looked around, but saw no person or thing that was calculated to produce the noise of walking."
1835C	"after some strugle"
1839JS	"[seized] upon by some power which entirely overcame me . . . [the power bound] my tongue so that I could not speak. Thick darkness gathered around me and it seemed . . . as if I were doomed to sudden destruction . . . I was ready to sink into despair and abandon myself to destruction."

Cause explanation (why it happened)

1835JS	He could not find an ordinary explanation ("he saw no person or thing").
1839JS	The feeling of being seized by a power was attributed to "this enemy." He said the cause was not imaginary. He was threatened "not [by] an imaginary ruin but [by] the power of some actual being from the unseen world who had a marvelous power as I had never before felt in any being."

Unintended experience event (what happened)

1832JS	"While in the attitude of prayer . . . a piller of light [brighter than the sun at noon] came down from above and rested upon me and I was filled."
1835JS	"I kneeled again my mouth was opened and my toung liberated, and I called on the Lord in mighty prayer, a pillar of fire appeared above my head, it presently rested down up[on] me ~~head~~, and filled me with Joy unspeakable."'
1839JS	"Just at this moment of great alarm I saw a pillar [of] light exactly over my head above the brightness of the sun, which descended . . . upon me. . . . I found myself delivered from the enemy which held me bound."

Cause explanation (why it happened)

1832JS	Image of pillar of fire/light associated with "shekinah" in the Old Testament; the filling attributed to the "spirit of god."
1835JS	No cause is given for the "pillar of fire"; it is implicitly understood as a response to prayer.
1839JS	No cause is given for the light; it is implicitly understood as a response to "great alarm."

Unintended experience event (what happened)

1832JS	"the Lord opened the heavens . . . I saw the Lord . . . he spake to me saying . . . thy sins are forgiven thee" (the Lord's speech continues in an apocalyptic vein and ends with a promise to "come quickly")
1833A	"angel came and that [glory?] and trees seemed to be consumed in blaze and he was there entrusted with this information that darkness covered the earth that the great mass of Christian world universally wrong their creeds all upon uncertain foundation now as young as you are I call upon you from this obscurity go forth and build up my kingdom on the earth"
1835JS	"a personage appeard in the midst of this pillar of flame which was spread all around, and yet nothing consumed, another personage soon appeard like unto the first, he said unto me thy sins are forgiven thee, he testifyed unto me that Jesus Christ is the Son of God; and I saw many angels in this vision"
1835C	"the Lord manifested to him that the different sects were [w]rong also that the Lord had a great work for him to do"
1839JS	"I saw two personages . . . standing above me in the air. One of [them] spake unto me . . . and said (pointing to the other) 'This is my beloved Son, Hear him.' . . . No sooner . . . did I get possession of myself so as to be

able to speak, than I asked the personages who stood above me in the light, which of all the sects was right, (for at this time it had never entered into my heart that all were wrong) and which I should join. I was answered that I must join none of them, for they were all wrong, and the Personage who addressed me said that all their Creeds were an abomination in his sight, that those professors were all corrupt, that 'they draw near to me with their lips but their hearts are far from me, they . . . [have] a form of Godliness but they deny the power thereof.' "*

Unintended experience event (what happened)

1832JS	"my soul was filled with love and for many days I could rejoice with great joy and the Lord was with me"
1835JS	No indication of what happened next.
1839JS	"When I came to myself again I found myself lying on [my] back looking up into Heaven."

Intended behavior event [what he did]

1832JS	"[I] could find none that would believe the hevnly [sic] vision nevertheless I pondered these things in my heart."
1839JS	"Some few days later after I had this vision I happened to be in company with one of the Methodist Preachers who was very active in the before mentioned religious excitement and conversing with him on the subject of religion I took occasion to give him an account of the vision which I had had. I was greatly surprised at his behavior, he treated my communication not only lightly but with great contempt, saying it was all of the Devil, that there was no such thing as visions or revelations in these days, that all such things had ceased with the apostles and that there never would be any more of them."

* This quotation could be broken down further but is left together because themes align with other material in this section of the chart.

CHART 4

BILL WILSON'S SUDDEN EXPERIENCE IN THE AA STORY

1939—"Bill's Story" in *Alcoholics Anonymous* (the Big Book), 1st ed.
1941 (March)—Jack Alexander, "Alcoholics Anonymous," *Saturday Evening Post* (second-hand, based on interviews).
1944 (June)—W.W., "The Fellowship of Alcoholics Anonymous," talk given at Yale Summer School of Alcohol Studies, reprinted in *Alcohol, Science, and Society* (1945).
1955—Foreword, *Alcoholics Anonymous*, 2nd ed.

UNINTENDED EXPERIENCE EVENT (WHAT HAPPENED)

1939	He had a "sudden and profound" experience.
1941	"Five months before coming to Akron, he had gone on the water wagon."
1944	He experienced a "sudden illumination," a "hot flash," a "sudden flash of Presence"—"the central experience of his life."
1955	"The broker had been relieved of his drink obsession by a sudden spiritual experience."

CAUSE EXPLANATION (WHY IT HAPPENED)

1939	He had "turn[ed] in all things to the Father of Light who presides over us all" and "God" had come to him following Ebby T.'s intervention.
1941	"the ministration of the Oxford Group in New York"
1944	He called upon God, "if there is a God, . . . [to] show Himself" following Ebby T.'s intervention.
1955	"following a meeting with an alcoholic friend . . . in contact with the Oxford Groups"

UNINTENDED EXPERIENCE EVENT (WHAT HAPPENED)

1939	"While I lay in the hospital the thought came that there were thousands of hopeless alcoholics who might be glad to have what had been so freely given me. Perhaps I could help some of them. They in turn might work with others."

1941	Absent
1944	"I actually thought . . . that God had selected me, by this sudden flash of Presence, to dry up all the drunks in the world."

CAUSE EXPLANATION

1939	No cause given
1941	None
1944	"I had the conceit . . . to believe . . . that God has selected me to dry up all the drunks."

INTENDED BEHAVIOR EVENT (WHAT HE DID)

1939	"My wife and I abandoned ourselves with enthusiasm to the idea of helping other alcoholics to a solution of their problems" (*AA*, 15).
1941	"Fascinated by the problem of alcoholism, he had many times gone back as a visitor to a Central Park West [Towns] detoxicating hospital, where he had been a patient, and talked to the inmates."
1944	"I worked like thunder for 6 months."
1955	"Prior to his journey to Akron, the broker had worked hard with many alcoholics."

REASON EXPLANATION (WHY HE DID IT)

1939	"My friend has emphasized the absolute necessity of demonstrating these principles in all my affairs. Particularly it was imperative to work with others as he had worked with me. Faith without works was dead" (*AA*, 14).
1941	No reason given
1944	"God had selected me . . . to dry up all the drunks in the world . . . Divine Appointment"
1955	"on the theory that only an alcoholic could help an alcoholic"

UNINTENDED EXPERIENCE EVENT (WHAT HAPPENED)

1939	"I would be amazingly lifted up and set on my feet" when he went "to [his] old hospital in despair" and talked to a man there (*AA*, 15).
1941	He found . . . he could stave off his own craving . . . by working on other alcoholics [but] he effected no recoveries."

1944	"not one alcoholic got dried up"
1955	"but he had succeeded only in keeping sober himself"

CAUSE EXPLANATION

1939	No reason given
1941	No reason given
1944	He believed "it had to happen in some particular way just like [his] or else it would be of no use."
1955	No reason given.

UNINTENDED EXPERIENCE EVENT (WHAT HAPPENED)

1939	"Led . . . [to Dr. Bob] . . . who . . . was nearing the nadir of alcoholic despair . . . he has not had a drink since" (*AA*, 155–56).
1941	"Dr. Armstrong became Griffith's first real disciple."
1944	"came across Dr. 'Bob' S. out in Akron . . . and Bob S. recovered"
1955	"the Akron physician . . . sobered, never to drink again"

CAUSE EXPLANATION (WHY IT HAPPENED)

1939	He remembered "his responsibilities . . . [to] other alcoholics," phoned a random church in the directory, and "related his experience" to the other alcoholic.
1941	He knew that working on other alcoholics could stave off his own craving, but no particular reason is given for success in this case as compared to others.
1944	He realized that "talk[ing] with another alcoholic[,] even though [he] failed with him, was better than to do nothing." His motivation, he said, had shifted. "No longer was I preaching from any moral hilltop or from the vantage point of a wonderful spiritual experience. No, this time I was looking for another alcoholic, because I felt that I needed him twice as much as he needed me."
1955	"He [Bill] suddenly realized that in order to save himself he must carry his message to another alcoholic."

UNINTENDED EXPERIENCE EVENT (WHAT HAPPENED)

1939   "Thus we grow" (*AA*, 162).

1941   "Progress was slow."

1944   "[P]rogress was very slow."

CAUSE EXPLANATION (WHY IT HAPPENED)

1939   Message (as laid out in the Big Book) was passed on from one alcoholic to another.

1941   No reason given.

1944   They started "preaching" again, assuming things had to happen "in some particular way," instead of looking at things from the other's point of view.

UNINTENDED EXPERIENCE EVENT (WHAT HAPPENED)

1944   They realized that AA was not a "set of fixed ideas, but . . . a growing thing, growing out of experience" and that recovery originated in "a spiritual awakening growing out of painful adversity" (and not a particular "spiritual experience").

LATER ACCOUNTS

1945—John J., "Man's Triumvirate" (secondhand account of talks given by Bill W. and Dr. Bob at the Tenth Anniversary commemoration in Cleveland), *AA Grapevine* 2/2 (July).

1951—Bill W., Speech in Chicago, February 1951. Fitzpatrick Archives, www.recovery-speakers.org. In Michael Fitzpatrick, *Dr. Bob and Bill W. Speak* (Hazelden, 2012), 37–39.

1954a—Bill W., Talk at LeMoyne College, Syracuse, New York, April 1954. Transcript. AA Archives.

1954b—Bill W., dictated autobiography, fall 1954. Published as *Bill W.: My First 40 Years; An Autobiography by the Cofounder of Alcoholics Anonymous* (Hazelden, 2000), 144–55.

1957—Anonymous, *Alcoholics Anonymous Comes of Age*.

1966—Bill W., Speech, AA International Doctors Conference, Indianapolis, 1966. Fitzpatrick Archives, www.recoveryspeakers.org. In Michael Fitzpatrick, *Dr. Bob and Bill W. Speak* (Hazelden, 2012), 37–39.

CHART 5

WINCHESTER CATHEDRAL IN "BILL'S STORY"

	Cathedral (1918)	Ebby T.'s visit (Nov. 1934)	Towns (Dec. 1934)
Original Story (SSFA), Unpublished ca. 1938	"I stood in Winchester Cathedral . . . with head bowed . . . A feeling of despair settled down on me . . . suddenly in that moment of darkness, He was there. I felt an all enveloping, comforting, powerful presence. Tears stood in my eyes, and as I looked about, I saw on the faces of others nearby, that they too had glimpsed the great reality. Much moved, I walked out into the Cathedral yard, where I read the following inscription on a tombstone . . ."	Ebby appeared "radiant of something which soothed my troubled spirit as tho the fresh clean wind of a mountain top blowing thru and thru me—I saw and felt and in a great surge of joy I realized that the great presence which had made itself felt to me that war time day in Winchester Cathedral had again returned."	Not discussed
"Bill's Story" (GSOA), Unpublished ca. Spring 1938	"I stood in Winchester Cathedral with head bowed . . . Suddenly in that moment of darkness—He was there! I felt an enveloping comforting Presence. Tears stood in my eyes. I had glimpsed the great reality. Much moved, I wandered through the Cathedral yard . . ."	Listening to Ebby, "That war time day in Winchester Cathedral came back again . . . He was on a different footing. His roots grasped new soil. Thus was I convinced . . . The real significance of my experience in the Cathedral burst upon me."	"I felt lifted up, as though the great clean wind of a mountain top blew through and through."

	Cathedral (1918)	Ebby T.'s visit (Nov. 1934)	Towns (Dec. 1934)
"Bill's Story" (*OWM*), Unpublished Feb.–March 1939	"I visited Winchester Cathedral. Much moved, I wandered outside. My attention was caught by a doggerel on an old tombstone . . ."	Listening to Ebby, "That war-time day in old Winchester Cathedral came back again . . . He was on a different footing. His roots grasped new soil. Thus was I convinced . . . The real significance of my experience in the Cathedral burst upon me."	"I felt lifted up, as though the great clean wind of a mountain top blew through and through."
"Bill's Story" (BB:1939), Published April 1939	"I visited Winchester Cathedral. Much moved, I wandered outside. My attention was caught by a doggerel on an old tombstone . . ."	Listening to Ebby, "That war-time day in old Winchester Cathedral came back again . . . He was on a different footing. His roots grasped new soil. [Section on choosing own conception of God inserted here.] Thus was I convinced . . . The real significance of my experience in the Cathedral burst upon me."	"I felt lifted up, as though the great clean wind of a mountain top blew through and through."
Autobiography (1954), Posthumously published	Describes spiritual experiences at Newport and on the *Lancashire* prior to his visit to Winchester Cathedral. "I have been in many cathedrals since and have never experienced anything like it. Returning there in 1950, I went through a similar experience. There was within those walls a tremendous sense of presence."	No mention of Winchester Cathedral.	Remembers experiences at Newport on the *Lancashire* and at the cathedral just prior to his sudden experience.

CHART 6

COMPARISON OF BILL WILSON'S EXPERIENCES AT
WINCHESTER CATHEDRAL (1938) AND AT TOWNS
HOSPITAL (1939–66)

Cathedral Experience *Sources*: See Chart 5	Towns Experience *Sources*: See Chart 7
1938 (SSFA and GSOA): "Across the Channel thousands were perishing that day. Where now was the **God of the preachers? Why did He not come?**"	1939: Fully accepted he must turn to "the Father of Light." 1944: "When he had gone away, I fell into a very deep depression, the **blackest** that I had ever known. And in that desperation, I cried out, 'If there is a God, **will He show Himself?**' " 1951–66: Similar to 1944.
1938 (SSFA and GSOA): "**Suddenly** in that moment of **darkness**—He was there!"	1944: "Then came a **sudden** experience in which it seemed the room lit up. It felt as though I stood on the top of a mountain, that a great clean wind blew, that I was free." 1951–66: Similar
1938 (SSFA and GSOA): "I felt an enveloping comforting **Presence**."	1944: Absent 1951: "Surrounded by a **Presence**" 1954a: "Lay on bed . . . perceived another world . . . surrounded by a **Presence** . . . great peace . . . assurance" 1954b: "Saw wall of room . . . great peace . . . conscious of **presence** . . . seemed like . . . sea of living spirit . . . shores of new world" 1966: "Lying on bed . . . in a new dimension . . . part of the great universe"
1938 (SSFA and GSOA): "Tears stood in my eyes. I had glimpsed the **great reality**."	1944: The sublime paradox of strength coming out of weakness. 1951, 1954a,b: "This is the **God of the preachers**." 1954b: "The **great reality**" 1966: "The great universe"

Framing: In 1938 (SSFA and GSOA), Bill's cathedral and Towns experiences are framed very differently. His cathedral experience occurs in a "moment of darkness" when he was thinking about the "thousands [who] were perishing . . . across the Channel" and asked himself, "Where now was the God of the preachers? . . . Why did He not come?" In the 1938 (SSFA & GSOA) and BB:1939 versions of his Towns experience, the event is precipitated by "full acceptance." Beginning with his 1944 account of his Towns experience, the two experiences are framed similarly. In both, he cries out to God in desperation and the experience comes "suddenly" out of "darkness."

Content: In the longer (uncut) versions of his cathedral experience, the experience was one of a comforting presence; at Towns, the consistent aspects were first light and then wind on a mountaintop. Phrases associated with his cathedral experience begin to appear in the third, more variable portion of his Towns experience in the fifties; thus, he feels "surrounded by a Presence" in accounts from the fifties (1951, 1954a,b) and interprets his experience using similar phrases—"the God of the preachers" (1951, 1954a,b) and "the great reality" (1954b).

CHART 7

COMPARISON OF ACCOUNTS OF BILL W.'S SUDDEN EXPERIENCE AT TOWNS HOSPITAL, 1934

1939—"Bill's Story," published in *Alcoholics Anonymous* (the Big Book) in 1939.
1944—W.W., "The Fellowship of Alcoholics Anonymous," talk given at the Yale Summer School of Alcohol Studies, June 1944.
1951—Bill W., Speech in Chicago, February 1951. Fitzpatrick Archives, www.recovery-speakers.org. In Michael Fitzpatrick, *Dr. Bob and Bill W. Speak* (Hazelden, 2012), 37–39.
1954a—Bill W., Talk at LeMoyne College, Syracuse, New York, April 1954. Transcript. AA Archives.
1954b—Bill W., dictated autobiography, fall 1954. Published as *Bill W.: My First 40 Years; An Autobiography by the Cofounder of Alcoholics Anonymous* (Hazelden, 2000), 144–55.
1966—Bill W., Speech, AA International Doctors Conference, Indianapolis, 1966. Fitzpatrick Archives, www.recoveryspeakers.org. In Michael Fitzpatrick, *Dr. Bob and Bill W. Speak* (Hazelden, 2012), 37–39.

First Event Begins

SUBEVENT I:
UNINTENDED EXPERIENCE EVENT (WHAT HAPPENED)

1939	"The effect was electric."
1944	"it seemed the room lit up"
1951	"The room lighted up . . . caught up in ecstasy"
1954a	"Whole room lit up in a great white light . . . caught up into an ecstasy"
1954b	"The effect was instant, electric . . . room blazed with an indescribably white light . . . ecstasy."
1966	"Instantly the place seemed to light up in a blinding glare . . . I was instantly transported into an ecstasy."

CAUSE EXPLANATION (WHY IT HAPPENED)

1939	Fully accepted that he must turn to "the Father of Light"
1944–66	Cried out to God

SUBEVENT 2:
UNINTENDED EXPERIENCE EVENT (WHAT HAPPENED)

1939	"Lifted up, as though . . . wind . . . mountain top blow"
1944	"It felt as though I stood on the top of a mountain, that a great clean wind blew."
1951	"As though . . . on top of mountain . . . wind blew"
1954a	"Seemed . . . on a mountain . . . wind . . . blowing"
1954b	"Mountain . . . in the mind's eye . . . on summit . . . great wind blew"
1966	"Seemed . . . on a mountain . . . great wind . . . blowing"

CAUSE EXPLANATION (WHY IT HAPPENED)

1939–44	None
1951–66	Attributed to "spirit" not air
1966	Also attributed to "God of the preachers"

SUBEVENT 3A:
UNINTENDED EXPERIENCE EVENT (WHAT HAPPENED)

1938	"Sense of victory"*
1944	"that I was free"
1951	Absent
1954a,b	"Blazing thought . . . 'You're a free man!' "
1966	Absent

CAUSE EXPLANATION (WHY IT HAPPENED)

None given, but implicitly linked to wind/spirit

SUBEVENT 3B:
UNINTENDED EXPERIENCE EVENT (WHAT HAPPENED)

1939	"Peace and serenity . . . utter confidence"*
1944	Absent

*Starred phrases are in a sentence that precedes the wind and mountain sentence in the earliest version. The events line up between all versions if the order of these two sentences is switched.

1951	"Surrounded by a Presence"
1954a	"Lay on bed . . . perceived another world . . . surrounded by a Presence . . . great peace . . . assurance"
1954b	"Saw wall of room . . . great peace . . . conscious of presence . . . seemed like . . . sea of living spirit . . . shores of new world"
1966	"Lying on bed . . . in a new dimension . . . part of the great universe"

CAUSE EXPLANATION

1939	None given
1944	"The sublime paradox of strength coming out of weakness"
1951	"This is the God of the preachers"
1954a,b	"This is the God of the preachers"
1954b	"The great reality"
1966	"The great universe"

Second Event Begins

UNINTENDED BEHAVIOR EVENT (WHAT HAPPENED)

1939	"I was alarmed."
1944, 1951	Not indicated
1954(a,b)–66	Fears he was hallucinating

INTENDED BEHAVIOR EVENT (WHAT HE DID)

1938	"I . . . called my friend, the doctor, to ask if I were still sane."
1944	"So I called in the doctor and tried to tell him, as best I could, what had happened."
1951	Absent
1954a	"I called in this little doctor."
1954b	"I told him the story . . . I feared to give him the full impact of it. But the essential facts, toned down somewhat emotionally, I did relate to him. . . . Lois . . . I'd hardly begun my tale before she, too, knew that I was well."
1966	"I . . . summoned him [Dr. Silkworth]."

BIBLIOGRAPHY

ARCHIVES

AA General Service Office Archives, New York
Rhine-Wilson Correspondence, Parapsychology Laboratory Records, 1893–1984, David M. Rubenstein Rare Book and Manuscript Library, Duke University
Stepping Stones Foundation Archives, Katonah, New York

BIBLIOGRAPHY

Aarts, Henk. 2007. Unconscious authorship ascription: The effects of success and effect-specific information priming on experienced authorship. *Journal of Experimental Social Psychology* 43 (1): 119–26.

Aarts, Henk, Ruud Custers, and Hans Marien. 2009. Priming and authorship ascription: When nonconscious goals turn into conscious experiences of self-agency. *Journal of Personality and Social Psychology* 96 (5): 967–79.

Albanese, Catherine L. 2007. *A Republic of Mind and Spirit: A Cultural History of American Metaphysical Religion*. New Haven: Yale University Press.

Aleman, André, and Frank Larøi. 2008. *Hallucinations: The Science of Idiosyncratic Perception*. Washington, DC: American Psychological Association.

Alexander, Jack. 1941. Alcoholics Anonymous. *Saturday Evening Post*, March 1. Available at http://www.barefootsworld.net/aajalexpost1941.html.

———. 1945 (May). The history of how the article came to be. *AA Grapevine*. Available at http://www.barefootsworld.net/aajalexpost1941.html.

Allen, James B. 1992. The significance of Joseph Smith's "first vision" in Mormon thought. In *The New Mormon History: Revisionist Essays on the Past*, ed. D. Michael Quinn, 37–52. Salt Lake City: Signature Books.

American Psychiatric Association. 2013. *Diagnostic and Statistical Manual of Mental Disorders*. 5th ed. Arlington, VA: American Psychiatric Publishing.

Anderson, Richard L. 2005. Attempts to redefine the experience of the eight witnesses. *Journal of Mormon Studies* 14 (1): 18–31, 125–27.

Anonymous. 1939. *Alcoholics Anonymous*. 1st ed. New York: AA World Services.

———. 1953. *Twelve Steps and Twelve Traditions*. New York: AA World Services.

———. 1955. *Alcoholics Anonymous*. 2nd ed. New York: AA World Services.

———. 1957. *Alcoholics Anonymous Comes of Age: A Brief History of A.A.* New York: AA World Services.

———. 1976. *Alcoholics Anonymous*. 3rd ed. New York: AA World Services, 1976.

———. 1980. *Dr. Bob and the Good Oldtimers: A Biography, with Recollections of Early AA in the Midwest*. New York: AA World Services.

———. 1984. *"Pass It On": The Story of Bill Wilson and How the A.A. Message Reached the World*. New York: AA World Services.

———. 2010. *Alcoholics Anonymous: The Book that Started It All; The Original Working Manuscript of Alcoholics Anonymous*. Center City, MN: Hazelden.

Ashurst-McGee, Mark. 2000. A pathway to prophethood. MA thesis, Utah State University.

———. 2006. Moroni as angel and treasure guardian. *FARMS Review* 18 (1): 34–100.

B., Dick. 1998. *Anne Smith's Journal, 1933–1939: A.A.'s Principles of Success*. 3rd ed. Kihei, HI: Paradise Research Publications.

B., Mel. 1998. *Ebby: The Man Who Sponsored Bill W*. Center City, MN: Hazelden.

Baker, Lynne Rudder. 2013. *Naturalism and the First-Person Perspective*. New York: Oxford University Press.

Barnier, A. J., and K. M. McConkey. 2004. Defining and identifying the highly hypnotizable person. In *The Highly Hypnotizable Person: Theoretical, Experimental, and Clinical Issues*, ed. M. Heap, R. Brown, and D. Oakley. London: Routledge.

Barnier, A. J., and C. J. Mitchell. 2005. *Looking for the Fundamental Effects of Hypnosis*. Invited address at the 35th Annual Congress of the Australian Society of Hypnosis (Scientific Program), Sydney, Australia.

Barnier, A. J., Z. Dienes, and C. J. Mitchell. 2008. How hypnosis happens: New cognitive theories of hypnotic responding. In *The Oxford Handbook of Hypnosis: Theory, Research and Practice*, ed. M. R. Nash and A. J. Barnier, 142–77. New York: Oxford University Press.

Barnier, A. J., and M. R. Nash. 2008. Introduction: A roadmap for explanation, a working definition. In *The Oxford Handbook of Hypnosis*, ed. Barnier and Nash, 1–18. New York: Oxford University Press.

Borchert, William. 2005. *When Love Is Not Enough: The Lois Wilson Story*. Center City, MN: Hazelden.

Bortolotti, Lisa. 2010. *Delusions and Other Irrational Beliefs*. Oxford: Oxford University Press.

Bowers, Maggie Ann. 2004. *Magic(al) Realism*. New York: Routledge.

Boyer, Pascal. 2013. Why "belief" is hard work: Implications of Tanya Luhrmann's *When God Talks Back*. *Journal of Ethnographic Theory* 3 (3): 349–57.

Brett, C.M.C., E. P. Peters, L. C. Johns, P. Tabraham, L. R. Valmaggia, and P. McGuire. 2007. Appraisals of Anomalous Experiences Interview (AANEX): A multidimensional measure of psychological responses to anomalies associated with psychosis. *British Journal of Psychiatry* 191 (51): s23–s30.

Brett, C.M.C., L. C. Johns, E. P. Peters, and P. K. McGuire. 2009. The role of metacognitive beliefs in determining the impact of anomalous experiences: A comparison of help-seeking and non-help-seeking groups of people experiencing psychotic-like anomalies. *Psychological Medicine* 39 (6): 939–50.

Brodie, Fawn. 1995. *No Man Knows My History: The Life of Joseph Smith*. 2nd ed. New York: Vintage Books.

Brooke, John L. 1994. *The Refiner's Fire: The Making of Mormon Cosmology, 1644–1844*. Cambridge: Cambridge University Press.

Brown, R. J., and D. A. Oakley. 2004. An integrative cognitive theory of hypnosis and high hypnotizability. In *The Highly Hypnotizable Person*, ed. Heap, Brown, and Oakley, 152–86. London: Routledge.

Brown, Sally, and David R. Brown. 2001. *A Biography of Mrs. Marty Mann: The First Lady of Alcoholics Anonymous*. Center City, MN: Hazelden.

Bulkeley, Kelly. 2014. Religious conversion and cognitive neuroscience. In *The Oxford Handbook of Religious Conversion*, ed. Rambo and Farhadian, 240–55. New York: Oxford University Press.

Bushman, Richard L. 1984. *Joseph Smith and the Beginnings of Mormonism*. Chicago: University of Illinois Press.

———. 2004. *Believing History: Latter-Day Saint Essays*. New York: Columbia University Press.

———. 2005. *Joseph Smith: Rough Stone Rolling*. New York: Alfred A. Knopf.

———. 2008. *Mormonism: A Very Short Introduction*. New York: Oxford University Press.

Carruthers, Peter. 2007. The illusion of conscious will. *Synthese* 159 (2): 197–213.

Cayce, Hugh Lynn. 1964. *Venture Inward: A Quest for Spiritual and Psychological Insight Based on the Psychic Discoveries of Edgar Cayce*. New York: Harper and Row.

Cheever, Susan. 2004. *My Name is Bill: Bill Wilson; His Life and the Creation of Alcoholics Anonymous*. New York: Washington Square Press.

Chesnut, Glenn F. 2006. *Changed by Grace: V. C. Kitchen, the Oxford Group, and A.A.* Lincoln, NE: iUniverse.

———. n.d. Bill Wilson's vision of the light at Towns Hospital, 14 December 1934. http://www.hindsfoot.org/lightbillw.pdf.

Collins, Randall. 2004. *Interaction Ritual Chains*. Princeton: Princeton University Press.

Cowdery, Oliver. 1839. *Defense in a Rehearsal of My Grounds for Separating Myself from the Latter Day Saints*. Norton, OH: Presley's Job Office.

Cox, Rochelle E., and Amanda J. Barnier. 2009. Hypnotic illusions and clinical delusions: A hypnotic paradigm for investigating delusions of misidentification. *International Journal of Clinical and Experimental Hypnosis* 57 (1): 1–32.

Craver, Carl F. 2007. *Explaining the Brain: Mechanisms and the Mosaic Unity of Neuroscience*. New York: Oxford University Press.

Craver, Carl F., and James Tabery. 2016. Mechanisms in science. In *The Stanford Encyclopedia of Philosophy*, ed. Edward N. Zalta. Spring edition. http://plato.stanford.edu/archives/spr2016/entries/science-mechanisms/.

Davidson, Karen Lynn, David J. Whittaker, Richard L. Jensen, and Mark Ashurst-McGee, eds. 2012. *Histories, Volume 1: Joseph Smith Histories, 1832–1844*. Vol. 1 of the Histories series of *The Joseph Smith Papers*, ed. Dean C. Jessee, Ronald K. Esplin, and Richard Lyman Bushman. Salt Lake City: Church Historian's Press.

Day, Samantha, and Emmanuelle Peters. 1999. The incidence of schizotypy in new religious movements. *Personality and Individual Differences* 27 (1): 55–67.

Deeley, Quinton. 2003. Social, cognitive, and neural constraints on subjectivity and agency: Implications for dissociative identity disorder. *Philosophy, Psychiatry, and Psychology* 10 (2): 161–67.

Deeley, Quinton, Natasha M. Maurits, Eamonn Walsh, David A. Oakley, Vaughan

Bell, Cristina Koppel, Mitul A. Mehta, and Peter W. Halligan. 2013. Using hypnotic suggestion to model loss of control and awareness of movements: An exploratory fMRI study. *PLoS One* 8 (10): e78324.

Deeley, Quinton, David A. Oakley, Eamonn Walsh, Vaughan Bell, Mitul A. Mehta, and Peter W. Halligan. 2014. Modelling psychiatric and cultural possession phenomena with suggestion and fMRI. *Cortex* 53:107–19.

Dennett, Daniel. 1992. The self as center of narrative gravity. In *Self and Consciousness: Multiple Perspectives*, ed. F. Kessel, P. Cole, and D. Johnson. Hillsdale, NJ: Erlbaum.

Dienes, Zoltán, and Josef Perner. 2007. Executive control without conscious awareness: The cold control theory of hypnosis. In *Hypnosis and Conscious States*, ed. Graham A. Jamieson, 293–314. Oxford: Oxford University Press.

Dijksterhuis, Ap, Jesse Preston, Daniel M. Wegner, and Henk Aarts. 2008. Effects of subliminal priming of self and god on self-attribution of authorship for events. *Journal of Experimental Social Psychology* 44 (1): 2–9

Doctrine and Covenants of the Church of Jesus Christ of Latter-day Saints. 1981. Salt Lake City: Church of Jesus Christ of Latter-day Saints.

Dreyfus, Hubert, and Sean Kelly. 2011. *All Things Shining: Reading the Western Classics to Find Meaning in a Secular Age*. New York: Free Press.

Dunn, Scott C. 2002. Automaticity and the dictation of the Book of Mormon. In *American Apocrypha: Essays on the Book of Mormon*, ed. Dan Vogel and Brent Lee Metcalfe, 17–46. Salt Lake City: Signature Books.

Durkheim, Emile. (1912) 1995. *The Elementary Forms of the Religious Life*. Trans. Karen Fields. New York: Free Press.

Easton-Flake, Amy, and Rachel Cope. 2014. Refiguring the archive: Women and the Book of Mormon translation. Paper presented at the Joseph Smith Translation Projects Workshop, Brigham Young University, 5 August.

Eddy, Mary Baker. 1919. *Science and Health*. Boston: Christian Science.

Egner, Tobias, and Amir Raz. 2007. Cognitive control processes and hypnosis. *Hypnosis and Conscious States: The Cognitive Neuroscience Perspective*, 29–50. New York: Oxford University Press.

Falby, Allison. 2008. *Between the Pigeonholes: Gerald Heard, 1889–1971*. Newcastle, UK: Cambridge Scholars Publishing.

Farias, Miguel, Gordon Claridge, and Mansur Lalljee. 2005. Personality and cognitive predictors of New Age practices and beliefs. *Personality and Individual Differences* 39 (5): 979–89.

Farias, Miguel, Raphael Underwood, and Gordon Claridge. 2013. Unusual but sound minds: Mental health indicators in spiritual individuals. *British Journal of Psychology* 104 (3): 364–81.

Festinger, Leon, Henry W. Riecken, and Stanley Schachter. (1956) 2008. *When Prophesy Fails*. London: Pinter and Martin.

Fitzgerald, Robert. 1995. *The Soul of Sponsorship: The Friendship of Fr. Ed Dowling, S.J. and Bill Wilson in Letters*. Center City, MN: Hazelden.

Fitzpatrick, Michael. 2012. *Dr. Bob and Bill W. Speak: AA's Cofounders Tell Their Stories*. Center City, MN: Hazelden.

Flake, Kathleen. 2007. Translating time: The nature and function of Joseph Smith's narrative canon. *Journal of Religion* 87 (4): 497–527.

Fleming, Stephen J. 2014. The secret tradition, part 9: Theurgy. *Juvenile Instructor.* Available at http://www.juvenileinstructor.org/the-secret-tradition-part-9-theurgy/.

Fluhman, J. Spencer. 2012. The spiritual environment of the restoration, 1790–1830. In *Mapping Mormonism*, ed. Brandon S. Plewe et al. Provo, UT: BYU Press.

Fuller, Robert. 2001. *Spiritual but Not Religious: Understanding Unchurched America.* New York: Oxford University Press.

Gallagher, Eugene V. 2014. *Reading and Writing Scripture in New Religious Movements: New Bibles and New Revelation.* New York: Palgrave Macmillan.

Gardner, Brant A. 2011. *The Gift and Power: Translating the Book of Mormon.* Salt Lake City: Greg Kofford Books.

Gazzaniga, Michael S. 1998. *The Mind's Past.* Berkeley: University of California Press.

George, Alexander L., and Andrew Bennett. 2005. *Case Studies and Theory Development in the Social Sciences.* Cambridge: MIT Press.

Gerrans, Philip. 2014a. *The Measure of Madness: Philosophy of Mind, Cognitive Neuroscience, and Delusional Thought.* Cambridge: MIT Press.

———. 2014b. Pathologies of hyperfamiliarity in dreams, delusions and déjà vu. *Frontiers in Psychology* 5:97.

Givens, Terryl. 2002. *By the Hand of Mormon: The American Scripture that Launched a New World Religion.* New York: Oxford University Press.

Glennan, S. S. Forthcoming. *Mechanisms and Mechanical Philosophy.* Oxford: Oxford University Press.

Goffman, Erving. 1974. *Frame Analysis: An Essay on the Organization of Experience.* New York: Harper and Row.

Gottschalk, Stephen. 2006. *Rolling Away the Stone: Mary Baker Eddy's Challenge to Materialism.* Bloomington: Indiana University Press.

Groeschel, Fr. Benedict J., CFR. 1993. *A Still, Small Voice: A Practical Guide on Reported Revelations.* San Francisco: Ignatius Press.

Gruss, Edmond C. 1984. A summary critique: God Calling. *Discerner*, April–June.

Hammer, Olav. 2001. *Claiming Knowledge: Strategies of Epistemology from Theosophy to the New Age.* Leiden, the Netherlands: Brill.

Handelman, Don. 2005. Microhistorical anthropology: Toward a prospective perspective. In *Critical Junctions: Anthropology and History Beyond the Critical Turn*, ed. Don Kalb and Herman Tak. New York: Berghahn.

Hardy, Grant. 2003. *The Book of Mormon: A Reader's Edition.* Urbana: University of Illinois Press.

———. 2010. *Understanding the Book of Mormon: A Reader's Guide.* New York: Oxford University Press.

Harper, Steven Craig. 2012. *Joseph Smith's First Vision: A Guide to the Historical Accounts.* Salt Lake City: Deseret Books.

Hartigan, Francis. 2001. *Bill W: A Biography of Alcoholics Anonymous Cofounder Bill Wilson.* New York: St. Martin's Griffin.

Haslam, S. Alexander, Inmaculada Adarves-Yorno, Tom Postmes, and Lise Jans. 2013. The collective origins of valued originality: A social identity approach to creativity. *Personality and Social Psychology Review* 17 (4): 384–401.

Heap, M., R. J. Brown, and D. A. Oakley. 2004. High hypnotizability: Key issues.

In *The Highly Hypnotizable Person*, ed. Heap, Brown, and Oakley. London: Routledge.

Heard, Gerald. (1941) 2007. *Training for the Life of the Spirit.* New York: Harper and Bros., repr. ed., Eugene, OR: Wipf and Stock.

———. (1949) 2007. *Prayers and Meditations.* New York: Harper and Bros.; repr. ed., Eugene, OR: Wipf and Stock.

Hedstrom, Matthew S. 2012. *The Rise of Liberal Religion: Book Culture and American Spirituality in the Twentieth Century.* New York: Oxford University Press.

Heriot-Maitland, Charles, Matthew Knight, and Emmanuelle Peters. 2012. A qualitative comparison of psychotic-like phenomena in clinical and non-clinical populations. *British Journal of Clinical Psychology* 51 (1): 37–53.

Hermans, Hubert. 2011. The dialogical self. In *The Oxford Handbook of the Self*, ed. Shaun Gallagher, 655–80. New York: Oxford University Press.

Hilgard, Ernest R. 1986. *Divided Consciousness: Multiple Controls in Human Thought and Action.* Expanded ed. New York: John Wiley and Sons.

Hood, Ralph W., Jr., Peter C. Hill, and Bernard Spilka. 2009. *The Psychology of Religion: An Empirical Approach.* New York: Guilford.

Horton, James E., and Helen J. Crawford. 2004. Neurophysiological and genetic determinants of high hypnotizability. In *The Highly Hypnotizable Person*, ed. Heap, Brown, and Oakley. London: Routledge

Houtman, Dick, and Birgit Meyer, eds. 2012. *Things: Religion and the Question of Materiality.* New York: Fordham.

Howe, Eber. (1834) 2015. *Mormonism Unvailed.* Ed. and intro. Dan Vogel. Salt Lake City: Signature Books.

Howe, Carol M. 2009. *Never Forget to Laugh: Personal Recollections of Bill Thetford, Co-Scribe of "A Course in Miracles."* N.p.: Carol M. Howe.

Huang, Julie Y., and John A. Bargh. 2014. The selfish goal: Autonomously operating motivational structures as the proximate cause of human judgment and behavior. *Behavioral and Brain Sciences* 37 (2): 121–35.

Hughes, Richard T. 1996. *Reviving the Ancient Faith: The Story of the Churches of Christ in America.* Grand Rapids, MI: Eerdmans.

Huxley, Aldous. 1945. *The Perennial Philosophy.* New York: Harper and Bros.

———. 1954. *The Doors of Perception.* New York: Harper and Bros.

———. (1956) 1990. *Heaven and Hell.* New York: Harper and Bros.

Jensen, Robin Scott, Robert J. Woodford, and Steven C. Harper, eds. 2009. Manuscript Revelation Books. Facsimile ed. Vol. 1 of the Revelations and Translations series of *The Joseph Smith Papers*, ed. Jessee, Esplin, and Bushman. Salt Lake City: Church Historian's Press.

Jessee, Dean C., Ronald K. Esplin, and Richard Lyman Bushman, eds. 2008–16. *The Joseph Smith Papers.* 14 vols. (to date). Salt Lake City: Church Historian's Press.

J., John. 1945. Man's Triumvirate [a report of Bill and Bob's talks at the Tenth Anniversary commemoration of AA's founding, Cleveland]. *AA Grapevine* Digital Archives 2/2.

Johnson, K. Paul. 1998. *Edgar Cayce in Context: The Readings; Truth and Fiction.* Albany, NY: SUNY Press.

Johnston, Hank, and John A. Noakes, eds. 2005. *Frames of Protest: Social Movements and the Framing Perspective.* Lanham, MD: Rowman and Littlefield.

Jung, C. G. 1997. *Encountering Jung: Jung on Active Imagination*. Ed. and intro. Joan Chodorow. Princeton: Princeton University Press.

Kirsch, I., E. Cardeña, S. Derbyshire, Z. Dienes, M. Heap, S. Kallio, et al. 2011. Definitions of hypnosis and hypnotizability and their relation to suggestion and suggestibility: A consensus statement. *Contemporary Hypnosis and Integrative Therapy* 28 (2): 107–11.

Köpetz, C. E., C. W. Lejuez, R. W. Wiers, and A. W. Kruglanski. 2013. Motivation and self-regulation in addiction: A call for convergence. *Perspectives on Psychological Science* 8 (1): 3–24.

Kurtz, Ernest. 1991. *Not-God: A History of Alcoholics Anonymous*. Center City, MN: Hazelden.

Lattin, Don. 2012. *Distilled Spirits: Getting High, then Sober, with a Famous Writer, a Forgotten Philosopher, and a Hopeless Drunk*. Berkeley: University of California Press.

Laurence, J. R., D. Beaulieu-Prévost, and T. du Chéné. 2008. Measuring and understanding individual differences in hypnotizability. In *The Oxford Handbook of Hypnosis*, ed. Nash and Barnier, 225–53. New York: Oxford University Press.

Lewis, James R. 2003. *Legitimating New Religions*. New Brunswick, NJ: Rutgers University Press.

Lifshitz, M., N. Aubert-Bonn, A. Fischer, I. F. Kashem, and A. Raz. 2012. Using suggestion to modulate automatic processes: From Stroop to McGurk and beyond. *Cortex* 49 (2): 463–73.

Liljencrants, Johan. 1918. *Spiritism and Religion: A Moral Study*. Washington, DC: Catholic University of America.

Luhrmann, Tanya. 2012. *When God Talks Back: Understanding the American Evangelical Experience*. New York: Alfred A. Knopf.

Lynn, S. J., I. Kirsch, J. Knox, O. Fassler, and S. O. Lilienfeld. 2007. Hypnosis and neuroscience: Implications for the altered state debate. In *Hypnosis and Conscious States*, ed. Graham A. Jamieson, 145–66. Oxford: Oxford University Press.

Lynn, S. J., I. Kirsch, and M. N. Hallquist. 2008. Social cognitive theories of hypnosis. In *The Oxford Handbook of Hypnosis*, ed. Nash and Barnier, 111–40. New York: Oxford University Press.

Lynn, S. J., and J. W. Rhue. 1991. An integrative model of hypnosis. In *Theories of Hypnosis: Current Models and Perspectives*, ed. S. J. Lynn and J. W. Rhue, 397–438. New York: Guilford Press.

McCubbins, Matthew D., and Mark Turner. 2012. Going cognitive: Tools for rebuilding the social sciences. In *Grounding Social Sciences in Cognitive Sciences*, ed. Ron Sun. Cambridge, MA: MIT Press.

MacKay, Michael, and Gerrit J. Dirkmaat. 2015. *From Darkness unto Light: Joseph Smith's Translation and Publication of the Book of Mormon*. Provo, UT: Brigham Young University.

MacKay, Michael, Gerrit Dirkmaat, and Robin Scott Jenson. 2013. The "Caractors" document: New light on an early transcription of the Book of Mormon characters. *Mormon Historical Studies* 14 (1): 131–52.

MacKay, Michael, Gerrit Dirkmaat, Grant Underwood, Robert Woodford, and William Hartley, eds. 2013. *Documents, Volume 1: July 1828–June 1831*. Vol. 1 of the Documents series of *The Joseph Smith Papers*, ed. Jessee, Esplin, and Bushman. Salt Lake City: Church Historian's Press.

MacLeod, C. M. 2011. Hypnosis and the control of attention: Where to from here? *Consciousness and Cognition* 20 (2): 321–24.

MacLeod, C. M., and P. W. Sheehan. 2003. Hypnotic control of attention in the Stroop task: A historical footnote. *Consciousness and Cognition* 12 (3): 347–53.

Malle, Bertram F. 2004. *How the Mind Explains Behavior: Folk Explanations, Meaning, and Social Interaction.* Cambridge, MA: MIT Press.

Manuscript Revelation Books. 2009. Facsimile ed. Ed. Robin Scott Jensen, Robert J. Woodford, and Steven C. Harper. Vol. 1 of the Revelations and Translations series of *The Joseph Smith Papers*, ed. Jessee, Esplin, and Bushman. Salt Lake City: Church Historian's Press.

Marien, H., R. Custers, R. R. Hassin, and H. Aarts. 2012. Unconscious goal activation and the hijacking of the executive function. *Journal of Personality and Social Psychology* 103 (3): 399–415.

Mazzoni, G., E. Rotriquenz, C. Carvalho, M. Vannucci, K. Roberts, and I. Kirsch. 2009. Suggested visual hallucinations in and out of hypnosis. *Consciousness and Cognition* 18 (2): 494–99.

Mazzoni, G., A. Venneri, W. J. McGeown, and I. Kirsch. 2013. Neuroimaging resolution of the altered state hypothesis. *Cortex* 49 (2): 400–10.

McConkey, Kevin M., and Amanda J. Barnier. 2004. High hypnotizability: Unity and diversity in behaviour and experience. In *The Highly Hypnotizable Person*, ed. M. Heap, R. Brown, and D. Oakley, 61–84. London: Routledge.

McConkey, K. M., M. I. Glisky, and J. F. Kihlstrom. 1989. Individual differences among hypnotic virtuosos: A case comparison. *Australian Journal of Clinical and Experimental Hypnosis* 17 (2): 131–40.

McGeown, W. J., G. Mazzoni, A. Venneri, and I. Kirsch. 2009. Hypnotic induction decreases anterior default mode activity. *Consciousness and Cognition* 18 (4): 848–55.

McGeown, W. J., A. Venneri, I. Kirsch, L. Nocetti, K. Roberts, L. Foan, and G. Mazzoni. 2012. Suggested visual hallucination without hypnosis enhances activity in visual areas of the brain. *Consciousness and Cognition* 21 (1): 100–16.

McKay, R., and D. Dennett. 2009. The evolution of misbelief. *Behavioral and Brain Sciences* 32:493–561.

Miller, Patrick D. 1997. *The Complete Story of the Course: The History, the People, and the Controversies Behind "A Course in Miracles."* Berkeley, CA: Fearless Press.

———. 2008. *Understanding "A Course in Miracles": The History, Message, and Legacy of a Spiritual Path for Today.* Berkeley, CA: Celestial Arts.

Nevid, Jeffrey. 2013. *Psychology: Concepts and Applications.* Belmont, CA: Wadsworth.

Novak, S. J. 1997. LSD before Leary: Sidney Cohen's critique of 1950s psychedelic drug research. *Isis: Journal of the History of Science Society* 88:87–110.

Oakley, D. A. 2006. Hypnosis as tool in research: Experimental psychopathology. *Contemporary Hypnosis* 23 (1): 3–14.

Oakley, D. A., and P. W. Halligan. 2013. Hypnotic suggestion: Opportunities for cognitive neuroscience. *Nature Reviews Neuroscience* 14 (8): 565–76.

Pace-Schott, E. F. 2013. Dreaming as a story-telling instinct. *Frontiers in Psychology* 4:159.

Pacherie, Elisabeth. 2011. Self-agency. In *The Oxford Handbook of the Self*, ed. Shaun Gallagher, 442–64. New York: Oxford University Press.

Palmer, Grant H. 2002. *An Insider's View of Mormon Origins*. Salt Lake City: Signature Books.

Paloutzian, Raymond F. 2014. Psychology of religious conversion and spiritual transformation. In *The Oxford Handbook of Religious Conversion*, ed. Lewis R. Rambo and Charles E. Farhadian, 209–39. New York: Oxford University Press.

Paloutzian, Raymond F., Sebastian Murken, Heinz Streib, and Sussan Rößler-Namini. 2013. Conversion, deconversion, and spiritual transformation. In *Handbook of the Psychology of Religion and Spirituality*, ed. Raymond F. Paloutzian and Crystal Park, 399–421. 2nd ed. New York: Guilford.

Papineau, David. 2015. Naturalism. In *The Stanford Encyclopedia of Philosophy*, ed. Edward N. Zalt. http://plato.stanford.edu/archives/fall2015/entries/naturalism/.

Persuitte, David. 2000. *Joseph Smith and the Origins of the Book of Mormon*. 2nd ed. Jefferson, NC: McFarland.

Perry, Robert. 2004 (August). The earlier versions and the editing of *A Course in Miracles*. *Miracles Monthly.* Available online at http://www.circleofa.org/library/acim-history-issues/copyright/earlier-versions/.

Peters, Emmanuelle, Samantha Day, Jacqueline McKenna, and Gilli Orbach. 1999. Delusional ideation in religious and psychotic populations. *British Journal of Clinical Psychology* 38 (1): 83–96.

Peterson, Daniel C. 2002. A response: What the manuscripts and eyewitnesses tell us about the translation of the Book of Mormon. In *Uncovering the Original Text of the Book of Mormon: History and Findings of the Critical Text Project*, ed. M. Gerald Bradford and Alison V. P. Coutts. Salt Lake City: Maxwell Institute.

———. 2005. Editor's introduction—Not so easily dismissed: Some facts for which counter explanations of the Book of Mormon will need to account. *FARMS Review* 17 (2): xi–xlix.

Postmes, Tom, and Nyla R. Branscombe, eds. 2010. *Rediscovering Social Identity*. New York: Psychology Press.

Powers, Thomas E. 1959. *First Questions in the Life of the Spirit*. New York: Harper and Bros.

———. 1990. *Invitation to a Great Experiment*. Expanded ed. of the 1959 ed. New York: Crossroads.

Quinn, Michael D. 1973. The first months of Mormonism: A contemporary view by Rev. Diedrich Willers. *New York History* 54 (4): 317–33.

———. 1998. *Early Mormonism and the Magic World View*. Rev. and enlarged ed. Salt Lake City: Signature Books.

Radden, Jennifer. 2011a. *On Delusion: Thinking in Action*. New York: Routledge.

———. 2011b. Multiple selves. In *The Oxford Handbook of the Self*, ed. Shaun Gallagher, 547–70. New York: Oxford University Press.

Radvansky, Gabriel, and Jeffrey M. Zacks. 2011. Event perception. *Wiley Interdisciplinary Reviews: Cognitive Science* 2 (6): 608–20.

———. 2014. *Event Cognition*. New York: Oxford University Press.

Raphael, Matthew J. 2000. *Bill W. and Mr. Wilson: The Legend and Life of A.A.'s Cofounder.* Amherst: University of Massachusetts Press.

Raz, Amir. 2005. Attention and hypnosis: Neural substrates and genetic associations of two converging processes. *International Journal of Clinical and Experimental Hypnosis* 53 (3): 237–58.

Raz, Amir, Theodore Shapiro, Jin Fan, and Michael I. Posner. 2002. Hypnotic suggestion and the modulation of Stroop interference. *Archives of General Psychiatry* 59 (12): 1155–61.

Raz, Amir, Irving Kirsch, Jessica Pollard, and Yael Nitkin-Kaner. 2006. Suggestion reduces the Stroop effect. *Psychological Science* 17 (2): 91–95.

Raz, Amir, Miguel Moreno-Íniguez, Laura Martin, and Hongtu Zhu. 2007. Suggestion overrides the Stroop effect in highly hypnotizable individuals. *Consciousness and Cognition* 16 (2): 331–38.

Rees, Robert A. 2006. The Book of Mormon and automatic writing. *Journal of Book of Mormon Studies* 15 (1): 5–17.

Renoux, Christian. 2001. *La prière pour la paix attribuée à saint François: Une énigme à résoudre.* Paris: Éditions franciscaines.

Ricks, Stephen D. 1993. Notes and communications: Translation of the Book of Mormon; Interpreting the evidence. *Journal of Book of Mormon Studies* 2 (2): 201–6.

Roberts, B. H. 1992. *Studies of the Book of Mormon.* 2nd ed. Salt Lake City: Signature Books.

Rosenthal, Robert. 2014. Personal communications via e-mail, November–December.

Rovane, Carol. 1998. *The Bounds of Agency.* Princeton: Princeton University Press.

Russell, A. J. 1945. *God Calling: A Devotional Diary.* New York: Dodd, Mead.

Saunders, David R., and Helen Schucman. 1962. Syndrome analysis: An efficient procedure for isolating meaningful subgroups in a non-random sample of a population. Paper presented at the Psychonomic Society, St. Louis.

Schjødt, Uffe, L. Hans Stødkilde-Jørgensen, Armin W. Geertz, Torben E. Lund, and Andreas Roepstorff. 2011. The power of charisma—perceived charisma inhibits the frontal executive network of believers in intercessory prayer. *Social Cognitive and Affective Neuroscience* 6 (1): 119–27.

Schucman, Helen. (1975) 2009. *Autobiography.* Mill Valley, CA: Foundation for Inner Peace.

———. (1976) 2006. A personal interview with Helen Schucman, PhD. Conducted by David Hammond. DVD. Mill Valley, CA: Foundation for Inner Peace.

———. 1977. How It Came—What It Is—What It Says. Pamphlet. Mill Valley, CA: Foundation for Inner Peace.

———. (1982) 2008. *The Gifts of God: Poems by the Scribe of "A Course in Miracles."* Mill Valley, CA: Foundation for Inner Peace.

———. 1990. Unpublished Writings of Helen Schucman. Vols. 1–22. Compiled by Kenneth Wapnick. Temecula, CA: FACIM.

Schucman, Helen, and William N. Thetford. 1968. Expressed symptoms and personality traits in conversion hysteria. *Psychological Reports* 23 (1): 231–43.

———. 1976. *A Course in Miracles.* 1st ed. New York: Foundation for Inner Peace.

———. 1992. *A Course in Miracles*. 2nd ed. Mill Valley, CA: Foundation for Inner Peace.

———. 2007. *A Course in Miracles*. 3rd ed. Mill Valley, CA: Foundation for Inner Peace.

Schucman, Louis. n.d. Interview. Conducted by Tamara Morgan. Unpublished manuscript. FIP Archives. Mill Valley, CA: Foundation for Inner Peace.

Sheehan, P. W. 1991. Hypnosis, context, and commitment. In *Theories of Hypnosis*, ed. S. J. Lynn and J. W. Rhue, 520–41. New York: Guilford Press.

Sherif, M., O. J. Harvey, B. J. White, W. R. Hood, and C. W. Sherif. 1961. *Intergroup Conflict and Cooperation: The Robbers Cave Experiment (Vol. 10)*. Norman, OK: University Book Exchange.

Shipps, Jan. 1974. The prophet puzzle: Suggestions leading to a more comprehensive interpretation of Joseph Smith. *Journal of Mormon History* 1:3–20.

Skousen, Royal. 1998. How Joseph Smith translated the Book of Mormon: Evidence from the original manuscript. *Journal of Mormon Studies* 7 (1): 22–31.

_____, ed. 2009. *The Book of Mormon: The Earliest Text*. New Haven: Yale University Press.

Skutch, Judith. 1977 (April). A *New Realities* interview with Judith R. Skutch. Conducted by James Bolen. *New Realities Magazine*. Available at http://acim -archives.org/Media/Interviews?Judy-Interview.html.

———. 1982 (March). The gifts of God. *New Realities Magazine*. Available at http://acim-archives.org/Media/articles/NR-1982_JudySkutch.html.

Skutch, Robert. 1984a. *Journey Without Distance: The Story Behind "A Course in Miracles."* Berkeley, CA: Celestial Arts.

———. 1984b. Author's note [accompanying "A Course in Miracles, the untold story," parts I and II, *New Realities Magazine*, July–August]. Available at http:// acim-archives.org/Media/articles/NR-1984_BobSkutch-AuthorsNote.html.

Skutch Whitson, Judith. 2014. Personal communications via e-mail, October– December.

Smith, L., S. Riley, and Emmanelle R. Peters. 2009. Schizotypy, delusional ideation and well-being in an American new religious movement population. *Clinical Psychology and Psychotherapy* 16 (6): 479–84.

Snow, David A. 2007. Framing processes, ideology, and discursive fields. In *The Blackwell Companion to Social Movements*, ed. David Snow, Sarah Soule, and Hanspeter Kriesi. Malden, MA: Blackwell.

Snow, David A., E. Burke Rochford Jr., S. K. Worden, and R. D. Benford. 1986. Frame alignment processes, micromobilization, and movement participation. *American Sociological Review* 51 (4): 464–81.

Spanos, Nicholas P. 1996. *Multiple Identities and False Memories: A Sociocognitive Perspective*. Washington, DC: American Psychological Association.

Staker, Mark L. 2009. *Hearken, O Ye People: The Historical Setting of Joseph Smith's Ohio Revelations*. Salt Lake City: Kofford Books.

Staker, Susan. 2002. Secret things, hidden things: The seer story in the imaginative economy of Joseph Smith. In *American Apocrypha: Essays on the Book of Mormon*, ed. Dan Vogel and Brent Lee Metcalfe. Salt Lake City: Signature Books.

Stark, Rodney 1999. A theory of revelations. *Journal of the Scientific Study of Religion* 38:287–308.

Stevens, Jay. 1987. *Storming Heaven: LSD and the American Dream*. New York: Harper and Row.

Streib, Heinz. 2014. Deconversion. In *The Oxford Handbook of Religious Conversion*, ed. Lewis Rambo and Charles Farhadian, 271–96. New York: Oxford University Press.

Sun, Ron, ed. 2012. *Grounding Social Sciences in Cognitive Sciences*. Cambridge, MA: MIT Press.

Tajfel, Henri. 1974. Social identity and intergroup behavior. *Social Sciences Information Sur les Sciences Sociales* 13:65–93. Reprinted in Postmes and Branscombe 2010.

Tasso, Anthony F., and Nicole A. Pérez. 2008. Parsing everyday suggestibility: What does it tell us about hypnosis? In *The Oxford Handbook of Hypnosis*, ed. Nash and Barnier, 311–36. New York: Oxford University Press.

Taves, Ann. 1999. *Fits, Trances, and Visions: Experiencing Religion and Explaining Experience from Wesley to James*. Princeton: Princeton University Press.

———— 2009. *Religious Experience Reconsidered: A Building-Block Approach to the Study of Religion and Other Special Things*. Princeton: Princeton University Press.

————. 2013. Building blocks of sacralities: A new basis for comparison across cultures and religions. In *Handbook of the Psychology of Religion and Spirituality*, ed. Paloutzian and Park. 2nd ed. New York: Guilford.

————. 2014. History and the claims of revelation: Joseph Smith and the materialization of the golden plates. *Numen* 61:182–207.

————. 2015. Reverse engineering complex cultural concepts: Identifying building blocks of "religion." *Journal of Cognition and Culture* 15:191–216.

Taves, Ann, and Michael Kinsella. 2014. Hiding in plain sight: the organizational forms of "unorganized religion." In *New Age Spirituality: Rethinking Religion*, ed. Steven J. Sutcliffe and Ingvild Saelid Gilhus. New York: Routledge.

Taves, Ann, and Egil Asprem. 2016. Experience as event: Event cognition and the study of (religious) experience. *Religion, Brain, and Behavior*, published online: 09 June.

Taves, Ann, and Steven C. Harper. 2016. Joseph Smith's first vision: New methods for the analysis of experience-related texts. *Mormon Studies Review* 3:53–84.

Taylor, Alan. 1999. Rediscovering the context of Joseph Smith's treasure seeking. In *The Prophet Puzzle: Interpretive Essays on Joseph Smith*, ed. Bryan Waterman, 141–54. Salt Lake City: Signature Books.

Thagard, Paul. 2006. *Hot Thought: Mechanisms and Applications of Emotional Cognition*. Cambridge, MA: MIT Press.

————. 2010. Explaining economic crises: Are there collective representations? *Episteme* 7:266–83. doi:10.3366/E1742360010000985.

————. 2012. Mapping minds across cultures. In *Grounding Social Sciences in Cognitive Sciences*, ed. Ron Sun. Cambridge, MA: MIT Press.

————. 2014. The self as a system of multilevel interacting mechanisms. *Philosophical Psychology* 27 (2): 145–63.

Thetford, William. (1983) 2009. *Life Story*. Mill Valley, CA: Foundation for Inner Peace.

————. 1984. A *New Realities* interview with William N. Thetford, PhD (part 1), by James Bolen. Available at http://acim-archives.org/Scribes/interviews/Bill-Apr1984.html.

Thompson, Doug, ed. 2008. *A Course in Miracles: Urtext Manuscripts; Complete Seven-Volume Combined Edition.* Jaffrey, NH: Miracles in Action Press, LLC.

Thomsen, Robert. 1999. *Bill W: The Absorbing and Deeply Moving Life Story of Bill Wilson, Co-Founder of Alcoholics Anonymous.* Center City, MN: Hazelden.

Tiebout, Harry M. 1944. Therapeutic mechanism of Alcoholics Anonymous. *American Journal of Psychiatry.* http://dx.doi.org/10.1176/ajp.100.4.468.

Tooby, John, and Leda Cosmides. 1992. The psychological foundations of culture. In *The Adapted Mind: Evolutionary Psychology and the Generation of Culture*, ed. J. H. Barkow, Leda Cosmides, and John Tooby, 19–136. Oxford: Oxford University Press.

———. 2005. Conceptual foundations of evolutionary psychology. In *The Handbook of Evolutionary Psychology*, ed. David M. Buss, 5–67. Hoboken, NJ: Wiley.

Tumminia, Diana G., and William H. Swatos, eds. 2011. *How Prophecy Lives.* Netherlands: Brill.

Turley, Richard E., Robin S. Jensen, and Mark Ashurst-McGee. 2015 (October). Joseph the Seer. *Ensign.* Available at https://www.lds.org/ensign/2015/10/joseph-the-seer?lang=eng.

Turner, John C., and Penelope J. Oakes. 2010. The significance of the social identity concept for social psychology with reference to individualism, interactionism, and social influence. In *Rediscovering Social Identity*, ed. Tom Postmes and Nyla R. Branscombe. New York: Psychology Press.

Vahle, Neal. 2009. *A Course in Miracles: The Lives of Helen Schucman and William Thetford.* San Francisco: Open View Press.

Van der Horst, Brian. 1977 (April). Simple, dumb, boring truths and *A Course in Miracles. New Realities Magazine.* Available at https://acim-archives.org/Media/articles/NR-1977_BrianVanderHorst.html.

Van Wagoner, Richard, and Steven Walker. 1982. Joseph Smith: The gift of seeing. *Dialogue: A Journal of Mormon Thought* 15 (2): 48–68.

Vaughan, Frances, and Roger Walsh, eds. 1983. *Accept This Gift: Selections from "A Course in Miracles."* Los Angeles: J. P. Tarcher.

Vogel, Dan, ed. 1996–2003. *Early Mormon Documents.* 5 vols. Salt Lake City: Signature Books.

———. 2002. The validity of the witnesses' testimonies. In *American Apocrypha: Essays on the Book of Mormon*, ed. Dan Vogel and Brent Metcalfe. Salt Lake City: Signature Books.

———. 2004. *Joseph Smith: The Making of a Prophet.* Salt Lake City: Signature Books.

Von Hippel, William, and Robert Trivers. 2011. The evolution and psychology of self-deception. *Behavioral and Brain Sciences* 34:1–56.

W., Bill. 1945. The fellowship of Alcoholics Anonymous. In *Alcohol, Science and Society: Twenty-Nine Lectures with Discussions as Given at the Yale Summer School of Alcohol Studies.* New Haven, CT: College and University Press. Available at http://www.barefootsworld.net/aabw1944talk.html.

———. 1946. The individual in relation to AA as a group. *AA Grapevine.*

———. 1954 (April). Talk at LeMoyne College. Syracuse, New York. GSOA Archives.

———. 1988. *The Language of the Heart: Bill W.'s Grapevine Writings.* New York: AA Grapevine, Inc.

———. 2000. *Bill W.: My First 40 Years; An Autobiography by the Cofounder of Alcoholics Anonymous.* Center City, MN: Hazelden.

W., Lois Burnham. 1949. The story of Alcoholics Anonymous. *Packer Alumna*, June 13–16. Stepping Stones Foundation Archives, Katonah, New York.

———. 1979. *Lois Remembers: Memoirs of the Co-Founder of Al-Anon and Wife of the Co-Founder of Alcoholics Anonymous.* New York: Al-Anon.

Walker, Ronald W. 1986. Martin Harris: Mormonism's early convert. *Dialogue: A Journal of Mormon Thought* 19 (4): 29–43.

Wallace, Anthony F. C. (1956) 2003. *Revitalization and Mazeways.* Lincoln: University of Nebraska Press.

Walsh, Eamonn, David A. Oakley, Peter W. Halligan, Mitul A. Mehta, and Quinton Deeley. 2015. The functional anatomy and connectivity of thought insertion and alien control of movement. *Cortex* 64:380–93.

Walsh, Eamonn, Mitul A. Mehta, David A. Oakley, D. N. Guilmette, A. Gabay, P. W. Halligan, and Quinton Deeley. 2014. Using suggestion to model different types of automatic writing. *Consciousness and Cognition* 26:24–36.

Walsh, Roger, and Frances Vaughan, eds. 1988. *A Gift of Healing: Selections from "A Course in Miracles."* Los Angeles, CA: J. P. Tarcher.

Wapnick, Gloria, and Wapnick, Kenneth. (1987) 2006. *Awaken from the Dream: A Presentation of "A Course in Miracles."* 3rd ed. Temecula, CA: FACIM.

Wapnick, Kenneth. n.d. The History of the Manuscripts of *A Course in Miracles.* Available at www.facimoutreach.org/qa/questions/ACIM_Manuscript_History.pdf.

———. 1978. *Christian Psychology in "A Course in Miracles."* Farmingdale, NY: Coleman.

———. 1983. *Forgiveness and Jesus: The Meeting Place of "A Course in Miracles" and Christianity.* Farmingdale, NY: Coleman.

———. 1989. *Love Does Not Condemn.* 1st ed. Temecula, CA: FACIM.

———. 1992. *Christian Psychology in "A Course in Miracles."* 2nd ed. Enlarged. Roscoe, NY: FACIM.

———. 1997. *Concordance of "A Course in Miracles."* New York: Viking Press.

———. 1999. *Absence from Felicity: The Story of Helen Schucman and Her Scribing of "A Course in Miracles."* 2nd ed. (1st ed., 1991.) Temecula, CA: FACIM.

———. 2009. *Love Does Not Condemn.* 2nd ed. Temecula, CA: FACIM.

Wapnick, Kenneth, and Gloria Wapnick. 1998. Interview conducted by Ian Patrick at the Foundation for *A Course in Miracles*, Roscoe, New York, September 11. Available at http://www.miraclestudies.net/InterviewIP.html.

Wapnick, Kenneth, and W. Norris Clarke, SJ. 1995. *"A Course in Miracles" and Christianity: A Dialogue.* Roscoe, NY: FACIM.

Ward, Thomas A., Keith J. Gaynor, Mike D. Hunter, Peter W. R. Woodruff, Philippa A. Garety, and Emmanuelle R. Peters. 2014. Appraisals and responses to experimental symptom analogues in clinical and nonclinical individuals with psychotic experiences. *Schizophrenia Bulletin* 40 (4): 845–55.

Watkins, Mary. 1986. *Invisible Guests: The Development of Imaginal Dialogues*. Hillsdale, NJ: Analytic Press.

Weber, Max. (1956) 1978. *Economy and Society*. Ed. Guenther Roth and Claus Wittich. Berkeley: University of California Press.

Wegner, Daniel. 2002. *The Illusion of Conscious Will*. Cambridge: MIT Press.

Welch, John W. 2005. *Opening the Heavens: Firsthand Accounts of Divine Manifestations, 1820–1844*. Provo, UT: Brigham Young University Press.

Wing, Nell. 1998. *Grateful to Have Been There: My 42 Years with Bill and Lois, and the Evolution of Alcoholics Anonymous*. 2nd ed. Center City, MN: Hazelden.

Znamenski, Andrei A. 2004. General introduction—adventure of the metaphor: Shamanism and shamanism studies. In *Shamanism: Critical Concepts in Sociology*, ed. Andrei A. Znamenski. New York: Routledge.

AUTHOR INDEX

SUBJECT INDEX